General Principles of Law and International Due Process

CILE Studies

Series Editor: Ronald A. Brand

CILE Studies is a series of monographs and edited volumes dedicated to the discussion of important issues and developments in public and private international law. Each volume is selected on the basis of its contribution to the literature with the objective to provide lasting commentary and innovative analysis.

Potential authors may contact:
Center for International Legal Education
University of Pittsburgh School of Law
Barco Law Building
3900 Forbes Avenue
Pittsburgh, PA 15260
U.S.A.
Phone: 412-648-7023
fax: 412-648-2648
email: cile@law.pitt.edu

Volumes 1 and 2 are available directly from the Center for International Legal Education at the above address. Volume 3 and later volumes can be ordered from Oxford University Press by visiting their website at: www.oup.com.

The Series

Volume 1

The Draft UNCITRAL Digest and Beyond: Cases, Analysis and Unresolved Issues in the U.N. Sales Convention,
(Franco Ferrari, Harry M. Flechtner, and Ronald A. Brand, editors)

Volume 2

Private Law, Private International Law, and Judicial Cooperation in the EU-US Relationship,
(Ronald A. Brand, editor)

Volume 3

Forum Non Conveniens—History, Global Practice, and Future Under the Hague Convention on Choice of Court Agreements,
(Ronald A. Brand and Scott R. Jablonski)

Volume 4

Drafting Contracts Under the CISG,
(Harry M. Flechtner, Ronald A. Brand, Mark S. Walter, editors)

Volume 5

Conflicts in a Conflict: A Conflict of Laws Case Study on Israel and the Palestinian Territories,
(Michael Karayanni)

Volume 6

General Principles of Law and International Due Process: Principles and Norms Applicable in Transnational Disputes,
(Charles T. Kotuby Jr. and Luke A. Sobota)

cile
Center for International Legal Education

General Principles of Law and International Due Process

Principles and Norms Applicable in Transnational Disputes

Charles T. Kotuby Jr. and Luke A. Sobota

OXFORD
UNIVERSITY PRESS

OXFORD
UNIVERSITY PRESS

Oxford University Press is a department of the University of Oxford. It furthers the University's objective of excellence in research, scholarship, and education by publishing worldwide. Oxford is a registered trademark of Oxford University Press in the UK and certain other countries.

Published in the United States of America by Oxford University Press
198 Madison Avenue, New York, NY 10016, United States of America.

Library of Congress Cataloging-in-Publication Data

Names: Kotuby, Charles T., Jr, author. | Sobota, Luke A., author.
Title: General principles of law and international due process : principles and norms applicable in transnational disputes / Charles T. Kotuby Jr. and Luke A. Sobota.
Description: New York : Oxford University Press, 2017. | Series: CILE studies; v. 6 | Includes bibliographical references and index.
Identifiers: LCCN 2016015294 | ISBN 9780190642709 hardback
Subjects: LCSH: Rule of law. | Due process of law. | International law.
Classification: LCC K3171 .K67 2017 | DDC 340/. 11— dc23 LC record available at https://lccn.loc.gov/2016015294

For Rebecca, Elizabeth, Thatcher, and Olivia Kotuby

and Anna, Jack, Elsa, and Jane Sobota.

Contents

Foreword

Hersch Lauterpacht's extraordinary career in international law was launched in 1927 with the publication of *Private Law Sources and Analogies of International Law*. The Author's Preface noted "the fact that general principles of law, recognized by civilised States and adopted by customary and conventional international law as a source of decision in international disputes, are for the most part identical with generally recognized principles of private law." Lauterpacht continued:

> The adoption, in Article 38(3) of the Statute of the Permanent Court of International Justice, of "general principles of law recognized by civilised States" as a binding—although, it seems, only supplementary—source of decision in the judicial settlement of international disputes signifies that that practice, hitherto unsupported by universal and authoritative international enactment, and regarded by many as derogating from the strictly judicial character of international arbitration, has now received formal approval on the part of practically the whole international community. There lies the outstanding and, to a certain, extent, revolutionary contribution made by the Statute to international law as a whole. This book is, in a sense, a commentary on Article 38(3) of the Statute and a respectful acknowledgment of the great service rendered to the cause of international law by the Committee of Jurists assembled in 1920 at The Hague. As a result of earnest and prolonged discussions, they arrived at a compromise which honours equally the representatives of both Continental and British-American jurisprudence, and places the judicial function of the Court upon a solid foundation.*

* At pages viii–ix. Much of Lauterpacht's scholarship, not only in that book but in others, was an elaboration of this theme. When he so prematurely died in 1960 at the age of 63, he had edited four editions of Oppenheim's classic treatise on *International Law*. His distinguished son, Sir Elihu Lauterpacht, recounts, in the first of five volumes of his father's *Collected Papers*, that his father prepared 364 typewritten pages that were to be the introductory section of the ninth edition of Oppenheim, meant to be later incorporated in a textbook of his own. In a section on "The basis of the validity of general principles of law," Judge Sir Hersch Lauterpacht expands upon the place of general principles in terms of exceptional interest. 1 Hersch Lauterpacht, International Law, Collected Papers, General Works 75–77 (E. Lauterpacht ed., 1970).

Why did Lauterpacht characterize the Statute's provision on general principles of law as its outstanding and revolutionary contribution to international law as a whole? Because it interred the hitherto dominant positivist contention that international law consisted solely of treaties and of customary international law established by State practice. Henceforth international decisions could confidently draw on the general principles of law as a source of international law.

In 1953, Bin Cheng published his seminal book examining the contents of salient general principles of law. As the authors of the present work observe, this book is an update of Cheng's. It carries Cheng onward and upward, especially in light of the fact that the number of arbitration awards that invoke general principles of law has increased with the advent of the International Centre for Settlement of Investment Disputes and the conclusion of some 3,000 bilateral investment treaties, as well as a trio of important multilateral treaties (NAFTA, CAFTA, and the Energy Charter Treaty) that enable foreign investors directly to require States to arbitrate disputes between them. Investor/State arbitration has ballooned, while international arbitration between States carries on. Moreover, although the World Court—an unofficial term that embraces the Permanent Court of International Justice and the International Court of Justice that replaced it—is much busier the last 35 years than before, it is no longer the only international court. There is today a high tide of international adjudication and arbitration, higher than ever before in the history of international law and relations. Recourse to general principles of law is a significant element of that high tide. Whether the tide will recede is unclear. Investor/State arbitration is currently the object of disproportionate and uninformed criticism that portends the regressive rather than the progressive development of international law.

This book makes a signal contribution to the progressive development of international law by its searching study of the place of general principles of law in contemporary international arbitration and their relationship to due process of law in international and national proceedings. It proceeds to expound the particulars of salient general principles in depth. It does so with scholarship, insight, and panache.

The authors, Chuck Kotuby and Luke Sobota, who are leading international counsel and advocates, have written a book that will be of genuine use to adjudicators, advocates, and scholars.

—Stephen M. Schwebel

Preface

From the signing of treaties at Alcáçovas in 1479, Tordesillas in 1494, and Westphalia in 1648, state practice as manifested in conventions and custom served as the primary source of international law. The law of nations regulated inter-state relations, but little more. That began to change near the turn of the twentieth century. The creation of ad hoc claims commissions to adjudicate private claims under international law indicated the need for a more comprehensive system of international law. Efforts such as the Hague Conferences of 1899 and 1907 and the Geneva Conventions of 1906 and 1929 led to the dawn of "human rights" under international law, and with it the codification of certain principles and norms that comprised the emerging system of international justice.

Notable among these advancements was Article 38 of the 1920 Statute of the Permanent Court of International Justice (PCIJ), which defined "international law" to include not only "custom" and "convention" *between* States but also "the general principles of law recognized by civilized nations" *within* their municipal legal systems. The architects of the post–World War I system sought to supplement the loose bundle of customary state practices with a repository of basic principles capable of regulating the myriad issues arising from international intercourse.

The "general principles" were seen as a necessary link between the developed systems of municipal law and the inchoate system of international justice. They provided a positive law footing upon which a system of international justice could function and a means to bind parties to basic juridical concepts to which no one could object, even if they had not been codified in the "law of nations." By design, this was not natural law or equity, to which the earlier claims commissions had resorted, but the determination that certain concrete legal principles obtaining in virtually all legal systems should also apply in the emerging international system. It was believed that a legal principle common to domestic legal systems across the globe would have the legitimacy and clarity to serve as a binding source of international law.

That belief solidified in 1945 when Article 38 was, with minor alteration, reiterated in the Statute of the International Court of Justice (ICJ). Shortly thereafter, Bin Cheng of University College London wrote his seminal book, *General Principles of Law as Applied by International Courts and Tribunals.* Published in 1953, the monograph sets out, in a descriptive rather than normative manner, five categories of substantive legal concepts recognized around the world. Notions such as pacta sunt servanda and *nemo auditur propriam turpitudinem allegans* are among these principles, often expressed in Latin maxims deriving from Roman law to demonstrate pedigree, permanence, and universality. Such *substantive* principles, which can provide a rule of decision for a particular controversy, join a set of core *procedural* requirements that are "simple and basic enough to describe the judicial processes of civilized nations"—what has been dubbed "the international concept of due process." The requirement of *nemo debet esse iudex in propria sua causa* and the principle of res judicata are fundaments of the procedural norms found in most judicial systems. Induced from the positive law of countries around the world, these general principles and procedural norms create a legal baseline for international law. They are meant not to define *a* rule of law, but rather *the* rule of law.

As originally conceived, these principles were primarily intended to ameliorate the non liquet of international relations among States, as there was little else on the international plane at that time. Private claims for denial of justice had waned and, with few exceptions, ad hoc claims commissions ceased to be a central feature in the development of international law. During the quarter century following World War II, apart from the invocation of general principles in some oil concession arbitrations, the ICJ proved to be the main engine for the continued development of the general principles. But its caseload of sovereign disputes—ranging from maritime and territorial claims to issues of diplomacy and wartime conflict—called chiefly for the explication of custom and convention; the relevance of general principles of national law and minimum norms of due process was limited. The ICJ judges overseeing such sensitive and politicized disputes, moreover, may have been reluctant to rely too heavily upon unwritten substantive principles lest they be accused of expanding the scope of their jurisdiction. The invocation of the general principles identified by Cheng ebbed during this time.

This has all changed. The ICJ today is no longer the only institution on the international stage and international law is no longer reserved for state-to-state disputes. With the growth of bilateral investment treaties and other international conventions promoting and protecting global commerce, private parties may now directly seek redress for violations of international law before institutions such as the International Center for the Settlement of Investment Disputes, which issued its first arbitral award in 1977. In this context, general principles can serve as substantive guarantees for the rights of private parties vis-à-vis each other and even foreign States, be it by guiding the application of governing law or defining what is "fair and equitable" for foreign investments. Domestic courts have also been called upon to apply international law with greater frequency, such as in deciding whether to recognize a foreign judgment or arbitral award, or in applying cross-border legislation such as the U.S. Alien Tort Statute.

The importance of international law has increased along with the number of venues applying it. Yet lacunae and ambiguities persist. In some cases, the law governing a particular issue may not be clear—a manifestation of the dualism of international and municipal law. In other cases, the governing law may be silent on a particular issue or may not readily apply to the situation presented. For these and various other reasons, courts and tribunals frequently invoke general principles and procedures found in municipal law. This, in turn, has served to elucidate their application in international law—not necessarily creating new principles, but affirming, clarifying, and applying those long established. Cheng's 1953 work is now among the most cited authorities in international arbitration.

Although the general principles are, by definition, basic and even rudimentary, they hold vital importance for the rule of law in international relations. This is no mean task. Reliable application of even the most abecedarian principles of due process remains elusive in scores of judicial systems. Despite being set quite low, the baseline standards for international conduct often go unmet. Greater adherence to general principles by both private and sovereign entities would mark a significant improvement on the status quo. States have successfully invoked the general principle of *nullus commodum capere potest de sua iniuria propria* to resist investment-treaty claims brought upon contracts procured by fraud; foreign companies and individuals have had international tribunals denounce domestic court processes marred by irregularities, bias, and external pressure. With tangible consequences for noncompliance, the guarantee of "international due process" becomes a real fixture in the law that inures to the benefit of all.

The chapters that follow summarize general principles of law and norms of international due process in the modern context, with a particular focus on the developments in the 60-odd years since Cheng's writing. This is not a comparative exercise based upon country-by-country surveys. Like Cheng's work, it relies upon the courts, tribunals, and governmental and nongovernmental organizations that have mined the laws of various judicial systems and identified core and common principles. It attempts to capture the articulation and invocation of these principles in various settings. This work diverges from Cheng's in one important sense: he primarily studied the general principles that govern *sovereign* interaction; this book is largely dedicated to the general principles of law applied to *private* conduct, including the substantive principles relating to state interaction with private parties and the procedural norms governing the adjudication of disputes arising from this interaction. The difference in focus is a reflection of how the system of international justice has evolved over the past half-century.

Chapter 1 discusses the history and genesis of general principles of law and norms of international due process as a source of international law, and the practical application of these principles and norms in various national and international fora. Chapters 2 and 3 undertake a substantive review of how the general principles identified by Cheng, both substantive and procedural, have been understood and applied in subsequent cases and scholarly work. The aim is to produce a practical resource for jurists, advocates, and scholars—to collect these principles and norms in a single volume and attempt to distill their meaning in light of their development and application throughout the world.

Acknowledgments

This book would not have been possible without the generous support and counsel of numerous arbitrators, scholars, and advocates. We would like to specially thank Judge Stephen Schwebel, Professor Ronald A. Brand, Thomas F. "Tim" Cullen, Jan Paulsson, Rahim Maloo, and David Weiss. With the disclaimer that all errors and omissions are our own, we would like to recognize the meticulous research and thoughtful editing of James Egerton-Vernon, Kiran Gore, Agustin Sanz, Ryan Mellske, Anastasiya Ugale, Eldy Roché, Hugh Carlson, Lindsay Reimschussel, Maria Pradilla Picas, Tammy Pilgrim, Caroline Edsall, Stephen Morrison, Lauren Beebe, Elizabeth Kiernan, William Sullivan, and Mehreen Imtiaz. Kelly Renehan, Alexis Sacasas, and Tendai Mukau provided tireless and invaluable assistance in preparing the manuscript.

Glossary of Latin Terms

Latin Phrase	English Translation
ad impossibilia nemo tenetur	no one is held to the impossible
actori incumbit onus probandi	the burden of proof belongs to the proponent
allegans contraria non est audiendus	a person making contradictory statements is not to be heard
audi alteram partem	listen to the other side
audiatur et altera pars	may the other side also be heard
clausula rebus sic stantibus	binding so long as circumstances remain the same
coram non iudice	not before a judge
damnum emergens	direct damages
ex aequo et bono	from equity and goodness
ex dolo malo non oritur actio	an action at law does not arise from grave deceit
ex re sed non ex nomine	look at the parties' acts rather than legal form
ex turpi causa non oritur actio	an action does not arise from a loathsome cause
exceptio inadimplenti contractus	affirmative defense in the case of an unfulfilled contract
expressio unius est exclusio alterius	the express statement of one is the exclusion of the other
extra compromisum arbiter nihil facere potest	the arbitrator cannot do anything outside the agreement
fraus omnia corrumpit	fraud corrupts all
in dubio pro reo	when in doubt, in favor of the defendant
iura novit curia	the court knows the law

Latin Phrase	**English Translation**
ius commune	common law
ius gentium	law of nations
jure causa proxima non remota inspicitur	the proximate cause rather than the remote one is to be looked to
lucrum cessans	lost profits
malitis non est indulgendum	malice is not be indulged
nemini dolos suus prodesse debet	no one can profit from his own wrongs
nemo auditur propriam turpitudinem allegans	no one is to be heard relying on his own turpitude
nemo contra factum suum venire potest	no one may argue contrary to her own actions
nemo debet esse iudex in propria sua causa	no one should be the judge in his own case
nemo iudex in causa sua	no one shall be the judge in her own case
non bis in idem	not twice for the same thing
non liquet	it is unclear
nullus commodum capere potest de sua iniuria propria	no advantage may be gained from one's own wrong
omnia praesumuntur rite esse acta	all things are presumed to have been done according to the right form
pacta sunt servanda	agreements are to be observed
petitum	claim
quod omnes tangit ab omnibus approbari debet	what touches all should be approved by all
restitutio in integrum	full restitution
ubi ius ibi remedium est	wherever there is a right, there is a remedy
ut res magis valeat quam pereat	let the thing have effect rather than perish
venire contra factum proprium	to come against one's own fact is not allowed
vis major	unpreventable event (force majeure)

CHAPTER 1

An Introduction to the General Principles of Law and International Due Process

> *As Wine and Oyl are Imported to us from abroad: so must ripe Understanding, and many civil Vertues, be imported into our minds from Forreign Writings, and examples of best Ages, we shall else miscarry still, and come short in attempts of any great Enterprise.*
>
> —John Milton[1]

The general principles of law can broadly be subdivided into two categories: (1) those that regulate substantive conduct, and therefore apply to both private parties and States, and (2) norms that regulate the exercise of sovereign or adjudicative powers, and therefore apply only to States and international tribunals. The first generally provide *rules of decision* that govern the conduct of persons and entities vis-à-vis each other. Whether sovereign, corporate, or individual, all are obligated to respect their contracts, act in good faith, and refrain from taking advantage of their own wrong—to name just a few. In contrast, the second category generally prescribes the process that is owed to all individuals before the law, whether that law is administered by a sovereign court or an international arbitral tribunal. These are the general principles of *due process*. When reduced to a common denominator of process that must obtain in any civilized legal system, this set of principles represents the core concept of "international due process."

---

1 *The Character of the Long Parliament* (1681), *reprinted in* XVIII The Works of John Milton 254 (1938).

Despite being codified almost a century ago as a source of international law, the general principles of law remain somewhat tenuous and remote, with extensive discourse over their proper derivation, identification, and application. The *first* purpose of this chapter is to trace the origins of general principles, from their early usage alongside concepts of natural law and equity to their positive footing in municipal law and their eventual inclusion in the organic Statutes of the Permanent Court of International Justice (PCIJ) and the International Court of Justice (ICJ). As discussed in Subchapter A, general principles primarily derive from commonalities of positive law in domestic legal orders around the world. Products of "international consensus," general principles embody "universal standards and rules of conduct that must always be applied."[2] Faced with parties from different legal and cultural traditions, a national judge, international court, or arbitral tribunal can revert to foundational principles that are steeped in, and enjoy the *imprimatur* of, the municipal laws of various States. Although general principles can operate independently to provide a rule of decision, courts and tribunals routinely resort to them as interpretive guides, definitional tools, or corrective fail-safes, especially when application of other sources of international law yields non liquet or when the strict application of domestic law yields an anomalous result.

The choice of substantive law is not the only challenge for the international legal order. The process by which an international dispute is resolved can also raise important issues of fairness and justice, and it is here that the precepts of international due process take hold. The *second* purpose of this chapter is to observe the incorporation of national concepts of due process into international law. As explored in Subchapter B, many of the same general principles explicated by Bin Cheng in 1953 cumulatively define the international minimum standard of treatment guaranteed to all litigants appearing before courts of law. In investment arbitration cases brought to address alleged denials of justice, the international standards provide the parameters of what sort of process will pass muster from a universal perspective. They play a similar role in cases implicating the treaty guarantees of "effective means" and "fair and equitable treatment" when the conduct at issue involves adjudicative acts. National courts, too, have occasion to assess the procedural and substantive adequacy of foreign decisions and arbitral awards when they are asked to recognize and enforce them as their own. These courts typically evaluate the propriety of a foreign adjudication by measuring it against international, rather than parochial, standards of due process. The case law arising from this process itself reveals an accepted and legitimate definition of international justice.

2 *Inceysa Vallisoletana S.L. v. Republic of El Salvador*, ICSID Case No. ARB/03/26, Award, ¶¶ 226–27 (Aug. 2, 2006).

Although general principles of law have long been the subject of theoretical debate, the varied fora and circumstances where these principles and processes have been and continue to be applied cannot be denied. As a recognized source of "international law," general principles have been invoked pursuant to Article 31(3)(c) of the Vienna Convention on the Law of Treaties, which calls for "any relevant rules of international law applicable in relations between the parties" to be taken into account in treaty interpretation. They have also been applied under Article 42 of the Convention on the Settlement of Investment Disputes Between States and Nationals of Other States (ICSID Convention), which provides for ICSID tribunals, in the absence of a choice-of-law provision, to apply domestic law and "such rules of international law as may be applicable." The International Law Commission has recognized in its Model Rules on Arbitral Procedure general principles as a source of law applicable in the "absence of any agreement between the parties concerning the law to be applied."[3]

A system of international adjudication without concepts such as good faith, estoppel, or procedural equality would not long survive, and the myriad applications of the general principles—both implicit and explicit—attest to the vital position they hold in the international juridical order. As Cheng put it, "[t]hey lie at the very foundation of the legal system and are indispensable to its operation."[4]

A. The Origin and Evolution of the General Principles of Law

> *[I]t is impossible to disregard a fundamental principle of justice in the application of law, if this principle clearly indicates certain rules, necessary for the system of international relations, and applicable to the various circumstances arising in international affairs.*
>
> —Baron Édouard Descamps[5]

---

3 Report of the Commission to the General Assembly, Doc. A/3859, at art. 10(1)(c), *reprinted in* 2 YEARBOOK OF THE INTERNATIONAL LAW COMMISSION 84 (1958).

4 BIN CHENG, GENERAL PRINCIPLES OF LAW AS APPLIED BY INTERNATIONAL COURTS AND TRIBUNALS 390 (Cambridge Univ. Press 1953).

5 Permanent Court of International Justice: Advisory Committee of Jurists, *Procès-verbaux of the Proceedings of the Committee, June 16th–July 24th 1920, with Annexes* [hereinafter *Procès-verbaux*], at 324 Annex No. I (speech by Baron Descamps).

The contemporary prominence of general principles of law in international law is the product of a shift over a century ago from equity to concrete norms. Notions of equity played an important part in the early development of international law. They proved "helpful, some three centuries ago, to build up a new law of nations" at a time when there was little by way of shared ethos to guide state-to-state conduct.[6] Equity retained its importance in the eighteenth and nineteenth centuries.[7] The 1794 Jay Treaty between the United States and Great Britain, for example, provided that claims would be decided "according to the merits of the several cases, and to justice, equity, and the law of nations."[8] Similarly, Spanish and U.S. negotiators of a 1795 commercial treaty and a related 1802 indemnification agreement also settled on language referring to "'justice, equity and the law of nations.'"[9]

By the turn of the twentieth century, however, equity had come under criticism. Notions of equity, often associated with natural law, were criticized as too malleable to form "a durable foundation" of the emerging international justice system, so they gradually gave way to notions of "positive international law, as recognized by nations and governments through their acts and statements."[10] The devastation of the First World War made the need for explicit sources of international law acute. The treaties ending the War frequently made provision for the settlement of international disputes implicating the interests of private parties. Such "massive entry of private interests into the field of international law" created a need for clear decisional rules.[11]

The international community's shift away from abstract equity was made concrete in Article 38 of the PCIJ and ICJ Statutes. First promulgated in 1920, Article 38 defined "international law" as those rules emerging from "international conventions," "international custom," and "the general principles of law recognized by civilized nations."[12] It also recognized "judicial decisions and the teachings of

---

6 *North American Dredging Company of Texas (U.S.A.) v. United Mexican States* (Mar. 31, 1926), 4 R.I.A.A. 26, ¶ 12.

7 *See generally* Louis B. John & Russell Gabriel, *Equity in International Law*, 82 Proceedings of the Annual Meeting (American Society of International Law) 277 (Apr. 20–23, 1988).

8 Ruth Lapidoth, *Equity in International Law*, 22 Israel L. Rev. 161, 167 (1987).

9 Robert Renbert Wilson, The International Law Standard in Treaties of the United States 46–48 (1953).

10 *North American Dredging Company of Texas (U.S.A.) v. United Mexican States* (Mar. 31, 1926), 4 R.I.A.A. 29, 30.

11 *Texaco Overseas Petroleum Co. (TOPCO) v. Gov't of the Libyan Arab Republic*, 17 I.L.M. 1, 14 (1978) (quotation marks and citation omitted).

12 Statute of the Permanent Court of International Justice art. 38(1).

the most highly qualified publicists of the various nations" as "subsidiary means for the determination of rules of law."[13]

Excluded from Article 38 is the notion of equity, at least as a freestanding source of "international law."[14] Equity of course continues to exist. The ICJ has referred to "considerations of equity" when tasked with applying the law of diplomatic protection in *Barcelona Traction*;[15] incorporated "equitable principles" into its determination of maritime boundaries in the *North Sea Continental Shelf* cases,[16] and searched for an "equitable solution derived from the applicable law" in the *Fisheries Jurisdiction* cases.[17] But the unbridled exercise of equity, untethered to any definite metrics, is difficult to characterize as law. As Judge André Gros wrote in his *Gulf of Maine* dissent:

> Controlled equity as a procedure for applying the law would contribute to the proper functioning of international justice; equity left, without any objective elements of control, to the wisdom of the judge reminds us that equity was once measured by "the Chancellor's foot". I doubt that international justice can long survive an equity measured by the judge's eye. When equity is simply a reflection of the judge's perception, the courts which judge in this way part company from those which apply the law.[18]

Thus, under Article 38(2), a case may be decided *"ex aequo et bono"* only "if the parties agree thereto."[19] By contrast, an international court or tribunal duly seised of jurisdiction requires no special consent from the parties in order to apply "international law," which is expressly defined in Article 38 to include "the general principles of law recognized by civilized nations."

---

13 *Id.*

14 P. Van Dijk, *Equity: A Recognized Manifestation of International Law?*, *in* INTERNATIONAL LAW AND ITS SOURCES: LIBER AMICORUM MAARTEN BOS 11 (Wybo P. Heere ed., 1989) ("a majority [of the Advisory Committee of Jurists] did not accept equity as an independent source of international law").

15 *Barcelona Traction, Light & Power Co., Ltd. (Belg. v. Spain)*, Second Phase, Judgment, 1970 I.C.J. 3, ¶ 93 (Feb. 5).

16 *North Sea Continental Shelf Cases (Ger./Den. and Ger./Neth.)*, Judgment, 1969 I.C.J. 3, ¶¶ 47, 55, 85, 88, 90, 98 (Feb. 20).

17 *Fisheries Jurisdiction Cases (U.K. v. Ice.)*, Merits, Judgment, 1974 I.C.J. 3, ¶ 78 (July 25).

18 *Delimitation of the Maritime Boundary in the Gulf of Maine Area (Can. v. U.S.)*, Judgment, 1984 I.C.J. 246, 386 (Oct. 12) (dissenting opinion of Judge Gros).

19 As Hugh Thirlway has explained:

> [T]he text [of Article 38(2)] is generally understood as meaning that the Court would decide simply on the basis of what it thought was fair in the circumstances, however much the solution so arrived at might depart from what would have resulted from the application of law. While a

Despite a similarity of function in terms of filling lacunae and tempering the application of other laws, general principles are quite distinct from equity. General principles of law are discrete decisional norms. As Cheng cautioned, it is "essential" that the scope and substance of the general principles "be clearly defined and understood" to avoid "the risk of [their] being exploited as an ideological cloak for self-interest."[20] This appreciation is reinforced by Article 38(1)(c)'s use of the definite article before "general principles of law," which denotes an identifiable and finite source of "international law." Legal concepts that expressly call for "equitable" consideration are now understood to encompass general principles. Thomas Wälde explained that the "fair and *equitable* treatment" (FET) standard found in most bilateral investment treaties (BITs) "can not be derived from subjective personal or cultural sentiments; it must be anchored in objective rules and principles."[21] As discussed in chapter 2.C, the FET standard is partly defined by reference to the general principles of law described in Article 38.

This is not to say that general principles are some newfangled creation of the twentieth century. The modern trend away from equity carries echoes of the evolution of *ius gentium* during Roman times. Because the civil law applied only to Roman citizens, *ius gentium* arose to provide a legal framework for the influx of peregrine, or non-Romans, into the capital:

> There was no positive law which could be applied to legal disputes between foreigners of different nationalities or between peregrini and Roman citizens. In such cases the Praetor Peregrinus had thus to decide *ex aequo et bono*. But as more and more people came to Rome from abroad so that the application of foreign legal principles became an everyday matter, it became increasingly evident that certain basic ideas and principles of law were common to all people. In due course, these generally accepted principles developed into a system of law which was initially quite independent of the civil law, but in the later days of the Empire was merged into one single system.[22]

> decision so given would be a judicial one, it would by definition not be a legal one, in the sense of based on law, and in no sense therefore can paragraph 2 of Article 38 be regarded as indicating a source of international law.

Hugh Thirlway, The Sources of International Law 104–05 (2014).

20 Cheng, *supra* note 4, at xiv.

21 *Int'l Thunderbird Gaming Corp. v. United Mexican States*, UNCITRAL, Separate Opinion of Thomas Wälde, ¶ 30 (Dec. 1, 2005).

22 Hermann Mosler, The International Society as a Legal Community 123 (1980); see also Clifford Ando, Law, Language and Empire in the Roman Tradition 2–4 (2011).

Examples of shared concepts cited by Roman jurists include the basic contracts of sale (*emptio venditio*) and lease (*locatio conductio*).[23] The revival of the study of Roman law in eleventh-century Northern Italy, [24] some five hundred years after the publication of the last major texts of Roman law, directed the energies of medieval and early modern scholars toward the problem, never really resolved, of determining the precise nature and content of the *ius gentium*.[25] After the Lutheran and Calvinist Reformations of the sixteenth century had ruptured the legal and political unity of Europe,[26] seventeenth-century jurists beginning with Hugo Grotius began to redeploy the concept of *ius gentium* to regulate relations between sovereigns. Grotius and his contemporaries followed the classical Roman jurists in conceiving of the *ius gentium* as a body of norms that applied to disputes of an international character and that consisted of fundamental and universally shared legal concepts drawn from Roman private law. For Grotius these concepts included, among other things, *pacta sunt servanda*.[27]

The articulation of general legal maxims in Roman law has also influenced the development of the general principles of law. Classical Roman jurists preferred to develop the law case by case, leaving the underlying general concepts and rules of law implicit in their discussion of specific facts.[28] On occasion, however, Roman jurists and practitioners formulated "working rules of thumb" to guide their reasoning.[29] These rules of thumb, intended to apply to specific legal situations but often expressed in general terms, were gathered into collections and published starting in the second century A.D., and later compiled in a *Digest* in the sixth century.[30] Medieval specialists in canon law, the law of the Roman Catholic Church, joined in this scholarly effort by compiling their own collections of general rules of canon law that were drawn from or modeled on the rules in the *Digest*.[31] Medieval jurists also devised their own legal maxims, called brocards,

---

23 Max Kaser, Das Romanische Privatrecht 202–05 (2d ed. 1971).

24 *See generally* S. Kuttner, *The Revival of Jurisprudence*, *in* Renaissance and Renewal in the Twelfth Century 299 (Robert L. Benson & Giles Constable eds., 1982).

25 See 2 Enno Cortese, Il Diritto Nella Storia Medievale 93–5 (1995).

26 On the unifying role of the Roman Catholic Church in the development of medieval Western law, see generally Harold Berman, Law and Revolution 51–118 (1983).

27 *See* Franz Wieacker, Privatrechtsgeschichte der Neuzeit 288–301 (2d ed. 1967) (discussing Grotius and contemporary natural law theorists).

28 *See* Franz Wieacker, Vom römischen Recht 9 (2d ed. 1961); Fritz Pringsheim, *The Inner Relationship Between English and Roman Law*, 5 Cambridge L.J. 347 (1935).

29 Peter Stein, Regulae iuris 81 (1966).

30 *See id.* at 79–83, 101.

31 *See* Peter Stein, *The Digest Title, De diversis regulis iuris antiqui and the General Principles of Law*, *in* 1 Essays in Jurisprudence in Honor of Roscoe Pound 1 (Ralph A. Newman ed., 1962).

that they gathered together into freestanding collections.[32] Article 38(1)(c) of the PCIJ Statute is thus situated in this rich tradition of studying and compiling general principles of law.

It should thus come as no surprise that, "[l]ong before Article 38 of the Statute of the Permanent Court of International Justice made the 'general principles of law recognized by civilized states' a source of common international law, foreign offices and arbitral tribunals had relied on such general principles to work out a loose minimum which they applied constantly in interstate practice."[33] The Anglo-American Board of Commissioners established under Article VII of the Jay Treaty of 1794, for instance, referred to shared legal principles in its discussion of international law.[34] The constitutions and codes of the newly emancipated States in the Americas followed suit in the nineteenth century.[35] The failed Central American Court of Justice, established in 1907, was similarly bound to apply "the principles of international law."[36] Subsequent courts and tribunals have variably used the terms "traditional principles,"[37] "principle[s] generally accepted,"[38] and "well-known rules"[39] when referring to general principles of law. A tribunal sitting in 1872 applied "principles of universal jurisprudence," specifically that of *actori incumbit onus probandi*, and felt justified in doing so because "the legislation of all nations" recognizes it.[40] The Permanent Court of Arbitration (PCA) in the *Russian Indemnity Case* held in 1912 that it was generally accepted that interest on a contract price forms part of compensatory relief

32 *See* Albert Lang, *Zur Entstehungsgeschichte der Brocardasammlungen*, 62 Zeitschrift der Savigny-Stiftung für Rechtsgeschichte: Kanonistische Abteilung 106 (1942).

33 Edward Borchard, *The "Minimum Standard" of the Treatment of Aliens*, 38 Mich. L. Rev. 445, 448–49 (1940).

34 Cheng, *supra* note 4, at 387.

35 The 1863 Constitution of the United States of Colombia provided that "ius gentium is an integral part of national legislation" (art. 91). The 1853 Argentine Constitution also recognized the applicability of *ius gentium* for extraterritorial prosecution (art. 118), whereas international treaties were the "supreme law of the land" together with the Constitution itself and municipal law (art. 31). The 1822 Chilean Constitution specifically empowered the judiciary to hear cases under *ius gentium* (art. 166). The 1863 statute regulating the federal jurisdiction in Argentina (still applicable, as amended) provided that courts are to apply, inter alia, "the general principles of ius gentium" (§ 21, Law No. 48).

36 Convention for the Establishment of a Central American Court of Justice art. 21, Dec. 20, 1907.

37 *Delimitation of the Polish-Czechoslovakian Frontier (Question of Jaworzina)*, Advisory Opinion ¶ 79, 1923 P.C.I.J. (Ser. B) No. 8 (Dec. 6).

38 *Factory at Chorzów (Germ. v. Pol.)*, Jurisdiction, Judgment No. 8, 1927 P.C.I.J. (Ser. A) No. 9, at 31 (July 26).

39 *Interpretation of Article 3, Paragraph 2, of the Treaty of Lausanne (Frontier between Turkey and Iraq)*, Advisory Opinion, 1925 P.C.I.J. (Ser. B) No. 12, at 32 (Nov. 21).

40 *Sentence du 26 mars 1872 (Affaire du Queen)*, at 708 (Albert De la Pradelle & Nicolas Politis eds.).

when payment on the contract is delayed. In the PCA's words, this principle can be derived from "all the private legislation of the States forming the European concert, [as well as] Roman law."[41] And, on the domestic plane, the U.S. Supreme Court deemed the principle of res judicata to be a "rule of fundamental and substantial justice" nearly a century ago.[42]

Against this backdrop, the recognition of general principles in Article 38 of the PCIJ Statute did not materially "add to the armoury" of law available to an international jurist.[43] It instead marked an attempt to distill and articulate the past practice of international courts and tribunals.[44] The text of Article 38 notably places general principles on the same footing as treaties and custom. During the negotiating history of the Statute, the words "in the order following" ("*en ordre successif*") in the introductory phrase of the draft article were deleted, thus eliminating hierarchy among these three sources of international law.[45] At the same time, general principles escape classification as "subsidiary" sources of law alongside judicial decisions and scholarly opinions, which are modes of applying and explicating the law, not sources of law themselves.

General principles are in some ways conceptually similar to "international custom." The primary difference, as elaborated in Subchapter A.2, is that general principles derive from the positive laws promulgated *within* States. Custom, on the other hand, is typically moored in the practice *among* States and accepted

---

41 *Russian Indemnity Case (Russ. v. Turk.)*, PCA, Award, 11 (Nov. 11, 1912).

42 *Hart Steel Co. v. Railroad Supply Co.*, 244 U.S. 294, 299 (1917). There is a lively debate in the United States as to whether foreign or international law should be applied in deciding constitutional questions. *See generally* STEPHEN BREYER, THE COURT AND THE WORLD (2015); Prepared Remarks of U.S. Attorney General Alberto R. Gonzales at the University of Chicago Law School, 9 Nov. 2005, *available at* http://www.justice.gov/archive/ag/speeches/2005/ag_speech_0511092.html; Ganesh Sitaraman, *The Use and Abuse of Foreign Law in Constitutional Interpretation*, 32 HARV. J.L. & PUB. POL'Y 653 (2009). There is, in contrast, little dispute about the propriety of resorting to general principles in those domestic cases in which international or foreign laws are directly at issue.

43 CHENG, *supra* note 4, at 19.

44 *See* FABIÁN RAIMONDO, GENERAL PRINCIPLES OF LAW IN THE DECISIONS OF INTERNATIONAL CRIMINAL COURTS AND TRIBUNALS 21–26 (2008).

45 The laws do interact in a hierarchical manner, which may vary depending upon use and context. *See* CHENG, *supra* note 4, at 393 ("From the juridical point of view, the superior value of general principles of law over customs and treaties cannot be denied; for these principles furnish the juridical basis of treaties and customs and govern their interpretation and application. From the operative point of view, however, the hierarchical order is reversed. Rules of law though in derogation of general principles of law are binding."). As explained by Lord Phillimore during the drafting process, the sequencing of Article 38(1) reflects the "logical order in which these sources would occur to the mind of the judge." *Procès-verbaux*, *supra* note 5, at 333.

by them as law.[46] The requirement in Article 38(1)(c) that general principles be recognized by "civilized nations" evinces a modicum of legal cultivation, consensus, and continuity, such that state consent to the principles as binding law may be safely presumed.[47] The same can, and has, been said of customary international law.[48] But the term "civilized nation" is antiquated and has rightly been the subject of extensive criticism.[49] ICJ Judge Giorgio Gaja has speculated that "this inappropriate wording may partly explain why the ICJ has been so far reluctant to refer to specific rules of one or other municipal system, lest it imply that some other systems had to be regarded as less civilized."[50] If that is so, one might hope for alteration in the ICJ's approach given that there is no basis to exclude consideration of the written laws of any State in assessing the existence of a general principle.[51]

Still, consistent with Article 38 of its enabling statute, the ICJ has routinely identified and relied upon the general principles, albeit often without any uniform

---

46 *See* Thirlway, *supra* note 19, at 56–57 (explaining that customary international law typically requires "sufficient State practice (i.e. sufficient examples of consistent following of the alleged custom), and that this should have been accompanied by . . . the view (or conviction) that what is involved is (or, perhaps, should be) a requirement of the law, or of necessity") (quotations marks and citations omitted); *North Sea Continental Shelf (Ger./Den. and Ger./Neth.)*, Judgment, 1969 I.C.J. 3, ¶ 77 (Feb. 20) ("Not only must the acts concerned amount to a settled practice, but they must also be such, or be carried out in such a way, as to be evidence of a belief that this practice is rendered obligatory by the existence of a rule of law requiring it."); Olufemi Elias & Chin Lin, *General Principles of Law, Soft Law and the Identification of International Law*, 28 Neth. Y.B. Int'l L. 3, 26 (1997).

47 A modern, but still ambiguous, permutation of the phrase can be found in the 2012 U.S. Model BIT, which speaks to principles and processes "embodied in the principal legal systems of the world." 2012 U.S. Model Bilateral Investment Treaty art. 5.2(a) (emphasis added), *available at* http://www.state.gov/documents/organization/188371.pdf (last visited Jan. 11, 2014).

48 *See* J. Starke, Introduction to International Law 34–38 (Butterworth's 9th ed. 1984).

49 *See, e.g.*, *North Sea Continental Shelf (Ger./Den. and Ger./Neth.)*, 1969 I.C.J. 3, 133–34 (Feb. 20) (separate opinion of Judge Ammoun) (arguing that "[t]he discrimination between civilized nations and uncivilized nations . . . is the legacy of the period, now passed away, of colonialism" and that "international law [] has become . . . a universal law able to draw on the internal sources of law of all States whose relations it is destined to govern").

50 Giorgio Gaja, *General Principles of Law*, *in* 4 Max Planck Encyclopedia of Public International Law ¶ 2 (Rüdiger Wolfrum ed., 2012).

51 *See* Thirlway, *supra* note 19, at 95 n.8; Mosler, *supra* note 22, at 122 (arguing that the phrase "civilized nations" must "in present day circumstances be interpreted as meaning recognition by the international community" in light of "the concept of the sovereign equality of States"); *North Sea Continental Shelf (Ger./Den. and Ger./Neth.)*, 1969 I.C.J. 3, 134 (Feb. 20) (separate opinion of Judge Ammoun) (Article 38(1)(c) "cannot be interpreted otherwise than by attributing to it a universal scope involving no discrimination between the members of a single community based upon sovereign equality"); Alain Pellet, *Article 38*, *in* The Statute of the International Court of Justice: A Commentary 837 (Andreas Zimmermann et al. eds., 2d ed. 2012) ("all States must be considered as 'civilized nations' ").

reference, label, or comparative analysis.[52] Shortly after its inception, the ICJ in *Corfu Channel* pointed out that circumstantial evidence "is admitted in all systems of law, and its use is recognized by international decisions."[53] A few years later, it noted in *Administrative Tribunal* that it is a "well-established and generally recognized principle of law [that] a judgment rendered by [a] judicial body is *res judicata* and has binding force between the parties to the dispute."[54] Principles such as estoppel and abuse of rights continue to mark ICJ jurisprudence.[55] As will be discussed in chapter 2, other courts and tribunals have done even more with the general principles than the ICJ.[56]

Notwithstanding their extensive use in international adjudication, there has long been and continues to be extensive debate about the proper source of general principles. In drafting Article 38(1)(c) of the PCIJ Statute, the primary concern of the Advisory Committee of Jurists was the situation of non liquet, with the PCIJ being rendered powerless in cases where treaty and customary international law did not directly speak to the issues presented.[57] Baron Édouard Descamps proposed that, in these situations, resort should be had to "rules of international law as recognized by the legal *conscience* of civilized nations," which he understood to mean "objective justice."[58] Perhaps because of an inadequate translation of the word "conscience," which in Baron Descamps's original French did not

52 *See* CLARENCE WILFRED JENKS, THE PROSPECTS OF INTERNATIONAL ADJUDICATION 268–305 (Stevens & Sons Ltd. 1964); HERSCH LAUTERPACHT, THE DEVELOPMENT OF INTERNATIONAL LAW BY THE INTERNATIONAL COURT 158–72 (Cambridge Univ. Press 1982); Jaye Ellis, *General Principles and Comparative Law*, 22 EUR. J. INT'L L. 949, 955 (2011) (noting that judges on the ICJ "have continued to assert the existence of general principles without reference to comparative studies of domestic law, often making reference to concepts much more at home in a natural law conception."); Michelle Biddulph & Dwight Newman, *A Contextualized Account of General Principles of International Law*, 26 PACE INT'L L. REV. 286, 292 (2014).

53 *Corfu Channel (U.K. v. Alb.)*, Judgment, Merits, 1949 I.C.J. 4, 18 (Apr. 9).

54 *Effect of Awards of Compensation Made by the United Nations Administrative Tribunal*, Advisory Opinion, 1954 I.C.J. 47, 53 (July 13).

55 *Case concerning the Arbitral Award Made by the King of Spain on 23 December 1906 (Hond. v. Nicar.)*, Judgment, 1960 I.C.J. 192, 209, 213 (Nov. 18); *Case concerning the Temple of Preah Vihear (Cambodia v. Thai.)*, Judgment, Merits, 1962 I.C.J. 6, 23, 31, 32 (June 15); *id.* at 39–51 (separate opinion of Vice-President Alfaro).

56 *See, e.g.*, Ole Kristian Fauchald, *The Legal Reasoning of ICSID Tribunals—An Empirical Analysis*, 19 EUR. J. INT'L L. 301, 312 (2008) (reporting that of 98 ICSID decisions, only eight examined the general principles as a separate legal basis).

57 *See generally* Pellet, *supra* note 51, at 739–42 ("Most of the members of the Committee shared the view that a declaration of non liquet would amount to a denial of justice and was consequently inconceivable.").

58 *Procès-verbaux*, *supra* note 5, at 310, 311, 323 (emphasis added).

necessarily carry moral overtones, the American statesman Elihu Root objected that the meaning was unclear, and opposed its inclusion on the ground that it could deter States from assenting to the jurisdiction of the PCIJ.[59] The text was then revised by Lord Phillimore, who understood the "general principles of law recognized by civilised nations" referenced in his draft to be those "accepted by all nations *in foro domestic*."[60] Baron Descamps and the other members of the Advisory Committee readily assented to the revision. As Cheng observed, with "[t]he views of Phillimore and Descamps being in substance the same, there is no foundation for the assertion that the solution adopted constituted a rejection of the views of Descamps and the adoption of the original view of Elihu Root"—"the exact opposite is the case."[61] Yet drawing upon differences, whether real or perceived, between the positions of Descamps, Phillimore, and Root, jurists and scholars have long debated whether general principles may be taken solely from municipal laws or whether they can also find footing in international and other legal sources.[62] These points of academic disagreement were well developed at the time of Cheng's writing,[63] and persist today.[64] During the Cold War, publicists from socialist and developing countries objected to derivation of general principles from the municipal laws of "capitalist powers," viewing this as "an effort to proclaim principles of the bourgeois legal systems as binding for all."[65] Many

---

59 CHENG, *supra* note 4, at 7–10. Mr. Root initially took the view that nations "will not submit to such principles as have not been developed into positive rules supported by an accord between all States." *Procès-verbaux, supra* note 5, at 287.

60 *Procès-verbaux, supra* note 5, at 335.

61 CHENG, *supra* note 4, at 15.

62 Like Cheng's own study, the primary purpose of this monograph is to determine what the general principles are in substance and the manner in which they have been applied, not to resolve long-standing debates over their normative legitimacy, theoretical basis, or proper classification.

63 *See* CHENG, *supra* note 4, at 2–5.

64 *See, e.g., Pulp Mills on the River Uruguay (Arg. v. Uru.)*, Judgment, 2010 I.C.J. 14, 156 (Apr. 20) (separate opinion of Judge Cançado Trindade) (reviewing literature on the general principles, arguing against their being grounded solely in domestic law, and asserting that they emanate from "the universal juridical conscience"); Ellis, *supra* note 52, at 954 (critiquing the rationale behind, and the methodology for determining, general principles: "In a heterogeneous society defined by significant power imbalances, in which law-making processes can be described as democratic only in a very loose sense, one has good reason to be wary of general principles as a source of law. At the same time, this source arguably has a very important role to play both in the settlement of individual disputes and in the development of international law."); Stephan W. Schill, *General Principles of Law and Investment Law*, *in* INTERNATIONAL INVESTMENT LAW: THE SOURCES OF RIGHTS AND OBLIGATIONS 133, 138–39 (2012) (reciting criticisms that general principles are "residual and weak" and only "fill gaps" with "technical issues of law," are "highly dependent upon subjective evaluations of arbitrators," and are "misused" to favor "foreign investors" and "capital-exporting . . . States").

65 GRIGORIJ I. TUNKIN, THEORY OF INTERNATIONAL LAW 198 (1974); *see also* FARHAD MALEKIAN, THE SYSTEM OF INTERNATIONAL LAW: FORMATION, TREATIES, RESPONSIBILITY 37–39 (1987).

rejected this criticism, which ultimately did not have a meaningful effect on the use or derivation of general principles.[66]

The orthodox approach is to define general principles by reference to *private* law found in *municipal* systems,[67] but this has not rendered other sources of law irrelevant. Judges and arbitrators have also resorted to "[p]rinciples grounded in the very nature of the international community or in other words 'general principles of international law.' "[68] Indeed, as a matter of practice, those who attempt to document the genesis of a particular general principle tend to point to *all* supporting authority, including non-domestic sources where available.[69] The

66 *See, e.g.*, GODEFRIDUS J.H. HOOF, RETHINKING THE SOURCES OF INTERNATIONAL LAW 141 (1983) ("Whatever the differences between 'bourgeois' law and socialist law may be . . . [a]t the very least they are both systems of law and, therefore, have in common their functions of ordering and regulating relations in society."); RAIMONDO, *supra* note 44, at 39 ("Tunkin's argument has no major impact on current scholarship, probably because the Soviet doctrine of international law collapsed with the Soviet Union.").

67 CHENG, *supra* note 4, at 25; *see also* HERSCH LAUTERPACHT, PRIVATE LAW SOURCES AND ANALOGIES OF INTERNATIONAL LAW 71 (Longmans, Green & Co. Ltd. 1927) ("general principles of law are for the most practical purposes identical with general principles of *private* law") (emphasis added); R. JENNINGS & A. WATTS, OPPENHEIM'S INTERNATIONAL LAW 36–37 (Pearson 9th ed. 1992) ("[t]he intention is to authorise the Court to apply the general principles of *municipal* jurisprudence, in particular of *private* law, in so far as they are applicable to relations of States") (emphasis added); Johan G. Lammers, *General Principles of Law Recognized by Civilized Nations, in* H.F. VAN PANHUYS, ESSAYS ON THE DEVELOPMENT OF THE INTERNATIONAL LEGAL ORDER 53, 56 (Martinus Nijhoff 1980) (noting that many scholars believe that the general principles "consist only of principles generally recognized—implicitly or explicitly—in national legal systems or of principles basic to law in general"); Biddulph & Newman, *supra* note 52 (arguing that there is a purely "domestic approach" and a "hybrid approach" to analyzing general principles, with most deriving general principles from domestic legal systems and some also taking account the structure of the international system itself) (citation omitted).

68 *Pulp Mills on the River Uruguay (Arg. v. Uru.)*, Judgment, 2010 I.C.J. 14, 146, ¶ 27 (separate opinion of Judge Cançado Trindade) (arguing that looking solely at municipal law "seems to amount to a static, and dogmatic position," and that there "is epistemologically no reason not to have recourse to general principles of law as recognized in domestic as well as international law"); *South West Africa (Eth. v. S. Afr.; Liber. v. S. Afr.)*, Second Phase, Judgment, 1966 I.C.J. 6, 287–98 (July 18) (dissenting opinion of Judge Kōtarō Tanaka) (arguing that human rights are protected under Article 38(1)(c) irrespective of recognition in domestic law); GEBHARD BÜCHELE, PROPORTIONALITY IN INVESTOR-STATE ARBITRATION 31–32 (Oxford 2015); Stephan W. Schill, *Enhancing International Investment Law's Legitimacy: Conceptual and Methodological Foundations of a New Public Law Approach*, 52 VA. J. INT'L L. 57, 90 (2011) ("The general principles of law comprise principles generally recognized in domestic law, general principles deriving from international relations, and general principles inherent in every kind of legal order."); Lammers, *supra* note 67, at 69 (advocating in favor of "principles of international law," which are "[p]rinciples induced from more specific rules of customary international law" that "exceed . . . the scope of the specific rules of customary international law from which they are induced" and include expressions of "general legal" conviction of States that have "found application in state practice").

69 Biddulph & Newman, *supra* note 52, at 291 (general principles "have been identified in municipal systems of states, in the underpinning of the international legal system as a whole, in natural law, as inchoate custom, in the tenets of legal logic, and in non-binding 'soft law' instruments") (citations omitted).

ICJ, for example, situated the general principles invoked in *Factory at Chorzów* and *Corfu Channel* in both municipal law and international jurisprudence.[70] More recently, an ICSID tribunal looked at international law and human rights law, in addition to domestic law, to flesh out an investor's legitimate expectations where there has been no specific promise by the State to refrain from exercising its regulatory powers.[71] Grounding general principles in municipal law nonetheless remains the norm in part because there is "no consensus on the correct methodology for identifying and applying general principles on the international plane."[72] Furthermore, from a theoretical standpoint, general principles emanating from the will of sovereign States carry a greater sanction of legitimacy.

But there is no a priori reason for restricting principles to issues of private law. Although Sir Hersch Lauterpacht emphasized the primacy of private law, he also recognized the role of public law, general maxims, and jurisprudence in forming general principles.[73] Half a century ago, Wolfgang Freidmann wrote that the "neat distinction of the categories of public and private law has long ceased to be expressive of the realities of contemporary municipal, as well as international, law"—he thus advocated for grounding general principles "both in public international law ... and in principles extracted from recognized national systems of law."[74] The justification for doing so has only strengthened since that time:

> [W]ith the increasing role of non-State actors in international law, comparative law analysis in other areas [besides private law] become more and more important. Issues involved in human rights cases and investor-State arbitrations often resemble situations for which domestic legal systems have developed solutions in their administrative or constitutional

70 *Factory at Chorzów*, Jurisdiction, Judgment No. 8, 1927 P.C.I.J. (Ser. A) No. 9, at 31 (July 26) (explaining the principle that a party cannot complain of a breach caused by the acts of the complaining party is "generally accepted in the jurisprudence of international arbitration, as well as by municipal courts"); *Corfu Channel (U.K. v. Alb.)*, Merits, Judgment, 1949 I.C.J. 4, 18 (Apr. 9) (holding that indirect evidence is "admitted in all systems of law, and its use is recognized by international decisions").

71 *Total S.A. v. Argentine Republic*, ICSID Case No. ARB/04/01, Decision on Liability, ¶¶ 111–34 (Dec. 27, 2010).

72 Biddulph & Newman, *supra* note 52, at 290–91.

73 *See* Hersch Lauterpacht, The Function of Law in the International Community 65, 123–26, 408 (1933).

74 Wolfgang Friedmann, *The Uses of "General Principles" in the Development of International Law*, 57 Am. J. Int'l L. 279, 281, 284 (1963).

> law jurisprudence. There is no reason why international tribunals should not draw on this experience.[75]

In investment cases concerning a State's exercise of its regulatory powers, for instance, both foreign investors and sovereigns would presumably benefit from any clarity that might be gleaned from domestic administrative law jurisprudence.

> Engaging in comparative public law analysis, and in the quest to uncover general principles of public law, helps international investment law to benefit from the experience other public law regimes have developed, not only in limiting the exercise of state powers, but also in empowering the state by illustrating the extent of regulatory space they are generally accorded.[76]

In this way, general principles become vital to the continued functioning and progression of international dispute resolution. By virtue of general principles being recognized as among the sources of international law, an international tribunal is empowered to choose and adapt common legal elements from developed systems in reaching its decision. The benefit of general principles "may be systemic ('general principles' as 'constitutional' rules), logical ('general principles' as those principles logically presupposed by the concept of law itself) and/or substantive (that ordinary positive law must bow to certain 'higher' natural law principles, even if these principles are 'soft')."[77] In identifying and applying a general principle, the tribunal melds it into the corpus of international law. General principles have thus been likened to the "bees of law," promoting "a great fluidity of the main legal ideas, which can be transported by way of analogy from one branch [of international law] to the other, from one legal system to the other."[78]

For a regime beset by fragmentation, cross-pollination is necessary to the proper functioning of the international system of justice:

> Private [domestic] law, being in general more developed than international law, has always constituted a sort of reserve store of principles upon

75 BÜCHELE, *supra* note 68, at 33; Stephan W. Schill, *General Principles of Law and Investment Law*, *in* T. GOZZINI ET AL., INTERNATIONAL INVESTMENT LAW: THE SOURCES OF RIGHTS AND OBLIGATIONS 133, 136 (2012) ("General principles of law could help overcome the frictions between the public international law framework and the private law dispute settlement mechanism if those engaged in investor-State arbitrations do not only consider general principles of *private* law, but recognize the potential of principles of *public* law to reshape investor-State arbitration and investment law.").

76 Schill, *supra* note 68, at 100 (arguing that international investment law "shares core functional similarities with domestic administrative and constitutional review of government conduct" and should be "analyzed from a comparative public law perspective").

77 Elias & Lin, *supra* note 46, at 6.

78 Robert Kolb, *Principles as Sources of International Law (With Special Reference to Good Faith)*, 53 NETH. INT'L L. REV. 1, 27 (2006).

> which the latter has been in the habit of drawing . . . for the good reason that a principle which is found to be generally accepted by civilized legal systems may fairly be assumed to be so reasonable as to be necessary to the maintenance of justice under any system.[79]

This exercise of importing more developed principles of law finds footing in most systems of jurisprudence. Where there is no adequate law to regulate certain conduct, judges the world over will revert to existing principles from which they can draw an appropriate rule of decision.[80] The general principles inform this process in international disputes, "enabl[ing] the Court to replenish, without subterfuge, the rules of international law by principles tested within the shelter of more mature and closely integrated legal systems."[81] As Saul Levmore has suggested, *uniformity* among different legal systems can often be explained by the fact that legal rules in all but the most tightly knit communities must control self-interested behavior that threatens the general welfare, whereas *variety* often arises with respect to rules that are not that important for the community or that raise issues about which reasonable people (even in the same culture) could disagree.[82] In explaining its own consultation of general principles, the International Criminal Tribunal for the Former Yugoslavia explained that "[t]he value of these sources is that they may disclose 'general concepts and legal institutions' which, if common to a broad spectrum of national legal systems, disclose an international approach to a legal question which may be considered as an appropriate indicator of the international law on the subject."[83]

None of this is particularly surprising. Inductive reasoning from common municipal laws is intuitive for most international jurists, who, having been educated and having practiced in their home countries, can be expected to rely upon their

---

79 *Doe v. Exxon Mobil Corp.*, 654 F.3d 11, 54 (D.C. Cir. 2011) (Kavanaugh, J., dissenting) (quoting J.L. Brierly, The Law of Nations 62–63 (6th ed. 1963)).

80 The authority to conduct this exercise is often part of national civil codes and procedural rules. *See, e.g.*, Argentinean Civil Code of 1869 art. 16; Austrian Civil Code of 1811 art. 7; Chilean Civil Code art. 24; Brazilian Civil Code of 1917 art. 7; Italian Civil Code art. 12; Mexican Federal Civil Code art. 19; Peruvian Civil Code of 1852 art. IX; Russian Civil Code art. 6; Swiss Civil Code art. 1; Ecuadorean Civil Code art. 18; Venezuelan Code of Civil Procedure art. 8; Ecuadorean Code of Civil Procedure art. 274.

81 Georg Schwarzenberger, *Foreword* to Bin Cheng, General Principles of Law as Applied by International Courts and Tribunals, at xi (1953).

82 Saul Levmore, *Variety and Uniformity in the Treatment of the Good-Faith Purchaser*, 16(1) J. Legal Stud. 43, 44 (Jan. 1987).

83 *Prosecutor v. Kunarac et al.*, Case Nos. IT-96-23-T and IT-96-23/1-T, Judgment, ¶ 439 (Int'l Crim. Trib. For the Former Yugoslavia) (Feb. 22, 2001).

domestic training and experience when they don the role of international adjudicator.[84] René-Jean Dupuy, for instance, frequently cited French law in support of his application of the "international law of contracts" in the *TOPCO* award.[85] Generally speaking, this is to the good. As the ICJ indicated in the *Barcelona Traction* case, if "the Court were to decide [its] case[s] in disregard of the relevant institutions of municipal law it would . . . lose touch with reality, for there are no corresponding institutions of international law to which the Court could resort." The general principles, unlike equity or natural law, situate international law in *positive* domestic law that runs through the legal orders of sovereigns around the world.

1. Identifying General Principles

Divining the precise content of a general principle of law can be a "formidable task."[86] As Lord Mustill rhetorically asked, "[h]ow can any tribunal, however cosmopolitan and polyglot, hope to understand the nuances of the multifarious legal systems?"[87] The historical reality is that few have even tried. Cheng observed that "recourse to a comprehensive comparative method is extremely rare."[88] Many of the general principles included in Cheng's work were first recognized by courts and tribunals on the basis of intuitive presumption, not comparative analysis. This trend continues today: three major international courts recognized the general principle of proportionality in the 1970s and 1980s "without explicit justification or citation to authority."[89] But beyond those core maxims that brook little dissent,[90] for general principles to be accepted as legitimate in different quarters

84 *Anglo-Iranian Oil Co. (U.K. v. Iran)*, Preliminary Objections, 1952 I.C.J. 151, 161 (July 22) (dissenting opinion of Judge Levi Carneiro) ("It is inevitable that everyone of us in this Court should retain some trace of his legal education and his former legal activities in his country of origin. This is . . . justified because in its composition the Court is to be representative of 'the main forms of civilization and of the principal legal systems of the world' (Statute art. 9), and the Court is to apply 'the general principles of law recognized by civilized nations.'").

85 *Texaco Overseas Petroleum Co. (TOPCO) v. Gov't of the Libyan Arab Republic*, 17 I.L.M. 1 (1978).

86 Otto Sandrock, *How Much Freedom Should an International Arbitrator Enjoy? The Desire for Freedom from Law vs. the Promotion of International Arbitration*, 3 AM. REV. INT'L ARB. 30, 50 (1992).

87 Michael Mustill, *The New* Lex Mercatoria: *The First Twenty-Five Years*, 4(2) ARB. INT'L 86, 114 (1988).

88 CHENG, *supra* note 4, at 392.

89 Alec Stone Sweet & Giancinto della Cananea, *Proportionality, General Principles of Law, and Investor-State Arbitration: A Response to Jose Alvarez*, 46 N.Y.U. J. INT'L L. & POL. 911–18 (2014); *see also* Fauchald, *supra* note 56, at 312.

90 JAN PAULSSON, THE IDEA OF ARBITRATION 15 (2013) ("There are very few of them [fundamental principles of law], and their strength lies in their simple intuitive appeal. Procedurally, disputants expect to be heard not because the law so directs, but because it cannot tolerably be otherwise. Substantively,

of the world, the process of identifying them should be more transparent, objective, and coherent. Locating the common denominator of municipal laws is becoming less difficult with the expanding scope of international law and the wider availability of translated sources of foreign law. "Linguistic provincialism [can no longer] excuse intellectual provincialism."[91]

Judges and arbitrators are on the front lines of this process. Their decisions and awards identify, define, and apply general principles, and thereby "flatten [some] paths in the jungle of the different national laws to be consulted."[92] This process is made easier by scholarly efforts such as the TransLex Principles, which collate the blackletter text of general principles that have been applied by judges and tribunals and provide comparative law references taken from domestic statutes, court decisions, doctrine, awards, and uniform law.[93] The Comparative Constitutions Project also provides access (in English) to all existing constitutions, including every amendment introduced throughout their history.[94] When domestic principles have been subsumed into international law, their application by international tribunals leads to their further enhancement, clarification, and refinement, as reflected in the wealth of jurisprudence discussed in chapters 2 and 3. If a general principle is recognized as such through the process of induction (i.e., distilling a common principle from various domestic legal systems), that principle, once established, can serve as the basis for deductive reasoning (e.g., applying the principle of good faith to specific conduct). In this way, the role of general principles in international law remains dynamic and continues to evolve over time.

For those "flattening the paths" for the first time, the process for identifying general principles of law typically proceeds in three stages. *First*, the tribunal drills down vertically into established legal rules to extract the underlying legal principle. *Second*, after that, it moves horizontally among a variety of national legal systems to determine whether that principle is universally recognized.[95] *Third*, before being

---

they expect redress for the breach of an important bargain upon which they have relied not because that is what a code provides, but because it is a fundamental premise of social life.").

91 *Bodum USA, Inc. v. La Cafetiere, Inc.*, 621 F.3d 624, 633 (7th Cir. 2010) (Posner, J., concurring).

92 Otto Sandrock, *How Much Freedom Should an Arbitrator Enjoy?*, 3 Am. Rev. Int'l Arb. 30, 50 (1992).

93 *See Trans-Lex Principles*, Trans-Lex.org Law Research, *available at* http://www.trans-lex.org/principles (last visited Sept. 6, 2016).

94 *See* online at http://comparativeconstitutionsproject.org/ (last visited Sept. 6, 2016).

95 For a further discussion of this "vertical" and "horizontal" framework, see generally Raimondo, *supra* note 44, at 1–2; Michael D. Nolan & Frederic G. Sourgens, *Issues of Proof of General Principles of Law*, 3 World Arb. & Mediation Rev. 505 (2009).

elevated to the international plane, the principle may undergo further modification "to suit the particularities of international law."[96]

a) Principles That Are General

The first step is one of distillation. At the outset, principles must be contrasted with rules, which tend to express concrete requirements setting forth the circumstances and conditions in which they are to apply.[97] Principles are anterior and more general—they provide the juridical foundation for rules and the starting points for legal reasoning.[98] Ronald Dworkin wrote that a principle is "a standard that is to be observed . . . because it is a requirement of justice or fairness or some other dimension of morality."[99] As Sir Gerald Fitzmaurice put it, a principle of law "is chiefly something which is not itself a rule, but which underlies a rule and explains or provides the reason for it."[100] Principles tend to express the fundamental values that undergird a judicial regime, bringing together positive rules and normative ideas.[101] General principles "are not inventions of the law," they "are antecedent of law."[102] In order to be considered "general," a principle must possess such a heightened degree of reason that all parties ex ante appreciate its normative value, whatever view they might take after a dispute has arisen.

A case study illustrates the generality of these principles in practice. Cheng correctly observed that "there seems little, if indeed any question as to res judicata

96 Jaye Ellis, *General Principles and Comparative Law*, 22 EUR. J. INT'L L. 949, 954 (2011); Lammers, *supra* note 67, at 62 (arguing that it is "required that the national situations to which the principle initially applied, and the interstate situations to which they are to be applied, are sufficiently similar to justify the application of those principles at the international level").

97 *See* Ronald M. Dworkin, *The Model of Rules*, 35 U. CHI. L. REV. 14, 25 (1967) ("Rules are applicable in an all-or-or-nothing fashion. If the facts a rule stipulates are given . . . the answer it supplies must be accepted. . . ."); Kolb, *supra* note 78, at 9 ("The generality of the [legal] principles puts them beyond the realm of operation or simple rules. On the one hand, their legal content is not so narrow, it is not so defined in an as precise way as it is in rules; but at the same time it is not so broad as general political concepts or words used in the social fashion of a given moment.").

98 *See generally* Max Rheinstein, Review of Josef Esser, *Grundsatz und Norm in der richterlichen Fortbildung des Privatrechts*, 24 U. CHI. L. REV. 597 (1957).

99 Dworkin, *supra* note 97, at 23.

100 Gerald Fitzmaurice, *The General Principles of International Law Considered from the Standpoint of the Rule of Law*, 92 RECUEIL DES COURS 7 (1957).

101 Jan Wouters et al., *The Influence of General Principles of Law*, at 4–5 (Leuven Working Paper No. 70, July 2011).

102 PAULSSON, *supra* note 90, at 15.

being a general principle of law."[103] As discussed in chapter 3.F, the principle of res judicata in municipal systems obliges the parties to adhere to a final judgment and bars them from raising the same claims again before another court. This principle originated in Roman civil law and enjoys near universal adherence today.[104] The principle promotes finality and repose: respect for what was already argued and decided ensures the stability and certainty of juridical relationships. Permutations as to the scope and application of res judicata exist in different systems—only civil law countries, for example, grant settlement agreements (*contratos de transacción*) the effect of res judicata[105]—but the normative principle remains constant across jurisdictions. It is that core aspect of res judicata that is abstracted from the municipal plane and placed on the international plane. The idiosyncrasies of local law are discarded; the focus is on deciphering the Platonic form of res judicata.[106] By ignoring peculiar manifestations in different regimes,

103 Cheng, *supra* note 4, at 336.

104 *See* 3 Digest of Justiniano, Book 44 (Alan Watson, ed., 2009). *See, e.g., Hart Steel Co. v. Railroad Supply Co.*, 244 U.S. 294, 299 (1917) (deeming the principle of res judicata to be a "rule of fundamental and substantial justice"); Canada: *Hill v. Hill*, 57 D.L.R. 2d 760 (1966); Donald J. Lange, The Doctrine of Res judicata in Canada 4–10 (Butterworth's 2d ed. 2004); Australia: *Ramsay v. Pigram*, 42 Austl. L.J.R. 89 (1968); Keith Handley, *Res Judicata: General Principles and Recent Developments*, 18 Aust. Bar Rev. 214 (1999); Enid Campbell, *Res Judicata and Decisions of Foreign Tribunals*, 16 Sydney L. Rev. 311 (1994); France: Civil Code art. 1351; New Zealand: *NZ Building Trades Union v. NZ Federated Furniture*, [1991] 1 ERNZ 331; *Langland v. Stevenson*, [1995] 2 NZLR 474; England: 16(2) Halsbury's Laws of England (4th ed. reissue 2003); Germany: Zivilprozessordnung [Civil Code] §§ 322–27; Belgium: Code Civil [C. Civ.] art. 23–27 (Belg.); Italy: Code of Civil Procedure art. 324; Sweden: Code of Judicial Procedure arts. 17:11 and 30:1; Latin America: Código Federal de Procedimientos Civiles [Federal Civil Procedure Code] arts. 354–57 (Mex.); Código Procesal Civil y Comercial de la Nación [Civil and Commercial Procedure Code] art. 347(6), 544(9) and 517 (Arg.); Russia: Code of Civil Procedure art. 209 (Russ.); Japan: Code of Civil Procedure art. 114; China: PRC Arbitration Law of 1994 art. 9; India: *Hope Plantation Ltd. v. Taluk Land Board* (1999) 5 SCC 590 (Sup. C) (stating that the application of res judicata is broad in Indian courts); South Africa: *Horowitz v. Brock & Others*, 1988 (2) SA 160; *see generally* Peter R. Barnett, Res Judicata, Estoppel, and Foreign Judgments: The Preclusive Effects of Foreign Judgments in Private Law (2001).

105 French Civil Code art. 2052 ("Transactions [a contract by which the parties put an end to an existing controversy, or prevent a future contestation] have, between the parties, the authority of res judicata of a final judgment."); Chilean Civil Code art. 2460 ("The transaction [a contract by which the parties extra-judicially put an end to an existing controversy, or prevent eventual litigation] has the effect of Res Judicata in last resort . . . ."); Ecuadorian Civil Code art. 2362 ("The transaction has the effect of Res Judicata in last resort . . . ."); Colombian Civil Code art. 2483 ("The transaction has the effect of Res Judicata in last resort . . . .").

106 *See generally Barcelona Traction, Light & Power Co., Ltd. (Belg. v. Spain)*, Second Phase, Judgment, 1970 I.C.J. 3 (Feb. 5) (separate opinion of Judge Fitzmaurice); Raimondo, *supra* note 44, at 49 ("The task of deriving general principles of law from national laws should not consist of looking mechanically for coincidences among legal rules, but of determining their common denominator."); *Prosecutor v. Kunarac et al.*, Case Nos. IT-96-23-T and IT-96-23/1-T, Judgment, ¶ 439 (Int'l Crim. Trib. for the Former Yugoslavia) (Feb. 22, 2001) ("In considering these national legal systems the Tribal Chamber

the core of the *principle* is ascertained.[107] It is this shared legal corpus that may be considered for inclusion among the general principles of law, thereby promoting a fundamental and international concept.[108]

b) Principles That Are Universal

According to the *Restatement (Third) of Foreign Relations Law of the United States*, the "rule[s] of international law" are ones that have been "accepted as such by the international community of states ... by derivation from general principles common to the major legal systems of the world."[109] As this definition indicates, the underlying legitimacy of general principles stems from their universal acceptance;[110] they "represent a consensus among civilized nations on the proper ordering of relations between nations and the citizens thereof."[111] In this way, "every municipal law is a vehicle for the general principles of law [to be] a source of international law."[112] With this grounding in domestic law, general principles possess "a degree of reasonableness and appropriateness," such that "a State which acts in a contrary manner [will] have been conscious of a possibility that a rule of law might point in the opposite direction."[113] Although general principles are not derived from express sovereign consent, they carry the *imprimatur* of inclusion in Article 38 of the ICJ Statute—a treaty accepted by most States.

---

does not . . . identify a specific legal provision . . . but to . . . identify certain basic principles."); *contrast* United States v. Fishbine, 1 Fletch 80, 95 (1985) (holding that a man subjected to potential incineration while wearing another man's suit is entitled to U.S. $10,000 in airline tickets). As Dworkin described it, it is the search for the function of "justice or . . . fairness or some other dimension of morality" in the normative concept. RONALD DWORKIN, TAKING RIGHTS SERIOUSLY 22 (1977).

107 STEPHAN W. SCHILL, INTERNATIONAL INVESTMENT LAW AND COMPARATIVE PUBLIC LAW 30 (2010) ("[C]omparative law is not a mechanical quantitative process, but one of abstraction, weighing, and qualitative evaluation. While comparative analysis must not become uncritical towards differences of national legal systems, it must analyze them in a functional perspective and against a sufficiently elevated level of abstraction.").

108 H.C. GUTTERIDGE, COMPARATIVE LAW 65 (Auvermann ed., 2d ed. 1949).

109 RESTATEMENT (THIRD) FOREIGN RELATIONS LAW OF THE UNITED STATES § 102(1) (AM. LAW INST. 1987).

110 Biddulph & Newman, *supra* note 52, at 298–99 (discussing the theory that the "consent [of States] can be implied from the common existence of a principle in the domestic legal systems of a majority of the world's states").

111 *Banco Nacional de Cuba v. Sabbatino*, 376 U.S. 398, 453 (1964) (White, J., dissenting).

112 *Texaco Overseas Petroleum Co. (TOPCO) v. Gov't of the Libyan Arab Republic*, 17 I.L.M. 1, 18 (1978).

113 H.W.A. Thirlway, *The Law and Procedure of the International Court of Justice: 1960–1989: Part Two*, 61 BRIT. Y.B. INT'L L. 1, 113 (Martinus Nijhoff 1990).

Ensuring that a general principle abides in many legal systems—the concept reflected in Article 38(1)(c)'s archaic "recognized by civilized nations" requirement—promotes its legitimacy and acceptance. A horizontal survey simultaneously ensures a level of consensus and solidity while guarding against the imposition of legal precepts that are incipient, evolving, or unsettled.[114] Not all claims to the title of "general principle" have been accepted. In the *South West Africa Cases*, for instance, a plea that the ICJ should allow a resident to bring an action in vindication of the public interest (*actio popularis*) was rejected because "a right of this kind may be known to certain municipal systems of law," but "it is not known to international law as it stands at present," and therefore could not be "regard[ed] as imported by the 'general principles of law' referred to in Art. 38, paragraph 1(c)."[115] Similarly, the *TOPCO* tribunal observed that although the "theory of administrative contracts," under which States may unilaterally amend contractual provisions, had been "consecrated by French law and by certain legal systems which have been inspired by French law," it "was unknown in many other legal systems which are as important as the French system."[116] Recalling that "general principles of law postulate that they should be 'sufficiently widely and firmly recognized in the leading legal systems of the world,'" the sole arbitrator determined that the theory of administrative contracts "has not been accepted by international law."[117] In contrast, where a principle is otherwise sufficiently recognized, perceived outliers will not defeat the existence of a general principle as such—it has never been the practice of the ICJ or international arbitral tribunals to insist upon proof of the widespread manifestation of a principle in every known legal system.[118] If unanimity were required, "it would amount to granting a veto power to those legal systems incorporating the most isolated tendencies," which runs contrary to the very purpose of the exercise.[119]

---

114 Vladimir Degan, Sources of International Law 70 (1997).

115 *South West Africa (Eth. v. S. Afr.; Liber. v. S. Afr.)*, Second Phase, Judgement, 1966 I.C.J. 6, at 240, ¶ 88 (July 18).

116 *Texaco Overseas Petroleum Co. (TOPCO) v. Gov't of the Libyan Arab Republic*, 17 I.L.M. 1, 21 (1978).

117 *Id.* (quoting Wolfgang Friedman, The Changing Structure of International Law 196 (1964)). In the *Abu Dhabi* case, the English law principle of interpretation *unius est exclusio alterius* was held to be a principle "rooted in the good sense and common practice of the generality of civilised nations," but the English rule that grants by a sovereign should be construed against the grantee (which was thought peculiarly English) was not. *See Petroleum Dev. (Trucial Coast) Ltd. v. Sheikh of Abu Dhabi*, 18 Int'l L. Rep. 144, 149 (1951).

118 *See, e.g.*, Nolan & Sourgens, *supra* note 95, at 510–13 (describing a "critical mass" approach); Friedman, *supra* note 74, at 284 (stating that "it is not necessary that the principle should be found to exist in identical form in every system of civilized law").

119 Emmanuel Galliard, *Use of General Principles of International Law in International Long-Term Contracts*, 27 Int'l Bus. Law. 214, 216 (1999).

To avoid selection bias, a comparative analysis should be as comprehensive as possible. Yet international courts and tribunals rarely reveal the methods they employ to determine general principles of law, and hardly ever refer to comparative law research.[120] It may be that this work is being done without being reflected in the final decision, but, if so, the lack of explication detracts from the coherence and credibility of the enterprise.[121] In all events, there are an abundance of sources to assist in the task. Comparative scholars have long observed that "the areas of agreement among legal systems are larger than those of disagreement."[122] In many ways, identifying cross-system similarities is the raison d'être of the mainstream comparative discipline, which has been thoroughly explicated in such works as Rudolf Schlesinger's *Comparative Law* and *The Oxford Handbook on Comparative Law*; monographs such as Reinhard Zimmermann and Simon Whittaker's *Good Faith in European Contract Law*, Kraus Peter Berger's *The Creeping Codification of the* Lex Mercatoria, and Sir Roy Goode's *Transnational Commercial Law: International Instruments and Commentary*; and soft law codifications such as the Lando Principles of European Contract Law and the International Institute for the Unification of Private Law (UNIDROIT) Principles of International Commercial Contracts.[123] The common principles identified and reiterated by comparative scholars can, in many cases, be deemed adequately "recognized" by the legal systems of the world.[124]

Failing prior scholarly identification of a principle the direct examination of the various national laws can begin by researching the various "families of law." Despite their unique histories, the world's legal systems have sufficient commonalities that baseline legal principles can be discerned. Aspects of the

120 *See* Hermann Mosler, *To What Extent Does the Variety of Legal Systems of the World Influence the Application of the General Principles of Law within the Meaning of Article 38(I)(c) of the Statute of the International Court of Justice?*, *in* International Law and the Grotian Heritage 179–82 (T.M.C. Asser Instituut ed. 1985).

121 *See* Raimondo, *supra* note 44, at 58.

122 Rudolph Sleshinger et al., Comparative Law 39 (5th ed. 1988).

123 As noted by one tribunal, the UNIDROIT Principles of International Commercial Contracts "are a reliable source of international commercial law in international arbitration for they contain in essence a restatement of those 'principles directeurs' that have enjoyed universal acceptance and, moreover, are at the heart of those most fundamental notions which have consistently been applied in arbitral practice." *Andersen Consulting Bus. Unit Member Firms v. Arthur Andersen Bus. Unit Member Firms and Andersen Worldwide Societe Coop.*, ICC Award No. 9797, July 28, 2006, *excerpted in* ICC Int'l Ct. Arb. Bull., Fall 2001, at 88.

124 It has been suggested that the most "pertinent and useful" comparisons may be made within a particular system of law (e.g., civil or common law) given the differences among them. *B.E. Chattin (U.S.) v. United Mexican States*, Decision of Commissioner Nielsen (July 23, 1927), 4 R.I.A.A. 282, 296. Although that may be appropriate in particular cases, system-specific principles that do not find resonance elsewhere cannot plausibly claim an international status.

Anglo-American common law have been incorporated into the law of a number of States through colonialism, whereas the French and Germanic civil law systems have been influential in Latin America and, to a lesser extent, in parts of Africa, Asia, and the Middle East. The Egyptian Civil Code of 1948, for example, was a result of the legislative process of reconciling the principles of Sharia law and the provisions of European Civil Codes, in particular the French Civil Code.[125] Albeit with competing nomenclature, comparative scholars generally identify two legal "families" (Romano-Germanic civil law and the common law), and further divide those families into eight[126] legal systems: common law, Romanistic civil law, Germanic civil law,[127] Nordic law,[128] Socialist law,[129] Far Eastern law,[130] Islamic law,[131] and Hindu law.[132] Whether one compares the selected principle in restatements and scholarly works among the two primary legal families, or goes further and considers all eight of the legal systems,[133] this categorization is still much more efficient than independently researching the law of some 200 different countries.[134] This rough division of legal traditions finds echo in the manner

---

125 Today, most Arab countries have modern civil codes based fully or partly on the Egyptian Civil Code. *See generally* W. Ballantine, Essays and Addresses on Arab Laws 5–8, 210–13, 248 (Cuzon Press 2000); Joseph Schacht, *Islamic Law in Contemporary States*, 8 Am. J. Comp. L. 133, 134–36 (1959).

126 There are seemingly as many formulations of these categories as there are categories. For a good discussion of other formulations, see Patrick Glenn, Legal Traditions of the World (4th ed. 2010) and Rene David & Camille Jauffret-Spinosi, Les grands systemes de droit contemporains (2d ed. 2002).

127 For an introduction to the history and various principles of Germanic law, see Rudolf Huebner, A History of Germanic Private Law (Francis S. Philbrick trans., Little, Brown & Co. 1918).

128 For an introduction to various principles of Nordic law, see Nordic Law—Between Tradition and Dynamism (Jaakko Husa et al. eds., 2007); Camilla Baasch Andersen, *Scandinavian Law in Legal Traditions of the World*, 1 J. Comp. L. 140 (2006); Ole Lando, *Nordic Countries, a Legal Family? A Diagnosis and a Prognosis*, 1 Global Jurist Advances 1535 (2001).

129 For an introduction to various principles of Socialist law, see Anita Naschitz, Introduction to Socialist Law (1967).

130 For an introduction to the many legal systems in Asia, see James V. Feinerman, *Introduction to Asian Legal Systems*, *in* Introduction to Foreign Legal Systems (Richard A. Danner & Marie-Louise H. Bernal eds., 1994).

131 For an introduction to various principles of Islamic law, see Wael B. Hallaq, An Introduction to Islamic Law (2009). The constitutions of Egypt, Syria, Kuwait, Bahrain, Qatar, and the United Arab Emirates refer to Sharia as either *the* or *a* source of law.

132 For an introduction to various principles of Hindu law, see J. Duncan M. Derrett, An Introduction to Modern Hindu Law (1963).

133 *See* Bruno Simma & Andreas Paulus, *Le role relatif des diferentes sources du droit international penal; dont les principes generaux du droit*, *in* Droit international penal 55–69 (Herve Ascensio et al. eds., 2000); Antonio Cassese, International Criminal Law 32–33 (2003); *cf.* Vladimir Degan, *On the Sources of International Criminal Law*, 4 Chinese J. Int'l L. 45, 81 (2005).

134 One need only include in the comparative law study those national legal systems that have experience in connection with the legal issue at hand. For instance, the law of Mongolia or Paraguay or Botswana—or other landlocked states—is not typically relevant to determine general principles regarding the high

of electing members to the ICJ, whose organic statute calls for electors to ensure that the 15-member tribunal represents "the main forms of civilization and of the principal legal systems of the world."[135]

For good or ill, the civil and common law systems of Germany, France, England, and the United States are referenced most often because "these legal orders are easily accessible and, above all, have influenced the public law systems of many other countries."[136] ICJ Judge Bruno Simma, for example, grappled with the issue of multiple tortfeasors by reviewing relevant authorities in the United States, Canada, France, Switzerland, and Germany, concluding that "the question has been taken up and solved by these legal systems with a consistency that is striking."[137] At bottom, as H.C. Gutteridge put it, in determining whether a principle is "universal" or "general," the judge or arbitrator "must satisfy himself that it is recognized in substance by all the main systems of law, and that in applying it he will not be doing violence to any of the fundamental concepts of any of those systems."[138]

The strength of the claim for a particular general principle will turn, as in all cases of inductive reasoning, upon the strength of the supporting data.[139] An adjectival rule that has been routinely followed in both domestic and international legal systems has a better claim to being a "general principle" than one that has been adopted only in, say, a handful of common law countries. Bald proclamations of universality are just that, and general principles so justified are

---

seas. In this same way, there is nothing to stop the application of principles recognized by States in a certain region, just as customary international law has developed regionally. *See, e.g.*, M. Akehurst, *Equity and General Principles of Law*, 25 INT'L & COMP. L.Q. 824 (1976).

135 Statute of the International Court of Justice art. 9. A variation of this can be seen in *Texaco Overseas Petroleum Co. (TOPCO) v. Gov't of the Libyan Arab Republic*, 17 I.L.M. 1, 30 (1978), in which the tribunal had to determine which of competing resolutions of the U.N. General Assembly best reflected customary law on an issue of expropriation. It ultimately eschewed those resolutions with the most numerical votes because they introduced "new principles which were rejected by certain representative *groups of States*"; instead, it recognized the resolution "supported by a majority of Member States representing all of the various groups," viz., industrialized and developing states.

136 Schill, *supra* note 68, at 93.

137 *Oil Platforms (Iran v. U.S.)*, Judgment, 2003 I.C.J. 161, 324, ¶¶ 66–74 (Nov. 6) (separate opinion of Judge Bruno Simma).

138 H.C. GUTTERIDGE, COMPARATIVE LAW 65 (Auvermann ed., 2d ed. 1949).

139 William Thomas Worster, *The Inductive and Deductive Methods in Customary International Law Analysis: Traditional and Modern Approaches*, 45 GEO. J. INT'L L. 445, 447–48 (2014) (defining "induction" as "drawing inferences from specific observable phenomena to general rules," such that "[t]he degree to which the conclusion is probably true is based on the quality of the evidence used to support it").

unlikely to gain many adherents.[140] The case of *Klöckner v. Cameroon* presents a cautionary tale against the ipse dixit invocation of supervening international law.[141] The *Klöckner* arbitration was governed by Cameroonian law, and the parties agreed that the dispute should be governed by the law applicable in the part of Cameroon whose law traces to France. Rather than discern the content of Cameroonian law, the tribunal instead based its decision exclusively on the "basic principle" of "frankness and loyalty" as divined from "French civil law," which the tribunal noted—without citation—was also a "universal requirement" that inheres in all "other national codes which we know of" and both "English law and international law."[142] On an application for annulment, the ad hoc ICSID Committee found that this truncated reasoning amounted to a failure to apply the proper law:

> Does the "basic principle" referred to by the Award . . . as one of "French civil law" come from positive law, i.e., from the law's body of rules? It is impossible to answer this question by reading the Award, which contains no reference whatsoever to legislative texts, to judgments, or to scholarly opinions. . . . [The Tribunal's] reasoning [is] limited to postulating and not demonstrating the existence of a principle or exploring the rules by which it can only take concrete form.[143]

Accordingly, the award was annulled because the tribunal did not apply "the law of the Contracting State," but instead based its decision "more on a sort of general equity than on positive law . . . or precise contractual provisions."[144] The Committee's decision has been criticized by academics and practitioners for too readily annulling a final arbitration award,[145] but it still serves as a cautionary tale: general principles of law must be supported by reference to positive rules of municipal or other relevant law.

---

140 Friedmann, *supra* note 74, at 284 ("Since nations and individuals appear to be unable to agree on the substantive content of natural law, the clothing of any particular controversy in the terminology of natural law does not advance us towards a solution of the problem at hand.").

141 *Klöckner Industrie-Anlagen GmbH v. United Republic of Cameroon*, ICSID Case No. ARB/81/2, Award (Oct. 21 1983), 2 ICSID Rep. 9 (Klöckner Award); Decision on Annulment (May 3, 1985), 2 ICSID Rep. 95 (1994) (Klöckner Annulment).

142 Klöckner Award, 2 ICSID Rep. at 105–06.

143 Klöckner Annulment, ¶ 71, 2 ICSID Rep. at 113.

144 *Id.* at 139.

145 *See, e.g.*, Alan D. Redfern, *ICSID—Losing Its Appeal?*, 3 Arb. Int'l 98, 109 (1987); W. Michael Reisman, *The Breakdown of the Control Mechanism in ICSID Arbitration*, 89 Duke L.J. 739, 762 (1989); W. Michael Reisman, *Repairing ICSID's Control System: Some Comments on Aron Broches' Observations on the Finality of ICSID Awards*, 7 ICSID Rev. 196, 200 (1992); *see also* Paul Friedland & Paul Brumpton,

To be coherent and to avoid arbitrariness, the process for identifying a general principle should be marked by transparency and objective criteria. A systematic survey of municipal law along the lines described above would satisfy these requirements. And if support is sought from sources outside of domestic fora, there should be some modicum of evidence demonstrating actual use or acceptance of the principle within those other sources.[146] Whatever the precise methodology, the process cannot be "the equivalent of entering a crowded cocktail party and looking over the heads of the guests for one's friends."[147] As Christoph Schreuer has explained, "[g]eneral principles of law are not an expression of general feelings of justice or equity but are part of the body of international law which, in a particular case, must be proven and not presumed."[148] Although the induction of general principles to date has hardly been a science, the touchstone of any legitimate process should be the existence of an objective metric by which to assess the commonality of the principle.

c) Principles That Are International

Even when a general principle is deemed to be universally recognized, it is never transposed into international law "lock, stock and barrel."[149] As Sir Gerald Fitzmaurice wrote, "conditions in the international field are sometimes very different from what they are in the domestic," such that domestic rules "may be less capable of vindication if strictly applied when transposed into the international level."[150] It is indeed rare to encounter a general principle transferred to international law with the same characteristics and limitations of domestic law. The third step in the process is thus to discern the catholic aspects of a shared legal principle and to apply those as a rule of decision to the international dispute at hand.[151] This process furthers the denationalization of international law, which is an important aspect of international adjudication.

Rabid Redux: The Second Wave of Abusive ICSID Annulments, 27 AM. U. INT'L L. REV. 727, 729–30 (2012) (characterizing *Klöckner* as symptomatic of "ICSID's annulment virus" of the 1980s).

146 Lammers, *supra* note 67, at 62 ("[T]he comparative law method has the merit of scientific verifiability, and constitutes a proper defense against complaints of subjectivism in the determination of general principles of law.").

147 *Conroy v. Aniskoff*, 507 U.S. 511, 519 (1993) (Scalia, J., concurring).

148 CHRISTOPH H. SCHREUER ET AL., THE ICSID CONVENTION: A COMMENTARY art. 42, ¶ 182 (2d ed. 2009).

149 *Int'l Status of South-West Africa*, Advisory Opinion, 1950 I.C.J. 128, 148 (July 11) (separate opinion of Lord McNair).

150 *Barcelona Traction, Light & Power Co., Ltd. (Belg. v. Spain)*, Second Phase, Judgment, 1970 I.C.J. 3, 64 (Feb. 5) (separate opinion of Judge Fitzmaurice).

151 *See* LAUTERPACHT, *supra* note 67, at 81–87.

In the diverse family of nations, with States in differing stages of economic, political, and social development, on-the-ground adherence to these fundamental precepts is bound to differ—especially when their application turns on inquiries such as whether a specific course of conduct is "reasonable" or "abusive." As illustrated in the decisions and awards discussed throughout this book, violations of general principles are legion. This unfortunate reality is what gives the general principles their continued salience. Although it might seem that this nonadherence calls into question the recognition of general principles as such, just as the absence of de facto state practice would prevent recognition as customary international law, there is no paradox. When it comes to general principles, the focus is on what national law *says*, not what a particular party *does*. That is because the inclusion of a principle in the written laws of many legal systems is itself validation of the principle.[152] Such laws are written ex ante, without necessarily any thought of their eventual incorporation into international law or their possible invocation by or against the State and its citizens. Whereas customary international law derives its legitimacy from state usage, the general principles derive their legitimacy from state recognition. To borrow from John Rawls, all legal systems, in the "veil of ignorance,"[153] recognize a priori the importance of pacta sunt servanda, even if, say, a particular government finds it expedient to ignore the State's contractual obligations to a particular foreign investor.

The identification and acceptance of new general principles will proceed incrementally. If a municipal court or international tribunal were to characterize a principle as one of general and universal applicability, it would not instantly bind other parties in their international affairs.[154] That decision would simply enter

152 *Texaco Overseas Petroleum Co. (TOPCO) v. Gov't of the Libyan Arab Republic*, 17 I.L.M. 1, 24 (1978) ("The fact that various nationalization measures in disregard of previously concluded agreements have been accepted in fact by those who were affected, either private companies or by the States of which they are nationals, cannot be interpreted as recognition by international practice of such a rule[.]").

153 *See generally* John Rawls, A Theory of Justice (Belknap Press 1971).

154 There is of course no rule of stare decisis in the system of investor-state arbitration, but prior arbitration awards are cited by both tribunals and counsel in virtually all international law proceedings. Although an issue of some debate, several prominent jurists have argued that these awards have become de facto sources for the development of international law. *See, e.g.*, Jan Paulsson, *The Role of Precedent in Investment Arbitration*, *in* Arbitration under International Investment Agreements 699, 718 (Katia Yannaca-Small ed., 2010) ("[I]n the end, there is no contradiction between the task of deciding an individual case—in principle the sole duty of ephemeral tribunals—and consciousness of contributing to the accretion of international norms."); Stephen Schwebel, *A Bit about ICSID* (2010) TDM 1, 5 (positing that the investor-state arbitration system has become so widely accepted that it has created a separate corpus of customary international law, "with the result that [it is] binding on all States including those not parties to BITs").

the fray of all international judicial decisions, where some shine as "bright[] beacons" and others "flicker and die near instant deaths."[155] This is a function of the Darwinian and non-hierarchical international legal system. "Good [decisions] will chase the bad, and set standards which will contribute to a higher level of consistent quality."[156] A new maxim will emerge only if the decision is cogent, the characterization defensible, and the principle universal.

Ultimately, international norms developed through "discursive synthesis," that is, the interaction of many different legal traditions and principles, are "more likely to be implemented [in national legal systems] and less likely to be disobeyed [on the international level]."[157] The general principles may thus be seen as an illustration of what Harold Koh calls the "Transnational Legal Process"—they are divined from the interaction of legal systems, they are internalized into a country's normative system, and they create new legal rules that will guide future transnational interactions.[158] This process of internalization quickens where international law is backed by efficacious remedies, as are now provided under various BITs and mutilateral conventions. So enforced, general principles are one of the few legal sources that can legitimately claim to support a compliance pull toward the rule of law, for state and private parties alike.

2. Typical Usage of General Principles

Whether denominated as such, the use of general principles is ubiquitous and varied. The parties to a contract or treaty may expressly designate general principles in their choice-of-law provision. The concession agreements nationalized by Libya in the early 1970s, for instance, were governed by "the general principles of law."[159] In addition, general principles "may be resorted to as an independent source of law . . . when there has not been practice by states sufficient to give the

155 Paulsson, *supra* note 154, at 704.

156 *Id.* at 710.

157 THOMAS M. FRANCK, FAIRNESS IN INTERNATIONAL LAW AND INSTITUTIONS 481 (1995).

158 Harold Hongju Koh, *Why Do Nations Obey International Law?*, 106 YALE L.J. 2599, 2646 (1997); Harold Hongju Koh, *The Transnational Legal Process*, 75 NEB. L. REV. 181, 204–05 (1996).

159 *Texaco Overseas Petroleum Co. (TOPCO) v. Gov't of the Libyan Arab Republic*, 17 I.L.M. 1 (1978); *Libyan American Oil Co. (LIAMCO) v. Gov't of the Libyan Arab Republic*, 62 INT'L L. REP. 141 (1977), and *BP Exploration Co. (Libya) Ltd. v. Gov't of the Libyan Arab Republic*, 53 INT'L L. REP. 297 (1974). *See generally* R. Doak Bishop, *International Arbitration of Petroleum Disputes: The Development of a* Lex Petrolea, 23 Y.B. COMM. ARB. 1131, 1146–47 (1998); André von Walter, *Arbitration on Oil Concession Disputes*, *in* MAX PLANCK ENCYCLOPEDIA OF PUBLIC INTERNATIONAL LAW 948 (Rudiger Wolfrum ed., 2012).

particular principle status as customary law and the principle has not been legislated by general international agreement."[160] In these circumstances, general principles act as substantive legal principles that can be dispositive of the merits, such as application of the principle against unjust enrichment.[161]

Even when not applicable in their own right, general principles may usefully play an auxiliary role, clarifying ambiguities and filling interstices. As explained by Lord Phillimore during the drafting process, the sequencing of Article 38(1) reflects the "logical order in which these sources would occur to the mind of the judge."[162] The ICJ "will usually only resort to [general principles] in order to fill a gap in the treaty or customary rules available to settle a particular dispute and, what is even more apparent, will decline to invoke them when such other rules exist."[163] The preference for positive law is almost reflexive, and where that law is clear, reversion to the general principles need not be undertaken.[164] But these primary sources of law are oftentimes unclear, yielding results that are, for a host of reasons, unsatisfactory or inadequate. It is here where the general principles do

---

160 Restatement (Third) Foreign Relations Law of the United States § 102 cmt. L (Am. Law Inst. 1987); Jennings & Watts, *supra* note 67, at 40 ("General principles of law . . . do not just have a supplementary role, but may give rise to rules of independent legal force."); *Georges Pinson (Fr.) v. United Mexican States*, Decision No. 1 (Oct. 19, 1928), 5 R.I.A.A. 327, 422 ("Every international convention must be deemed tacitly to refer to general principles of international law for all questions which it does not itself resolve in express terms and in a different way."); Michel Virally, *The Sources of International Law*, *in* Manual of Public International Law 143–45 (M. Soresen ed., 1968) ("When both customary and conventional law will not suffice, the I.C.J. is empowered by Article 38(1) of its Statute to resort to the rules of municipal law for the disposal of cases submitted to it, or, to put it technically, Article 38 authorizes the use of analogy.").

161 *See* Friedmann, *supra* note 74, at 290–99; Lammers, *supra* note 67, at 64–65 (discussing "'the gap-filling function' . . . which the framers of Article 38 had in mind").

162 *Procès-verbaux*, *supra* note 5, at 333.

163 Pellet, *supra* note 51, at 850.

164 Lammers, *supra* note 67, at 66 ("[P]rovisions of treaties and customary international law are, by nature, more direct emanations of the will of states and are often also more specifically related to the subject matter envisaged by those provisions than are the general principles of national law."). Sometimes, the lines between these sources of law become blurred. For example, although it is settled as a matter of international law that expropriations must be fully compensated, this is not properly considered a general principle, because it is primarily rooted in bilateral and multilateral treaties codifying state usage. *See, e.g.*, Andrew Newcombe & Lluís Paradell, Law and Practice of Investment Treaties: Standards of Treatment §§ 7.5, 7.6 (2009). Yet it has been mistakenly labeled as a general principle. *See, e.g.*, *Benvenuti et Bonfant v. People's Republic of the Congo*, Award (Aug. 15, 1980), 21 I.L.M., 740, 758 ("This principle of compensation in the event of nationalization is in accordance with the Congolese Constitution and is one of the generally recognized principles of international law[.]").

the brunt of their work, which falls into three general categories: interpretative, definitional, and corrective.[165]

The *first*, and least ambitious, invocation of general principles is to place them *alongside* the governing positive law as an interpretive guide.[166] In an ICC arbitration governed by the laws of Ecuador, for instance, an insurance company filed a request for arbitration against a state-owned entity, which in turn objected to the tribunal's jurisdiction by citing an Ecuadorian constitutional provision barring public entities from submitting to "a foreign jurisdiction."[167] Due to this prohibition, the contract containing the arbitration clause was, according to the respondent, null and void under the Ecuadorian Civil Code. The tribunal studied the text of the Ecuadorian laws at issue, their legislative history, and domestic court decisions interpreting them, and then concluded that those laws did not oust its jurisdiction.[168] But the tribunal was also "comforted in the above conclusion by the fact that it accords with . . . established principles of international arbitration" and the general principle of "*venire contra factum proprium*."[169] Such an outcome, Jan Paulsson has argued, "is shown not to be an international imposition on national law," but a "vibrant affirmation" of the foundational core of that law, as recognized in myriad other national legal systems.[170] As this example attests, however, an "interpretation" of domestic law may be perceived as an alteration or correction of it—especially to a State that takes a different view of its own law.

Second, general principles can be used to define the depth and contours of broad or amorphous legal provisions. The "fair and equitable treatment" standard

---

165 Schill, *supra* note 68, at 90–91 (explaining that general principles "have been frequently used by international courts and tribunals . . . as a source of substantive rights and obligations, to fill lacunae in the governing law, and to aid in the interpretation and the further development of international law") (citations omitted).

166 PETER MALANCZUK AKEHURST'S MODERN INTRODUCTION TO INTERNATIONAL LAW 48–49 (Routledge 7th ed. 2002) (general principles are "not so much a source of law as a method of using existing sources"); Friedmann, *supra* note 74, at 287–90, 284 (discussing use of general principles such as good faith as "principles . . . of interpretation"); Lammers, *supra* note 67, at 64–65 (discussing "'the interpretative function' . . . [w]hen conventional or customary international law contains or relates to certain notions derived from, or to be appreciated in the light of, the national legal systems of States, such as the concept of property, the legal separation between companies and shareholders, or the international minimum treatment of aliens").

167 ICC Arb. No. 10947/ESR/MS (June 2002), *reprinted in* 22 ASA BULL. 2/2004 (June).

168 *Id.* ¶¶ 11–28.

169 *Id.* ¶ 30.

170 *See* Jan Paulsson, *The Lalive Lecture, Geneva: Unlawful Laws and the Authority of International Tribunals (May 27, 2009), in* 23(2) ICSID REV. 215, 230 (2008).

common to most modern BITs, for instance, can be viewed as a "variable standard,"[171] that is, an incomplete norm that entrusts arbitrators with considerable discretion in applying the standard to a given set of facts.[172] An ICSID tribunal expressly adverted to general principles in determining the "precise content" of the FET standard because "[t]reaties and international conventions . . . are not of great help to this end, as for the most part, they also contain rather general references to fair and equitable treatment and full protection and security without further elaboration."[173] Provisions such as this can be made more concrete by reference to foundational legal principles. Although it is a form of interpretation, this use of general principles goes a step further by providing specific elements or attributes that are not expressly included in the governing law itself. For example, the FET standard was deemed violated where a host state seized and auctioned an investor's property after providing notice that, although compliant with local law, was viewed as inadequate when measured against universal norms.[174] In this way, specific precepts common to all legal systems give shape to broad investment protections.

The *third* and most aggressive use of the general principles is to *displace* perceived failures in otherwise applicable law.[175] Take the famous *Abu Dhabi Case*. The Sheikh of Abu Dhabi entered into a written contract with a foreign oil company whereby the company was given the "exclusive right to drill for and win mineral oil within a certain area in Abu Dhabi."[176] A dispute arose, and although the contract contained an arbitration clause, it was silent on applicable law. The arbitrator cast aside the law of Abu Dhabi, despite its obvious connection to the case, because the Sheikh was exclusively in charge of administering "discretionary

---

171 *See* Herbert Hart, The Concept of Law 128–36 (2d ed. 1994) (distinguishing between "the open texture of the law," which means that courts must develop governing standards in light of "competing interests which vary in weight from case to case," and more determinate and rigid rules that demand the same outcome for each application).

172 *See generally* Sweet & della Cananea, *supra* note 89, at 911.

173 *Merrill & Ring v. Canada*, NAFTA Award, ¶¶ 186–87 (Mar. 31, 2010).

174 *Middle East Cement Shipping & Handling Co. S.A. v. Arab Republic of Egypt*, ICSID Case No. ARB/99/6, Award, ¶¶ 140–43 (Apr. 12, 2002), *reprinted in* 7 ICSID Rep. 173 (2005).

175 Lammers, *supra* note 67, at 64–65 (discussing "'the corrective function'" under which general principles "may set aside or modify provisions of conventional or customary international law"); *Amco Asia Corp. et al. v. Republic of Indonesia*, ICSID Case No. ARB/81/1, Resubmitted Case, Award, ¶¶ 37–40 (May 31, 1990) (reading Article 42 of the ICSID Convention to allow the tribunal to (1) apply international law where "there are no relevant host-state laws" and (2) "check[]" host-state law "in case of conflict": "the Tribunal believes that its task is to test every claim of law in this case first against [host-state] law, and then against international law").

176 *Petroleum Dev. (Trucial Coast) Ltd. v. Sheikh of Abu Dhabi*, 18 Int'l L. Rep. 144 (1951).

justice" there,[177] such that the application of that law would violate elementary notions of fairness. In its stead, the arbitrator chose to apply "the principles rooted in the good sense and common practice of the generality of civilized nations."[178] For the sole arbitrator in that case, Lord Asquith of Bishopstone, this meant the acceptance of basic principles of a highly developed system of laws and the concomitant rejection of others that were of historic or national peculiarity. In doing so, Lord Asquith accepted and applied certain principles of English law he viewed as universal, such as the interpretive rule *expressio unius est exclusio alterius*, but rejected others that he deemed parochial, such as the feudally inspired principle that grants by a sovereign are to be construed against the grantee. In the end, "the decision-making [wa]s no longer affected by the idiosyncrasies of local law, but [wa]s rather detached from the constraints of domestic dogmatism."[179] Although not free of controversy,[180] the corrective power of general principles allows judges and arbitrators in appropriate circumstances to "play their proper role in ensuring that law does not present itself as a blank sheet of paper upon which any dictator or dominant group can write laws illegitimate within the legal order, and thereby debase law itself."[181]

One law displacing another is not a rarity in international disputes. Conflicts of law are inherent in this setting, and the primacy of one law invariably entails the defeasance of another. But as opposed to a domestic court refusing application of a foreign law (on grounds of public policy, for instance), the application of the

177 *Id.* at 149; *see also Int'l Petroleums Ltd. v. Nat'l Iranian Oil Co. (Sapphire)*, 35 INT'L L. REP. 136, 172–73 (1967) (applying general principles to agreement between Canadian company and Iran's state-owned oil company where the agreement's call for execution "in a spirit of good faith and reciprocal good will" was deemed "scarcely compatible" with Iranian law).

178 *Petroleum Dev. (Trucial Coast) Ltd. v. Sheikh of Abu Dhabi*, 18 INT'L L. REP. 144, 149 (1951).

179 Klaus Peter Berger, *General Principles of Law in International Arbitration—How to Find Them, How to Apply Them*, 5 WORLD ARB. & MEDIATION REV. 97, 105 (2011). Lord Asquith infelicitously characterized Abu Dhabi as a "very primitive region" that lacked "any law sufficiently elaborated that it can be applied to modern commercial contracts." 18 INT'L L. REP. at 149, Commentators have rightly taken issue with this characterization and have even concluded that a faithful application of Islamic law in that case would have reached the same result as applying general principles of law. *See, e.g.*, Ibrahim Fadlallah, *Is There a Pro-Western Bias in Arbitral Awards?*, 9 J. WORLD INV. & TRADE 101, 102 (2008); *see* Ibrahim Fadlallah, *Arbitration Facing Conflicts of Culture—The 2008 Annual School of International Arbitration Lecture sponsored by Freshfields Bruckhaus Deringer LLP*, 25 ARB. INT'L 303 (2009). So it turned out that the salient principles applied to the case were indeed "rooted in the good sense and common practice of the generality of civilized nations"—Islamic nations included.

180 Lammers, *supra* note 67, at 65–66 (arguing that general principles cannot trump conventional or customary international law, but perhaps can displace other principles of law).

181 JAN PAULSSON, THE IDEA OF ARBITRATION 242 (2013).

general principles to govern the outcome of a transnational case is less intrusive, and perhaps less arbitrary as well.[182] Even when it is completely displaced, the otherwise applicable law is not discarded as contrary to a *parochial* sense of "good morals [or] some deep-rooted tradition of the common weal" of the forum.[183] Rather, it is made consonant with *international* standards derived from the commonalities of positive law on the municipal plane. This is also what differentiates the general principles from *lex mercatoria*, which traditionally has little formal basis in a consensus of domestic laws.[184]

A microcosm of these various roles can be found in the European Court of Justice's (ECJ) invocations of "the general principles common to the laws of the Member States,"[185] which enjoy constitutional status and are binding on Union Institutions and Member States.[186] In identifying such a principle, the "most important source" for the ECJ is "the laws of Member States."[187] In assessing the commonality of a principle across Member States, the "ECJ will by no means search for a common denominator but will seek the 'best' and 'most progressive' solution of legal problems that commonly arise in the national legal orders."[188]

182 *See, e.g., Davies v. Davies*, [1887] 36 Ch. D. 359, 364 (Kekewich, J.) ("Public policy does not admit of definition and is not easily explained.... [It] is a variable quantity; ... it must vary and does vary with the habits, capacities, and opportunities of the public."); *Besant v. Wood*, [1879] 12 C.D. 605, 620 (Jessel, M.R.) ("It is impossible to say what the opinion of a man or a Judge might be as to what public policy is.").

183 *Loucks v. Standard Oil Co.* of New York, 224 N.Y. 99, 111 (1918); *see also World Duty Free Co. Ltd. v. Republic of Kenya*, ICSID Case No. ARB/00/7, Award, ¶¶ 140, 147 (Oct. 4, 2006) ("Domestic courts generally refer to their own international public policy," even though "some judgments" do refer to a "universal conception of public policy").

184 *Lex mercatoria* is historically understood as the body of customs and practices followed by medieval Italian merchants to supplement the often incomplete rules applied by autonomous private courts, which then spread to other principal trading centers across Europe. *See* Mark Janis, International Law 301 (Aspen 2012); Ernst Von Caemmerer, *The Influence of the Law of International Trade on the Development and Character of the Commercial Law in the Civil Law Countries, in* The Sources of the Law of International Trade 88 (Schmittoff ed., 1964); Andreas F. Lowenfeld, Lex Mercatoria: *An Arbitrator's View*, 1990 Arb. Int'l 133. Although certain authors have identified a modern *lex mercatoria* arising out of national legislation, others favor the traditional non-sovereign approach steeped in commercial self-regulation, where freedom of contract and international commercial arbitration awards continue to play a critical role in the law's development. *See* Bernardo Cremades & Steven L. Plehn, *The New* Lex Mercatoria *and the Harmonization of the Laws of International Commercial Transactions*, 2 B.U. Int'l L.J. 317 (1984).

185 European Union, Consolidated Version of the Treaty on the Functioning of the European Union (TFEU) art. 340 (2007).

186 Annekatrien Lenaerts, *The Role of the Principle* Fraus Omnia Corrumpit *in the European Union: A Possible Evolution towards a General Principle of Law?*, 32 Y.B. Euro. L. 460, 462 (2013).

187 *Id.*

188 *Id.* at 463.

Once identified, the general principles of Union law are called upon to interpret, or to fill gaps in, the governing law:

> Since general principles stand at the highest level of hierarchy of norms alongside the Treaties themselves, an *interpretation* that is consistent with a general principle is preferred to one that would negate or contradict the general principle. . . . [G]eneral principles [also] constitute a crucial tool for the creation of a "common law of Europe." According to this gap-filling function, the Court may *complete* existing Union rules with additional unwritten rules of law in order to achieve Union objectives. Moreover, . . . the Court may in certain situations *correct* the strict application of existing Union rules on the basis of fundamental, unwritten principles such as good faith, fairness, or justice in order to avoid undermining Union objectives.[189]

Although the process by which the ECJ identifies the general principles of Union law is seemingly more fluid than that on the international plane, both sets of general principles serve the vital function of completing and unifying Union and international law, respectively.

3. Invocations of General Principles

Supplanting notions of equity, the sources of international law codified in Article 38 of the PCIJ and ICJ Statutes have provided a stable foundation that has proven critical to the development of the international legal system. As principles common to almost all legal systems, their existence bears witness to a fundamental unity of law, which gives them legitimacy and makes them obligatory. The general principles are predicates to the rule of law, both in the municipal and international setting. They are, as Cheng said, "the paths which civilised mankind has learned in its long experience in the municipal sphere to be those leading to justice and which it would perforce have to follow if it wished to establish Law and Justice among Nations."[190]

This pedigree legitimates the use of general principles in all manner of international dispute resolution. In commercial arbitration between private parties, the application of transnational law can isolate the peculiarities of national law that may hinder the fair resolution of an individual case, and there is a discernible

---

189 *Id.* at 463–64 (emphasis added).

190 CHENG, *supra* note 4, at 386.

trend for the general principles to play this role. General principles carry even more weight when the arbitration is conducted under a sovereign compact against a respondent State. In this scenario, to ensure that the application of state law does not fall below minimum international standards, general principles may be invoked either as an interpretive, definitional, or corrective mechanism, especially when the strict application of the respondent State's law would yield an idiosyncratic result. National courts seised with a transnational case have used the general principles in the same manner. The varied places and circumstances where the general principles have been applied are a testament to the vital position they hold in the international juridical order.

a) Arbitral Tribunals

General principles are found in all forms of international arbitration. International commercial arbitrators routinely exercise the power to apply nonstate law to resolve disputes between private parties, especially where the parties have no explicit agreement on *lex contractus*.[191] It is easy to see why this is an appealing option:

> [I]nternational standards . . . apply uniformly and are not dependent on the peculiarities of any particular national law. They take due account of the needs of international intercourse and permit cross-fertilization between systems that may be unduly wedded to conceptual distinctions [rather than] a pragmatic and fair resolution in the individual case.[192]

This is true regardless of whether a sovereign party is involved in the case. Indeed, given that they stem primarily from *private* municipal law, general principles are perhaps the ideal source of international law to guide private arbitral tribunals. Some commentators have observed a "trend among international arbitrators . . . to challenge the adequacy of applying national laws when resolving transnational disputes," even purely private disputes, in order to "show[] that the national solutions on which they rely have a transnational status."[193]

---

191 *See* Emmanuel Gaillard, *General Principles of Law in International Commercial Arbitration—Challenging the Myths*, 5 World Arb. & Mediation Rev. 161, 165–66 (2011) (arguing that, whenever the parties' are silent as to their choice of law, but have chosen to have their dispute governed by the rules of the ICC, the LCIA, the ICDR, the HKIAC, or the KCAB, arbitrators enjoy the discretion to resort to general principles of law in the same way they can select a given national law).

192 ICC Case No. 8385, Collection of ICC Arbitral Awards 1996–2000, at 474 (comments of Yves Derains).

193 Yves Derains, *The Application of Transnational Rules in ICC Arbitral Awards*, 51 World Arb. & Mediation Rev. 173, 193 (2011). The application of non-domestic law will generally not hinder the

Commercial arbitrators frequently invoke general principles in the realm of contract law. As discussed further in chapter 2, general principles have been relied upon to guide or even correct the application of otherwise applicable domestic law when that law is underdeveloped, unsuited for a transnational dispute, or—in extreme cases—unable to meet minimum standards of propriety and fairness.[194] For instance, a claim brought under a contract promising commissions for an agent's efforts in securing public works contracts for a foreign investor was rejected on jurisdictional grounds, notwithstanding the fact that the claim was arbitrable under *lex arbitri* (French law) and *lex contractus* (Argentine law).[195] Finding that the agent had engaged in public bribery, the sole arbitrator admonished that such conduct "can have no countenance in any court . . . in any . . . civilized country."[196] "[G]eneral principles" preclude entertaining private disputes of this nature, irrespective of any "national rules on arbitrability."[197] Similarly, general principles apply where a state entity invokes local law to evade an agreement to arbitrate. It has been held that an arbitral tribunal's plenary interpretation of local law permits reference to basic precepts such as *venire contra factum proprium*.[198]

Reliance upon general principles in relation to domestic law creates greater sensitivities when a sovereign is party to the dispute. States have historically been the main subjects of international law. In 1953, Cheng wrote against a near-exclusive backdrop of inter-state dispute resolution, and the "International Courts and Tribunals" referenced in the title to his book were limited to the ICJ (and its predecessor, the PCIJ) and episodic ad hoc claims tribunals. In this context, Cheng described the principle of good faith in terms of forbidding a *State* from abusing

enforceability of that award in a national court. *See* Ole Lando, *The* Lex Mercatoria *in International Commercial Arbitration*, 34 Int'l & Comp. L.Q. 747 (1985) (surveying enforcement of arbitral awards based on non-national sources of law in European countries). This may not be true, however, for contracts governed by the laws of countries whose statutes, constitutions, and treaties preclude or restrict the application of non-domestic law to certain types of contracts, as is the case in several Latin American countries. *See* Alden F. Abbott, *Latin American and International Arbitration Conventions: The Quandary of Non-Ratification*, 17 Harv. Int'l L.J. 131, 137–40 (1976); Donald B. Straus, *Why International Commercial Arbitration Is Lagging in Latin America: Problems and Cure*, 33 Arb. J. 21 (1978). In contrast, French law explicitly permits an arbitrator to resort to non-national sources of law even where the parties did not agree upon its application. *See* French Civil Code art. 1496; Philippe Fouchard, *L'arbitrage international en France apres le decret du 12 Mai 1981*, 109 J. Droit Int'l (Clunet) 374, 394 (1982).

194 *See, e.g.*, ICC Case No. 8486, 10(2) ICC Bull. 69 (1999); ICC Case No. 8223, 10(2) ICC Bull. 58 (1999).

195 ICC Case No. 1110, Award (1963), 10(3) Arb. Int'l 282 (1994).

196 *Id.* at 291.

197 *Id.*

198 ICC Arb. No. 10947/ESR/MS (June 2002), *reprinted in* 22 ASA Bull. 2/2004, ¶ 30 (June).

its rights, taking advantage of its own wrongs, or taking inconsistent positions to another sovereign's detriment. His explication of the principle of *pacta sunt servanda* was largely done in the context of international treaties—not private contracts. Private parties were largely dependent upon diplomatic protection to vindicate their rights on the international plane, that is, outside of the host State's courts. The weight and complexity of other facets of foreign relations often trumped the grievances of a particular investor, and States proved to be unreliable advocates for their constituents.[199]

Although the number and type of international tribunals have since burgeoned, the disputes between investors and States that had arisen prior to 1953 were of a similar ilk as those seen today. Then, as now, foreign investors were vulnerable to social and political upheaval in the host State. Then, as now, rulers nullified contracts with foreign investors and expropriated their assets. Then, as now, laws would change to reflect new political platforms. The confiscation of foreign assets after the Cuban Revolution of 1959, for example, was enabled by changes in Cuban law that purported to insulate the expropriating government from providing compensation.[200] About 40 years later, the Nicaraguan legislature enacted a special law to facilitate lawsuits against select foreign companies for alleged injuries caused by pesticides.[201] Although violative of international law, measures such as these are often supported by a nationalistic populace and ratified

199 Although there were early cases brought before the PCIJ by certain countries to enforce awards rendered in favor of their nationals, *see, e.g., Mavrommatis Palestine Concessions (Greece v. U.K.)*, Judgment, 1924 P.C.I.J. (Ser. A) No. 2 (Aug. 30); *Société Commerciale de Belgique (Belg. v. Greece)*, Judgment, 1939 P.C.I.J. (Ser. A/B) No. 78 (June 15), diplomatic-protection actions were not commonplace. As Judge Stephen Schwebel has explained, "[t]he exercise of diplomatic protection . . . was replete with rules which allowed the government of the alien to escape the diplomatic burdens of espousal, such as the local remedies rule and that of continuity in the nationality of claims." Keynote Address at the 22d ICCA Congress Miami: In Defence of Bilateral Investment Treaties (Apr. 6, 2014). In addition, the practice of diplomatic protection by capital-exporting countries triggered strong opposition from host countries in Latin America and other parts of the world, as reflected in the *Calvo* and *Drago* doctrines. *See, e.g.*, Horacio Grigera Naón, Lecture, *Arbitration and Latin America: Progress and Setbacks*, 21 Arbitration Int'l 127 (2005). Although diplomatic protection has receded further with the advent of investor-state arbitration, the pendulum may yet swing back. The frustration faced by many prevailing parties in having investment awards enforced could trigger a new era of diplomatic protection efforts to secure payment. *See* Victorino J. Tejera Perez, *Diplomatic Protection Revival for Failure to Comply with Investment Arbitration Awards*, 3(2) J. Int'l Disp. Settlement 445 (2012); *see also* Wenhua Shan, *Is Calvo Dead?*, 55(1) Am. J. Comp. L. 123 (Winter 2007).

200 *See First Nat'l City Bank (FNCB) v. Banco Para el Comercio Exterior de Cuba* (Bancec), 462 U.S. 611 (1983).

201 *See Osorio v. Dole Food Co.*, 665 F. Supp. 2d 1307 (S.D. Fla. 2009), *aff'd sub nom.* Osorio v. Dow Chem. Co., 635 F.3d 1277 (11th Cir 2011).

by local judges. The travails of foreigner Jacob Idler before the handpicked judges of revolutionary Venezuela, for instance, remain well known and relatable over 150 years later.[202] Reliable application of the rule of law continues to be absent in many countries, and this inevitably leads to international strife.

What has changed since Cheng's writing is the availability of direct recourse for private parties affected by allegedly abusive sovereign acts. Today, the rise of international arbitration under BITs and similar instruments has empowered investors to act on their own behalf. Private parties are no longer relegated to take foreign local courts as they find them, and they no longer depend on the discretion of their own government to exercise diplomatic protection.[203] They can bring an international claim directly against host States that have waived their sovereign immunity in binding arbitration clauses.[204] Arbitrators are thus empowered to apply international law to resolve what are often regulatory disputes: the legal protections afforded by BITs and other investment treaties, combined with a neutral forum in which to adjudicate them, form what has been called the world's first "comprehensive form of global administrative law."[205] Investment treaties confer upon private parties both substantive and procedural rights in the host State, such as "fair and equitable treatment," adequate compensation for expropriation, and protection against discriminatory or arbitrary legislation. Some BITs even allow foreign investors to bring ordinary contract claims before an international arbitral tribunal rather than domestic courts,[206]

202 *Compare Idler v. Venezuela*, 4 MOORE INT'L ARBS. 3491 (1885), *with Bridgeway Corp. v. Citibank*, 201 F.3d 134 (2d Cir. 2000).

203 *See generally* M. SORNARAJAH, THE SETTLEMENT OF FOREIGN INVESTMENT DISPUTES 61–84 (2000); Karl-Heinz Böckstiegel, *Arbitration of Foreign Investment Disputes—An Introduction*, *in* NEW HORIZONS IN INTERNATIONAL COMMERCIAL ARBITRATION AND BEYOND 125 (Albert Jan van den Berg ed., 2005); JOHN COLLIER & VAUGHAN LOWE, THE SETTLEMENT OF DISPUTES IN INTERNATIONAL LAW: INSTITUTIONS AND PROCEDURES 1–15 (1999).

204 This is because most contemporary BITs include compulsory clauses for the settlement of disputes that may arise between foreign investors and the host State, allowing such investors to bring claims against the host State before international arbitral tribunals. These arbitration clauses operate as advance consent of the host State to arbitrate any and all disputes, at the investor's initiative, over the treaty's meaning and application. *See, e.g.*, *Republic of Ecuador v. Chevron Corp.*, 638 F.3d 384 (2d Cir. 2011).

205 *See also* Gus Van Harten & Martin Loughlin, *Investment Treaty Arbitration as a Species of Global Administrative Law*, 17 EUR. J. INT'L L. 121, 123 (2006); Sabino Cassese, *Administrative Law without the State? The Challenge of Global Regulation*, 37 N.Y.U. J. INT'L L. & POL. 663 (2005); Benedict Kingsbury, Nico Krisch & Richard B. Stewart, *The Emergence of Global Administrative Law*, 68 L. & CONTEMP. PROBS. 15 (2005); Gus Van Harten, *The Public-Private Distinction in the International Arbitration of Individual Claims against the State*, 56 INT'L & COMP. L.Q. 371 (2007).

206 *See, e.g.*, US-Romania Bilateral Investment Treaty art. II(2)(c) (signed May 28, 1992, entered into force January 15, 1994) ("[e]ach Party shall observe any obligation it may have entered into with regard to

thus "transform[ing] municipal law obligations into obligations directly cognizable in international law."[207] Although this has expanded the number of such claims, thorny choice-of-law issues persist. The contracts are typically governed by the laws of the host State, either as the rule of decision or as an important datum;[208] the aggrieved investor may thus be liberated from local courts, but it remains bound by local laws. This is where general principles of law fit in.

As noted, it is not uncommon for international arbitral tribunals to employ general principles as a tool for the proper interpretation and even correction of applicable local law. This is seen in the seminal case of *Amco v. Indonesia*.[209] In 1964, an Indonesian company began construction of a hotel in Jakarta but stopped short the following year due to a lack of funds. By order of the Indonesian Government, the company was reorganized under the new name of P.T. Wisma and placed

---

investments"); *see generally* Stanimir A. Alexandrov, *Breaches of Contract and Breaches of Treaty—The Jurisdiction of Treaty-Based Arbitration Tribunals to Decide Breach of Contract Claims in* SGS v. Pakistan *and* SGS v. Philippines, 5 J. World Inv't & Trade 555 (2004).

207 *Nobles Ventures v. Romania*, ICSID Case No. ARB/01/11, Award, ¶¶ 53–55 (Oct. 12, 2005).

208 *See generally* Yas Banifatemi, *The Law Applicable in Investment Treaty Arbitration*, *in* Arbitration under International Investment Agreements 196–98 (K. Yannaca-Small ed., Oxford Univ. Press 2010). Choice-of-law rules reflect the tenuous "balance . . . between the law of the host State and international law." *Id.* at 201. For instance, resolution of contract claims under a BIT umbrella clause first starts with a State's internal law to determine the terms of the contract and whether it has been breached, and then moves to international law as a subsidiary matter to determine the State's responsibility owing to the breach. In contrast, arbitrators reviewing an expropriatory measure look first to international law to determine whether an illicit expropriation has occurred, and then to national law as a subsidiary matter to fill any lacunae that might exist. Determining the proper role and sequencing of domestic and international law is necessarily case and issue specific. *Compare CME Czech Republic B.V. v. Czech Republic*, UNCITRAL, Final Award, ¶ 402 (Mar. 14, 2003) ("There is no ranking in the application of the national law of the host State, the Treaty provisions or the general principles of international law. Further there is no exclusivity in the application of these laws."), and *Wena Hotels Ltd. v. Arab Republic of Egypt*, ICSID Case No. ARB/98/4, Decision on Application for Annulment ¶ 40 (Feb. 5, 2002), 41 I.L.M. 933, 941 (2002) ("The law of the host State can indeed be applied in conjunction with international law if this is justified. So too international law can be applied by itself if the appropriate rule is found in this other ambit."), *with Klöckner Industrie-Anlagen GmbH v. United Republic of Cameroon*, ICSID Case No. ARB/81/2, Decision on Annulment, ¶ 69 (May 3, 1985), 2 ICSID Rep. 95, 122 (1994) ("Article 42(1) therefore clearly does not allow the arbitrator to base his decision solely on the 'rules' or 'principles of international law.'"), *and Amco Asia Corp. et al. v. Republic of Indonesia*, Decision on the Application for Annulment, ¶ 20 (May 16, 1986), 1 ICSID Rep. 509, 515 (1993) ("Article 42(1) of the Convention authorizes an ICSID tribunal to apply rules of international law only to fill up lacunae in the applicable domestic law and to ensure precedence to international law norms where the rules of the applicable domestic law are in collision with such norms.").

209 *Amco Asia Corp. et al. v. Republic of Indonesia*, ICSID Case No. ARB/81/1, Award on the Merits (Nov. 21, 1984), *reprinted in* 24 I.L.M. 1022 (1985). For a good summary of the decision in *Amco*, see generally International Investment Law and Arbitration: Leading Cases from the ICSID, NAFTA, Bilateral Treaties and Customary International Law 262 *et seq.* (Todd Weiler ed., 2005).

under the control of an entity established under Indonesian law for the welfare of Indonesian army personnel. In 1968, P.T. Wisma identified a U.S. investor, Amco, as being interested in both completing the construction of the hotel and undertaking its management for a limited period of time. Amco obtained the necessary investment license from the Indonesian Government to enter into a "Lease and Management Agreement." After construction was completed, a dispute arose with regard to Amco's management of the hotel. In 1980, P.T. Wisma enlisted the Indonesian armed forces to take control of the hotel and persuaded the Indonesian Government to revoke Amco's investment license without notice. The legality of the revocation of the investment license was affirmed by an Indonesian court and upheld on appeal.

In 1981, Amco commenced an ICSID arbitration against the Indonesian Government, alleging, inter alia, that the revocation of its investment license constituted a breach of contract. As a threshold matter, the tribunal determined that it was not bound by the decision of the Indonesian courts; were it otherwise, the arbitral process would be meaningless.[210] Asked to decide whether the investment license was a contract capable of being breached, the tribunal examined "Indonesian law as well as general principles of law drawn from the main legal systems, which constitute a source of international law applicable *together* with Indonesian law in the instant case."[211] Holding that the contract could be breached, the tribunal continued that "the withdrawal of the investment authorization, decided without due process being granted to the investor, . . . commits the liability of the Republic of Indonesia under Indonesian *as well as* under international law, that is to say under the two systems of law applicable in the instant case."[212] The result was an affirmation of

210 *Amco Asia Corp. et al. v. Republic of Indonesia*, ICSID Case No. ARB/81/1, Award on the Merits, ¶¶ 177–78 (Nov. 21, 1984), *reprinted in* 24 I.L.M. 1022 (1985) ("[A]n international tribunal is not bound to follow the result of a national court. One of the reasons for instituting an international arbitration procedure is precisely that parties—rightly or wrongly—feel often more confident with a legal institution which is not entirely related to one of the parties. If a national judgment was binding on an international tribunal, such a procedure could be rendered meaningless. Accordingly, no matter how the legal position of a party is described in a national judgment, an International Arbitral Tribunal has the right to evaluate and examine this position without accepting any res judicata effect of a national court. In its evaluation, therefore, the judgments of a national court can be accepted as one of the many factors which have to be considered by the arbitral tribunal.").

211 *Id.* ¶¶ 181–83 (emphasis added) (surveying French, Dutch, Belgian, Italian, Danish and secondary sources under the common law), ¶ 188.

212 *Id.* ¶¶ 244–50 (emphasis added). The Government of Indonesia filed an application for the annulment of the award under Section VII of the ICSID Convention. Among other things, Indonesia challenged the tribunal's reference to equitable considerations, asserting that such reference amounted to an excess of power. Although the ad hoc annulment committee agreed with Indonesia that the tribunal had not

the host State's law in line with, and buttressed by, the "legal provisions common to a number of nations."[213]

Another recurring theme is the application of hortatory general principles of law by arbitral tribunals to trump refractory local custom. Bribery and other forms of corruption—although universally condemned—are a lamentable reality in many societies. In *World Duty Free Company Ltd. v. Kenya*,[214] the claimant, a British company, had concluded an agreement in 1989 with the Kenyan Government for the construction, maintenance, and operation of duty-free complexes at the Nairobi and Mombassa airports. Later, the Government expropriated and liquidated the claimant's local assets—including its rights under the 1989 agreement. The claimant sought, inter alia, restitution for breach of the contract. Kenya defended by saying that the 1989 agreement was "tainted with illegality" and thus unenforceable because it was procured upon the payment of a U.S. $2 million bribe from the claimant to the former president of Kenya.[215] The claimant did little to rebut the factual basis of the defense, instead arguing that "it was routine practice to make such donations in advance of doing business in Kenya" because "said practice had cultural roots" and was "regarded as a matter of protocol by the Kenyan people."[216] "[S]ufficient regard to the *domestic* public policy," the claimant argued, required the tribunal to uphold the contract notwithstanding the bribe.[217]

The ICSID tribunal first divined and then applied "an international consensus as to universal standards and accepted norms of conduct that must be applied in

been authorized to decide the case *ex aequo et bono*, and ultimately annulled the award because the tribunal had failed to consider certain justifications for the revocation decision under Indonesian law, the committee rejected the claim that the tribunal exceeded its powers by basing its decision in part on the general principles of law. *See Amco Annulment Decision* ¶¶ 19–22 (May 16, 1986), *reprinted in* 1 Int'l Lab. Rep. 649 (1986). When the case was resubmitted, the second ICSID tribunal continued to employ international law as a supplemental and corrective set of norms, and explained its task as testing every claim of law first against Indonesian law and then against international law. *Amco Asia Corp. et al. v. Republic of Indonesia*, ICSID Case No. ARB/81/1, Resubmitted Case, Award, ¶¶ 37–40 (June 5, 1990). After so doing, the second tribunal found that although certain substantive grounds might have existed for the revocation of the license under Indonesian law, the circumstances surrounding the decision fell below minimum standards of due process and required compensation to be paid by the State. *Id.* ¶ 139.

213 *Amco Asia Corp. et al. v. Republic of Indonesia*, ICSID Case No. ARB/81/1, Award on the Merits, ¶ 180 (Nov. 21, 1984), *reprinted in* 24 I.L.M. 1022 (1985) (internal question marks omitted).

214 *World Duty Free Co. Ltd. v. Republic of Kenya*, ICSID Case No. ARB/00/7, Award (Oct. 4, 2006).

215 *Id.* ¶¶ 135, 182.

216 *Id.* ¶ 120.

217 *Id.*

all fora."[218] After surveying arbitral jurisprudence, a number of international conventions, decisions of domestic courts, and various domestic laws (including the Kenyan Prevention of Corruption Act), the tribunal concluded that "bribery and influence peddling . . . [is] sanctioned by criminal law in most, if not all, countries."[219] Finding bribery to be illegal as a matter of English and Kenyan law, the tribunal deemed it unnecessary "to consider the effect of a local custom which might render legal locally what would otherwise violate transnational public policy."[220] Even "[i]f it had been necessary," the tribunal continued, it would have been "minded to decline . . . to recognize any local custom in Kenya purporting to validate bribery committed by the claimant in violation of international public policy."[221] Thus, the claimant "is not legally entitled to maintain any of its pleaded claims in these proceedings on the ground of *ex turpi causa non oritur actio*."[222]

Based upon the facts there, the *World Duty Free* tribunal did not impute the bribe of Kenya's president to the State itself.[223] It nonetheless went on, ex hypothesi, to note that even if Kenya were charged with receipt of the bribe, the tribunal would nonetheless allow it to invoke the defense of *ex turpi causa non oritur actio*. Quoting Lord Mansfield, the tribunal acknowledged that "'the objection, that a contract is immoral or illegal as between plaintiff and defendant, sounds at all times very ill in the mouth of the defendant,'" but reiterated the importance, as a "'matter of public policy,'" of a court not lending its aid to "'an immoral or illegal act.'"[224] This underscores the risk to those engaged in corruption: having formed a contract in violation of the rule of law, neither party can reliably call upon the rule of law to aid it if the other side breaches.

Consistent with the nature of general principles, the ICSID tribunal elevated Kenyan *written* law over allegedly widespread Kenyan *practice* with respect to bribery. Because general principles of law remain aspirational in many countries,

---

218 *Id.* ¶ 139.

219 *Id.* ¶ 142.

220 *Id.* ¶ 172.

221 *Id.*

222 *Id.* ¶ 179; *see also Metal-Tech Ltd. v. Republic of Uzbekistan*, ICSID Case No. ARB/10/3, Award, ¶ 372 (Oct. 4, 2014) (dismissing BIT claim for lack of jurisdiction where investment was tainted by corruption).

223 *Id.* ¶ 169.

224 *Id.* ¶ 181 (quoting *Holman v. Johnson* (1775) 1 Cowp. 341, 343). The tribunal also noted that, if receipt of the bribe had been attributed to Kenya at an earlier point, it is possible the Kenya could have waived its right to rescind the contract for fraud such that the contract would have been fully enforceable against it. *See id.* ¶¶ 164, 183–85. Relying upon English and Kenyan law, the tribunal stated that "'[i]f . . . an improper inducement is offered by B (acting on behalf of Y) to A (acting on behalf of X) which

they cannot be divined from a comparative review of de facto practices around the world. Instead, in ascertaining the general principles, international tribunals accept what countries decree the law to be in their codes and constitutions (e.g., trial before impartial and independent tribunals) and hold them to it. This contrasts with the process by which customary international law is determined, with its review of actual state practice with respect to the norm at issue. As noted in Subchapter A.2, general principles of law obtain their status as such not because of actual adherence on the ground, but because they emanate from the positive law of many States and are widely deemed essential to a functioning rule of law. There is thus an immutability in general principles that is not found in customary international law, whose principles "can be, and have been developed, eroded or otherwise altered by practice."[225]

The power to apply general principles emanates from the very essence of an international arbitral tribunal's legal authority. Its application of the law is plenary. This means that, in a given case, it is proper for it to refuse to apply "unlawful laws,"[226] viz., those otherwise applicable laws that run afoul of superior national norms or the minimum standards of international law. General principles of law can apply in their stead. They provide baselines against which laws can be measured and to which they can be corrected, and thus play a key role in shaping the rules of foreign investment protection.[227] The "law of the host state can indeed be applied" where there is no conflict, but general principles will "prevail over domestic rules that might be incompatible with them," modifying or supplanting those national laws that are discordant with minimum international standards.[228] Thus, where a tribunal found that Egyptian law governed the contract at issue, it further concluded, under Article 42 of the ICSID Convention, that

causes or contributes to the making of a contract; and if this fact is afterwards discovered, . . . (a) X is entitled at his option to rescind the contract [or] (b) X . . . may choose to waive his right to rescind the contract; keep the contract alive and enforce it according to its terms.'" *Id.* ¶ 164 (quoting the expert legal opinion of Lord Mustill submitted by Kenya). This raises a possible tension: the respondent could have waived its right to rescind a fraudulent contract, such that it is valid and enforceable, but the claimant may nonetheless be prevented from pressing its claim under the doctrine *ex turpi causa non oritur actio*. Because it found that Kenya had timely acted to rescind the contract, the *World Duty Free* tribunal did not have cause to address whether a tribunal could hear a claim based upon a contract procured by fraud where the respondent had waived its option to rescind the contract.

225 Elias & Lin, *supra* note 46, at 29.

226 Paulsson, *supra* note 154, at 224, 230.

227 *See* M. Sornarajah, The International Law on Foreign Investment 94 (2d ed. 2004).

228 *Wena Hotels Ltd. v. Arab Republic of Egypt*, ICSID Case No. ARB/98/4, Decision on Application for Annulment, ¶¶ 40–44 (Feb. 5, 2002), 41 I.L.M. 933 (2002); *accord Amco Asia Corp. et al. v. Republic of Indonesia*, ICSID Case No. ARB/81/1, Award on the Merits ¶ 40 (Nov. 21, 1984), *reprinted in* 24 I.L.M.

"Egyptian law must be construed so as to include [general] principles ... [and the] national laws of Egypt can be relied upon *only in as much as they do not contravene said principles.*"[229]

A similar result can obtain from voluntarily negotiated choice-of-law provisions. In *TOPCO*, for instance, concession agreements between Libya and two foreign oil companies provided for international law to check and, where necessary, substitute for municipal law: " 'This concession shall be governed and interpreted by [i] the principles of the law of Libya common to the principles of international law and [ii] in the absence of such common principles then by and in accordance with the general principles of law. . . .' "[230] At the first level, principles of Libyan law could be applied only where they conformed with "principles of international law," which the sole arbitrator read broadly to include "international law as it is applied between all nations belonging to the community of states."[231] Where Libyan law diverged from those international principles, it no longer obtained; instead, the issue would be governed by "the general principles ... mentioned in Article 38 of the Statute of the International Court of Justice."[232] As the tribunal explained, "these clauses tend to remove all or part of the agreement from the internal law and to provide for its correlative submission to ... a system which is properly an international law system."[233] This was intentional: "The recourse to general principles ... is justified by the need for the private contracting party to be protected against unilateral and abrupt modifications of the legislation in the contracting State: it plays, therefore, an important role in the contractual equilibrium intended by the parties."[234]

1022 (1985) ("applicable host-state laws ... must be checked against international laws, which will prevail in case of conflict").

229 *SPP (Middle East) Ltd & Southern Pacific Projects v. Egypt & EGOTH*, ICSID Case No. ARB/84/3, Award, ¶ 84 (May 20, 1984), *reprinted in* 32 I.L.M. 933 (1993) ("When ... international law is violated by the exclusive application of municipal law, the Tribunal is bound ... to apply directly the relevant principles and rules of international law. . . . [S]uch a process will not involve the confirmation or denial of the validity of the host State's law, but may result in not applying it where that law, or action taken under that law, violates international law.") (citations omitted).

230 *Texaco Overseas Petroleum Co. (TOPCO) v. Gov't of the Libyan Arab Republic*, Award, ¶ 8, 53 INT'L L. REP. 389, 404 (1979).

231 *Id.* ¶ 41, 53 INT'L L. REP. at 453.

232 *Id.* ¶ 50, 53 INT'L L. REP. at 461.

233 *Id.* ¶ 45, 53 INT'L L. REP. at 456.

234 *Id.* ¶ 42, 53 INT'L L. REP. at 454.

From a theoretical perspective, general principles are just as well suited for resolving investor-state disputes as they are for resolving international commercial disputes. As noted, unlike treaties and custom that derive entirely from inter-state conduct, general principles derive in the main from domestic laws that regulate private parties—the usual claimants in such cases. To ensure compliance with international legal commands, the precise content of the principle is determined with reference to more than just one territorial system.[235] The body of published decisions from the Iran-United States Claims Tribunal is illustrative.[236] The judges on the Tribunal have broad discretion to determine the substantive law to be applied[237] and have identified and applied general principles of law in cases presenting issues of unjust enrichment,[238] force majeure,[239] and good faith performance of contracts.[240] As would be expected, the Tribunal has relied heavily upon Iranian and U.S. law in the comparative analyses it has undertaken, as well as French law because it serves as the basis for the Iranian Civil Code. It has taken a broader analysis on occasion, though more rarely.[241]

---

235 *See* Christoph Schreuer, *International and Domestic Law in Investment Disputes. The Case of ICSID*, 1 AUSTRIAN REV. INT'L & EUR. L. 89, 107 (1996); *see also* Norber Wühler, *Application of General Principles, in* ICCA CONGRESS SERIES n.7, 553 (1996); Lord McNair, *The General Principles of Law Recognized by Civilized Nations*, 33 BRIT. Y.B. INT'L L. 1, 15 (1957).

236 Richard Lillich, *Preface* to THE IRAN-UNITED STATES CLAIMS TRIBUNAL 1981–83, at vii (Richard Lillich ed., 1984). For background on the Tribunal, see *Symposium on the Iran-United States Claims Tribunal*, 16 L. & POL'Y INT'L BUS. 667 (1984).

237 *See generally* John Crook, *Applicable Law in International Commercial Arbitration: The Iran-US Claims Tribunal Experience*, 83 AM. J. INT'L L. 278 (1989); Grant Hanessian, *General Principles of Law in the Iran-U.S. Claims Tribunal*, 27 COLUM. J. TRANSNAT'L L. 309 (1988–89) (explaining that the Iran-U.S. Tribunal performed a "[c]omparative analysis of municipal legal systems" in determining general principles of law, giving "particular attention to the laws of Iran and the United States" but also consulting "the laws of various nations, including common and civil law countries").

238 *Schlegel Corp. v. Nat'l Iranian Copper Indus. Co.*, 14 Iran-U.S. Cl. Trib. Rep. 176 (1987); *Flexi-Van Leasing, Inc. v. Islamic Republic of Iran*, 12 Iran-U.S. Cl. Trib. Rep. 335 (1986); *Shannon & Wilson, Inc. v. Atomic Energy Org. of Iran*, 9 Iran-U.S. Cl. Trib. Rep. 397, 402 (1985).

239 *Sylvania Technical Sys., Inc. v. Islamic Republic of Iran*, 8 Iran-U.S. Cl. Trib. Rep. 298, 309, 312 (1985) (international contracts); *Queens Office Tower Ass'n (QUOTA) v. Iran Nat'l Airlines Corp.*, 2 Iran-U.S. Cl. Trib. Rep. 247, 254 (1983); *Am. Bell Int'l, Inc. v. Islamic Republic of Iran*, 12 Iran-U.S. Cl. Trib. Rep. 170 (1986).

240 *See, e.g., General Dynamics Corp. v. Islamic Republic of Iran*, 5 Iran-U.S. Cl. Trib. Rep. 386, 398 (1984) (obligation under "general principles of law" to perform contract with due diligence); *PepsiCo, Inc. v. Islamic Republic of Iran et al.*, 13 Iran-U.S. Cl. Trib. Rep. 3 (1986) (ratification of contract by conduct); *Harnischfeger Corp. v. Ministry of Rds. and Transp.*, 8 Iran-U.S. Cl. Trib. Rep. 119, 133 (1985) (applying a "generally accepted principle in various legal systems that an essential error regarding the conditions upon which a party has entered into a contract may relieve that party from liability, at least where the other party knew or should have known about the error"); *Questech, Inc. v. Ministry of Nat'l Defense of the Islamic Republic of Iran*, 9 Iran-U.S Cl. Trib. Rep. 107 (1985) (applying the general principle of changed circumstances despite a contract clause choosing Iranian law).

241 *See, e.g., Dames & Moore v. Islamic Republic of Iran*, 4 Iran-U.S. Cl. Trib. Rep. 212, 229, 232 (1983) (dissenting opinion of Judge Richard M. Mosk to dismissal of claims on jurisdictional grounds) (referring

For instance, in *CMI International Inc. v. Ministry of Roads and Transportation* (MORT), an Oklahoma corporation alleged a breach and repudiation of two purchase order contracts for heavy equipment, both of which expressly stated that they would be governed by Idaho law.[242] The tribunal held that MORT was liable for damages because it breached the contracts by failing to establish letters of credit to pay for the machines, as required by the purchase orders. In the meantime, CMI had secured a "substantial[]" profit on the resale of some of the machines, but it argued that, under the quantum law of Idaho, it was not required to account for any profits on resale. The tribunal rejected this (idiosyncratic) facet of Idaho law, holding that it was not "rigidly tied to the law of the contract, at least insofar as the assessment of damages is concerned."[243] The tribunal instead held that "under general principles of law, compensation normally requires accounting for profits made on resales, and the Tribunal believes they should be taken into account here by being deducted from the damages for which compensation is awarded."[244]

The same corrective function of the general principles is found in the more recent ICSID case of *Inceysa Vallisoletana v. El Salvador*.[245] The claimant there, a Spanish company, signed a contract to install equipment and provide industrial services to the Republic of El Salvador. It alleged before an ICSID tribunal that the Republic breached that contract and expropriated the claimant's rights thereunder. For its part, El Salvador contended that the claimant had procured the contract through fraud, and therefore could not claim the protections of the Spain-El Salvador BIT,

---

to national laws and the International Encyclopedia of comparative law). Early in the Tribunal's existence, one scholar expressed the hope that it might "augur well for the possible elaboration . . . of normative commercial law principles having a transnational legal dimension." Thomas Carbonneau, *The Elaboration of Substantive Legal Norms and Arbitral Adjudication: The Case of the Iran-United States Claims Tribunal*, *in* THE IRAN-UNITED STATES CLAIMS TRIBUNAL 1981–83, at 104, 105 (Richard Lillich ed., 1984). He challenged the Tribunal to employ comparative law methodology and produce a "corpus of commercial law principles from the statutory and decisional law of various national legal systems, allowing it to resolve disputes according to a principled substantive consensus among legal systems." *Id.* Although the general principles of law have indeed served an important role in many decisions of the Tribunal, the explication of general principles by the parties appearing before that Tribunal has been mixed, with some being exemplary and others bordering on ipse dixit. As Judge Mosk has noted, "determining the law of any jurisdiction, especially without the assistance of the parties, can be difficult." *Harnischfeger Corp. v. Ministry of Rds. and Transp.*, 8 Iran-U.S. Cl. Trib. Rep. 119, 140–41 (1985) (dissenting opinion from final award).

242 *CMI Int'l, Inc. v. Ministry of Rds. and Transp. (MORT) and the Islamic Republic of Iran*, 4 Iran-U.S. Cl. Trib. Rep. 263 (1983).

243 *Id.* at 267–68.

244 *Id.* at 270.

245 *Inceysa Vallisoletana S.L. v. Republic of El Salvador*, ICSID Case No. ARB/03/26, Award (Aug. 2, 2006).

which only protected investments made "in accordance with the laws of the host state."[246] The claimant, however, was armed with two separate decisions of the Supreme Court of El Salvador sustaining the legality of the bidding process for the contract, and pled them as res judicata over the matter.[247]

The ICSID tribunal agreed that the legality of the contract turned upon the "laws and governing legal principles in El Salvador applicable to ... investment."[248] Chief among those laws was the BIT itself, which was incorporated into domestic law by the El Salvador Constitution and provided for the application of "international law" to disputes regarding foreign investments.[249] Because "the general principles of law are an autonomous and direct source of international law," the tribunal held that they may be applied as "general rules on which there is international consensus" and "rules of law on which the legal systems of [all] States are based."[250] With these principles in mind, the tribunal reviewed the legality of the investment contract de novo, without regard for the decisions of the El Salvador Supreme Court. Just as the tribunal in *Amco*, it viewed this as a necessary consequence of its competence; holding otherwise would in every case allow the State, through its courts, "to redefine the scope and content of its own consent to the jurisdiction of the [Tribunal] unilaterally and at its own discretion."[251]

In reviewing the procurement of the contract, the tribunal concluded that the claimant violated at least three general principles of law. *First*, it violated the "supreme principle ... of good faith"—which, in the context of contractual relations, requires the "absence of deceit and artifice in the negotiation and execution of [legal] instruments."[252] *Second*, it violated the principle of *nemo auditur propriam turpitudinem allegans*, which prevents a party from "seek[ing] to benefit from an investment effectuated by means of [an] illegal ac[t]."[253] *Third*, "the acts committed by [the claimant] during the bidding process [we]re in violation of the legal principle that prohibits unlawful enrichment."[254] Accordingly, "the

246 *Id.* ¶¶ 45, 47–48.

247 *Id.* ¶ 67.

248 *Id.* ¶ 218.

249 *Id.* ¶¶ 219–20.

250 *Id.* ¶¶ 226–27.

251 *Id.* ¶ 213. In addition, the Tribunal also held that the "basic requisites of *res judicata* are not met, namely the (i) identity of parties and (ii) identity of claims." *Id.* ¶ 214.

252 *Id.* ¶¶ 230–31.

253 *Id.* ¶¶ 240, 242.

254 *Id.* ¶ 253.

systematic interpretation of the [El Salvadorian] Constitution . . . [and] the general principles of law" barred the cause of action.[255] The tribunal in *Inceysa* thus invoked the general principles to ensure a holistic application of local law, which resulted in the correction of an apparent injustice in the local courts.[256] It is notable that this process, and the inclusion of general principles within it, ultimately inured to the benefit of the State.

There are also general principles unique to discrete areas of international law, such as the precautionary principle in environmental law and *in dubio pro reo* in criminal law.[257] Inter-state disputes also have their own general principles, such as a sovereign's obligation to warn of the existence of a minefield in its territorial waters.[258] These are specialized fields unto themselves, and the use of general principles within them tends to be sui generis and evolving. Chapter 2 focuses upon those general principles that are endemic to any legal order and thus transcend and crosscut all fields of international law.

b) National Courts

International courts and arbitral tribunals have led the way in applying the general principles of law to transnational cases, but, as those principles have their roots in positive domestic law, national courts have embraced their usage

255 *Id.* ¶ 263 (emphasis added). *See generally* Rahim Moloo & Alex Khachaturian, *The Compliance with the Law Requirement in International Investment Arbitration*, 34 FORDHAM INT'L L.J. 1473, 1479–81 (2011).

256 The "in accordance with the law" clause in the Spain-El Salvador BIT did not dictate this decision; the violation of general principles of law can bar the admissibility of a claim *sua sponte*. In *Plama Consortium Ltd. v. Republic of Bulgaria*, ICSID Case No. ARB/03/24, Award, ¶¶ 141–43 (Aug. 27, 2008), the tribunal held that the claimant's fraudulent procurement of government approval of its investment violated the general principle of *nemo auditur propriam turpitudinem allegans*, which violated international law and rendered its claim inadmissible, even though the Energy Charter Treaty (ECT) contains no such requirement of legality. This application of the principle was instead couched in terms of the objective of the ECT to "strengthen[] the rule of law on energy issues"—not to undercut it. *Id.* ¶ 138; *Gustav F.W. Hamester GmbH & Co. K.G. v. Republic of Ghana*, ICSID Case No. 07/24, Award, ¶ 123 (June 18, 2010) ("an investment will not be protected if it has been created in violation of national or international principles of good faith," and "these are general principles that exist independently of specific language to this effect in the Treaty").

257 Biddulph & Newman, *supra* note 52, at 288 (discussing and contrasting the use of general principles in international disputes involving the environment, investment, crime, and indigenous rights, and finding "contextually-differentiated approaches within specialized areas of international law that respond to the unique nature of each area").

258 *Corfu Channel Case (U.K. v. Alb.)*, Merits, Judgment, 1949 I.C.J. 4, 22 (Apr. 9) (discussing "general and well-recognized" principles relating to a State's maritime obligations).

as well. In the immediate aftermath of World War II, the continental tradition of mechanically applying written laws was partially blamed for some of the grave injustices perpetuated by the courts of Germany and occupied nations, and general principles (or *principes generaux*) obtained special favor in France as a reaction against judicial enforcement of totalitarian enactments during the Vichy period.[259] General principles offered an alternative source to effectuate justice where the written law failed to do so.[260] This is of a piece with long-standing civil law tradition: to fill lacunae, many civil codes refer judges to general principles of law.[261] Although tradition and training have made some civil law judges reticent to apply anything but the norms imposed by the local legislature—to avoid what the French might condemn as a *gouvernement de juges*[262]—many modern scholars have eschewed such a cramped view of the proper role of civil law judges.[263] Article 230 of the Colombian Constitution, for instance, identifies "*foreign* general principles of law" as among those "auxiliary sources" upon which a judge may rely to impart justice.[264] Like other civil law countries, Colombia recognizes the need for judges to apply, in interpreting the Code, general principles of procedural law "so as to comply with the constitutional guarantee of due process, to respect the right to a defense and maintain equality between the parties."[265] In this vein, the Chilean and Argentine Supreme Courts have referenced general principles of international law in the context of determining the validity of statutes of limitations in cases of violation of human rights.[266]

---

259 Vivian Grosswald Curran, *Fear of Formalism: Indications from the Fascist Period in France and Germany of Judicial Methodology's Impact on Substantive Law*, 35 Cornell Int'l L.J. 101, 103, 142–48 (2001–2002) (citing, inter alia, Jacques Ghestin & Gilles Goubeaux, Traite De Droit Civil: Introduction Generale (1977)).

260 *Id.* at 142, 147.

261 *See, e.g.*, Spanish Civil Code art. 1; Quebec Civil Code, Preliminary Provision; Ecuadorean Civil Code art. 18(7); Venezuelan Civil Code art. 4; Argentinean Civil and Commercial Code art. 16.

262 *See* Curran, *supra* note 259, at 148.

263 *See id.* at 144 (citing, inter alia, Jean Boulanger, *Principes genereaux du droit et droit positif*, *in* 1 Le Droit Francais au Mileau du xx e siècle: Etudes offertes a Georges Ripert (1951)).

264 Colombian Constitution art. 230 (1991) (emphasis added).

265 *See* Colombian Code of Civil Procedure art. 4; Judgment No. C-029/95, issued by the Constitutional Court of Colombia (Feb. 2, 1995) (holding that Article 4 of the Code of Civil Procedure was constitutional and in line with the 1991 Constitution).

266 *See*, inter alia, *Caso Chena*, Appeal, Rol No. 3125-2004, ¶ 37 (Mar. 13, 2007); *Caso Molco*, Appeal, Rol No. 559-2004, 5 *et seq.* (Dec. 13, 2006); *Simón, Julio Héctor y otros*, Fallos: 328:2056 (June 14, 2005); *Priebke, Erich*, Fallos 318:2148 (Nov. 2, 1995).

The general principles of law have achieved even greater acceptance in the common law systems, where inductive judicial reasoning is more commonplace. An early case from the U.S. Supreme Court, for instance, surveyed civil and common law codes to arrive at a universal definition of "piracy" under the law of nations.[267] The same exercise pervades U.S. judicial interpretation of the Alien Tort Statute (ATS), which expressly designates the "law of nations" as the governing standard.[268] General principles play a key role in issues of liability under the ATS because the law of nations on questions of civil obligations can rarely be stated with much accuracy. There is, as the U.S. Supreme Court has noted, no "public code recognized by the common consent of nations"[269]—courts thus look to the general principles, steeped in various municipal codes, to fashion one. This is the "reserve store of principles upon which [international law] has been in the habit of drawing."[270]

In *Kuwait Airways Corp. v. Iraqi Airways*, for instance, Kuwait Airways brought an action for conversion in the United Kingdom against Iraq Airways, alleging that during the 1990 Iraqi invasion of Kuwait, 10 commercial airplanes belonging to Kuwait Airways were seized by Iraq. In transnational cases such as this, English courts typically apply the "double actionability rule," which requires that the act be tortious in England *and* civilly actionable in the relevant foreign country (here Iraq) before an action will lie.[271] Under a special provision of Iraqi law, the seized aircraft were legally transferred to Iraqi Airways after the war, and the defendant invoked that law as a defense. Kuwait Airways conceded the existence and applicability of this law, but argued that the English court should "altogether disregard" it.

267 *United States v. Smith*, 18 U.S. (5 Wheat.) 153, 163 (1820).

268 *See, e.g., Sosa v. Alvarez-Machain*, 542 U.S. 692, 732 (2004) ("federal courts should not recognize private claims under federal common law for violations of any international law norm with less definite content and acceptance among civilized nations than the historical paradigms familiar when [the ATS] was enacted"); *Doe VIII v. Exxon Mobil Corp.*, 654 F.3d 11, 54 (D.C. Cir. 2011) (Kavanaugh, J., dissenting) (arguing for the application of a "principle which is found to be generally accepted by civilized legal systems"); *Sarei v. Rio Tinto*, PLC, 550 F.3d 822, 827–31 (9th Cir. 2008) (en banc) (looking to general principles to decide exhaustion of domestic remedies requirements); *Jean v. Dorelien*, 431 F.3d 776, 782 (11th Cir. 2005) (same, in the context of the Torture Victim Protection Act); *see generally* David W. Rivkin, *A Survey of Transnational Legal Principles in U.S. Courts*, 5 WORLD ARB. & MEDIATION REV. 231, 234–37 (2011); Luke A. Sobota & David Wallach, *Alien Tort Statute, in* INTERNATIONAL LITIGATION TREATISE (ABA) (forthcoming).

269 *United States v. Smith*, 18 U.S. (5 Wheat.) 153, 159 (1820) (Story, J.).

270 *Doe VIII v. Exxon Mobil Corp.*, 654 F.3d 11, 54 (D.C. Cir. 2011) (Kavanaugh, J., dissenting).

271 *Kuwait Airways Corp. v. Iraqi Airways*, [2002] UKHL 19, ¶ 12.

The English court acknowledged that the "normal position" on choice of law was to apply "the laws of another country even though those laws are different from the law of the forum court," but declared that "blind adherence to foreign law can never be required of an English court."[272] In exceptional cases, the court continued, "a provision of foreign law will be disregarded when it would lead to a result wholly alien to fundamental requirements of justice. . . . [That is,] when it would violate some fundamental principle of justice, some prevalent conception of good morals, some deep-rooted tradition of the common weal."[273] In that situation, "the court will decline to enforce or recognise the [offensive] foreign decree to whatever extent is required in the circumstances"[274]—even though it will continue to apply that foreign law as a whole.

The court found that the ad hoc Iraqi decree transferring legal title of foreign seized property violated international law: "Having forcibly invaded Kuwait, seized its assets, and taken [Kuwait Airways'] aircraft from Kuwait to its own territory, Iraq adopted this decree as part of its attempt to extinguish every vestige of Kuwait's existence as a separate state."[275] The decree could therefore not be invoked by Iraqi Airways to obtain the protection of the "double actionability rule." According to the English court, "[a]n expropriatory decree made in these circumstances and for this purpose is simply not acceptable today . . . [and constitutes] a gross violation of established rules of international law of fundamental importance."[276] Implicit in the decision is the principle of *nullus commodum capere potest de sua iniuria propria*. The decree that would have otherwise governed the case was excised from Iraqi law and entirely ignored; this allowed Kuwait Airlines to sustain its claims because the torts of conversion and usurpation were recognized in both England and Iraq.

Another illustration arises out of the decision in 1960 of the new Cuban Government to expropriate and nationalize all of Citibank's assets within the country. A letter of credit issued by Citibank arising from a sugar transaction with a Canadian company was acquired by Banco Para el Comercio Exterior de Cuba (Bancec), which had been established by the Government around the same time to serve as an official and autonomous credit institution for foreign trade.

272 *Id.* ¶¶ 15–16.
273 *Id.* ¶¶ 16–17.
274 *Id.*
275 *Id.* ¶ 28.
276 *Id.* ¶ 29.

When Bancec brought suit on the letter of credit in the United States, Citibank counterclaimed, asserting a right to set-off the value of its seized Cuban assets. This counterclaim was premised upon Bancec being deemed the *alter ego* of the Cuban Government, and thus responsible for the expropriation. The natural choice of law, however, was that of Cuba, which effectively immunized Bancec by establishing de jure separation between the company and the State. Bancec's primary argument was thus that the law of the place of its incorporation—Cuba—should govern the substantive questions relating to its structure and internal affairs.[277]

The case wound its way through the federal courts: the district court sided with Citibank on finding Bancec sufficiently aligned with the Government of Cuba, but the Second Circuit Court of Appeals—strictly applying Cuban law—reversed. The case ultimately came before the U.S. Supreme Court, which ruled for Citibank. The Court acknowledged that, "[a]s a general matter," the law of the State of incorporation typically governs to achieve "certainty and predictability" for "parties with interests in the corporation."[278] It nonetheless disclaimed blind adherence to Cuban law, or even U.S. law, and instead applied "principles of equity common to international law and federal common law."[279] Referring to various authorities on European civil law[280] and international decisions collecting "the wealth of practice already accumulated on the subject in municipal law[s]" around the world,[281] the Court held that Bancec's independent corporate status could be disregarded in this instance. The Court explained that "[t]o give conclusive effect to the law of the chartering state in determining whether the separate juridical status of its instrumentality should be respected would permit th[at] state to violate with impunity the rights of third parties under international law while effectively insulating itself from liability in foreign courts."[282] In lieu of Cuban law, the Court applied "principles . . . common to both international law and federal common law," as explicated by "governments throughout the world,"[283] and held Bancec answerable in U.S. court for the expropriatory acts of the Cuban Government. Although cast in terms of "equity," this decision can be seen as an offshoot of the

277 *First Nat'l City Bank (FNCB) v. Banco Para el Comercio Exterior de Cuba (Bancec)*, 462 U.S. 611, 613 (1983).

278 *Id.* at 621.

279 *Id.* at 613.

280 *Id.* at 628 n.20.

281 *Id.*

282 *Id.* at 622.

283 *Id.* at 623–24.

principle of *nemo iudex in causa sua*,[284] with resort to general principles "to avoid the injustice that would result from permitting a foreign state to reap the benefits of our courts while avoiding the obligations of international law."[285]

B. The Origin and Evolution of International Due Process

> *However imperfect due process, it has a protective faculty which cannot be removed.... It is the natural enemy and the unyielding foe of tyranny, whether popular or otherwise. As long as due process subsists, courts will put in despotism's path a resistance, more or less generous, but which always serves to contain it.... There is in due process something lofty and unambiguous which forces judges to act respectably and follow a just and orderly course.*
>
> —Benjamin Constant[286]

With the ascension of republicanism and other responsive forms of government, certain general principles of procedural law have come to constrain States in their exercise of sovereign power. These principles direct the process that is due to all individuals before the law. This guarantee ensures that official adjudicative proceedings adhere to certain procedural rules and places restraints on the arbitrary exercise of governmental power. At its core, the notion of "due process" is an effort to "reduce the power of the State to a comprehensible, rational, and principled order, and to ensure that citizens are not deprived of life, liberty, or property except for good reason."[287] Although this inquiry may raise normative questions of reasonableness and proportionality, the very notion that there exists a conceptual limit on government power "invites—indeed, requires—courts ... to take seriously the idea that there are real answers to such normative questions."[288] The fact that adjectival principles tend to be broad, with fluid and contextual application, does not diminish their importance or necessity. "[L]aw and arbitrary command ... genuinely differ," and the norm of due process "depends

284 *See* Cheng, *supra* note 4, at 279.

285 *First Nat'l City Bank (FNCB) v. Banco Para el Comercio Exterior de Cuba (Bancec)*, 462 U.S. 611, 633–34 (1983).

286 Principles of Politics Applicable to All Governments 155 (E. Hofman ed., 2003) (1815).

287 Timothy Sandefur, *In Defense of Substantive Due Process, or the Promise of Lawful Rule*, 35 Harv. J.L. & Pub. Pol'y 283, 285 (2012).

288 *Id.*

on recognizing that difference."[289] When due process is reduced to its underlying precepts, which define a threshold of process that must obtain in every modern legal system, the result is a loose code of "international due process." These are the baseline standards of fairness in the administration of justice that everyone is due before a court of law, and from which no State can deviate.

1. A Process Grounded in General Principles

Due process has been the halting work of millennia. The *Lex Duodecim Tabularum* (or Twelve Tables) codified Roman law in 450 B.C. as part of the transition to the Republic. Tables I and II articulated adjectival requirements such as the right of parties "to state their cases . . . by making a brief statement in the presence of the judge, between the rising of the sun and noon; and, both of them being present, let them speak so that each party may hear";[290] the obligation of the judge to "render his decision in the presence of the plaintiff and the defendant" before "[t]he setting of the sun";[291] and the ability of "anyone [who] is deprived of the evidence of a witness . . . [to] call him with a loud voice in front of his house, on three market-days."[292] Sources from the imperial period make clear that legal procedure was the subject of exensive regulation by Roman provincial officials;[293] according to Livy, the Twelve Tables arose in part as a response to plebeian demands for written rules to avoid capricious and biased adjudication by patricians.[294]

Although the Twelve Tables were limited in scope, *praetors*[295] and other magistrates would interpret and apply them to fill lacunae, and those decisions would

289 *Id.*

290 Twelve Tables, Table I, Law VIII, *available in English at* http://www.constitution.org/sps/sps01_1.htm (last visited Sept. 6, 2016).

291 *Id.* Table I, Laws IX–X.

292 *Id.* Table II, Law III.

293 *See, e.g.*, DIG. 48.3.6.1 (Marcian, De iudiciis publicis 2).

294 *See* TITUS LIVIUS, THE HISTORY OF ROME, vol. I, 292–93, *available at* http://oll.libertyfund.org/titles/livy-the-history-of-rome-vol-1?q=twelve+tables#Livy_1023-01_226 (last visited Sept. 6, 2016). *See also* Raymond Westbrook, *The Nature and Origins of the Twelve Tables*, *in* ZEITSCHRIFT DER SAVIGNY-STIFTUNG FÜR RECHTSGESCHICHTE. ROMANISTISCHE ABTEILUNG, vol. 105, Issue 1, at 74–121 (Aug. 1988). A similar tension had been addressed in Athens during the sixth century B.C.: following demands of equal treatment by serfs, Solon the Poet proposed a set of laws to rule Athens, including notions such as appellate review. *See* PLUTARCH, THE PARALLEL LIVES, published in vol. I of the Loeb Classical Library Edition, 1914, at 453, *available at* http://penelope.uchicago.edu/Thayer/E/Roman/Texts/Plutarch/Lives/Solon*.html.

295 The *praetor* was "a specialized magistracy . . . established in 367 b.c. to relieve the consuls of the administration of justice. It remained at first reserved for the *patricians*, but thirty years later the plebians

then be followed in subsequent decisions, allowing the creation of an evolving body of law reflected in various edicts.[296] Major efforts to codify existing law were made under Hadrian in the *Perpetual Edict* in the second century A.D.[297] and under Justinian in the *Corpus iuris civilis* of the sixth century A.D.[298] The latter purported to be exhaustive and, although issued after the fall of the Western Roman Empire, became the cornerstone of the civil law tradition.

As Christianity spread during the last centuries of the Roman Empire, different versions and iterations of what were originally purported to be the canons on morality, liturgy, and religious life accepted by the Apostles became the basis for the law of the Roman Catholic Church, regulating both the clergy and "Christ's faithful" on a wide range of procedural and substantive issues.[299] A decisive stage in the development of fundamental principles of procedure was reached after the revival of Roman law in the eleventh century and the nearly simultaneous rise of

---

gained access to it. In the beginning there was only one *praetor*, but by 242 b.c. a second one was added. Henceforth, the first *praetor* was charged with the administration of justice between Roman citizens, while the second one took care of the affairs between citizens and aliens and among aliens." Hans Julius Wolff, Roman Law: An Historical Introduction 33 (1951).

296 *Aediles* and other "praetors had the right to issue public notices (edicta) to the People. . . . As the praetor's flexibility in applying private law increased, at some point he started to promulgate in a written edict issued at the beginning of his term the general principles according to which he would act in this sphere: the *edictum perpetuum*, valid for the entire year of his magistracy. . . . In its developed form, the praetor's edict specified (most importantly) the conditions under which he would grant formulae, the various *exceptiones* he would admit into those formulae, and also the remedies he would introduce where the civil law gave no action." T. Corey Brennan, The Praetorship in the Roman Republic, Origins to 122 B.C., vol. I, 132–33 (2001).

297 Under Hadrian,

> the praetorship of Salvius Julian, an eminent lawyer, was inmortalized by the composition of the perpetual edict. This well-digested code contained everything of value in the previous praetorian edicts; and although it was only perpetual in the same sense as the former edicts, namely, that the magistrate could not change them during his year of office, yet, after the labours of so many men distinguished in jurisprudence, the framing of the Perpetual Edict of Julian attained such perfection that no alteration was made in it, and it became the invariable standard of civil jurisprudence.

Edward Gibbon, The History of the Decline and Fall of the Roman Empire 343 (Harper & Brothers 1857).

298 Under Justinian's reign, "the civil jurisprudence was digested in the immortal works of the Code, the Pandects and Institutes [the parts in which the *Corpus* was organized]: the public reason of the Romans has been silently or studiously transfused into the domestic institutions of Europe, and the laws of Justinian still command the respect or obedience of independent nations." *Id.* at 340–41.

299 After the New Testament, "the *Didache* or Teaching of the Twelve Apostles, an anonymous collection of moral, liturgical, and disciplinary instructions, is one of the first and most precious post-apostolic writings. It was written about the year 100. . . . They were not issued by any formal authority. They were simply compiled customs." James A. Coriden, An Introduction to Canon Law 11 (2004).

the study of canon law within the Roman Catholic Church.[300] As Christianity spread during the last centuries of the Roman Empire, different versions and iterations of what were originally purported to be the canons on morality, liturgy, and religious life accepted by the Apostles became the basis for the law of the Roman Catholic Church, regulating both the clergy and "Christ's faithful" on a wide range of procedural and substantive issues. At this time, both canon law and Roman law coexisted, cross-pollinated,[301] and evolved to become the *ius commune* of the old continent.[302] Evidence of this scholarly interest in due process is seen in the appearance of the legal genre of the *ordo iudiciarius*, a manual specifying the procedure to be followed in different types of proceeding,[303] and the procedural treatise of William Durant the Elder known as the *Speculum iudiciale*, which was first composed towards the end of the thirteenth century[304] and remained in print well into the sixteenth century.[305] Many of the basic elements of contemporary due process have their historical roots in this literature of the Middle Ages. The

---

300 From the sixth to the eleventh century, small political units (*villae*) were grouped together in *centearii*, which in turn fell under the umbrella of *comitatus* (counties), where a

> count acting on behalf of the king summoned to his court all the freemen of the district to transact public affairs, including adjudication of disputes. From among the freemen jurors were chosen. Civil and criminal cases were heard by jurors who pronounced the law and made findings of fact, while the count presided over the proceedings and carried out the sentence.... During the 9th and 10th centuries feudal custom was extremely diversified.... By the 11th century such arbitrariness gave way to objective and universal norms of conduct.

ELLEN GOODMAN, THE ORIGINS OF THE WESTERN LEGAL TRADITION: FROM THALES TO THE TUDORS 174 (1995).

301 Gratian, author of the twelfth century codification of canon law known as *Decretum Gratiani*, which survived, with additions, as the *Codex Iuris Canonici* of the Roman Catholic Church from 1140 through to 1918,

> built upon the work of Romanists, in particular the Corpus Iuris Civilis of Justinian; he built upon the work of earlier canonists and upon the work of students of law at Bologna.... Gratian's *Decretum* received almost immediate recognition as an authoritative statement of the canon law. It was cited by popes, churches, councils and ecclesiastical courts; it provided a foundation for judicial decisions and legislation, and soon legal scholars provided glosses, commentaries, treatises and summaries.

GOODMAN, *supra* note 300, at 211.

302 Roman law and canon law "were taught side-by-side at the nascent universities. Students at Oxford, for example, learned a curriculum comprising of Roman and canon law with the term *utrumque ius* referring to those who studied both laws.... The melding of these two legal traditions comprised the medieval *ius commune*. It was a system of general principles drawn either from Roman or canon law, depending upon the issue in question." Melodie Eichbauer, *Medieval Inquisitorial Procedure: Procedural Rights and the Question of Due Process in the 13th Century*, HISTORY COMPASS 12/1, 73 (2014).

303 *See generally* LINDA FOWLER-MAGERL, *ORDINES IUDICIARII* AND *LIBELLI DE ORDINE IUDICIORUM* (1994).

304 *See* JAMES A. BRUNDAGE, MEDIEVAL CANON LAW app'x 2 (1995).

305 *E.g.*, WILLIAM DURANT THE ELDER, SPECULUM IURIS GULIELMI DURANDI, EPISCOPI MIMATENSIS, I.V.D. CVM IOAN. ANDREAE, BALDI DE VBALDIS, ALIORUMQ[UE] ALIQUOT PRAESTANTISSIMORUM IURISCONSULTORUM THEOREMATIBUS, 4 pts. in 3 vols. (Venice, Ex officina Gasparis Bindoni, 1576).

principle of *ne ultra petita*, for example, was first elaborated by medieval jurists seeking to interpret particular passages drawn from the *Code* of Justinian and from canon law.[306] Procedural rules that impose restrictions on the exercise of executive power can also be found in medieval canon law, such as the rule *quod omnes tangit ab omnibus approbari debet*.[307] Both before and after the sixteenth-century English Reformation, this amalgam of Roman and canon law was taught in English universities and played an important role in international areas of law (e.g., admiralty), thereby bridging to some extent the two main Western legal traditions.[308]

Another influence on the civil law conception of due process was the issuance, circa 1265, of *Livro de las Legies* by King Alfonso X of Castilla, Leon, and Galicia. Known today as the *Partidas*, it was a compilation of procedural, substantive, and organizational rules prepared by a commission of prominent jurists.[309] Not unlike the Magna Carta sealed at Runnymede 50 years earlier, the *Partidas* contained traces of what have become staples of civil law due process, although it did not place any mandatory restrictions on the king himself but rather identified

---

306 *See* Knut Wolfgang Nörr, Zur Stellung des Richters im gelehrten Prozess der Frühzeit (1967) (discussing the rule *iudex secundum allegata non secundum conscientiam iudicat*).

307 *See* Gaines Post, Studies in Medieval Legal Thought 91–238 (1964) (discussing *plena potestas* and *quod omnes tangit ab omnibus approbari debet*).

308 As Richard Helmholz describes it,

> The influence of *ius commune* in England was not limited to university faculties or tribunals of specialized jurisdiction. It was known and employed by common lawyers and government officials in a variety of ways and situation.... Even in later eras, which were dominated by greater levels of legal nationalism, some interchange occurred. The *ius commune* was long used when it was needed to confront questions of constitutional moment and diplomatic import.... The *ius commune* was also of moment in the conduct of foreign affairs.... At the same time, the *ius commune* never occupied the central place in the development of English legal institutions that it did on the Continent. English lawyers destined for practice in the common law courts did not share university training in Roman and canon laws with the English civilians, as did their counterparts in Italy, France, Germany, and Spain. The common lawyers learned the law at the Inns of Court in London and in the royal courts themselves—in any event, separately from the civilians who were to make their careers in the courts of the church or the Admiralty.

R.H. Helmholz, The *ius commune* in England: Four Studies (2001).

309 It has been suggested that the

> authors of this notable work borrowed extensively from Roman sources, although ... they carefully avoid confessing that fact.... The Corpus Juris Civilis, as the latest embodiment of the Roman Law, would naturally be most resorted to though it is not to be supposed that preceding jurists were ignored. The Canon Law, which had already attained so considerable a development in Italy, was another important source.

Charles Sumner Lobingier, *Las Siete Partidas and Its Predecessors*, 1 Calif. L. Rev. 487, 494 (1912–1913).

certain types of desirable behavior.[310] According to the *Partidas*, positive law was needed to "unite men by love, i.e., by law and reason, because that is how justice is made."[311] The king was thus to appoint judges bound to apply the written laws,[312] whose "language . . . must be clear so every man understands them and remembers them."[313] The third *Partida* provided for appellate review,[314] set forth certain evidentiary rules,[315] and required that sentences be "read [] publicly" and "so worded that [they] may be understood without any doubt."[316] The *Partidas* had great significance in Latin America after 1492, and was especially influential in the post-emancipation codification movement (1822–1916).[317] It also served as the legal foundation for the formation of the governing juntas in both Spain and Spanish America after the imprisonment of King Fernando VII during the Peninsular War with Napoleon.[318]

Notwithstanding the import of these and other legal developments in medieval Europe,[319] it was not until the French Revolution and the adoption of the 1791 Constitution that the king was unquestionably subject to the rule of law in the

---

310 Alfonso X believed the king to be God's representative on earth, put there for the fulfillment of justice: "'It is fitting that a man should be ruler so as to destroy discord among men, to make *FUEROS* and laws, to break down the proud and evil-doers and to protect the Faith.'" Madaline W. Nichols, *Las Siete Partidas*, 20 CALIF. L. REV. 260, 266 (1932) (quoting *Partida* II).

311 *Partida* I, Law 7.

312 *Partida* I, Law 12.

313 *Partida* I, Law 8. *See also* Partida I, Law 13.

314 *Partida* III, Title 4, Law 1.

315 *Partida* III, Title 17.

316 *Partida* III.

317 *See* Nichols, *supra* note 310. Modern codification under Roman civil law influence was widespread both in Europe and the Americas, including in Canada and the U.S. state of Louisiana. From the Bavarian Codex of 1756 to the Napoleonic Code of 1804 to the German Civil Code (or BGB) of 1900, European codification efforts extended to every corner of the Continent and to the colonies under European domain, including Latin America, where existing regal legislation was also incorporated. By the end of the nineteenth century most every country in Latin America had a Civil Code, with Andrés Bello's Code in Chile having special influence in Ecuador (1858), El Salvador (1859), Venezuela (1862), Nicaragua (1867), Honduras (1880), Colombia (1887), and Panama (1903). *See generally* JOHN H. MERRYMAN & ROGELIO PÉREZ-PERDOMO, THE CIVIL LAW TRADITION (2007).

318 When King Ferdinand VII was imprisoned by Napoleon, local political bodies argued, based on the *Partidas*, that "absent the King, sovereignty reverted to the people" of the colonies. *See* HISTORIA DE AMÉRICA ANDINA: CRISIS DEL RÉGIMEN COLONIAL E INDEPENDENCIA 162 (G. Carrera Damas ed., 2003).

319 The thirteenth century has been regarded as "one of the great culminations of Western civilization":

> Extraordinary as it was in other fields, it was particularly important in law. It saw a great outburst of juristic activity, doctrinal, administrative and legislative. In Italy, it was the period of the Glossators. In France, it was the period of St. Louis and the *Ordonnances*, of the apocryphal

civil law tradition.[320] The 1789 Declaration of the Rights of Man and Citizen had proclaimed that "any society in which the guarantee of rights is not assured, nor the separation of powers determined, has no Constitution."[321] The distrust of existing aristocratic courts, however, initially made the French chary to redress administrative excess through the process of judicial review. The power of a court to pass on the constitutionality of a government act was seen as an encroachment on the people's sovereignty and a violation of the equality principle enshrined in the Declaration.[322] The Declaration nonetheless contained provisions of due process that have survived the successive adoption of constitutions by the different Republics, such as Article XVII's mandate that "[p]roperty being an inviolable and sacred right, no one can be deprived of private usage, if it is not when the public necessity, legally noted, evidently requires it, and under the condition of a just and prior indemnity."

Although certainly influenced by these and other legal events in Europe, including the first Spanish-language constitution, the 1812 Cadiz Constitution,[323] the new nations of Latin America also looked to the constitutional experience of the United States.[324] In particular, many States in South America did not share

> *Establissements* and of the redaction of the Coutumes by Beaumanoir and others. In England it saw the birth of the Royal Courts, the development of the Council and the legislation of Edward I. But if national opinion may be any guide, it nowhere produced a more splendid result than the medieval Code of Spain usually called *Las Siete Partidas*, The Seven Parts, and attributed to Alfonso X of Castile and Leon, known as the "Wise," *El Sabio*. It took ten years to prepare, the years 1256–1265, and was received from the first with enthusiastic admiration.

Nichols, *supra* note 310.

320 As the 1791 Document framed it *"Le Roi ne règne que par [la loi]"* (the king does not reign but for the law). See *Constitution Française du Septembre 1791*, Chapter II, *De la royauté de la régence et des ministres*.

321 *Déclaration des Droits de l'Homme et du Citoyen de 1789*, Article XVI.

322 Article VI provides that

> [t]he law is the expression of the general will. All the citizens have the right of contributing personally or through their representatives to its formation. *It must be the same for all, either that it protects, or that it punishes.* All the citizens, being equal in its eyes, are equally admissible to all public dignities, places and employments, according to their capacity and without distinction other than that of their virtues and of their talents.

(emphasis added.)

323 *See generally* Alberto Ricardo Dalla Via, "La constitución de Cádiz de 1812: su influencia en el movimiento emancipador y en el proceso constituyente," Revista de Derecho Político UNED, No. 84, 2012; José Gamas Torruco, México y la Constitución de Cádiz, UNAM, México, 2012; Felipe Westermeyes Hernández, *Chile y la Constitución de Cádiz: Un Primer Acercamiento a una Relación Preterida*, *in* Cuando las Cortes de Cádiz. Panorama Jurídico de 1812 (Luis Martí Mingarro ed., 2012).

324 *See* Rodolfo Piza Rocafort, "Influencia de la Constitución de los Estados Unidos en las Constituciones de Europa y de América Latina," Cuadernos de CAPEL, Nov. 23, 1987.

France's concern with judicial review and adopted a model of separation of powers closer to that of the U.S. Constitution.[325] Due process standards were explicitly set down in the new constitutions,[326] and courts were charged with securing compliance with them. One Latin American innovation was the *amparo*, or constitutional injunction, which provides an expedited and specialized channel to redress alleged violations of basic rights and liberties.[327]

The inchoate notions of due process set forth in the Twelve Tables have had perhaps their most robust expression in modern human rights conventions. The Inter-American Convention on Human Rights (IACHR)[328]—building upon the principles set forth "in the Charter of the Organization of American States, in the American Declaration of the Rights and Duties of Man, and in the Universal Declaration of Human Rights"[329]—imposes upon States the obligation to "respect the rights and freedoms" it enshrines "without any discrimination."[330] Included is the "right to a hearing, with due guarantees and within a reasonable time, by a competent, independent, and impartial tribunal, previously established by law."[331] The European Convention for the Protection of Human Rights and Fundamental Freedoms[332] follows a similar pattern, providing, inter alia, that "everyone is entitled to a fair and public hearing within a reasonable time by an independent and impartial tribunal established by law."[333]

---

325 Jorge Ulises Carmona Tinoco, "La División de Poderes y la Función Jurisdiccional," Revista Latinoamericana de Derecho, Año IV, Nov. 7–8, 2007, at 178.

326 *See, e.g.*, Argentine Constitucion of 1853 (Article 18); Chilean Constitution of 1822 (Articles 115–17); Peruvian Constitution of 1823 (Articles 193–94).

327 Mexico, in its 1857 Constitution, was the first country to provide for an expedited court action to secure individual rights and guarantees. That action was named *amparo*, a term then used in many other jurisdictions. In Argentina, for example, the *amparo* was a creation of the Supreme Court in 1957, followed by regulation by statute in 1966. The *amparo* was further enshrined as part of the 1994 Constitutional Amendment. *See* Patricio Alejandro Maraniello, "El amparo en Argentina. Evolución, rasgos y características especiales," Revista IUS, 2011, vol. 5, No. 27, at 9, 12–18.

328 Inter-America Convention on Human Rights, adopted in San Jose, Costa Rica, Nov. 22, 1969 (entered into force July 18, 1978). The IACHR was ratified by Argentina, Barbados, Bolivia, Brazil, Chile, Colombia, Costa Rica, Dominica, Ecuador, El Salvador, Grenada, Guatemala, Haiti, Honduras, Jamaica, Mexico, Nicaragua, Panama, Paraguay, Peru, Dominican Republic, Suriname, Trinidad & Tobago, and Venezuela.

329 According to its Preamble, the signatory states considered that "these principles have been set forth in the Charter of the Organization of American States, in the American Declaration of the Rights and Duties of Man, and in the Universal Declaration of Human Rights, and that they have been reaffirmed and refined in other international instruments, worldwide as well as regional in scope."

330 IACHR art. 1(1).

331 *Id.* at art. 8(1).

332 Adopted in Rome, Italy, Nov. 4, 1950, effective since 1953, and ratified by all 47 members of the Council of Europe.

333 *Id.* at art. 6(1).

In the common law tradition, reference to the Magna Carta is almost obligatory in any discussion of due process. The actual events surrounding the Great Charter's sealing in 1215 differ markedly from the near-mythical gloss that surrounds it today. The document was not particularly novel.[334] "[T]he idea that the King was subject to law had for a very long time been part of the orthodoxy of medieval constitutional thought both in England and elsewhere,"[335] and "equivalent charters" were issued by "[t]he Golden Bull in Hungary of 1222 and 1231, . . . the Holy Roman Emperor in 1120 and 1231 and . . . King of Aragon in 1283 and 1287."[336] Nor was the charter especially ambitious. The only institutional method for enforcement was set out in Clause 61, which called for a committee of 25 barons to enforce promises given by the king, but that clause was deleted in the reissue of the charter the following year.[337] The Magna Carta, moreover, was sealed by King John at Runnymede under the coercion and duress of an impending civil war.[338] In only three months' time, King John had breached several of its provisions and persuaded Pope Innocent III to annul it, leading the barons of northern England to resume the rebellion that they had temporarily suspended upon its conclusion.[339]

But, unlike other charters from that epoch, the Magna Carta endured. It "constitute[d] the first comprehensive state statement in written form, formally promulgated to the whole English population, of the requirements of good governance and the limits upon the exercise of political power."[340] King Henry III reissued a modified version in 1225, and it also featured prominently in the summonsing of the first Parliament in 1265.[341] Writing in the fifteenth century, Sir John Fortescue, then Chief Justice of the King's Bench, declared that " 'the King of England cannot alter nor change the lawes of his Realme at his pleasure. . . . [H]e can neither change Lawes without the consent of his subjects, nor yet charge

---

334 *See generally* R.H. Helmholz, *Magna Carta and the* Ius Commune, 66 U. Chi. L. Rev. 297 (1999).

335 Lord Sumption, *Magna Carta Then and Now*, Address to the Friends of the British Library, at 6–7 (Oct. 1, 2015).

336 Lord Judge, *Magna Carta: Destiny or Accident?*, UNSW, at 1 (Feb. 19, 2015).

337 James Spigelman, *Magna Carta and Its Medieval Context*, Address to Banco Court, Supreme Court of South Wales, Sydney, at 8–12 (Apr. 22, 2015).

338 Lord Judge, *Magna Carta: Destiny or Accident?*, Middle Temple, at 2 (Oct. 1, 2015).

339 Lord Neuberger, *Magna Carta: The Bible of the English Constitution or a Disgrace of the English Nation?*, Guildford Cathedral, ¶¶ 11–13 (June 18, 2015); Lord Sumption, *Magna Carta Then and Now*, Address to the Friends of the British Library, at 11 (Mar. 9, 2015).

340 Spigelman, *supra* note 337 at 19.

341 Lord Neuberger, *supra* note 339, ¶ 17.

them with strange impositions against their wils.' "[342] Although the Magna Carta was scarcely mentioned in legal writings during the fifteenth and sixteenth centuries, Sir Edward Coke revived (and arguably overread) the Magna Carta at the beginning of the seventeenth century to promote the rule of law and to challenge the royal absolutism of Charles I.[343] Since that time, the document has taken on a stature far greater than its tenuous origins might have foretold, playing a significant role in the English Bill of Rights of 1689 and the U.S. Constitution in 1789. Thus, "[g]radually, in social conditions and societies which are remote from [that of England], Magna Carta and what Magna Carta was believed to stand for became part of the fabric of our political thinking."[344]

"The rule of law can be said to permeate the whole of the Great Charter, in that each clause is a provision which limits the power of the King or controls the actions of the powerful."[345] Specifically, the Magna Carta's "law of the land" provision recognized the need for procedural regularity in the exercise of governmental powers.[346] This is how it codified the notion that when the crown acted against an individual, it would do so in accordance with certain general and accepted principles:

> No free man shall be seized or imprisoned, or stripped of his rights or possessions, or outlawed or exiled, or deprived of his standing in any other way, nor will we proceed with force against him, or send others to do so, except by the lawful judgement of his equals or by *the law of the land.*[347]

In these last five words, King John essentially promised to act according to the rule of law and not his own mere will. Up to that point, the judicial court was largely an extension of the king's court. The king personally presided over cases involving the baronage and knights, and "[t]here was a large political element in many of his decisions": "He unquestionably sold justice, by demanding

342 Baroness Hale of Richmond, *Magna Carta: Did She Die in Vain?*, at 10–11, Gray's Inn (Oct. 19, 2015) (quoting SIR JOHN FORTESCUE, IN PRAISE OF THE LAWS OF ENGLAND, ch. 9, at 25 b. (1616 ed.), *reproduced in* G.G. COULTON, SOCIAL LIFE IN BRITAIN FROM THE CONQUEST TO THE REFORMATION, ch. 15 (2004)).

343 Lord Sumption, *supra* note 339, at 13–15; Lord Neuberger, *supra* note 339, ¶¶ 17–22.

344 Lord Judge, *supra* note 336, at 2; *see also* Lord Neuberger, *supra* note 339, ¶ 34 ("the 1215 Magna Carta can fairly be said to represent an almost undetectable first step towards democracy").

345 Lord Neuberger, *supra* note 339, ¶ 42.

346 *Murray's Lessee v. Hoboken Land & Improvement Co.*, 59 U.S. (18 How.) 272, 276 (1856).

347 *The Magna Carta 339, in* BRITISH DOCUMENTS OF LIBERTY 41–46 (Henry Marsh ed., 1971).

large sum, known as 'proffers' in return for access to his court. And on occasion he denied justice. The baronage therefore found themselves squeezed . . . [and] dependent on the vagaries of the King's will for their claims against each other."[348]

In the 1354 statutory reissue of the Charter, these words were replaced with "due process of law." As Sir Edward Coke later explained, the terms "law of the land" and "due process of law" were virtually synonymous,[349] and—when applied to constrain court processes—represented a regular procedure for summoning citizens to trial and adjudicating their liability.[350] Presiding over the *Bagg's* case of 1615 as Chief Justice of the King's Bench, Coke cited the Magna Carta in holding that the general principle *audiatur et altera pars* was violated when a civil servant was not permitted to make his case before being sacked.[351] The "law of the land" provision was subsequently adapted and adopted in the form of due process clauses included in American colonial and state constitutions,[352] and later the federal Constitution.[353] These provisions have been construed to require, inter alia, "a law which hears before it condemns, which proceeds upon inquiry and renders judgment only after trial," as famously explicated by Daniel Webster in his *Dartmouth College v. Woodward* argument.[354]

These artfully vague terms tend to shroud whether "due process" and "law of the land" clauses limit the *type* of laws imposed by the sovereign or only the *means* by which those laws are adopted and applied. It certainly has the latter role: "The history of American freedom is, in no small measure, the history of procedure."[355] Certain baseline procedural rules have thus been identified as the core of "due process." They include, for example, the right to notice reasonably calculated to

348 Lord Sumption, *supra* note 339, at 9.

349 Edward Coke, *Institutes*, *in* 1 The Selected Writings and Speeches of Sir Edward Coke 858 (Steve Sheppard ed., 2003) ("For the true sense and exposition of these words ['law of the land'], see the Statute of 37. Edw. 3. cap. 8. where the words, by the law of the Land, are rendered, without due process of Law. . . .").

350 *See* Rhonda Wasserman, Procedural Due Process: A Reference Guide to the United States Constitution 2 (2004).

351 *James Bagg's Case*, (1615) 77 E.R. 1271, 1280.

352 Eight of the 13 colonies had a "law of the land" provision, or its equivalent, in their constitutions. *See* Hannis Taylor, Due Process of Law and the Equal Protection of the Laws 13–15 (Callaghan 1917).

353 U.S. Const. amends. V and XIV.

354 *Dartmouth College v. Woodward*, 17 U.S. 518, 581 (1819).

355 *Malinski v. New York*, 324 U.S. 401, 414 (1945) (concurring opinion of Frankfurter, J.).

apprise interested parties of the pendency of an action,[356] the ability to be heard at a meaningful time and in a meaningful manner,[357] the opportunity to present every available defense;[358] the requirement that criminal guilt or civil liability be based on public evidence;[359] and the need for the judge to be impartial, unbiased, and objective.[360] The generic nature of these rights is intentional. "[N]o single model of procedural fairness, let alone a particular form of procedure, is dictated by the Due Process Clause. 'The very nature of due process negates any concept of inflexible procedures universally applicable to every imaginable situation.' "[361] Intrinsic to the right itself, the amount of process due varies in accordance with the circumstances of each individual case.[362]

But the principle of due process has also been held to place certain limits on the types of laws that may be enacted. After independence, the U.S. Supreme Court

---

356 *Mullane v. Central Hanover Bank & Trust Co.*, 339 U.S. 306, 314 (1950).

357 *Mathews v. Eldridge*, 424 U.S. 319, 333 (1976) (citing *Armstrong v. Manzo*, 380 U.S. 545, 552 (1965) and *Grannis v. Ordean*, 234 U.S. 385, 394 (1914)).

358 *American Surety Co. v. Baldwin*, 287 U.S. 156, 168 (1932); *see also Philip Morris U.S.A. v. Williams*, 549 U.S. 346 (2007).

359 *Fiore v. White*, 531 U.S. 225 (2001) (failure to prove a basic element of a crime renders a criminal conviction void for lack of due process); *Thompson v. Louisville*, 362 U.S. 199, 206 (1961) ("it is a violation of due process to convict and punish a man without evidence of his guilt"); *Garner v. Louisiana*, 368 U.S. 157 (1961) (same); *United States ex rel. Vajtauer v. Commissioner of Immigration*, 273 U.S. 103, 106 (1927) ("Deportation without a fair hearing or on charges unsupported by any evidence is a denial of due process"); *Greene v. McElroy*, 360 U.S. 474, 496–97 (1959) ("Certain principles have remained relatively immutable in our jurisprudence. One of these is that where governmental action seriously injures an individual, and the reasonableness of the action depends on fact findings, the evidence used to prove the Government's case must be disclosed to the individual so that he has an opportunity to show that it is untrue.... [While we] have formalized these protections in the requirements of confrontation and cross-examination, [t]hey have ancient roots, and [t]his Court has been zealous to protect these rights from erosion. It has spoken out not only in criminal cases, but also in all types of cases where administrative and regulatory actions were under scrutiny.") (citations omitted).

360 *Caperton v. A.T. Massey Coal Co.*, 556 U.S. 868 (2009); *see also Mooney v. Holohan*, 294 U.S. 103, 112 (1935) (due process "cannot be deemed to be satisfied by mere notice and hearing if a State has contrived a conviction through the pretense of a trial which in truth is but used as a means of depriving a defendant of liberty through a deliberate deception of court and jury by the presentation of testimony known to be perjured").

361 *Kremer v. Chem. Constr. Corp.*, 456 U.S. 461, 483 (1982) (quoting *Mitchell v. W.T. Grant Co.*, 416 U.S. 600, 610 (1974)).

362 For instance, the balancing test that the Supreme Court in *Mathews v. Eldridge* outlined for addressing procedural due process claims "dictates that the process due in any given instance is determined by weighing 'the private interest that will be affected by the official action' against the Government's asserted interest, 'including the function involved' and the burdens the Government would face in providing greater process." *Hamdi v. Rumsfeld*, 542 U.S. 507, 529 (2004) (quoting *Mathews v. Eldridge*, 424 U.S. 319, 335 (1976)).

interpreted the federal due process clause to restrain the legislative as well as the executive and judicial branches; Congress, it held, was not "free to make any process 'due process of law' by its mere will."[363] This reflects the notion that due process ensures the protection of not just *any* process, but a process of *law*.[364] The U.S. Supreme Court described

> the traditional and common-sense notion that the Due Process Clause, like its forebear in the Magna Carta, was intended to secure the individual from the arbitrary exercise of the powers of government. By requiring the government to follow appropriate procedures when its agents decide to "deprive any person of life, liberty, or property," the Due Process Clause promotes fairness in such decisions. And by barring certain government actions regardless of the fairness of the procedures used to implement them, it serves to prevent governmental power from being used for purposes of oppression.[365]

The latter promise assures, for instance, that duly enacted legislation does not single out a particular person for no legitimate reason.[366] This "implies that lawfulness is a function of an action's underlying logic or correspondence to principle.... By pledging that government will comply with [these] deeper principles of lawfulness, [it] guarantees that government will act in a manner for which it can give a rational account."[367] Not unlike the FET clauses found in many BITs, the standards that have developed are marked by fluid concepts such as regularity, fairness, and rationality, which gauge the propriety of the process and the reasonableness of a particular enactment. According to the U.S. Supreme Court, "there is wisdom ... in the ... gradual process of judicial inclusion and exclusion" on what due process requires.[368]

As countries in the civil law tradition have moved toward republican forms of government, the adjectival rules of Roman law have similarly been applied to check the

363 *Murray's Lessee v. Hoboken Land & Improvement Co.*, 59 U.S. 272, 276 (1856). This conclusion was consistent with contemporaneous conclusions of state courts interpreting their own constitutional due process clauses. *See, e.g., Wynehamer v. People*, 13 N.Y. 378, 392 (1856) (concluding that state constitutional due process clauses "are imposed by the people as restraints upon the power of the legislature"); *see also Hoke v. Henderson*, 15 N.C. 1, 15–16 (1833) (interpreting "law of the land" clause).

364 *See Of the Nature of Laws in General*, *in* WILLIAM BLACKSTONE, COMMENTARIES ON THE LAWS OF ENGLAND § 2 (J.B. Lippincott Co. 1839).

365 *Daniels v. Williams*, 474 U.S. 327, 331 (1986) (citations and quotation marks omitted).

366 *See, e.g., U.S. Dep't of Agriculture v. Moreno*, 413 U.S. 528, 532–33 (1973) (legislation singling out class of persons to be denied public funding invalidated under the due process clause of the U.S. Constitution).

367 Sandefur, *supra* note 287, at 292–93.

368 *Davidson v. New Orleans*, 96 U.S. 97, 104 (1877).

exercise of governmental power. The foundations of French administrative law were developed almost entirely as a product of certain general principles of process and procedure. At the close of World War II, the *Conseil d'Etat* decided two leading cases, *Aramu*[369] and *Dame Veuve Trompier Gravier*,[370] concerning the right to be heard in defense against adverse government decisions. In both, existing law did not impose a duty on the decision-making authority to inform the affected individual of the measure that it would take. Nonetheless, in *Dame Veuve Trompier-Gravier*, the *Conseil d'Etat* declared that a measure that adversely affects individual interests could not "legally" be taken without providing the individual with notice and an opportunity to contest it.[371] In *Aramu*, the *Conseil d'Etat* went further, proclaiming that an act of the executive branch was illegal if it violated the "applicable general principles of law, even in the absence of a [legal] text."[372] Seemingly bold pronouncements for a civil law tribunal, the *Conseil d'Etat* insisted that "when the judge applies general principles, he interprets the presumed will of the legislator and does not create law." Whatever is made of this characterization, it is now settled that general principles may trump administrative acts and, in certain circumstances, can even prevail against statutes.[373]

Supranational courts have also contributed to the development of due process. Upon conclusion of the Treaty of Paris of 1951, the inaugural members of what would become the European Union (EU) did not enact codes of procedure but instead left the details to be worked out by the institutions then being established.[374] As a result, the attributes of due process were for over 60 years generated solely by the ECJ as general principles.[375] In 1962, the ECJ announced that due process required a hearing prior to termination of public employment as a matter of "generally accepted principle[s] of administrative law" in the legal systems of the Member States, even though it had no textual warrant for doing so.[376] Later,

369 *Aramu*, CE Ass., Oct. 26, 1945, Rec. Lebon 213.

370 *Aramu*, CE Sect., May 5, 1944, Rec. Lebon 133.

371 *Id.*

372 *Aramu*, CE Ass., Oct. 26, 1945, Rec. Lebon 213.

373 *See* Sweet & della Cananea, *supra* note 89, at 946.

374 *See* Eva Nieto-Garrido & Isaac Martin Delgado, European Administrative Law in the Constitutional Treaty 113–14 (2007) ("The legal status of the general principles of law is one of the most important characteristics of Community law: the ECJ has, through these principles, given form to the law of the EU while at the same time expanding the protection of the rights of citizens. The absence of a general law on administrative procedure and the resulting plethora of measures has made the ECJ the protagonist in developing general rules on procedure through these principles.").

375 *See generally* Mario P. Chiti, *The Role of the European Court of Justice in the Development of General Principles and Their Possible Codification*, 3–4 Rivista italiana di diritto pubblico comunitario 661–71 (1995).

376 *Alvis v. Council*, Case 32/62, [1963] E.C.R. 49, 54–55.

in *Transocean Marine Paint Association v. Commission*, the ECJ held that the principle of *audi alteram partem* was common to the legal orders of the Member States and could therefore be invoked by private parties despite its absence in any applicable treaty.[377] Today, these and other general principles applied under the rubric of "good and fair administration" are codified as Article 41 of the Charter of Fundamental Rights of the EU, which includes the right "to be heard" and the right to administrative proceedings that are "handled impartially, fairly, and within a reasonable period of time."[378]

These concepts of due process, developed through application in myriad contexts throughout the world, derive from and overlap with the general principles of law discussed in Cheng's monograph. For instance, as Cheng observed, judgments rendered without service of process or notice are *coram non iudice* and contrary to "immutable principle[s] of natural justice."[379] Proper service has long been a "fundamental conditio[n]" that is "universally prescribed in all systems of law established by civilized countries."[380] Judgments rendered without proper notice usually will be denied recognition and enforcement outside of their country of origin[381] and may even give rise to responsibility under international law if they lead to the seizure of property or other harm.[382]

Cheng also devoted a chapter of his book to the notion of *audiatur et altera pars*, which translates in practice to the "fundamental requirement of equality between the parties in judicial proceedings" and their equal right to be heard.[383] Elsewhere, he discussed the maxim *nemo debet esse iudex in propria sua causa*, or the

---

377 *Transocean Marine Paint Ass'n v. Commission*, Case 17/74, [1974] E.C.R. 1063.

378 Charter of Fundamental Rights of the European Union (2000/C 364/01) art. 41, *signed and proclaimed by* the Presidents of the European Parliament, the Council and the Commission at the European Council meeting, Nice (Dec. 7, 2000).

379 *Hollingsworth v. Barbour*, 29 U.S. (4 Pet.) 466, 475 (1830).

380 *Twining v. New Jersey*, 211 U.S. 78, 111 (1908).

381 *Hilton v. Guyot*, 159 U.S. 113, 166–67 (1895) ("Every foreign judgment, of whatever nature, in order to be entitled to any effect, must have been rendered by a court having jurisdiction of the cause, and upon regular proceedings, and due notice."); *Int'l Transactions, Ltd. v. Embotelladora Agral Regiomontana*, SA de CV, 347 F.3d 589, 594 (5th Cir. 2003) ("Notice is an element of our notion of due process and the United States will not enforce a judgment obtained without the bare minimum requirements of notice."); German Code of Civil Procedure 328(1)2 ("The defendant, who has not entered an appearance in the proceedings and who takes recourse to this fact, has not duly been served the document by which the proceedings were initiated, or not in such time to allow him to defend himself.").

382 *See, e.g., Middle East Cement Shipping & Handling Co. S.A. v. Arab Republic of Egypt*, ICSID Case No. ARB/99/6, Award, ¶¶ 140–43 (Apr. 12, 2002), *reprinted in* 7 ICSID Rep. 173 (2005).

383 Cheng, *supra* note 4, at 291–98.

"universally accepted doctrine that no one can be judge in his own cause,"[384] and the principle *extra compromisum arbiter nihil facere potest*, meaning that tribunals may exercise only that jurisdiction authorized by law.[385] All three of these general principles form part of international due process. For instance, the European Convention on Human Rights marks an early attempt to codify an intra-European baseline of due process, and it includes the guarantee that "everyone is entitled to [i] *a fair and public hearing* within a reasonable time [ii] by an *independent and impartial tribunal* [iii] *established by the law*."[386] Judgments falling short on any of these elements will typically not be recognized in the European Union.[387]

Modern soft law codifications, such as the American Law Institute (ALI) and the International Institute for the Unification of Private Law (UNIDROIT) Principles of Transnational Civil Procedure, include many principles underlying international due process. The first three articles of that instrument address the "independence [and] impartiality" of judges, their "jurisdiction over parties," and the "procedural equality of the parties."[388] The general principle that judgments cannot be rendered without due notice follows in Article 5.[389] That Article further catalogues a number of general principles that have been applied in various fora, including the requirement of "effective . . . notice" at the outset of proceedings and the "right to submit relevant contentions of fact and law and to offer supporting evidence."[390] When pulled together into a "Transnational [Code of] Civil Procedure," as ALI and UNIDROIT have done, these individual principles form a set of minimum "standards for adjudication of transnational commercial disputes."[391]

2. The Concept of International Due Process

For nearly as long as individuals have been engaging each other across national borders, a rudimentary code of "international due process" has existed, that is,

384 *Id.* at 279.

385 *Id.* at 259–66.

386 Convention for the Protection of Human Rights and Fundamental Freedoms art. 6(1) (Rome, Nov. 4, 1950).

387 *See Yukos Capital S.A.R.L. v. OAO Rosneft, Amsterdam Court of Appeal*, Case No. 200.005.269/01, Decision (Apr. 28, 2009); Case of *Oao Neftyanaya Kompaniya Yukos v. Russia*, App. No. 14902/04, Eur. Ct. H.R. (Sept. 20, 2011).

388 ALI/UNIDROIT Principles of Transnational Civil Procedure princ. 1-3, 2004-4 UNIF. L. REV. 758–66.

389 *Id.* at 768.

390 *Id.*; *see, e.g.*, *Hilton v. Guyot*, 159 U.S. 113, 159 (1895) (To be recognized, a foreign judgment must be the product of "due allegations and proofs, and the opportunity to defend against them . . . .").

391 ALI/UNIDROIT Principles of Transnational Civil Procedure, 2004-4 UNIF. L. REV. 758.

"certain minimum standards in the administration of justice of such elementary fairness and general application in the legal systems of the world that they have become international legal standards."[392] These precepts can apply in myriad settings, serving as "devices devoted to the enforcement of the rules of substantive law" or as "rules determining the organization, the competence and the functioning of [adjudicative] organs."[393] These standards have been culled from and reflect essential adjectival requirements found in different legal traditions.

Modern applications and explications of this international standard can be found in the ad hoc claims commissions formed to address alleged mistreatment of aliens by local courts at the beginning of the nineteenth century. International law was forced to grapple with domestic courts that were "not independent"; "judges [who were] removable at will [and] not superior, as they ought to be, to local prejudices and passions"; and judicial systems that failed to "afford to the foreigner the same degree of impartiality which is accorded to citizens of the country, or which is required by the common standard of justice obtaining throughout the civilized world."[394] Cases and commentary addressing themselves to the proper articulation of principles of state responsibility toward aliens flourished. There was convergence around a legal standard that demanded "[f]air courts, . . . administering justice honestly, impartially, without bias or political control."[395] As famously stated by Elihu Root, the minimum standard of treatment requires "justice, very simple, very fundamental, and of such general acceptance by all civilized countries as to form a part of the international law of the world."[396]

It was thus understood that the "due process" required in reciprocal-protection treaties signed by the United States shortly after World War I was "not the due

392 Friedmann, *supra* note 74, at 290 (discussing use of general principles to establish "procedural standards of fairness"); Schill, *supra* note 68, at 90 (explaining that general principles "have been used frequently by international courts and tribunals . . . to develop the procedural law of international adjudication, as a source of substantive rights and obligations, to fill lacunae in the governing law, and to aid in the interpretation and the further development of international law") (citations omitted)).

393 Robert Kolb, *General Principles of Procedural Law*, *in* The Statute of the International Court of Justice: A Commentary 873 (Andreas Zimmermann et al. eds., 2d ed. 2012).

394 Elihu Root, *The Basis of Protection to Citizens Residing Abroad*, 4 Proc. Am. Soc'y Int'l L. 16, 25 (1910).

395 Borchard, *supra*, note 33, at 460; *see also* Georg Schwarzenberger, International Law 613, 619 (Stevens 3d ed. 1957) ("[i]ndependence from the executive" on the part of the judiciary is required by "the rule on the minimum standard of international law").

396 Root, *supra* note 394, at 21.

process of the United States Constitution, but the due process required by international law, since the standard of 'due process of law,' whether procedural or substantive, of one of the parties is not controlling and does not necessarily reflect international law."[397] This reflects the reality that the "twist[s] and turn[s]" and "idiosyncratic jurisprudence" of Anglo-American due process are not shared in all legal systems around the world.[398] In *The Affaire du Capitaine Thomas Melville White*, for instance, the British Government complained to an arbitral tribunal that the arrest of one of its citizens in Peru was illegal under standards of English law. The tribunal, however, had "little doubt" that "the rules of procedure to be observed by the courts in [Peru] are to be judged solely and alone according to the legislation in force there," and not those half a world away.[399] But despite the fact that many rules of procedure differ between the common and civil law (such as the use of juries and live witnesses), the *idea* of due process "is not alien to that code which survived the Roman Empire as the foundation of modern civilization" in Continental Europe and much of the world.[400]

The related notion of denial of justice as a source for international liability also took root, with tribunals identifying specific circumstances under which a judicial decision might be condemned: where it is the product of "corruption, threats, unwarrantable delay, flagrant abuse of judicial procedure"; where the winner was "dictated by the executive"; or where the resolution is "so manifestly unjust that no court which was both competent and honest could have given it."[401] The jurisprudence on denial of justice includes several basic principles of international due process, including that no one shall be subjected to liability without a hearing, that there shall be no common interest between the parties and the judge, and that every party shall be given a fair opportunity to be heard.[402] The failure of a State to provide these guarantees may attract responsibility under international law.

---

397 R.R. WILSON, UNITED STATES COMMERCIAL TREATIES AND INTERNATIONAL LAW 113–15 (1960).

398 *Soc'y of Lloyd's v. Ashenden*, 233 F.3d 473, 476–77 (7th Cir. 2000).

399 *Decision de la commission, chargée, par le Senat de la Ville libre hanséatique de Hambourg, de prononcer dans la cause du capitaine Thomas Melville White, datée de Hambourg du 13 avril 1864, in* PASICRISIE INTERNATIONALE, 1794–1900, HISTOIRE DOCUMENTAIRE DES ARBITRAGES INTERNATIONAUX 48 (Henri La Fontaine ed., 1997).

400 *Holdon v. Hardy*, 169 U.S. 366, 388 (1898).

401 *Barcelona Traction, Light & Power Co., Ltd. (Belg. v. Spain)*, Second Phase, Judgment, 1970 I.C.J. 3, 155–56 (Feb. 5) (separate opinion of Judge Tanaka); *see also* Harvard Law School, Research in International Law, *Draft Convention on the Law of Responsibility of States for Damage Done in Their Territory to the Person or Property of Foreigners*, 23 AM. J. INT'L L. 133, 173, 180–81 (Special Supp. 1929).

402 *See generally* JAN PAULSSON, DENIAL OF JUSTICE IN INTERNATIONAL LAW (2005).

These minimum standards of due process also come to the fore where the courts of one nation are asked to recognize and enforce the judgment of another. "Nations are not inexorably bound to enforce judgments obtained in each other's courts."[403] In the United States, recognition of a foreign money judgment is granted by rote "where there has been opportunity for a full and fair trial abroad before a court of competent jurisdiction, ... after due citation or voluntary appearance of the defendant, and under a system of jurisprudence likely to secure an impartial administration of justice, ... and there is nothing to show either prejudice in the court ... or fraud in procuring the judgment."[404] Conversely, recognition of foreign judgments will be denied where the court lacked jurisdiction; where "trials [were not] held in public"; where the case was "highly politicized"; where the judge could not "be expected to be completely impartial toward [foreign] citizens"; and where the judgment debtor was denied the ability to appear personally, to "obtain proper legal representation," and to obtain witnesses on its behalf.[405] The enforcement of a foreign judgment thus turns on whether "it was obtained in a manner that [did or] did not accord with the basics of due process."[406] A similar requirement redounds throughout the world.[407]

The enforcement of arbitral awards can also turn upon satisfaction of certain general principles of international due process. Article V of the New York Convention, which provides the bases for refusing recognition and enforcement of a foreign arbitral award, includes fundamental tenets of due process such as notice of the proceedings, equality in the opportunity to present one's case, and a prohibition on tribunals acting in excess of their jurisdiction.[408]

403 *Bank Melli Iran v. Pahlavi*, 58 F.3d 1406, 1410, 1413 (9th Cir. 1995).

404 *Hilton v. Guyot*, 159 U.S. 113, 202–03 (1895).

405 *Bank Melli Iran v. Pahlavi*, 58 F.3d 1406, 1407–13 (9th Cir. 1995).

406 *Id.* at 1413.

407 *See, e.g.*, Inter-American Convention on Extraterritorial Validity of Foreign Judgments and Arbitral Awards of 1979 (requiring "[t]hat the defense of the parties has been guaranteed" prior to recognition of foreign judgments); Argentina, Federal Code of Procedures art. 517(2) (same); *Beals v. Saldanha*, [2003] 3 S.C.R. 416, 2003 SCC 72 (Can.) (requiring that defendants receive "minimum standards of fairness" in the foreign proceeding: "Fair process is one that, in the system from which the judgment originates, reasonably guarantees basic procedural safeguards such as judicial independence and fair ethical rules governing the participants in the judicial system."); Bangladeshi Civil Procedure Code § 13(d) (no recognition of foreign judgment based upon proceedings "opposed to natural justice"); *Al-Bassam v. Al-Bassam*, [2004] EWCA Civ 857 (U.K.) (reviewing foreign judgment with respect to article 6 of the European Convention on Human Rights, which requires "a fair and public hearing within a reasonable time by an independent and impartial tribunal established by law").

408 *See, e.g.*, ICCA's Guide to the Interpretation of the 1958 New York Convention: A Handbook for Judges (2011), http://www.arbitration-icca.org/media/1/13890217974630/judges_guide_english_composite_final_jan2014.pdf; *see generally* Marike Paulsson, The 1958 New York Convention in Action (2016).

The New York Convention also states that a foreign arbitral award may be refused recognition if the award is "contrary to the public policy of [the forum] country."[409] In some States, this provision is understood to refer to supranational, not domestic, public policies, such that only those values essential to the international legal order constitute a basis to deny enforcement.[410] To read the public policy defense as "a parochial device protective of national political interests would," explained a U.S. court, "seriously undermine the Convention's utility."[411]

The requirements of due process established in these contexts are quite minimal notwithstanding the importance of the rule of law to international intercourse, yet there is a marked hesitancy by municipal and international bodies alike to sit in judgment of another country's judicial system. As a result, almost all reviewing courts indulge the presumption that justice has been fairly and regularly meted out. As an international tribunal wrote in 1927, "it is a matter of the greatest political and international delicacy for one country to disacknowledge the decision of a court of another country."[412] This hesitancy is motivated in part by notions of comity, including that the mutual recognition of legal rights, judgments, and awards depends in large measure upon a "spirit of cooperation" among sovereigns.[413] In addition, international relations are guided by "many values" beyond substantive justice in a particular case—"among them predictability, fairness, ease of commercial interactions, and stability through satisfaction of mutual expectations."[414] Translated into practice, few successful challenges to municipal judgments and arbitral awards succeed on procedural grounds.

---

409 United Nations Convention on the Recognition and Enforcement of Foreign Arbitral Awards art. V(2)(b), June 10, 1958, 21 U.S.T. 2517, T.I.A.S. No. 6997, 330 U.N.T.S. 38.

410 The New York Convention left this question open to signatory states, and allows each enforcement jurisdiction to decide for itself whether the public policy defense will be defined by national or supranational norms. *See generally* James D. Fry, *Désordre Public International under the New York Convention: Wither Truly International Public Policy*, 8 CHINESE J. INT'L L. 81 (2009). Although the great majority of national arbitration laws provide that courts may refuse enforcement based on the public policy of the forum, *id.* at 95–96, a number of other States expressly cabin this defense to violations of international public policy (or, to the French, *ordre public international*), *id.* at 96–97.

411 *Parsons & Whittemore Overseas Co., Inc. v. Societe Generale De Industrie Du Papier*, 508 F.2d 969, 973–74 (2d Cir. 1974).

412 *B.E. Chattin (U.S.) v. United Mexican States*, Decision of Commissioner Nielsen (July 23, 1927), 4 R.I.A.A. 282, 288 (quotation marks and citation omitted).

413 *Societe Nationale Industrielle Aerospatiale v. United States Dist. Ct.*, 482 U.S. 522, 543 n.27 (1987).

414 *Id.* at 567 (Blackman, J., concurring in part and dissenting in part) (citations omitted).

3. Specific Invocations of International Due Process

The application of principles of international due process has increased along with the growth of international disputes. Investment tribunals seised to adjudicate a denial-of-justice claim will refer to concepts embedded in the notion of international due process to help them define the cause of action and to provide the parameters of what sort of process will pass muster from a universal perspective. They will undertake a similar analysis when applying treaty guarantees of "fair and equitable treatment" and "effective means." National courts, too, have occasion to assess the procedural and substantive adequacy of foreign decisions when they are asked to recognize them as their own. In each of these contexts, the process of measuring the administration of justice in a particular case against a baseline standard that is accepted by all modern legal regimes reveals an accepted definition of international justice.

a) Arbitral Tribunals

Although an alien usually must take a foreign legal system as he finds it, with all its deficiencies and imperfections,[415] "[t]he sovereign right of a state to do justice cannot be perverted into a weapon for circumventing its obligations toward aliens who must seek the aid of its courts."[416] As noted, there is an international minimum standard of justice that must be respected in all systems. At its foundation, international due process requires States to provide "fair courts, readily open to aliens, administering justice honestly, impartially, without bias or political control."[417] These procedural requirements apply to all organs of the State, including administrative proceedings.[418] Only those processes falling short of this threshold will result in state liability on the international plane.[419]

The requirements of international due process are minimal, but cases before international tribunals over the past century reveal several notorious instances in which

415 *See Salem (U.S.) v. Egypt*, Award (June 8, 1932), 2 R.I.A.A. 1161, 1202.

416 J. Irizarry y Puente, *The Concept of Denial of Justice in Latin America*, 43 MICH. L. REV. 383, 406 (1944).

417 Borchard, *supra* note 33, at 460.

418 As stated by Sir Gerald Fitzmaurice, denial of justice can concern "such actions in or concerning the administration of justice, whether on the part of the courts or of some other organs of the state." G.G. Fitzmaurice, *The Meaning of the Term "Denial of Justice,"* 13 BRIT. Y.B. INT'L L. 93, 94 (1932). Jan Paulsson also explains that "[i]f it is established that justice has been so maladministered, it is impossible to see why the state should escape sanction because the wrong was perpetrated by one category of its agents rather than another." PAULSSON, *supra* note 402, at 44.

419 *See* A.O. Adede, *A Fresh Look at the Meaning of the Doctrine of Denial of Justice under International Law*, 14 CAN. Y.B. INT'L L. 73, 91 (1976).

they have been breached. An early example is found in *Chattin v. United Mexican States*.[420] That case concerned an American citizen, B.E. Chattin, who, in 1910, was arrested and subsequently fined and jailed in Mexico. Upon being released, Chattin returned to the United States and brought a claim for damages before the U.S.-Mexico Claims Commission. In reviewing the Mexican process, the Commission noted, inter alia, that there was "no trace of an effort to have the two foremost pieces of evidence explained" and that no "oral examination or cross-examination of any importance [was] attempted."[421] The absence of these processes, in the Commission's view, rendered the hearings in open court "a mere formality,"[422] and it admonished the Mexican legal process for its "astonishing lack of seriousness."[423]

Putting this process "to the test of international standards," the Commission asked "whether the treatment of Chattin amounts even to an outrage, to bad faith, to willful neglect of duty, or to an insufficiency of government action recognizable by every unbiased man."[424] Answering this procedural question was the Commission's only mandate: "It is not for the Commission to endeavor to reach from the record any conviction as to the innocence or guilt of Chattin and his colleagues."[425] After evaluating the entirety of the process by which Chattin was tried, the Commission concluded that it "would render a bad service to the Government of Mexico if it failed to place the stamp of its disapproval and even indignation on a criminal procedure so far below international standards of civilization as the present one."[426]

Modern awards continue to relate international claims for denial of justice to the international minimum standards of due process. NAFTA tribunals, for instance, have defined denial of justice to mean a "[m]anifest injustice in the sense of a lack of due process leading to an outcome which offends a sense of judicial propriety,"[427]

420 *B.E. Chattin (U.S.) v. United Mexican States*, Decision of Commissioner Nielsen (July 23, 1927), 4 R.I.A.A. 282.

421 *Id.* at 292.

422 *Id.* at 295.

423 *Id.* at 292.

424 *Id.* at 295.

425 *Id.* at 292. The tribunal did, however, consider whether there was a *sufficiency* of evidence, albeit reluctantly: "An international tribunal can never replace the important first element, that of the Judge's being convinced of the accused's guilt; it can only in extreme cases, and then with great reserve, look into the second element the legality and sufficiency of the evidence." *Id.* at 293.

426 *Id.* at 292.

427 *E.g., Loewen Grp., Inc. & Raymond L. Loewen v. United States of America*, ICSID Case No. ARB(AF)/98/3, Award, ¶ 132 (June 26, 2003), *reprinted in* 42 ICM 811 (2003).

that is, a judicial decision that is "clearly improper and discreditable."[428] The prevailing standard is "the common standard of justice obtaining throughout the civilized world."[429] There will be a denial of justice where "the legal system ... has performed ... so badly that it falls short of international minimum standards."[430] These stringent procedural and substantive requirements—coupled with the minimal standards of due process and the disinclination of judges and arbitrators to condemn foreign courts—make it difficult to prosecute successful denial-of-justice claims.[431] Denials of justice nonetheless exist.[432]

In *Loewen v. United States*, a Canadian company and its chief executive officer, claimants before a NAFTA tribunal, alleged that a state jury trial against them in Mississippi had been tainted by appeals to local favoritism, and that the assessment of punitive damages violated their right to due process. The tribunal began

428 *Mondev Int'l Ltd. v. United States of America*, ICSID Case No. ARB (AF)/99/2, Award, ¶ 127 (Oct. 11, 2002).

429 Root, *supra* note 394.

430 Paulsson, *supra* note 402, at 229; *see also Loewen Grp., Inc. & Raymond L. Loewen v. United States of America*, ICSID Case No. ARB(AF)/98/3, Award, ¶¶ 121, 137 (June 26, 2003), *reprinted in* 42 I.L.M. 811 (2003); *Philip Morris Brands Sàrl, Philip Morris Products S.A. and Abal Hermanos S.A. v. Oriental Republic of Uruguay*, ICSID Case No. ARB/10/7, Award, ¶ 500 (July 8, 2016).

431 *See, e.g., Int'l Thunderbird Gaming Corp. v. United Mexican States*, UNCITRAL, Separate Opinion of Thomas Wälde (Dec. 1, 2005) (where a claimant is given an opportunity to be heard, the domestic administrative decision cited both the facts and the law upon which it was based, and the claimant had an opportunity for judicial review of the administrative decision, minor irregularities in the proceedings will not "shock a sense of judicial propriety" and thereby breach the minimum standard); *Frank Charles Arif v. Republic of Moldova*, ICSID Case No. ARB/11/23, Award (Apr. 8, 2013) (holding that, although there were admittedly some procedural irregularities, none rose to the level of a denial of justice because there was no "[decision] so egregiously wrong that no competent and honest court would use them," no "procedures that [we]re so void of reason that they breathe bad faith," no "violation[s] of fundamental principles of procedure," or any "egregious misapplication of procedural law [or] a procedure which is tainted by bad faith").

432 It has been said that "the rule of law is pure illusion for most of our fellow travelers on this planet." Jan Paulsson, Speech at the Rule of Law Conference at the University of Richmond: Enclaves of Justice (Apr. 12, 2007), *available at* http://www.arbitration-icca.org/media/0/12254618965440/speech-richmond_enclaves_of_justice.pdf. Only 90 of 215 countries enjoyed a positive score (on a scale of -2.5 to 2.5) in the 2015 World Bank governance indicator for "rule of law." *See* http://info.worldbank.org/governance/wgi/index.aspx#home (last visited Sept. 6, 2016). According to the World Justice Project's 2015 Rule of Law Index, 68 of 102 countries score below 0.60 (on a 1.00 scale) in terms of their provision of "civil justice," with 40 of those countries scoring below 0.50. *See* http://worldjusticeproject.org/sites/default/files/roli_2015_0.pdf (last visited Sept. 6, 2016). As reflected in Transparency International's 2014 Corruption Perceptions Index, on a scale of 0 (highly corrupt) to 100 (very clean), only 54 of 174 countries had scores at or above 50. *See* Transparency International, Corruption Perceptions Index 2014: Results, *available at* https://www.transparency.org/cpi2014/results (last visited Sept. 6, 2016). In terms of protecting property rights, the Heritage Foundation's 2015 Index of Economic Freedom scores over half of the countries surveyed (116 out of 186) at less than 50 on a 100 point scale. http://www.heritage.org/index/explore (last visited Sept. 6, 2016). Reflecting upon data such as this, Jan Paulsson

by noting the limitations on its inquiry, explaining that it "need not resolve the domestic procedural disputes which arose at the trial."[433] Instead, the question was whether the "whole trial and its resultant verdict" satisfied minimum standards of international law.[434] Acknowledging that "mistakes and errors will occur" even before the most even-handed judge, the tribunal stated that international law neither anticipates "perfect trials" nor countenances "nitpicking a trial record and the rulings of a trial judge."[435] Even under the rigorous standard it articulated, the *Loewen* court found a denial of justice because "the trial court permitted the jury to be influenced by persistent appeals to local favouritism as against a foreign litigant."[436] It further held that the "excessive" punitive damages award—issued after only a "minimal" hearing on the question—was "the antithesis of due process."[437]

Denial of justice has been viewed as part of the "fair and equitable treatment" standard, which is prevalent in BITs and has come to encompass "the international law requirements of *due process*, . . . obligations of good faith and natural justice."[438] This international rule of decision is not "derived from subjective personal and cultural sentiments," but rather is "anchored" in "objective rules and principles" present in a

---

wrote that "[t]he error is to think that injustice is abnormal. It may be more realistic to think and act on the assumption that justice is a surprising anomaly." Paulsson, *supra* note 402, at 2.

433 *Loewen Grp., Inc. & Raymond L. Loewen v. United States*, ICSID Case No. ARB(AF)/98/3, Award, ¶ 121 (June 26, 2003), *reprinted in* 42 I.L.M. 811 (2003).

434 *Id.* ¶ 137.

435 *Id.* ¶ 120.

436 *Id.* ¶ 136; *see also id.* ¶ 135 (noting that international law attaches "special importance to discriminatory violations of municipal law") (citing the Harvard Law School, Research in International Law, *Draft Convention on the Law of Responsibility of States for Damage Done in Their Territory to the Persons or Property of Foreigners*, 23 AM. J. INT'L L. 133, 174 (Special Supp. 1929) ("a judgement is manifestly unjust, . . . if [it has] been inspired by ill-will towards foreigners, as such, or as citizens of a particular state"); Adede, *supra* note 420, at 91 ("a . . . decision which is clearly at variance with the law and discriminatory cannot be allowed to establish legal obligations for the alien litigant").

437 *Loewen Grp., Inc. & Raymond L. Loewen v. United States*, ICSID Case No. ARB(AF)/98/3, Award, ¶ 122 (June 26, 2003), *reprinted in* 42 I.L.M. 811 (2003). Despite criticizing the national court proceedings in the "strongest terms," the tribunal ultimately decided *against* the investor on jurisdictional grounds. *Id.* ¶¶ 220–40.

438 *S.D. Myers, Inc. v. Gov't of Canada*, UNCITRAL, Partial Award, ¶ 134 (Nov. 13, 2000); *see also Waste Mgmt., Inc. v. United Mexican States*, ICSID Case No. ARB(AF)/00/3, Award, ¶ 98 (Apr. 30, 2004), *reprinted in* 43 I.L.M. 967; *Jan de Nul N.V. & Dredging Int'l N.V. v. Arab Republic of Egypt*, ICSID Case No. ARB/04/13, Award, ¶ 187 (Nov. 6, 2008); *AMTO LLC v. Ukraine*, SCC Case No. 080/2005, Final Award, ¶ 75 (Mar. 26, 2008). Indeed, the 2004 U.S. Model BIT anchored the explanation of fair and equitable treatment in "principles of due process embodied in the principal legal systems of the world." 2004 U.S. Model BIT art. 5(2)(a). *See* CAMPBELL MCLACHLAN, LAURENCE SHORE & MATTHEW WEINIGER, INTERNATIONAL INVESTMENT ARBITRATION ¶ 7.176 (2007) (observing that "[t]he key terms ['fair and equitable treatment'] are expressive of 'general principles of law common to civilized nations' within the meaning of Article 38(1)(c) of the Statute of the International Court of Justice").

consensus of national laws.[439] It is typically invoked to challenge an alleged abuse of government power by a host State. For example, in the case of *Middle East Cement v. Egypt*, Egypt seized and auctioned the claimant's vessel after notice that, although arguably compliant with local law, was not "sufficient" to reach the claimant. The ICSID tribunal held that this process did not comport with "fair and equitable treatment," which it read in conjunction with the BIT's requirement of "due process."[440] In such cases, as another tribunal held, the validity of the local process under municipal law does not immunize the State from the mandates of international law.[441]

Other investment treaty guarantees also emanate from principles of international due process. Arbitrary treatment is condemned by many BITs, and is typically exemplified by "a willful disregard of *due process of law* . . . which shocks, or at least surprises, a sense of juridical propriety."[442] Some treaty provisions create *lex specialis* specific to procedural rights, with some States having undertaken to provide investors with "effective means of asserting claims and enforcing rights."[443] "Effective means" within a legal system has been held to require things such as an impartial judge[444] and timely adjudication[445]—core components of international due process. It also has been held to require the provision of legislation for the enforcement of property rights that meets a minimum "qualitative standard."[446] This substantive obligation jibes with other jurisprudence that "the clear and malicious misapplication of the law" can constitute a denial of justice and a violation of international due process insofar as it constitutes a "pretence of form" to mask a violation of international law.[447]

---

439 *Int'l Thunderbird Gaming Corp. v. United Mexican States*, UNCITRAL, Separate Opinion of Thomas Wälde, ¶¶ 28–30 (Dec. 1, 2005) (conducting a "comparative administrative law" survey, including decisions from EU authorities, the Court of Justice of the European Union, and World Trade Organization panels, to demonstrate the "contemporary state practice and the minimum standards of national and international [administrative] law" on the issue of legitimate expectations).

440 *Middle East Cement Shipping & Handling Co. S.A. v. Arab Republic of Egypt*, ICSID Case No. ARB/99/6, Award, ¶¶ 139–47 (Apr. 12, 2002), *reprinted in* 7 ICSID Rep. 173 (2005).

441 *Int'l Thunderbird Gaming Corp. v. United Mexican States*, UNCITRAL, Separate Opinion of Thomas Wälde, ¶¶ 25–26 (Dec. 1, 2005).

442 *Elettronica Sicula S.p.A. (ELSI) (U.S. v. It.)*, Judgment, 1989 I.C.J. 15, ¶ 128 (July 20).

443 *See, e.g.*, U.S.-Ecuador BIT art. II(7); Energy Charter Treaty art. 10(2).

444 *See, e.g.*, *Petrobart Ltd. v. Kyrgyz Republic*, SCC Case No. 126/2003, Award, 73–77 (Mar. 29, 2005).

445 *See, e.g.*, *Chevron Corp. and Texaco Petroleum Co. v. Republic of Ecuador*, UNCITRAL, PCA Case No. 34877, Partial Award on the Merits (Mar. 30, 2010); *Duke Energy Electroquil Partners & Electroquil S.A. v. Republic of Ecuador*, ICSID Case No. ARB/04/19, Award (Aug. 18, 2008); *White Industries Australia Ltd. v. Republic of India*, UNCITRAL, Award (Nov. 30, 2011).

446 *AMTO LLC v. Ukraine*, SCC Case No. 080/2005, Final Award, ¶ 87 (Mar. 26, 2008).

447 *Azinian v. United Mexican States*, ICSID Case No. ARB (AF)/97/2, Award, ¶¶ 99–103 (Nov. 1, 1999), *reprinted in* 39 I.L.M. 537.

b) National Courts

The standard of review employed by arbitral tribunals reviewing national court decisions for compliance with treaty obligations and international law is similar to that employed by national courts asked to recognize and enforce a foreign judgment.[448] By design and necessity, neither type of review is insular, and the latter is emphatically *not* "intended to bar the enforcement of all judgments of any foreign legal system that does not conform its procedural doctrines to the latest twist and turn of [local] courts."[449] This has underpinnings in comity—a presumptive respect for and deference to the judicial pronouncements of other sovereign countries.[450] The canonical definition of comity in the United States is found in *Hilton v. Guyot*:

> No law has any effect, of its own force, beyond the limits of the sovereignty from which its authority is derived. The extent to which the law of one nation, as put in force within its territory, whether by executive order, by legislative act, or by judicial decree, shall be allowed to operate within the dominion of another nation, depends upon what our greatest jurists have been content to call "the comity of nations." . . .

---

448 The focus of the analysis can differ, however. An arbitral tribunal assessing whether a denial of justice has occurred will focus on the *particulars* of that case, although systemic problems of politicization or corruption in the judiciary may also be taken into account on the theory that such conditions make the delict more likely. In contrast, some enforcement courts will only (or at least primarily) assess a country's provision of due process at a *systemic* level so as avoid sitting as a (foreign) court of appeal. *See, e.g., Bridgeway Corp. v. Citibank*, 201 F.3d 134 (2d Cir. 2000) and *Yukos Capital S.A.R.L. v. OAO Rosneft*, Amsterdam Court of Appeal, Case No. 200.005.269/01, Decision (Apr. 28, 2009). Irrespective of the legal standard, in practice arbitral tribunals and enforcement courts routinely consider *both* the particular case before them and the context in which it was issued. *See generally* Christina Weston, Comment, *The Enforcement Loophole: Judgment-Recognition Defenses as a Loophole to Corporate Accountability for Conduct Abroad*, 25 Emory Int'l L. Rev. 731, 743–47 (2011).

449 *Soc'y of Lloyd's v. Ashenden*, 233 F.3d 473, 476 (7th Cir. 2000). This approach is not unique to the United States, though the degree to which local predilections of "due process" will hold away tend to differ across jurisdictions. *See Beals v. Saldanha*, [2003] 3 S.C.R. 416, 448–49 (S.C.C.) (Can.) and *Society of Lloyd's v. Meinzer*, (2001), 55 O.R.(3d) 688, 704 (C.A.) (Can.); *Jacobson v. Frachon*, (1927) 138 LT 386 (Eng.).

450 Adrian Briggs, *The Principle of Comity in Private International Law*, 354 Recueil des cours 65, 91 (2012) ("As a starting position, the essential characteristics of the principle of the doctrine of comity should be understood as having two components, namely (1) placing and demonstrating mutual trust and confidence in foreign judicial institutions, not interfering with them, and determining the precise conditions by which this is to be done; and (2) giving full faith and credit to, or respecting the conclusiveness of, the acts of foreign institutions, and working out exactly what this means."); *see, e.g., Morguard Investments Ltd. v. De Savoye*, 3 S.C.R. 1077 at 1095 (Canada 1990) (explaining that comity is "the informing principle of private international law, which has been stated to be the deference and respect due by other states to the actions of a state legitimately taken within its territory").

> "Comity," in the legal sense, is neither a matter of absolute obligation, on the one hand, nor of mere courtesy and good will, upon the other. But it is the recognition which one nation allows within its territory to the legislative, executive or judicial acts of another nation, having due regard both to international duty and convenience, and to the rights of its own citizens or of other persons who are under the protection of its laws.[451]

In this spirit, federal and state enforcement law in the United States is uniform in providing that the foreign procedure need only be "*compatible* with the requirements of due process of law"[452] because "[i]t is a fair guess that no foreign nation has decided to incorporate [U.S. notions of] due process doctrines into its own procedural law."[453] A foreign legal system need not share every jot and tittle of U.S. jurisprudence, but it "must abide by fundamental standards of procedural fairness"[454] and "afford the defendant the basic tenets of due process,"[455] that is, "a concept of fair procedure simple and basic enough to describe the judicial processes of civilized nations, our peers."[456] U.S. Judge Richard Posner has called this "the 'international concept of due process' to distinguish it from the complex concept that has emerged from [domestic] case law," such as "the circumstances under which [U.S.] due process requires an opportunity for a hearing in advance of the deprivation of a substantive right rather than afterward."[457]

Over the past century, U.S. jurisprudence has developed a list of elements of the "international concept of due process." Writing of the federal common law

---

451 *Hilton v. Guyot*, 159 U.S. 113, 163–64 (1895).

452 *Soc'y of Lloyd's v. Ashenden*, 233 F.3d 473, 477 (7th Cir. 2000).

453 *Id.* at 476.

454 *Cunard Steamship Co. v. Salen Reefer Servs. AB*, 773 F.2d 452, 457 (2d Cir. 1985).

455 *Wilson v. Marchington*, 127 F.3d 805, 811 (9th Cir. 1997).

456 *Soc'y of Lloyds v. Ashenden*, 233 F.3d 473, 476–77 (7th Cir. 2000). This has long been the rule for international tribunals, too. *See Decision de la commission, chargee, par Ie Senat de la Ville libre hanseatique de Hambourg, de prononcer dans la cause du capitaine Thomas Melville White, datee de Hambourg du 13 avril 1864, in* PASICRISIE INTERNATIONALE, 1794–1900, HISTOIRE DOCUMENTAIRE DES ARBITRAGES INTERNATIONAUX 48 (Henri La Fontaine ed., 1997).

457 *Soc'y of Lloyd's v. Ashenden*, 233 F.3d 473, 477 (7th Cir. 2000). This differs from the enforceability of a foreign arbitration award under the New York Convention, where the questions whether the award debtor had "notice" and was "[]able to present his case" are decided with reference to the due process rules of the enforcing State—not an "international" concept of due process. *Id.; see also* Robert B. von Mehren, *Enforcement of Foreign Arbitral Awards in the United States*, 771 PLI/COMM 147, 156–57 (1998). The standard under the New York Convention is still minimal and deferential because courts tend to favor the enforcement of arbitral awards. *See Generica Ltd. v. Pharm. Basics, Inc.*, 125 F.3d 1123, 1129–30 (7th Cir. 1997) (holding that "an arbitrator must provide a fundamentally fair hearing," which it then defined as "one that meets the minimal requirements of fairness—adequate notice, a hearing on the evidence, and an impartial decision by the arbitrator").

in 1895, the U.S. Supreme Court held that there must be an "opportunity for [a] full and fair trial abroad before a court of competent jurisdiction"; "regular proceedings" and not ad hoc procedures; "due [notice] or voluntary appearance of the defendant"; "a system of . . . impartial administration of justice between the citizens of its own country and those of other countries"; and assurances against "fraud in procuring the judgment."[458] Other requirements noted in the *Restatement of Foreign Relations Law* include the assurance that "the judiciary was not dominated by the political branches of government or by an opposing litigant"; that the defendant was able to "obtain counsel, to secure documents or attendance of witnesses"; and that the parties "have access to appeal or review."[459] These "are not mere niceties of American jurisprudence" but are instead "the ingredients of 'civilized jurisprudence'" and "basic due process."[460]

These precepts are reflected in the recognition and enforcement laws of the 50 U.S. states, which are largely uniform in their requirements. In particular, a majority of states have enacted laws based on one of two model statutes drafted by the Uniform Law Commission, a nonprofit association that studies and proposes uniform model legislation for U.S. states. In 1962, the Commission proposed the Uniform Foreign Money Judgments Recognition Act, which provides that foreign judgments cannot be enforced if they were rendered "under a system which does not provide impartial tribunals or procedures compatible with the requirements of due process of law," but, based upon the understanding that an enforcement action should not be a form of appeal, it does not provide for review of the provision of due process in the specific case.[461] In 2005, the Commission released a revised model act, the Foreign-Country Money Judgment Recognition Act. The revised Act is not radically different from the original, but adds discretionary defenses to enforcement if (1) "the judgment was rendered in circumstances that raise substantial doubt about the integrity of the rendering court with respect to the judgment" or (2) "the specific proceeding in the foreign court leading to the judgment was not compatible with the requirements of due process of law."[462] Thus, unlike the original Act, the revised version allows enforcing

458 *Hilton v. Guyot*, 159 U.S. 113, 202 (1895).

459 Restatement (Third) Foreign Relations Law of the United States § 482 cmt. b (Am. Law Inst. 1987).

460 *Bank Melli Iran v. Pahlavi*, 58 F.3d 1406, 1413 (9th Cir. 1995) (citing *Hilton v. Guyot*, 159 U.S. 113, 205 (1985)); *see also British Midland Airways Ltd. v. Int'l Travel, Inc.*, 497 F.2d 869, 871 (9th Cir. 1974) ("It has long been the law that unless a foreign country's judgments are the result of outrageous departures from our own notions of 'civilized jurisprudence,' comity should not be refused.").

461 *See* Uniform Foreign Money-Judgments Recognition Act §§ 3–4 (1962).

462 Foreign-Country Money Judgments Recognition Act §§ 4(c)(7)–(8) (2005).

courts to examine the circumstances surrounding the *particular* judgment for which enforcement is sought, as opposed to evaluating only the foreign judicial "system" as a whole.

This is a welcome change as the standard in the original version has little to recommend it. Analyzing the specific judgment seeking to be enforced is not incompatible with according an appropriate level of deference.[463] Although systemic problems in a judiciary make it more probable that there has been a denial of justice in a particular case, this is not always true. Turmoil in a State's judiciary as the result of the political purge of the highest court may have little bearing on the fairness of a first-instance judgment concerning a commercial dispute between two private parties. Conversely, relative tranquility in a State's judicial system does not foreclose the risk of a specific miscarriage of justice wrought by a biased or corrupt magistrate, as *Loewen* reflects. Comity would also militate in favor of a focused inquiry into the judgment at issue, as denying recognition of a single judgment is preferable to making broad and negative pronouncements about the general health of another sovereign's judiciary.

In all events, the standard for enforcement is minimal and frequently satisfied. For example, a federal court in New York recognized a judgment issued in Romania in 1999, despite acknowledging that "the Romanian judicial system [wa]s far from perfect" and that "illegal behavior, particularly corruption by government officials" remained a "serious" problem during Romania's transition from authoritarian rule.[464] Notwithstanding the nascent and troubled state of the Romanian judiciary, the U.S. court determined that "no judicial system operates flawlessly," emphasizing that the Romanian Constitution "sets forth certain due process guarantees" and its judiciary law "establishe[d] the judiciary as an independent branch of government," backed up by "tenure for at least some judges" and "three levels of appellate review."[465] This sufficed for the U.S. court to conclude that the Romanian judicial system as a whole was not "devoid of impartiality or due process."[466]

463 *See* Jeff Todd, *The Rhetoric of Recognition*, 45 McGeorge L. Rev. 209, 222–39 (2013); Thomas Kelly, Note, *An Unwise and Unmanageable Anachronism: Why the Time Has Come to Eliminate Systemic Inadequacy as a Basis for Nonrecognition of Foreign Judgments*, 42 Geo. J. Int'l L. 555, 559 (2011); Virginia A. Fitt, Note, *The Tragedy of Comity: Questioning the American Treatment of Inadequate Foreign Courts*, 50 Va. J. Int'l L. 1021, 1030–32 (2010).

464 *S.C. Chimexim S.A. v. Velco Enters. Ltd.*, 36 F. Supp. 2d 206, 214–15 (S.D.N.Y. 1999).

465 *Id.* at 214.

466 *Id.* at 214–15.

A different result obtained with respect to judgments coming out of Nicaragua. In the 1990s, thousands of Nicaraguans filed suit against American companies in Nicaraguan courts, alleging that they were exposed to pesticides while working on foreign-owned plantations, causing them to become infertile. These lawsuits were aided by Special Law 364, which was enacted *post litem motam* by the National Assembly of Nicaragua specifically to handle these types of claims.[467] Special Law 364 favored the Nicaraguan plaintiffs by covering their costs, imposing minimum damage amounts, creating irrefutable presumptions of causation, providing summary proceedings, abolishing statutes of limitations, and curtailing appellate review.[468] Ultimately, Nicaraguan courts awarded over U.S. $2 billion in damages within the framework of Special Law 364.

When a group of Nicaraguan plaintiffs sought to enforce one of those judgments in Florida against Dole Food Company and the Dow Chemical Company, the judgment debtors objected on numerous grounds, including the lack of due process provided them in Nicaragua. The court in *Osorio v. Dole Food Company* evaluated Special Law 364 to determine whether it was "fundamentally fair":

> [T]he legal regime set up by Special Law 364 and applied in this case does not comport with the "basic fairness" that the "international concept of due process" requires. It does not even come close. "Civilized nations" do not typically require defendants to pay out millions of dollars without proof that they are responsible for the alleged injuries. Basic fairness requires proof of a connection between a plaintiff's injury and a defendant's conduct (i.e., causation) before awarding millions of dollars in damages. Civilized nations do not target and discriminate against a handful of foreign companies and subject them to minimum damages so dramatically out of proportion with damage awards against resident defendants. In summary, civilized nations simply do not subject foreign defendants to the type of discriminatory laws and procedures mandated by Special Law 364, and the Court cannot enforce the judgment because it was rendered under a legal system that did not provide "procedures compatible with the requirements of due process of law."[469]

467 *See Osorio v. Dole Food Co.*, 665 F. Supp. 2d 1307 (S.D. Fla. 2009), *aff'd sub nom. Osorio v. Dow Chem. Co.*, 635 F.3d 1277 (11th Cir. 2011).

468 *Id.* at 1314–15.

469 *Id.* at 1345 (citing, inter alia, *Soc'y of Lloyd's v. Ashenden*, 233 F.3d 473, 477 (7th Cir. 2000)).

Finding that Special Law 364 "target[ed] a handful of United States companies for burdensome and unfair treatment to which domestic Nicaraguan defendants are never subjected," the court held that the foreign judgment issued under it should not be recognized or enforced.[470]

Cases such as *Osorio* are rare, and courts in the United States have sustained against due-process challenges foreign judgments from countries including China,[471] St. Vincent,[472] France,[473] Israel,[474] and Austria.[475] In the related but less demanding context of *forum non conveniens* motions,[476] U.S. courts have suggested that countries such as India and Ukraine would provide adequate forums, notwithstanding complaints about the efficacy and fairness of the judicial systems in those countries.[477]

These results are mirrored when arbitral awards are at issue. Actions in domestic courts to set aside arbitral awards on procedural grounds have likewise met with very limited success.[478] As in the context of foreign judgments, the ready

470 *Id.*

471 *Hubei Gezhouba Sanlian Indus. Co., Ltd. v. Robinson Helicopter Co., Inc.*, No. 06-cv-01798, 2009 U.S. Dist. LEXIS 62782, at *16–*18 (C.D. Cal. July 22, 2009) (finding no evidence "that the PRC court system is one which does not provide impartial tribunals or procedures compatible with the requirements of due process of law," and refusing to consider challenge based on the particular foreign judgment at issue), *aff'd*, 425 F. Appx. 580 (9th Cir. 2011).

472 *Kingsland Holdings Inc. v. Bracco*, Civ. No. 14817, 1996 Del. Ch. LEXIS 28, at *14 (Del. Ch. Ct. Mar. 5, 1996) (noting that "St. Vincent Court was established in the tradition of the English court system").

473 *Pariente v. Scott Meredith Literary Agency, Inc.*, 771 F. Supp. 609, 616–17 (S.D.N.Y. 1991) (holding that court would not engage in "microscopic review" of French evidentiary rules).

474 *Kam-Tech Sys. Ltd. v. Yardeni*, 774 A.2d 644, 650 (N.J. App. Div. 2001) ("Our jurisprudence does not require that the procedures of a foreign court be identical to those used in the courts of the United States.").

475 Kreditverein Der Bank Austria Creditanstalt Fur Niederosterreich Und Burgenland v. Nejezchleba, No. 04-72, 2006 U.S. Dist. LEXIS 47011, at *8 (D. Minn. June 30, 2006) ("Although defendant has offered examples of differences between American law and Austrian law (e.g., differences in discovery procedures, evidentiary rules), there is nothing in the record to indicate that Austria's legal system is not 'fundamentally fair' or that it offends American ideas of 'basic fairness.'").

476 *See* Christopher A. Whytock & Cassandra Burke Robertson, *Forum Non Conveniens and the Enforcement of Foreign Judgments*, 111 Colum. L. Rev. 1444, 1450 (2011) ("Among other differences, the forum non conveniens doctrine's foreign judicial adequacy standard is lenient, plaintiff-focused, and ex ante, whereas the judgment enforcement doctrine's standard is stricter, defendant-focused, and ex post.").

477 *See In re* Union Carbide Corp. Gas Plant Disaster at Bhopal, India in Dec. 1984, 809 F.2d 195, 204–05 (2d Cir. 1987) (India); *In re Arbitration Between Monegasque de Reassurances S.A.M. v. Nak Nafotgaz of Ukraine*, 311 F.3d 488, 499 (2d Cir. 2002) (Ukraine).

478 *See* Kaj Hobér & Nils Eliasson, *Review of Investment Treaty Awards by Municipal Courts*, *in* Arbitration under International Investment Agreements: A Guide to the Key Issues 635–70 (Katia Yannaca-Small ed., 2010) (surveying 10 court cases, none of which overturned a decision based on due process violations).

enforceability of arbitral awards stems from the deferential standard of review. The awards are measured against a procedural baseline originating from two sources, viz., obligations imposed under the New York Convention and under the domestic law of the country of enforcement.[479] The former establishes "limited grounds"[480] for refusing enforcement of an award in cases of improper notice, a party's inability to "present his case," or a violation of the State's "public policy."[481] Domestic laws are generally no more demanding. The laws of jurisdictions favored for arbitration have converged toward a "very deferential approach" to reviewing procedural adequacy,[482] aided by the widespread adoption of the United Nations Commission on International Trade Law (UNCITRAL) Model Law on International Commercial Arbitration. As with foreign judgments, there have been notable commercial arbitrations in which procedural rulings have led to nonrecognition, including the denial of an opportunity for a party to present its claim[483] and the refusal of an arbitrator to admit key evidence.[484]

Under the ICSID Convention, investor-state awards are reviewed by ad hoc annulment committees rather than national courts. ICSID awards may be annulled only where there is "a serious departure from a fundamental rule of procedure."[485] One commentator has characterized this requirement as encompassing

---

479 *See, e.g.*, ICCA's GUIDE TO THE INTERPRETATION OF THE 1958 NEW YORK CONVENTION: A HANDBOOK FOR JUDGES (2011), http://www.arbitration-icca.org/media/1/13890217974630/judges_guide_english_composite_final_jan2014.pdf.

480 Gary Born, *The Principle of Judicial Non-interference in International Arbitral Proceedings*, 30 U. PA. J. INT'L L. 999, 1016–17 (2009).

481 *See* Convention on the Recognition and Enforcement of Foreign Arbitral Awards arts. V(1)(b), V(2)(b), June 10, 1958, 330 U.N.T.S. 3; Born, *supra* note 480, at 1015–20 (describing these two provisions as part of a baseline "international procedural public policy").

482 Born, *supra* note 480, at 1022; *see also id.* at 1020–25 (surveying domestic laws and judicial interpretations that favor deference to tribunals); Panel Discussion, *Annulment and Judicial Review—How "Final" Is an Award?*, *in* 2 INV. TREATY ARB. & INT'L L. 213–14 (Ian A. Laird & Todd Weiler eds., 2009) (observing that "the courts are less intrusive and . . . very conservative in terms of setting aside an arbiter award" and that non-ICSID arbitrations, particularly in the United States and United Kingdom, increasingly provide a degree of finality comparable to that of ICSID).

483 *Iran Aircraft Indus. v. Avco Corp.*, 980 F.2d 141, 146 (2d Cir. 1992) (refusing recognition of arbitral award where arbitrator had previously told the claimant that invoices may be submitted in summary form to prove its claims, only to switch course at the hearing on the merits and deny the claims for failure to submit the original invoices; "by so misleading [claimant], however unwittingly, the Tribunal denied Avco the opportunity to present its claim in a meaningful manner").

484 *Generica Ltd. v. Pharm. Basics, Inc.*, 125 F.3d 1123, 1130 (7th Cir. 1997) ("When the exclusion of relevant evidence actually deprived a party of a fair hearing, therefore, it is appropriate to vacate an arbitral award.").

485 Convention on the Settlement of Investment Disputes Between States and Nationals of Other States art. 52(1)(d), Mar. 18 1965, 4 I.L.M. 524 (1965).

the bare "minimum standards of due process,"[486] and ICSID ad hoc annulment committees interpreting this standard have thus looked for egregious conditions such as an "absence of deliberations"[487] or "manifest excess of powers."[488] Of the 336 ICSID cases concluded as of October 2015,[489] only one award was annulled under Article 52(1)(d) for violation of a "fundamental rule of procedure."[490] In *Fraport AG v. Philippines*, the ICSID ad hoc annulment committee found that the tribunal had relied upon evidence submitted after conclusion of the formal proceedings, thus denying the claimant its fundamental right to be heard.[491]

* * *

Many of the basic precepts of international due process are inseparably bound up with substantive general principles of law. Whereas general principles can correct or supplant a deficient foreign law, international due process provides a metric against which a foreign process may be assessed. Although forgiving, the requirements of international due process are sufficiently stringent to condemn judgments from those judicial systems in which judges cannot consistently be relied upon to apply the rule of law, whether because of corruption or subjugation to the political branches or some other factor external to the case itself. Together, the general principles and international due process coalesce around a minimum standard of treatment expected of all States at all times.

486 GEORGIOS PETROCHILOS, PROCEDURAL LAW IN INTERNATIONAL ARBITRATION 254 (2004).

487 *Klöckner Industrie-Anlagen GmbH v. United Republic of Cameroon*, ICSID Case No. ARB/81/2, Decision on Annulment ¶¶ 82–112 (May 3, 1985), *reprinted* at 2 ICSID Rep. 95 (1994).

488 *Id.* at ¶¶ 57–81, 135–69.

489 See *List of Concluded Cases*, INT'L CENTRE FOR SETTLEMENT OF INVESTMENT DISPUTES (ICSID) (Nov. 9, 2015).

490 CHRISTOPH H. SCHREUER ET AL., THE ICSID CONVENTION: A COMMENTARY 213 (2d ed. 2009). A search of published opinions since *Fraport* revealed no new successful challenges. Requests for annulment are infrequent; as of early 2008, there had been only 23 requests. *See* Panel Discussion, *supra* note 482.

491 *Fraport AG Frankfurt Airport Servs. Worldwide v. Republic of the Philippines*, ICSID Case No. ARB/03/25, Decision on the Application for Annulment, ¶¶ 197–247 (Dec. 23, 2010) (citing UNCITRAL Model Law in interpreting right to be heard).

CHAPTER 2

Modern Applications of the General Principles of Law

[The] comparison of systems is slippery business.

—Justice Ruth Bader Ginsburg[1]

The purpose of this chapter is to define the scope and contour of the general principles of law today by examining how they have been applied in national courts and international tribunals. The very concept of law requires good faith adherence to contractual obligations as they are undertaken and understood by the mutual consent of parties. There is a concomitant principle of good faith in the exercise of rights, such that actions taken under the pretense of law for an illicit purpose can claim no protection from the machinery of justice. The principle of good faith has numerous other filaments. For States, this principle is reflected in the principle of proportionality, which requires a rational relationship between the means and ends of a sovereign act and the protection of an investor's legitimate expectations. Other consequences of the principle of good faith are that parties are bound by their prior actions and precluded from taking advantage of their own wrongdoing. Municipal judicial systems universally acknowledge that proximate causation and attributable fault are essential preconditions to liability, and that those found responsible must eliminate all of the consequences of their wrongful acts. It is now also common ground that shareholders are distinct from the corporations in which they hold stock, which, except in rare circumstances, imposes a limitation on liability. In their various iterations and permutations, these principles are, as Bin Cheng remarked, the "logical consequence[s] flowing from the very conception of law" and the foundation of every legal order.[2]

---

1 *Intel Corp. v. Advanced Micro Devices, Inc.*, 542 U.S. 241, 263 n.15 (2004).

2 Bin Cheng, General Principles of Law as Applied by International Courts and Tribunals 389 (Cambridge Univ. Press 1953).

A. Good Faith in Contractual Relations

Pacta sunt servanda, now an indisputable rule of international law, is but an expression of the principle of good faith which above all signifies the keeping of faith, the pledged faith of nations as well as that of individuals. Without this rule, International law as well as civil law would be a mere mockery.

—Bin Cheng[3]

Good faith is "the fundamental principle of every legal system."[4] Binding individuals, juridical persons, and sovereigns alike, it essentially "converts a moral or ethical precept" into a legal principle—an obligation to act with fairness, reasonableness, and decency in the formation and performance of a contract.[5] It further requires fair dealing in the exercise of rights and prohibits parties from benefiting from their own illegitimate actions. Parties would not enter into contractual relations if there were not a mutual expectation that promises would be honored, that obligations would be performed, and that compensation would be provided in the event of breach. An integral facet of legal certainty, good faith is viewed as "the fundamental principle of the entire system"[6]—the "*Magna Carta* of international commercial law."[7] Despite variances in contractual formalities and canons of construction, good faith is the irreducible predicate for transnational

3 *Id.* at 113 (citation omitted).

4 *Id.* at 105. Good faith has been expressly recognized as a general principle in civil codes around the world. *See, e.g.*, Argentinean Civil Code of 1869 art. 1198 (contracts); Chilean Civil Code art. 1546; Brazilian Civil Code of 2002 art. 113; French Civil Code art. 1134; German Civil Code art. 242; Italian Civil Code art. 1337 (contracts); Mexican Federal Civil Code art. 1796; Swiss Civil Code art. 2.1.

5 *See, e.g.*, Commentary on the UNIDROIT Principles of International Commercial Contracts (PICC) 171 (Stefan Vogenauer & Jan Kleinheisterkamp eds., 2009).

6 Lord Mustill, *The New* Lex Mercatoria: *The First Twenty-Five Years*, 4(2) Arb. Int'l 86, 111 (1988). *See infra* note 16.

7 K.P. Berger, The Creeping Codification of the *Lex Mercatoria* 165 (Kluwer Law International 1999); *see also* Declaration on Principles of International Law concerning Friendly Relations and Co-operation among States in Accordance with the Charter of the United Nations ("Every State has the duty to fulfil in good faith its obligations under international agreements valid under the generally recognized principles and rules of international law."); Restatement (Third) Foreign Relations Law of the United States § 321 cmt. (a) (Am. Law Inst. 1987) (stating that the rule of pacta sunt servanda "lies at the core of the law of international agreements and is perhaps the most important principle of international law"); Michael Joachim Bonell, An International Restatement of Contract Law: The UNIDROIT Principles of International Commercial Contracts 127 *et seq.* (3d ed. 2004); T.O. Elias, New Horizons in International Law (1979).

intercourse. Good faith thus plays an integral role in (1) performing contracts, (2) excusing contracts, and (3) remedying the breach of contracts.

1. Pacta Sunt Servanda: Agreements Must Be Honored

A contract would not be a contract if not binding. The principle pacta sunt servanda is, in H.L.A. Hart's phrase, "the minimum content of Natural Law."[8] In 1969, the principle was codified for States in the Vienna Convention on the Law of Treaties,[9] which has been widely accepted as setting forth rules of customary international law.[10] With roots in both Western and Eastern legal systems, this principle has become a fixture in the international legal order precisely because "no international jurisdiction whatsoever has ever had the least doubt as to [its] existence."[11] "All civilizations, from the earliest, have recognized the rule, and it has been handed down throughout the centuries. . . . The oldest religions of Asia (Confucianism, Buddhism, Hinduism, and later Islam) paid special attention to the obligation of complying with agreements entered into."[12] In Sharia law, the principle of pacta sunt servanda is one of divine origin,[13] and is elevated to the

---

8 H.L.A. HART, THE CONCEPT OF LAW 193 (Oxford 2d ed. 1994).

9 Vienna Convention on the Law of Treaties art. 26, *opened for signature* May 23, 1969, 1155 U.N.T.S. 331 (entered into force Jan. 27, 1980) ("Every treaty in force is binding upon the parties to it and must be performed by them in good faith.").

10 *See, e.g., Arbitration regarding the Iron Rhine Railway* (*Belg. v. Neth.*), PCA, Award, 23 (May 24, 2005); *Dispute regarding Navigational and Related Rights (Costa Rica v. Nicar.)*, Judgment, 2009 I.C.J. 213, ¶ 47 (July 13); *Sovereignty over Pulau Ligitan and Pulau Sipadan (Indon. v. Malay)*, Judgment, 2002 I.C.J. 625, ¶¶ 37–38 (Dec. 17); *Kasikili/Sedudu Island (Bots. v. Namib.)*, Judgment, 1999 I.C.J. 1045, ¶ 18 (Dec. 13) (II); *Territorial Dispute (Libyan Arab Jamahiriya/Chad)*, Judgment, 1994 I.C.J. 7, ¶ 41 (Feb. 3); *Interpretation of the Agreement of 25 March 1951 between the WHO and Egypt*, Advisory Opinion, 1980 I.C.J. 73, ¶¶ 41–43 (Dec. 20) (good faith); *Legality of the Threat or Use of Nuclear Weapons*, Advisory Opinion, 1996 I.C.J. 226, ¶ 99 (July 8) (good faith).

11 *Texaco Overseas Petroleum Co. (TOPCO) v. Gov't of the Libyan Arab Republic*, Award (Jan. 19, 1974), 53 INT'L L. REP. 389, 462 (1979); *see also Inceysa Vallisoletana S.L. v. Republic of El Salvador*, ICSID Case No. ARB/03/26, Award, ¶¶ 223–33 (Aug. 2, 2006) ("[T]he maxim *Pacta Sunt Servanda* [is] unanimously accepted in legal systems"); *Texaco Overseas Petroleum Co. v. Gov't of the Libyan Arab Republic (TOPCO)*, 17 I.L.M. 1, 18–19 (1978) ("A contract must be performed in accordance with its contents and in compliance with the requirements of good faith."; "Surah 5 of the Koran . . . begins with the verse 'O ye believers, perform your contracts!'"); *Pacta Sunt Servanda, in* 7 ENCYCLOPEDIA OF PUBLIC INTERNATIONAL LAW 364 (Rudolf Bernhardt ed., 1984).

12 *Pacta Sunt Servanda*, *supra* note 11, at 364–65.

13 Anowar Zahid & Rohimi Shapiee, *Pacta Sunt Servanda: Islamic Perception*, 3 J. E. ASIA & INT'L L. 375, 384 (2010); *see also* Joseph Schacht, *Islamic Law in Contemporary States*, 8 AM. J. COMP. L. 133, 139 (1959) ("The rule *pacta sunt servanda* is one of the fundamental principles of Islamic law."); SARA MCLAUGHLIN & EMILIA JUSTYNA POWELL, DOMESTIC LAW GOES GLOBAL: LEGAL TRADITIONS AND INTERNATIONAL COURTS (2013); MARK W. JANIS & CAROLYN EVANS, RELIGION AND INTERNATIONAL LAW 98 (1999).

level of religious duty for believers of the Islamic faith.[14] Whatever the derivation, it would run contrary to simple logic if pacta were not servanda.[15]

This is all easy enough; *contracts should be respected and fulfilled.*[16] As more recent cases have demonstrated, the nature of the contract does not affect application of this foundational principle. Whether an agreement between private parties,[17] a contract undertaken by a State in its proprietary capacity,[18] or sovereign consent to arbitrate a dispute,[19] "pacta sunt servanda" means that agreements must

14 Janis & Evans, *supra* note 13; *see also Saudi Arabia v. Arabian American Oil Co.*, 27 Int'l L. Rep. 117, 163–64 (1963) ("All . . . types [of contracts] are viewed by Moslem jurists as agreements or pacts which must be observed, since God is a witness to any contract entered into by individuals or by collectivities; under Moslem law, any valid contract is obligatory, in accordance with the principles of Islam and the Law of God, as expressed in the Koran: 'Be faithful to your pledge to God, when you enter into a pact.' ").

15 Sir Gerald Fitzmaurice, *Some Problems regarding the Formal Sources of International Law*, *in* Symbolae Verzijl 153–76 (1958).

16 *See, e.g.*, *General Dynamics Corp. v. Islamic Republic of Iran*, 5 Iran-U.S. Cl. Trib. Rep. 386, 398 (1984) (obligation under "general principles of law" to perform contractual duties with due diligence); *Texaco Overseas Petroleum Co. (TOPCO) v. Gov't of the Libyan Arab Republic*, 1 I.L.M. 19 (1978) ("the maxim *pacta sunt servanda* is a general principle of law 'constituting' an essential foundation of international law"); *Sapphire Int'l Petroleums Ltd. v. Nat'l Iranian Oil Co.*, Award, 35 Int'l L. Rep. 136, 181 (1963) ("it is a fundamental principle of law, which is constantly being proclaimed by international courts, that contractual undertakings must be respected"); *Libyan American Oil Co. (LIAMCO) v. Gov't of the Libyan Arab Republic*, Award (Apr. 12, 1977), 6 Y.B. Comm. Arb. 89, 100 (1981) ("the principle of the sanctity of contracts . . . has always constituted an integral part of most legal systems. These include those systems that are based on Roman law, the Napoleonic Code (e.g., Article 1134) and other European civil codes, as well as Anglo-Saxon Common Law and Islamic Jurisprudence (*Shari'a*)"); *Bundesgerichtshof* (BGH), Oct. 14, 1992, 46 Neue Juristische Wochenschrift 259, 263 (Ger.) ("the notion of good faith is a supranational legal principle inherent in all legal systems"); *Nuclear Tests (Austl. v. Fr.)*, Judgment, 1974 I.C.J. 253, 267–68 (Dec. 20) ("One of the basic principles governing the creation and performance of legal obligations, whatever their source, is the principle of good faith."); *see also* UNIDROIT Principles of International Commercial Contracts art. 1.7 (2004); U.N. Convention on Contracts for the International Sale of Goods art. 7(1) (2010).

17 *See, e.g.*, *Zapata Hermanos Sucesores v. Hearthside Baking Co.*, 313 F.3d 385, 389 (7th Cir. 2002) (Posner, J.); *Bermudan company v. Spanish company*, ICC Case No. 5485, Award (1987), 14 Y.B. Comm. Arb. 156 (1989); *French contractor v. Yugoslav subcontractor*, ICC Case No. 3540, Award (1980), 7 Y.B. Comm. Arb. 124 (1982); *Two Israeli companies v. Government of an African State*, ICC Case No. 2321, Award (1974), 1 Y.B. Comm. Arb. 133 (1976); *Amco Asia Corp. et al. v. Republic of Indonesia*, ICSID Case No. ARB/81/1, Award on the Merits (Nov. 21, 1984), *reprinted in* 24 I.L.M. 1022 (1985); Sapphire Int'l Petroleums Ltd. v. Nat'l Iranian Oil Co., Award, 35 Int'l L. Rep. 136 (1963).

18 *Amco Asia Corp. et al. v. Republic of Indonesia*, ICSID Case No. ARB/81/l, Decision on Jurisdiction (Sept. 25, 1983), ICSID Review-Foreign Investment Law Journal, 166–90 (1998); *Libyan American Oil Co. (LIAMCO) v. Gov't of the Libyan Arab Republic*, Award (Apr. 12, 1977), 6 Y.B. Comm. Arb. 89, 103 (1981).

19 *Desert Line Projects LLC v. Republic of Yemen*, ICSID ARB/05/17, Award, ¶¶ 205–06 (Feb. 6, 2008). Although this book does not focus on treaty obligations in great detail, " '[t]reaties of every kind . . . are as obligatory upon nations as private contracts are binding upon individuals . . . and to be kept with

be "fully respected as definitely binding on both parties" by virtue of the "basic rules . . . shared by all . . . systems of law."[20]

Pacta sunt servanda also means that *obligations should be carried out according to the good faith and mutual intention of the parties*—that is to say, in Cheng's words, "carrying out the substance of [the parties'] mutual understanding honestly and loyally."[21] Contractual performance is dictated by contractual interpretation, and the dual inquiries into what a contract requires and how it must be fulfilled often collapse into one. The principle of good faith stands with, and informs the application of, other canons of contract construction.[22] It becomes the "major interpretative principle that is applied ancillary to [the] principal obligation" of pacta sunt servanda.[23] In this sense, the principle of good faith is as applicable to the judge or arbitrator charged with interpreting a contract as it is to the parties that executed it.

To interpret an agreement in good faith is, inter alia, to presume the contracting parties to have acted honestly; to have made real, not illusory, promises; to have intended nothing that would be unreasonable, absurd, contradictory,

---

the most scrupulous good faith.'" *Van Bokkelen v. Haiti (U.S. v. Haiti)* (1886), U.S. Foreign Relations 1034–35. "A treaty is a solemn compact between nations. It possesses in ordinary the same essential qualities as a contract between individuals, enhanced by the weightier quality of the parties and by the greater magnitude of the subject-matter." *Heirs of Jean Maninet (France v. Venezuela)*, XX R.I.A.A. 55, 78 (1905). "It cannot be that good faith is less obligatory upon nations than upon individuals in carrying out agreements." *Metzger & Co. (U.S. v. Haiti)* 1901 U.S.F.R. 262, 271.

20 *Desert Line Projects LLC v. Republic of Yemen*, ICSID ARB/05/17, Award, ¶¶ 205–06 (Feb. 6, 2008).

21 CHENG, *supra* note 2, at 114–15.

22 *See, e.g.*, W. LAURENCE CRAIG, WILLIAM W. PARK & JAN PAULSSON, INTERNATIONAL CHAMBER OF COMMERCE ARBITRATION § 35.02 (Oceana TM 3d ed. 2000) (citing sources); Mustill, *supra* note 6, at 110 ("A contract should be performed in good faith"); U.N. Convention on Contracts for the International Sale of Goods arts. 7(1), 9; UNIDROIT Principles of International Commercial Contracts arts. 1.7 & 1.9 (2010); *Ambiente Ufficio S.P.A. et al. v. Argentine Republic*, ICSID Case No. ARB/08/9, Decision on Jurisdiction and Admissibility, Dissenting Opinion of Santiago Torres Bernárdez, ¶ 245 (May 2, 2013), citing Report of the United Nations Conference of the Law of Treaties, First and second sessions, Vienna, March 26–May 24, 1968 and April 9–May 22, 1969, Documents of the Conference UN publication, Sales No. E.70.V.5 at 38, ¶ 5 ("international courts and tribunals are expected to bear constantly in mind, as noted by the International Law Commission, that 'the interpretation of treaties in good faith and according to the law is essential if the *pacta sunt servanda* rule is to have any real meaning'").

23 *Int'l Thunderbird Gaming Corp. v. United Mexican States*, UNCITRAL, Separate Opinion of Thomas Wälde, ¶ 25 (Dec. 1, 2005); *see also Nuclear Tests (Austl. v. Fr.)*, Judgment, 1974 I.C.J. 253, 267 (Dec. 20) ("the very rule of *pacta sunt servanda* in the law of treaties is based on good faith"); ICC Award No. 5953, 117 J. DROIT INT'L (CLUNET) 1056, 1060 (1990); *see also* ICC Case No. 3131, Award (1979), REV. ARB. 525, 531 (1983); 9 Y.B. COMM. ARB. 109 (1984); *Norsolor SA (Fr.) v. Pabalk Ticaret Sirketi SA (Turk.)*, T.G.I. Paris (Mar. 4, 1981), REV. ARB. 379, 465 (1983).

or impossible; and to have used terms as a reasonable person would ordinarily understand them under the circumstances (absent a definition giving those terms a special meaning).[24] These specific manifestations of the principle of good faith have been codified in the Vienna Convention on the Law of Treaties.[25] Notwithstanding questions about the proper role, and concerns over the indeterminacy, of canons of interpretation,[26] these precepts have been so well tread at the international level as to comprise general principles of law.[27] It has been said that the articles for contract interpretation set forth in the International Institute for the Unification of Private Law (UNIDROIT) Principles of International Commercial Contracts "can be regarded as 'general principles of law'" because, "despite the existing differences between the national approaches to contractual interpretation," the drafters "achieved their aim of extracting a balanced 'set of principles of rules which are universally adopted and recognised' from the heremeneutic criteria common to domestic systems and uniform laws."[28] The principles of pacta sunt servanda and good faith "merge ... into one" when it comes to interpreting and performing a contractual obligation, thus forming the principle of "*pacta sunt servanda bona fide*."[29]

The most elementary interpretive canon emanating from this general principle is that *the common intention of the parties at the time of contracting should dictate the obligations of a contract.* Because contracts are borne of consent of both sides, the test appropriately focuses on those points of mutual agreement. It is

24 Cheng, *supra* note 2, at 106–08.

25 Vienna Convention on the Law of Treaties, *opened for signature* May 23, 1969, 1155 U.N.T.S. 331 (entered into force Jan. 27, 1980). Article 31 provides: "A treaty shall be interpreted in good faith in accordance with the ordinary meaning to be given to the terms of the treaty in their context and in the light of its object and purpose.... A special meaning shall be given to a term if it is established that the parties so intended." Article 32 further provides: "Recourse may be had to supplementary means of interpretation ... to determine the meaning when the interpretation according to article 31 ... [l]eaves the meaning ambiguous or obscure ... or ... leads to a result which is manifestly absurd or unreasonable."

26 *See Commentary on Draft Articles*, 2 Y.B. Int'l L. Comm'n 218, ¶ 1 (1966); Karl N. Llewellyn, The Common Law Tradition: Deciding Appeals 521–35 (Little Brown and Co. 1960).

27 *See, e.g., Arbitration regarding the Iron Rhine Railway (Belg. v. Neth.)*, PCA, Award, ¶ 45 (May 24, 2005) (espousing the nature of Article 31 as a rule of customary international law). *See generally* Richard K. Gardiner, Treaty Interpretation 36–38 (2008) (espousing Article 31 of the VCLT as a set of "general principles" rather than hard and fast "rules"); *see also* Appellate Body Report, *United States—Import Prohibition of Certain Shrimp and Shrimp Products*, ¶ 158, WT/DS58/AB/R (Oct. 12, 1998) (*adopted* Nov. 6, 1998) (seeking "interpretative guidance" on an international obligation by reference to certain general principles of law codified in the Vienna Convention).

28 *See, e.g.*, Commentary on the UNIDROIT Principles of International Commercial Contracts (PICC) 495 (Stefan Vogenauer & Jan Kleinheisterkamp eds., 2009).

29 ICC Award 5953, 117 J. Droit Int'l (Clunet) 1056, 1061 (1990).

not unusual for a party, *post litem motam*, to fasten upon its own understanding or expectation during negotiations, but it is the shared intent of both parties, not the unilateral aspirations of one, that creates a binding contract. Although the method for determining the parties' common intent varies, domestic systems are unanimous that this is the ultimate inquiry. For example, the Honduran Civil Code states that if "the terms of a contract are clear and leave no doubt as to the contracting parties' intention, then its clauses will be interpreted according to their literal meaning. [But] [i]f the wording seems contrary to the parties' clear intent, then intent will prevail over wording."[30] The Civil Codes of Chile,[31] Paraguay,[32] and Ecuador[33] contain similar provisions, and the same concept is articulated in Swiss jurisprudence.[34] In common law jurisdictions, courts are also advised to consider the parties' intentions in contract interpretation. As one Canadian court has stated, "[t]he goal in interpreting an agreement is to discover, objectively, the parties' intention at the time the contract was made."[35] Courts in the United States have similarly noted the importance of intent in contract interpretation.[36]

The common intent of the parties can be discerned from the text and structure of the contract, the context in which it was signed, and the history of the negotiations. The principle of good faith informs and infuses all of these heuristics. This is by design: because it is neither practical nor efficient for parties to anticipate and address all conceivable disputes that might arise in the future, the principle of good faith ensures that the contract will be interpreted so as to reflect the mutuality, probity, and loyalty with which the agreement was originally concluded. It is trite to observe that contracts "ought to be interpreted conformably with the real mutual intention . . . between parties acting loyally and with reason,"[37]

---

30 Honduran Civil Code art. 1576.

31 Chilean Civil Code art. 1560.

32 Paraguayan Civil Code art. 708.

33 Ecuadorian Civil Code art. 1576.

34 *See, e.g., Judgment of 5 December 2008*, ¶ 7.3.1, 27 ASA BULL. 762, 769–70 (Swiss Federal Supreme Court) (2009) (reiterating that contracts should be interpreted pursuant to the real intent of the parties and not the literal meaning of the words, which can hide the true nature of the contract).

35 *Gilchrist v. Western Star Trucks Inc.* (2000), 73 B.C.L.R. (3d) 102 (C.A.), ¶ 17.

36 *See, e.g., Affordable Cmtys. of Mo. v. Fannie Mae*, 714 F.3d 1069, 1075 (8th Cir. 2013) ("The cardinal rule of contract interpretation is to ascertain the intention of the parties and to give effect to that intention.").

37 CHENG, *supra* note 2, at 107; *see also Mastrobuono v. Shearson Lehman Hutton, Inc.*, 514 U.S. 52, 63 (1995) (establishing that the courts are bound to interpret contracts in accordance with the expressed intentions of the parties—even if the effect of those intentions is to limit arbitration).

thereby "taking into account the consequences . . . [that] the parties . . . reasonably and legitimately envisaged."[38]

The weighing and harmonization of the text, context, and history of a contract is necessarily a casuistic exercise. The principle of good faith calls for adherence to the unambiguous language to which the parties assented. "When a deed is worded in clear and precise terms, when its meaning is evident and leads to no absurd conclusion, there can be no reason for refusing to admit the meaning which such deed naturally presents."[39] Clear text cannot be "enlarged by reading into it stipulations which are said to result from the proclaimed intentions of the authors of the [agreement], but for which no provision is made in the text itself."[40] Parties demonstrate their good faith by hewing to the text of a written obligation: where the text is clear and reflective of the parties' intent, background principles of construction cannot impose additional obligations not otherwise undertaken.[41] English law is particularly emphatic on this point.[42]

---

38 *Inceysa Vallisoletana S.L. v. Republic of El Salvador*, ICSID Case No. ARB/03/26, Award, ¶ 177 (Aug. 2, 2006) (quoting *Amco Asia Corp. et al. v. Republic of Indonesia*, ICSID Case No. ARB/81/1, Decision on Jurisdiction, ¶ 14 (Sept. 25, 1983)).

39 *Asian Agric. Prods. Ltd. v. Republic of Sri Lanka*, ICSID Case No. ARB/87/3, Award, ¶ 40 (June 27, 1990), 6 ICSID Rev. 526 (1991).

40 Cheng, *supra* note 2, at 116 (quoting the *Polish War Vessels in Danzig*, Advisory Opinion, 1931 P.C.I.J. (Ser. A/B) No. 43, at 144 (Dec. 11)).

41 Gardiner, *supra* note 27, at 156; *Regina v. Immigration Officer at Prague Airport ex parte European Roma Rights Centre*, [2004] UKHL 55, ¶ 19 (Dec. 9) ("there is no want of good faith if a state interprets a treaty as meaning what it says and declines to do anything significantly greater than or different from what it agreed to do"); *accord Keith Cox v. Canada*, Communication No. 539/1993, U.N. Doc. CCPR/C/52/D/539/19930, Concurring Opinion of Messrs. Kurt Herndl and Waleed Sadi (Oct. 31, 1994), *reprinted in* Office of the United Nations High Commissioner for Human Rights, 5 International Covenant on Civil and Political Rights: Selected Decisions of the Human Rights Committee under the Option Protocol 177–79 (2005).

42 The English position stems not so much from a rejection of the intrinsic value of good faith in commercial dealings, but from the prioritization of certainty, predictability, and alacrity in resolving commercial disputes. As articulated by Lord Millett: "Businessmen need speed and certainty; these do not permit detailed and leisurely examination of the parties' conduct. Commerce needs the kind of bright lines which the common law provides and which equity abhors." P.J. Millett, *Equity's Place in the Law of Commerce*, 114 L.Q. Rev. 214, 214 (1998). English law also places considerable emphasis upon the freedom of a party to pursue its own interests, which has been deemed to allow all but misrepresentations in contract negotiations. *See, e.g., Walford v. Miles*, [1992] 2 A.C. 128 (H.L.) 138. There are nonetheless a "range of situation-specific norms in English law that often lead to a very similar outcome as the application of a general good faith norm." Margarita N. Michael, *The "Good Faith" Movement: Swimming against the Tide*, *in* Eur. Middle E. & Afr. Arb. Rev. (2015). Parliament, for instance, included "good faith" in Section 61(3) of the Sale of Goods Act of 1979, and the Secretary of State added it to Regulation 5(1) of the Unfair Terms in Consumer Contracts Regulations of 1999. More recently, the English High Court held that good faith could be implied based upon the presumed intent of the parties. *See Yam Seng Pte Ltd. v. Int'l Trade Corp. Ltd.*, ¶ 114 [2013] EWHC 111 (Q.B.). As Lord Steyn observed, respect

The principle of good faith can also inform the interpretation of ambiguous terms and even temper a strictly textual analysis so as to provide a construction (and hence performance) that is not purely a "semantic exercise" dictated by "the literal meaning of a term."[43] Such use of the doctrine is, however, not without controversy and must be handled with care. Because it may be presumed that the parties carefully negotiated the terms of their contract, it is only when the negotiating history indicates "without any doubt" the parties' common aspirations that such extra-textual evidence may be considered.[44] In narrow circumstances, the principle of good faith permits an interpretation that might "run[] counter to the literal terms of an isolated phrase."[45]

For instance, where two private parties agree that disputes shall be submitted to judicial settlement only if they "cannot be settled by negotiation," "the condition in question does not mean ... that resort to the Court is precluded so long as the alleged wrongdoer may profess a willingness to negotiate" in perpetuity.[46] Although the alleged wrongdoer's dilatory tactics in this example might be condemned as an abuse of right (as discussed in chapter 2.B), the same result may be reached by simply interpreting the contract's terms in accordance with the "ordinary conceptions of fair dealing."[47] The parties, at the formation of the

---

for "the reasonable expectations of parties" under English law to some extent captures the concept of good faith in the sense that honest parties reasonably expect each other to faithfully perform their written promises, such that "[t]here is not a world of difference between the objective requirement of good faith and the reasonable expectations of the parties." Lord Steyn, *Contract Law: Fulfilling the Reasonable Expectations of Honest Men*, 113 L.Q. Rev. 433, 439 (1997). It thus may be that, some 250 years on, the seeds of good faith planted by Lord Mansfield are beginning to bear fruit in England. *See Carter v. Boehm*, (1766) 3 Burr 1905.

43 *Compañía de Aguas del Aconquija, S.A. and Vivendi (formerly Compagnie Générale des Eaux) v. Argentine Republic*, ICSID Case No. ARB/97/3, Award, ¶ 7.4.3 (Aug. 20, 2007); *Methanex Corp. v. United States of America*, NAFTA, Final Award, ¶ 16 (Aug. 3, 2005); *see also Judgment of 27 January 2010*, ¶ 2.1, 29 ASA Bull. 396, 401–02 (Swiss Federal Supreme Court) (2011) (finding that when the real intent of the parties cannot be ascertained, the arbitration agreement must be construed objectively so as to establish the meaning that the parties must have intended to attribute to their declarations of will, in good faith and taking into account the overall circumstances of the case); Gardiner, *supra* note 27, at 151.

44 *Inceysa Vallisoletana S.L. v. Republic of El Salvador*, ICSID Case No. ARB/03/26, Award, ¶ 195 (Aug. 2, 2006).

45 Cheng, *supra* note 2, at 116 (quoting *Paula Mendel and others (U.S) v. Germany, Germ.-U.S. Cls. Comm'n, Decision (Aug. 13, 1926)*, 7 R.I.A.A. 372; *see also id.* at 114 (citing *Boundaries in the Island of Timor (Neth. v. Port.)*, PCA, 1 H.C.R. 354, 365 (1914)).

46 Cheng, *supra* note 2, at 117 (quoting the *Mavrommatis Palestine Concessions Case (Greece v. U.K.)*, Objection to the Jurisdiction of the Court, Judgment, 1924 P.C.I.J. (Ser. A) No. 2, at 62 (Aug. 30) (dissenting opinion of Judge John Moore)).

47 Cheng, *supra* note 2, at 118.

contract, evidently intended to allow for judicial recourse, and an interpretation of the exhaustion requirement that would prevent such recourse is antithetical to that intent.[48] A similar construction is found in the *Inceysa* tribunal's interpretation of the term "investment" under the Spain-El Salvador BIT.[49] The term was not qualified by the phrase "in accordance with the law," but this was deemed implicit in the signatories' bona fide expectation that illicit investments would not be protected by the treaty.[50]

The principle of good faith can also, in some instances, give rise to additional obligations that flow from the principal obligation of the contract. New York law, for instance, holds that "neither party . . . shall do anything which has the effect of destroying or injuring the rights of the other party to receive the fruits of the contract."[51] Although the covenant of good faith and fair dealing cannot imply obligations "inconsistent with other terms of the contractual relationship,"[52] it does encompass "any promises which a reasonable person in the position of the promisee would be justified in understanding were included."[53] International tribunals have treated the same principle as a general one.[54] Were such rudimentary elements not implied, parties would face the tedious and time-consuming task of trying to anticipate and itemize all of the ways in which one of them might try to denigrate or destroy the contract in the future.

At times, these canons of contract construction can conflict and lead to diametrically opposed results—"one of which does and the other does not enable the [agreement] to have appropriate effects."[55] According to virtually every

---

48 *See Interpretation of Peace Treaties between Bulgaria, Hungary and Romania (Second Phase)*, Advisory Opinion, 1950 I.C.J. 221, 244 (July 18) (dissenting opinion of Judge Read) (noting that the principle against absurd interpretation of contractual terms "has been regarded as authoritative by the foreign offices of the world and by international lawyers and tribunals").

49 *See Inceysa Vallisoletana S.L. v. Republic of El Salvador*, ICSID Case No. ARB/03/26, Award, ¶¶ 190–207 (Aug. 2, 2006).

50 *Id.*

51 *See, e.g., M/A-COM Sec. Corp. v. Galesi*, 904 F.2d 134, 136 (2d Cir. 1990); *511 W. 232nd Owners Corp. v. Jennifer Realty Co.*, 98 N.Y.2d 144, 153 (Ct. App. 2002); *Van Valkenburgh, Nooger & Neville v. Hayden Publ. Co.*, 30 N.Y.2d 34, 45 (Ct. App. 1972).

52 *Murphy v. Am. Home Prods. Corp.*, 58 N.Y.2d 293, 304 (Ct. App. 1983).

53 *Rowe v. Great Atl. & Pac. Tea Co.*, 46 N.Y.2d 62, 69 (Ct. App. 1978).

54 *See, e.g.*, ICC Award 2291 (1975), 103 J. Droit Int'l (Clunet) 989, 990 (1976); ICC Award 9593, 10(2) ICC Bull. 107 (1999); ICC Case No. 2521, Award, 103 J. Droit Int'l (Clunet) 997 (1976); ICC Case No. 6294, Award, 118 J. Droit Int'l (Clunet) 1050 (1991); ICC Case No. 4629, Final Award (1989), 18 Y.B. Comm. Arb. 11 (1993).

55 *Commentary on Draft Articles*, 2 Y.B. Int'l L. Comm'n 219, ¶ 6 (1966).

international tribunal posed with this choice, the former should be adopted.[56] This is a manifestation of *ut res magis valeat quam pereat.*[57] Cheng understood this general principle to mean that *"[n]o construction shall be admitted which renders a [contract] null and illusive, nor which leaves it in the discretion of the party promising to fulfill or not his promise."*[58] This notion is elemental, and it governs private contracts[59] and treaties alike.[60]

An offshoot of this principle is to interpret an agreement as a whole to achieve its purpose and aim, which ensures that individual words or phrases within the agreement are given meaning, force, and effect (known as the principle of effectiveness).[61] It was thus held that a treaty purporting to fix "the frontiers" of a State by referencing international instruments that defined its international boundaries could not be read to exclude one of those boundaries.[62] "Any other construction would be contrary to the actual terms of [the treaty] and would render completely ineffective the reference to one or other of those instruments."[63] The entirety of an agreement—the words used by the parties and the agreement's

---

56 *See generally* GARDINER, *supra* note 27, at 160–61 (citing, *e.g.*, *Territorial Dispute (Libyan Arab Jamahiriya/Chad)*, Judgment, 1994 I.C.J. 6 (Feb. 3); Appellate Body Report, *Japan—Taxes on Alcoholic Beverages*, AB-1996-2, WT/DS8/AB/R, WT/DS10/AB/R & WT/DS11/AB/R (Oct. 4, 1996); Appellate Body Report, *Korea—Definitive Safeguard Measure on Imports of Certain Dairy Products*, ¶¶ 80–81, AB-1999-8, WT/DS98/AB/R (Dec. 14, 1999)); *Distributor v. Manufacturer*, ICC Case No. 7920, Partial Award (1993), *in* 23 Y.B COMM. ARB. 80–85 (Albert Jan van den Berg ed., Kluwer Law International 1998); *Eli Lilly do Brasil, Ltda v. Fed. Express Co.*, 502 F.3d 78, 81–82 (2d Cir. 2007) (applying "the well-settled 'presumption in favor of applying that law tending toward the validation of the alleged contract").

57 *See, e.g.*, *Asian Agric. Prods. Ltd. v. Republic of Sri Lanka*, ICSID Case No. ARB/87/3, Award (June 27, 1990), 6 ICSID REV. 526 (1991) ("nothing is better settled, as a canon of interpretation in all systems of law, than that a clause must be interpreted to give it meaning rather than so as to deprive it of meaning").

58 CHENG, *supra* note 2, at 106; Mustill, *supra* note 6, at 112. ICC Arbitrators have recognized this principle as being a "universally acknowledged principle of interpretation." ICC Case 1434/1975, ICC Award 263, at 267; ICC Cases 3460/1980, ICC Award 425; *see also* RESTATEMENT (SECOND) OF THE LAW OF CONTRACTS § 203 (Am. Law Inst. 1981) ("An interpretation which gives a reasonable, lawful, and effective meaning to all the terms is preferred to an interpretation which leaves a part unreasonable, unlawful, or of no effect.").

59 *See, e.g.*, ICC Case No. 1434, Award (1975), 102 J. DROIT INT'L (CLUNET) 982 (1976); ICC Case No. 3380, Award (1980), 7 Y.B. COMM. ARB. 116 (1982); ICC Case No. 8331, Award (1996), 125 J. DROIT INT'L (CLUNET) 1041 (1998).

60 GARDINER, *supra* note 27, at 148; *see, e.g.*, *Asian Agric. Prods. Ltd. v. Republic of Sri Lanka*, ICSID Case No. ARB/87/3, Award, ¶ 40(E) (June 27, 1990), 6 ICSID REV. 526 (1991).

61 GARDINER, *supra* note 27, at 148, 200–01 (citing *Territorial Dispute (Libyan Arab Jamahiriya/Chad)*, Judgment, 1994 I.C.J. 6 (Feb. 3)).

62 *See Territorial Dispute (Libyan Arab Jamahiriya/Chad)*, Judgment, 1994 I.C.J. 6, ¶¶ 43–47 (Feb. 3).

63 *Id.* ¶ 47.

overall purpose—must be fairly considered and weighed to give the contract its proper scope.[64]

Consistent with this principle and the overriding obligation of pacta sunt servanda, a party cannot unilaterally modify or terminate an agreement. Recognized in the *Chilean-Peruvian Accounts* case of 1875 and the *Oscar Chinn* case of 1934,[65] this principle has more recently been confirmed by the UNIDROIT Principles of International Commercial Contracts: "A contract . . . can only be modified or terminated in accordance with its terms or by agreement or as otherwise provided in these Principles."[66] Less a principle unto itself, this is a manifestation of the principle that contracts are to be fulfilled, enforced, and given effect.

Another interpretive principle recognized by Cheng was that of *contra proferentem in the interpretation of agreements, which precludes the party who proposed a provision from not honoring it on the ground that it is ambiguous*[67] *and which interprets ambiguous phrases against their author.*[68] This, too, derives from the general principle of good faith.[69] Applied against both sovereign and private

64 *See, e.g., CBA Int'l Dev. Corp. v. Islamic Republic of Iran*, 5 Iran-U.S. Cl. Trib. Rep. 177, 180–81 (1984) (holding that, as a general principle of law, contracts are to be interpreted so as to give meaning to their texts taken as a whole); *Compañía de Aguas del Aconquija, S.A. and Vivendi (formerly Compagnie Générale des Eaux) v. Argentine Republic*, ICSID Case No. ARB/97/3, Award, ¶ 7.4.3 (Aug. 20, 2007) (a "term is not to be examined in isolation or in abstracto, but in the context of the treaty and in the light of its object and purpose"); *Methanex Corp. v. United States of America*, NAFTA, Final Award, ¶ 16 (Aug. 3, 2005) (same).

65 Cheng, *supra* note 2, at 113.

66 UNIDROIT Principles of International Commercial Contracts art. 1.3 (2004); *see also* Arbitral Award, Arbitration Court of the Lausanne Chamber of Commerce and Industry (Jan. 25, 2002).

67 *See, e.g., First Travel Corp. v. Islamic Republic of Iran*, Case No. 34 (206-34-1), Award (Dec. 3, 1985), 12 Y.B. Comm. Arb. 257 (1987) (deciding that in face of ambiguity, it would apply the rule of contra proferentem and interpret the agreement against the drafter's interest so as to protect the party who did not draft the agreement).

68 *See, e.g., Telestat Canada v. Juch-Tech, Inc.*, Superior Court of Justice of Ontario (OSCJ), Case No. 11-29505, ¶¶ 57–65 (May 3, 2012); ICC Award No. 7110, 10(2) ICC Bull. 39, at 44 (1999) (determining that "it is a general principle of interpretation widely accepted by national legal systems and by the practice of international arbitral tribunals, including ICC arbitral tribunals, that in case of doubt or ambiguity, contractual provisions, terms or clauses should be interpreted against the drafting party"); *Cysteine Case*, China CIETAC Arbitration Proceeding, Award (Jan. 7, 2000); ICC Award No. 3460, J. Droit Int'l (Clunet) 939 (1981); UNIDROIT Principles of International Commercial Contracts art. 4.6 (2010); UNIDROIT at 528.

69 *See* UNIDROIT Principles of International Commercial Contracts art. 4.6 (2010). *See also* Commentary on the UNIDROIT Principles of International Commercial Contracts (PICC) 527 (Stefan Vogenauer & Jan Kleinheisterkamp eds., 2009) (stating that today the principle of contra proferentem is "part of the modern lex mercatoria" because the rule is recognized in many major legal systems and applicable to the interpretation of international conventions).

parties,[70] it seeks to guarantee the equality of parties to a contract. Contra proferentem typically applies to the party who proffered or drafted a provision that has at least two different meanings.[71] But it is usually invoked as a matter of last resort considering that the other party presumptively had the opportunity to read, and then acquiesced to, the ambiguous language before executing the contract. The principle is most apt where the party responsible for the language advances an interpretation in variance with "the meaning that the other party would reasonably and naturally have understood."[72]

The principle of good faith has also been applied to *affirm the existence of a contract—whether through the parties' contemporaneous conduct or their past course of dealings.*[73] For instance, a pro forma invoice and a letter of credit are not "contractually formative documents" in most legal systems, and parties are thus "not bound by any written agreement" without more; but those parties can create binding obligations when, in accordance with those documents, they "conduct[] themselves in such a way as to create a contract for the sale and purchase of [goods]."[74] Although this result might be explained as a form of estoppel, as discussed in chapter 2.C, it can also be seen as an emanation of good faith that "is

70 *See, e.g., Int'l Thunderbird Gaming Corp. v. United Mexican States*, UNCITRAL, Separate Opinion of Thomas Wälde, ¶ 50 (Dec. 1, 2005).

71 *See, e.g., Ceskoslovenska Obchodní Banka A.S. v. Slovak Republic*, ICSID Case No. ARB/97/4, Decision of the Tribunal on Objections to Jurisdiction, ¶ 51 (May 24, 1999); UNIDROIT at 528.

72 Cheng, *supra* note 2, at 108.

73 *See, e.g., DIC of Delaware, Inc. v. Tehran Redev. Corp.*, 8 Iran-U.S. Cl. Trib. Rep. 144, 161 (1985) (part performance of an oral contract as evidence of its existence "must be taken to constitute a general principle of law"); *accord Futura Trading, Inc. v. Nat'l Iranian Oil Co.*, 13 Iran-U.S. Cl. Trib. Rep. 99, 113 (1986); *Kimberly-Clark Corp. v. Bank Markazi Iran*, 2 Iran-U.S. Cl. Trib. Rep. 334, 339 (1983); *Iowa State Univ. v. Ministry of Culture*, 13 Iran-U.S. Cl. Trib. Rep. 271, 273–75 (1986); *Cal-Maine Foods, Inc. v. Islamic Republic of Iran*, 6 Iran-U.S. Cl. Trib. Rep. 52, 61–62 (1984); *Chas. T. Main Int'l, Inc. v. Khuzestan Water & Power Auth.*, 3 Iran-U.S. Cl. Trib. Rep. 156, 162 (1983); *R.N. Pomeroy v. Islamic Republic of Iran*, 2 Iran-U.S. Cl. Trib. Rep. 372, 380 (1983); *Pepsico, Inc. v. Islamic Republic of Iran*, 13 Iran-U.S. Cl. Trib. Rep. 3, 33 (1986); *United States v. Islamic Republic of Iran* (Case B29), 6 Iran-U.S. Cl. Trib. Rep. 12, 17 (1984).

74 *Futura Trading, Inc. v. Nat'l Iranian Oil Co.*, 13 Iran-U.S. Cl. Trib. Rep. 99, 112–13 (1986); *see also Framatome-Award*, 8 Y.B. Comm. Arb. 94, 101–17 (1983) ("B[y] . . . proceeding or causing the necessary work to be carried out on the site set aside for the performance of the Contract, ABC necessarily ratified the Contract. It cannot be claimed that the legal and material performance of the Contract over several months by the [opposing] party has no consequence. . . . It must be admitted that ABC, like the governmental authorities upon which it depended, considered the Contract perfectly valid and binding on both parties, at least until the occurrence of the dispute. If ABC was not of this opinion, however, the principle of good faith would have imposed upon it a duty to make its view known to the co-contractor.").

widely accepted by municipal systems of law," and thus "must be taken to constitute a general principle of law."[75]

A final corollary to good faith has developed not in contractual relations, but in the process of resolving modern disputes: *the duty to maintain the status quo in juridical relations*. Citing cases from 1844 to 1951, Cheng found that good faith requires a party to refrain from taking any action that would aggravate a dispute and prejudice the effectiveness of an eventual judicial decision or arbitral award.[76] Because dispute-resolution agreements would be set at naught if a party were free to take unilateral actions in its own self-interest, the general principle of good faith requires a party to preserve the status quo pending the resolution of a dispute. Of a piece with good faith conduct and the general prohibition of unilateral alterations of a contractual relationship, this principle has been reinforced by international conventions and institutional rules allowing international courts and tribunals to order provisional measures to prevent the aggravation or extension of the dispute.[77] Before the International Court of Justice (ICJ), a party seeking provisional measures must prove prima facie jurisdiction, plausible rights to be protected, and an imminent risk of irreparable prejudice to those rights.[78] This principle has since been recognized and applied by several ICSID tribunals.[79]

---

75 *DIC of Delaware, Inc. v. Tehran Redev. Corp.*, 8 Iran-U.S. Cl. Trib. Rep. 144, 161 (1985). This conclusion may obtain even where the otherwise applicable law does not recognize certain types of contracts, but the parties act as if they are in force. *Id.* In these situations, however, the application of the principle deserves special attention. Although acknowledging the principle, the *DIC* tribunal ultimately held that no contract was formed by the mere existence of "routine minutes of a meeting" indicating what one party wanted the other party to do. *Id.* at 160.

76 Cheng, *supra* note 2, at 140–41.

77 *See, e.g.*, Statute of the International Court of Justice art. 41, UNCITRAL Arbitration Rules art. 26, ICSID Convention art. 47, ICSID Arbitration Rules art. 39, and ICC Rules of Arbitration art. 28; Manila Declaration on the Peaceful Settlement of International Disputes art. 8, 68th Plenary Meeting, U.N. Doc. A/RES/37/10 (Nov. 15, 1982) ("States parties to an international dispute . . . shall refrain from any action whatsoever which may aggravate the situation so as to endanger the maintenance of international peace and security and make more difficult or impede the peaceful settlement of the dispute."); Vienna Convention on the Law of Treaties, Preamble, *opened for signature* May 23, 1969, 1155 U.N.T.S. 331, 332 (entered into force Jan. 27, 1980) ("Affirming that disputes concerning treaties, like other international disputes, should be settled by peaceful means and in conformity with the principles of justice and international law."); United Nations Charter art. 33(1) ("The parties to any dispute, the continuance of which is likely to endanger the maintenance of international peace and security, shall, first of all, seek a solution [by pacific settlement]."); *Armed Activities on the Territory of the Congo (New Application: 2002) (Dem. Rep. Congo v. Rwanda)*, Jurisdiction and Admissibility, Judgment, 2006 I.C.J. 6, ¶ 8 (Feb. 3) (declaration of Judge Elaraby) (confirming the "duty of States to settle their disputes peacefully and in accordance with international law").

78 *Elec. Co. of Sofia and Bulgaria (Belg. v. Bulg.)*, Judgment, 1939 P.C.I.J. (Ser. A/B) No. 79, at 199 (Dec. 5).

79 *See Holiday Inns S.A. and others v. Morocco*, ICSID Case No. ARB/72/1, Decision on Provisional Measures (July 2, 1972), 1 ICSID Rep. 645, 654 (1993); *Amco Asia Corp. et al. v. Republic of Indonesia*,

In *Quiborax v. Bolivia*, the tribunal found non-aggravation of the dispute and preservation of the status quo to be a freestanding right.[80] It ordered provisional measures to suspend criminal proceedings commenced by Bolivia against the claimant's witnesses because they threatened the procedural integrity of the ICSID proceedings, especially the claimant's access to evidence.[81]

2. Good Faith in Excusing Contractual Performance

The general principle of good faith has also guided courts and tribunals on when to *excuse* adherence to a contract. For instance, under most legal systems, one party may be entitled to treat itself as discharged from its obligations if the other has committed a substantial breach—*exceptio inadimplenti contractus*.[82] Similarly, where a party induces a contract through fraud or deceit, that party "violat[es] the principle of good faith" and excuses the other party from mandatory performance under the contract.[83] This latter principle—where a party seeks to benefit from its own wrongful or fraudulent conduct—will be discussed in more detail in chapters 2.D and 3.D.

ICSID Case No. ARB/81/1, Decision on Request for Provisional Measures, at 412 (Dec. 9, 1983), 1 ICSID Rep. 410 (1993); *Plama Consortium Ltd. v. Republic of Bulgaria*, ICSID Case No. ARB/03/24, Order, ¶ 40 (Sept. 6, 2005); *Occidental Petroleum Corp. and Occidental Exploration & Prod. Co. v. Republic of Ecuador*, ICSID Case No. ARB/06/11, Decision on Provisional Measures, ¶ 96 (Aug. 17, 2007); *City Oriente Ltd. v. Republic of Ecuador and Empresa Estatal Petróleos del Ecuador*, ICSID Case No. ARB/06/21, *Decision on Provisional Measures, ¶ 55 (Nov. 19, 2007); and Burlington Resources Inc. v. Republic of Ecuador*, ICSID Case No. ARB/08/5, Procedural Order No. 1, ¶¶ 61–68 (June 29, 2009).

80 *Quiborax S.A., Non Metallic Minerals S.A. and Allan Fosk Kaplún v. Plurinational State of Bolivia*, ICSID Case No. ARB/06/2, Decision on Provisional Measures, ¶¶ 133–36 (Feb. 26, 2010).

81 *Id.* ¶ 148; *see also Biwater Gauff v. United Republic of Tanzania*, ICSID Case No. ARB/05/22, Procedural Order No. 1, ¶¶ 84–98 (Mar. 31, 2006) and *AGIP S.p.A. v. People's Republic of the Congo*, ICSID Case No. ARB/77/1, Decision, at 310 (Jan. 18, 1979) (ordering provisional measures to preserve access to and integrity of evidence).

82 *See, e.g.*, United Nations Convention on Contracts for the International Sale of Goods arts. 49(1)(a) and 64(1)(a) ("The buyer/seller may declare the contract avoided if the failure by the seller/buyer to perform any of his obligations under the contract or this Convention amounts to a fundamental breach of contract."); ICC Case No. 3540, Award (Oct. 3, 1980), 7 Y.B. Comm. Arb. 124 (1982); ICC Case No. 2583, Award, 103 J. Droit Int'l (Clunet) 950 (1976); *Sapphire Int'l Petroleums Ltd. v. Nat'l Iranian Oil Co., Award*, 35 Int'l L. Rep. 136 (Mar. 15, 1963); *Diversion of Water from the Meuse (Neth. v. Belg.)*, Judgment, 1937 P.C.I.J. (Ser. A/B) No. 70 (June 28, 1937) (dissenting opinion of Judge Anzilotti). *See generally* Philip O'Neill et al., *Is the Exceptio Non Adimpleti Contractus Part of the New* Lex Mercatoria?, *in* Transnational Rules in International Commercial Arbitration 147 (Emmanuel Galliard ed., 1993).

83 *Inceysa Vallisoletana S.L. v. Republic of El Salvador*, ICSID Case No. ARB/03/26, Award, ¶¶ 234–39 (Aug. 2, 2006); *see also World Duty Free Co. Ltd. v. Republic of Kenya*, ICSID Case No. ARB/00/7, Award (Oct. 4, 2006).

So-called "excuse concepts" are not limited to the acts of one of the parties; they also arise where some unforeseen development has occurred without fault and beyond the control of the parties that affects contractual performance.[84] Cheng identified this principle broadly as *clausula rebus sic stantibus*.[85] Generally speaking, a fundamental and unforeseen change in circumstances can justify termination of a contract if (1) the maintenance of the original circumstances constituted an essential basis of the contractual bargain, and (2) the effect of the change is to significantly transform the extent of the obligations still to be performed.[86] This principle remains widely regarded as a general principle of law,[87] and is recognized in many national jurisdictions and by international courts and tribunals under the rubric of "changed circumstances," "hardship," or "impracticability."[88] As applied between sovereigns, the principle has been codified in Article 62 of the Vienna Convention on the Law of Treaties and has been analogized to the "state of necessity" defense under customary international law.[89] Because the test is one

84 Klaus Peter Berger, Private Dispute Resolution in International Business: Negotiation, Mediation, Arbitration Volume II: *Handbook* 486 (3d ed. 2015).

85 Cheng, *supra* note 2, at 113.

86 ICC Award No. 1512 (1971), 1 Y.B. Comm. Arb. 128 (1976) (also published in 101 J. Droit Int'l (Clunet) 905 (1974)).

87 *See Questech, Inc. v. Ministry of Nat'l Def. of the Islamic Republic of Iran*, 9 Iran-U.S. Cl. Trib. 107, Award No. 59 (191-59-1) (Sept. 25, 1985), 11 Y.B. Comm. Arb. 283 (1986); *Hungarian State Enter. v. Jugoslavenski Naftovod* (Yugoslav Crude Oil Pipeline), Ad Hoc Arbitration, Award (July 6, 1983), 9 Y.B. Comm. Arb. 69, 70 (1984).

88 *See, e.g.*, Uniform Commercial Code art. 2, ¶ 2-615 (contemplating impracticability such as hardship to be an exception to nonperformance); UNIDROIT Principles of International Commercial Contracts art. 6.2.2 (2004) (allowing parties to invoke hardship as an exception to nonperformance); *Scafom Int'l BV v. Lorraine Tubes S.A.S*, Belgium Court of Cassation Supreme Court, Case No. C.07.0289N (June 19, 2009) (finding that under rare circumstances the U.N. Convention on Contracts for the International Sale of Goods (CISG) allows for hardship as an excuse to contractual nonperformance); Hans van Houtte, *Changed Circumstances and Pacta Sunt Servanda*, *in* Transnational Rules in International Commercial Arbitration 113–14, 120 (Emmanuel Gaillard ed., 1993) (finding the principle of *clausula rebus sic stantibus* in English, German, Swiss, Italian, Dutch, Japanese, and Libyan law).

89 *See* Draft Articles on Responsibility of States for Internationally Wrongful Acts, with Commentaries art. 25, U.N. Int'l Law Comm'n, U.N. DOC. A/56/10 (2001) (providing that necessity may not be invoked by a State as an excuse for nonperformance of an international obligation unless the act is the only way to safeguard an essential interest against a grave and imminent peril, the State did not assume the risk of the peril, and the State did not contribute to the situation of necessity); Matthias Sherer, *Economic or Financial Crises as a Defence in Commercial and Investment Arbitration*, Czech Y.B. Int'l L. 219, ¶ 14.59 (2010) (noting that "even if the doctrines invoked in commercial and investment cases are different, the standards applied by the arbitrators share some of the same requirements," that is, the event is unforeseeable, the risk is not assumed in the contract/treaty, the circumstances represent a bouleversement, and both "hardship" and "necessity" defenses are exceptional and appropriate only in extreme circumstances); *Sempra Energy Int'l v. Argentine Republic*, ICSID ARB/02/16, Award, ¶ 353 (Sept. 28, 2007) (holding that a "State cannot invoke necessity if it has contributed to the situation

of degree, and because breaching parties can often point to some alteration in the circumstances so as to excuse their nonperformance, international courts and tribunals apply this principle restrictively,[90] viewing it as a "dangerous exception to the principle of sanctity of contracts."[91]

A changed circumstance that renders performance not just impracticable, but impossible, gives rise to the distinct but related principle of force majeure. "*Most, if not all, legal systems recognize* force majeure *as an excuse for contractual non-performance,*" *such that it* "*can be considered a general principle of law.*"[92] For example, Arab, European, and North American jurisdictions consistently recognize force majeure as an excuse for performance where an intervening event is unforeseen and unavoidable, and renders performance impossible.[93] Under this

giving rise to a state of necessity," in light of the "general principle of law devised to prevent a party from taking legal advantage of its own fault"); *see generally* Elizabeth A. Martinez, *Understanding the Debate over Necessity: Unanswered Questions and Future Implications of Annulments in the Argentine Gas Cases*, 23 Duke J. Comp. & Int'l L. 149, 157–60 (2013).

90 *See* van Houtte, *supra* note 88, at 105.

91 ICC Award No. 1512 (1971), 1 Y.B. Comm. Arb. 128, 129 (1976) ("The principle *Rebus sic stantibus* is universally considered as being of strict and narrow interpretation."); *see also Fisheries Jurisdiction (Fed. Rep. Ger. v. Ice.)*, Jurisdiction of the Court, Judgment, 1973 I.C.J. 3, 19 (Feb. 2) (to excuse a party from performance under a treaty the change in circumstances must be vital: it has to "imperil the existence or vital development of one of the parties."); *Vine Wax Case*, Bundesgerichtshof [BGH] [Federal Court of Justice] Mar. 24, 1999, Civil Panel VIII, CLOUT Case No. 271 (Ger.) and *Powder Milk Case*, Bundesgerichtshof [BGH] [Federal Court of Justice] Jan. 9, 2002 (Ger.) (requiring strict interpretation of force majeure under the CISG).

92 *See, e.g.*, *Anaconda-Iran, Inc. v. Islamic Republic of Iran*, 13 Iran-U.S. Cl. Trib. Rep. 199, 211 (1986); *Sylvania Technical Sys. Inc. v. Islamic Republic of Iran*, 8 Iran-U.S. Cl. Trib. Rep. 298, 312 (1985); *Queens Office Tower Assocs. v. Iran Nat'l Airlines Corp.*, 2 Iran-U.S. Cl. Trib. Rep. 247, 254 (1983); *Am. Bell Int'l, Inc. v. Islamic Republic of Iran*, 12 Iran-U.S. Cl. Trib. Rep. 170 (1986).

93 *See, e.g.*, ICC Award Nos. 3099 and 3100, 7 Y.B. Comm. Arb. 87-95 (1982) (also published in: 107 J. Droit Int'l (Clunet) 951 (1980)) (finding, under French law, that "[t]he concept is . . . defined by its three characteristics: externality, unavoidability and unforeseeability"); ICC Award No. 4462, 16 Y.B. Comm. Arb. 54-78 (1985) (also published in: I.L.M. 567 (1990)) (same; applying Libyan law); *Kel Kim Corp. v. Cent. Markets, Inc. et al.*, 70 N.Y.2d 900, 902 (1987) (holding that that a force majeure event means "destruction of the subject matter of the contract or [when] the means of performance makes performance objectively impossible"); Adnan Amkhan, *Force Majeure and Impossibility of Performance in Arab Contract Law*, 6 Arab L.Q. 297, 301–05 (1991) (finding that force majeure under Arab contract law requires an event that is unforeseeable, that is unavoidable, that renders performance impossible); Belal Hashmi & Abdulrahman Hammad, *Construction and Projects in Saudi Arabia: Overview*, Practical Law: A Thompson Reuters Legal Solution (Oct. 1, 2013) (reporting that "the Saudi default definition of force majeure generally includes only circumstances that make performance absolutely impossible, rather than just unduly burdensome"); *see also* United Nations Convention on Contracts for the International Sale of Goods art. 79 ("A party is not liable for a failure to perform any of his obligations if he proves that the failure was due to an impediment beyond his control and that he could not reasonably be expected to have taken the impediment into account at the time of the conclusion of the contract or to have avoided or overcome it, or its consequences.");

principle, the impossibility of performance caused by conditions beyond either party's control can be invoked by the contracting parties (or the tribunal) to terminate a contract, even when the underlying contract did not contemplate termination or the textual conditions for termination were not met.[94] Before making this determination, however, courts and tribunals will closely analyze "the context of the circumstances causing *force majeure*, taking into account the particular party affected by those circumstances and the specific obligations that party is prevented from performing."[95] Close scrutiny will be given, for instance, to a state-owned entity invoking an act of its own government as a *fait du prince*.[96] The French *Cour de Cassation* in the *Air France* case held that a government act is not considered extraneous when the government is organically linked to the normal functioning of the state-owned enterprise.[97] As ICJ Judge Eduardo Jiménez de Arechaga explained:

> [I]f the contract rests entirely subject to the law of the contracting state, one might fear that the state might exercise its sovereign powers contrary to its contractual obligations, by modifying its own law in order to escape from its responsibilities.... [T]he solution ... is to appeal to the fundamental

---

UNIDROIT Principles of International Commercial Contracts art. 7.1.7 (2004) ("Non-performance by a party is excused if that party proves that the non-performance was due to an impediment beyond its control and that it could not reasonably be expected to have taken the impediment into account at the time of the conclusion of the contract or to have avoided or overcome it or its consequences.").

94 *See, e.g.*, *Gould Marketing, Inc. v. Ministry of Defense*, 3 Iran-U.S. Cl. Trib. Rep. 147 (1983) and 6 Iran-U.S. Cl. Trib. Rep. 272 (1984); *Int'l Schools Servs., Inc. v. Nat'l Iranian Copper Indus. Co.*, 9 Iran-U.S. Cl. Trib. Rep. 187 (1985); *Blount Bros. Corp. v. Islamic Republic of Iran*, 10 Iran-U.S. Cl. Trib. Rep. 56, 75 (1986).

95 *Sylvania Technical Systems, Inc. v. Islamic Republic of Iran*, 8 Iran-U.S. Cl. Trib. Rep. 298, 30 (1985), summarized in 80 Am. J. Int'l L. 365 (1986); *see also Exxon Research & Eng'g Co. v. Islamic Republic of Iran*, 15 Iran-U.S. Cl. Trib. Rep. 3 (1987); *Am. Bell Int'l Inc., v. Islamic Republic of Iran*, 12 Iran-U.S. Cl. Trib. Rep. 170, 187 (1986); *Int'l Technical Prod. Corp. v. Islamic Republic of Iran*, 9 Iran-U.S. Cl. Trib. Rep. 206 (1985); *Amoco Int'l Fin. Corp. v. Islamic Republic of Iran*, 15 Iran-U.S. Cl. Trib. Rep. 189 (1987) (application of contract standard establishing consequences of force majeure).

96 As Karl-Heinz Böckstiegel has written, there is a "presumption that a State will not have its executive organs act to the detriment of its foreign trade organs, including state owned enterprise," such that laws targeted toward a specific contract or contracts "should in principle not be considered as force majeure." Karl-Heinz Böckstiegel, *Arbitration and State-Owned Enterprises: A Survey on the National and International State of Law and Practice*, International Chamber of Commerce 47–48 (1984); *see also* Karl-Heinz Böckstiegel, *Acts of State and Arbitration*, German Institution of Arbitration 143–47 (1997); Karl-Heinz Böckstiegel, The State as the Contracting Partner of Foreign Private Companies, Habilitation Thesis upon Recommendation by the School of Law of the University of Cologne, with the support of the German Research Community 54–75 (1971).

97 French *Cour de Cassation* (Labor Chamber), Decision No. 69-40253 (Apr. 15, 1970); *see also* Conclusions by General Counsel Robert Mellotée on the French *Cour de Cassation* (Labor Chamber) Decision No. 69-40253 (Apr. 15, 1970), *Recueil Dalloz*, Jurisprudence (1971).

> principles applicable in any legal system—the rule "Pacta sunt servanda" with its limitations, the abuse of law and good faith. . . . [T]he contracting state is not authorized to manipulate its legislation a posteriori, not in the public interest, but with the clear aim of specifically modifying the obligations resulting from a contract.[98]

Where the event is not imputable to the party invoking it as an excuse, the force majeure lasts as long as the event itself, which may be permanent. Instances of war or other armed conflict, acts or threats of terrorism sabotage, piracy, blockade, fires, explosions, plagues, certain governmental actions, and natural disasters such as storms, earthquakes, or droughts may constitute force majeure.[99] This is not to say that a force majeure event cannot be the subject of a warranty: "In the case of a binding promise that it shall rain tomorrow, the immediate legal effect of what the promisor does is, that he takes the risk of the event, within certain defined limits, as between himself and the promisee."[100]

3. Good Faith as a Factor in Remedying Nonperformance

It is a general principle of law that *reparation is a consequence of a party's failure to fulfill an agreement.*[101] Cheng noted that the principle of reparation obtains even where the duration of the breach is short or the extent of the breach is minor.[102] Where a breach occurs, courts and tribunals will consider a range of remedies that vary across national legal traditions. These differences, however, do not diminish the existence of the general principle.

---

98 Eduardo Jiménez de Arechaga, Commentary, *in* 60 YEARS OF ICC ARBITRATION, A LOOK AT THE FUTURE 207–09 (ICC-Publishing 1984).

99 KLAUS PETER BERGER & OLIVIA JOHANNA ERDELYI, FORCE MAJEURE IN INTERNATIONAL CONTRACT LAW 68–70 (2013). Events of a political, financial, or economic nature—such as a currency collapse or a peaceful change of government—may not constitute force majeure but nevertheless may alter the equilibrium of a contract so as to make it economically nonsensible, thereby implicating *clausula rebus sic stantibus. Id.*

100 Oliver Wendell Holmes, Jr., *The Common Law* (1881), *in* 3 THE COLLECTED WORKS OF JUSTICE HOLMES 268 (S. Novick ed., 1995).

101 CHENG, *supra* note 2, at 113, citing *Factory at Chorzów (Fed. Rep. Ger. v. Pol.)*, Merits, Judgment, 1928 P.C.I.J. (Ser. A.) No. 17 (Sept. 13). *Amco Asia Corp. et al. v. Republic of Indonesia*, ICSID Case No. ARB/81/1, Award, ¶¶ 265–68 (Nov. 20, 1984); *Enron Corp. and Ponderosa Assets, L.P. v. Argentine Republic*, ICSID Case No. ARB/01/03, Award, ¶ 360 (May 22, 2007); *Fedax N.V. v. Republic of Venezuela*, ICSID Case No. ARB/96/3, Award, ¶ 30 (Mar. 9, 1998), *reprinted in* 37 INTERNATIONAL LEGAL MATERIALS 1392–98 (1998).

102 CHENG, *supra* note 2, at 113–14.

In the civil law, for instance, the principle of pacta sunt servanda is "taken very seriously," as demonstrated by the fact that the civil law generally favors specific performance for breach of contract.[103] Some modern international sources also recognize specific performance as a matter of right.[104] But under the common law, reparation usually comes in the form of damages unless they are inadequate. "When we delve for reasons, we encounter Holmes's argument that practically speaking the duty created by a contract is just to perform or pay damages, for only if damages are inadequate relief in the particular circumstances of the case will specific performance be ordered."[105] Straddling this divide, international arbitration tribunals have the power to order non-pecuniary restitution and specific performance—depending on the *lex arbitri*, applicable substantive law, or constitutive contract[106]—but there are relatively few cases in which such remedies have been granted.[107] Instead, international tribunals generally trend toward awarding

103 *See* Richard Hyland, *Pacta Sunt Servanda: A Meditation*, 34 Va. J. Int'l L. 405 (1994) (explaining the differing commitment to pacta sunt servanda in the common and civil laws); Redfern & Hunter on International Arbitration § 9.52 (6th ed. 2015).

104 *See, e.g.*, UNIDROIT Principles of International Commercial Contracts § 2 (2004), "Right to Require Performance," art. 7.2.2 cmts. 1 & 2 ("In accordance with the general principle of the binding character of the contract . . ., each party should as a rule be entitled to require performance by the other party not only of monetary, but also of non-monetary obligations, assumed by that party. While this is not controversial in civil law countries, common law systems allow enforcement of non-monetary obligations only in special circumstances. Following the basic approach of the CISG (Art. 46) [UNIDROIT] adopts the principle of specific performance, subject to certain qualifications."). However, unlike the CISG approach, under UNIDROIT, "specific performance is not a discretionary remedy, i.e., a court must order performance, unless one of the exceptions laid down in [art. 7.2.2] applies." *Id.*

105 *Zapata Hermanos Sucesores v. Hearthside Baking Co.*, 313 F.3d 385, 389 (7th Cir. 2002) (citing Oliver Wendell Holmes, Jr., The Common Law 300–02 (1881)); Oliver Wendell Holmes, Jr., *The Path of the Law*, 10 Harv. L. Rev. 457, 462 (1897).

106 *See* Redfern & Hunter, *supra* note 103, § 9.52. This power is reflected in the command of *Chorzów Factory*: to "wipe out the consequences of the illegal act and re-establish the situation which would, in all probability, have existed if that act had not been committed." *Factory at Chorzów (Fed. Rep. Ger. v. Pol.)*, Merits, Judgment, 1928 P.C.I.J. (Ser. A.) No. 17, at 47 (Sept. 13).

107 *See, e.g.*, *Case concerning Rainbow Warrior Affair (N.Z. v. Fr.)*, Decision (Apr. 30, 1990), 20 R.I.A.A. 215; *Case concerning the Temple of Preah Vihear (Cambodia v. Thai.)*, Merits, Judgment, 1962 I.C.J. 6, 37 (June 15) (ordering Thailand to restore to Cambodia certain sculptures and other objects that it had removed from the temple); *Texaco Overseas Petroleum Co. (TOPCO) v. Gov't of the Libyan Arab Republic*, 17 I.L.M. 1 (1978); *Enron Corp. and Ponderosa Assets, L.P. v. Argentine Republic*, ICSID Case No. ARB/01/3, Decision on Jurisdiction, ¶¶ 79–81 (Jan. 14, 2004) (noting that the tribunal has the power to order pecuniary or non-pecuniary relief as part of its inherent power); *Ioan Micula, Viorel Micula and others v. Romania*, ICSID Case No. ARB/05/20, Award, ¶ 1309 (Dec. 11, 2013) (acknowledging its power to grant non-pecuniary relief as to provide an "effective remedy" and "redress the injuries suffered by the Claimants as a result of such internationally wrongful acts, within the limits of the parties' request for relief and provided that such relief is admissible under international law").

damages.[108] There are practical reasons for this. In the commercial arbitration context, "tribunals rightly tend to avoid making awards that are difficult to enforce."[109] In the investor-state context, this may be attributed to a concern that restitutio in integrum would infringe upon sovereign prerogatives or to the reality that suits are typically brought only when the "investment relationship ha[s] broken down," such that claimants are primarily interested in compensation.[110]

These variances aside, there remains a baseline principle that is universally applied in the event of a breach: *some* sort of reparation must follow. As Cheng observed, "[r]eparation is the indispensable complement of a failure to 'follow a contract' and there is no necessity for this to be stated in the [contract] itself."[111] Any breach of an engagement, whatever its duration or materiality, involves an obligation to make reparation so that each party may place entire confidence in the good faith of the other. General principles governing reparation are discussed in chapter 2.F.

B. Abuse of Rights and the Principle of Proportionality

There is no legal right, however well established, which could not, in some circumstances, be refused recognition on the ground that it has been abused.

—Sir Hersch Lauterpacht[112]

The negative corollary of the good faith exercise of a legal entitlement is the universal prohibition on abuse of rights. This principle relates not to how rights are obtained (viz., by law or contract), but to how they are exercised.[113] As Cheng

108 CRCICA Award No. 6/1985, *in* ARBITRAL AWARDS OF THE CAIRO REGIONAL CENTRE OF INTERNATIONAL COMMERCIAL ARBITRATION 189 (Mohie Eldin I. Alam Eldin ed., 2000) ("It is an established principle of law . . . that an aggrieved party is entitled to damages for losses suffered and profit lost which flow as a direct and normal consequence of the breach by the other party. In other words, the party must be put in the same position as he would have been in if the breach had not occurred. The Claimant was awarded damages on that basis."); *Karaha Bodas Co. L.L.C. v. Pertamina and PT. PLN (Persero)*, INT'L ARB. REP., at C-2, ¶ 79 (Mar. 2001) ("There can be no doubt that in case of breach of contract, the prejudiced party is entitled to damages. This general principle of law, which is part of Indonesian law, has not been disputed by either party.").

109 REDFERN & HUNTER, *supra* note 103, § 9.53.

110 Christoph Schreuer, *Non-pecuniary Remedies in ICSID Arbitration*, 20(4) ARB. INT'L 325, 332 (2004).

111 CHENG, *supra* note 2, at 113 (quoting *Factory at Chorzów (Fed. Rep. Ger. v. Pol.)*, Merits, Judgment, 1928 P.C.I.J. (Ser. A.) No. 17, at 29 (Sept. 13)).

112 SIR HERSCH LAUTERPACHT, THE DEVELOPMENT OF INTERNATIONAL LAW BY THE INTERNATIONAL COURT 164 (1958).

113 *See* GARDINER, *supra* note 27, at 148.

observed, "[e]very right is the legal protection of a legitimate interest, [so] [a]n alleged exercise of a right not in furtherance of such an interest, but with the malicious purpose of injuring others can no[t] claim the protection of the law."[114] To determine whether a proscribed abuse has occurred, particularly on the part of a State, international courts and tribunals have developed the related principle of proportionality. This chapter discusses both.

1. The General Prohibition on the Abuse of Rights

When the term "general principles" was being inserted in the PCIJ Statute, Arturo Ricci-Busatti, the Italian member of the Committee, referred to "abuse of rights" as one of the general principles of law.[115] Since then, numerous judges, arbitrators, and scholars have considered abuse of rights to be part of international law, whether as a general principle of law or as part of customary international law.[116] The principle of abuse of rights has been invoked by States in defense or prosecution of international claims;[117] frequently cited by the ICJ;[118] and applied by interstate,[119] investor-state,[120] and private arbitration panels.[121]

---

114 Cheng, *supra* note 2, at 122–23.

115 Permanent Court of International Justice: Advisory Committee of Jurists, *Procès-verbaux of the Proceedings of the Committee, June 16th–July 24th 1920, with Annexes*, at 314–15, 335; *Saipem S.p.A. v. People's Republic of Bangladesh*, ICSID Case No. ARB/05/7, Decision on Jurisdiction, ¶¶ 154–58 (Mar. 21, 2007); *Waguih Elie George Siag & Clorinda Vecchi v. Arab Republic of Egypt*, ICSID Case No. ARB/05/15, Decision on Jurisdiction, ¶¶ 119, 125, 213 (Apr. 11, 2007).

116 Michael Byers, *Abuse of Rights: An Old Principle, A New Age*, 47 McGill L.J. 389, 397 (2002).

117 A number of States have argued for the applicability of abuse of rights in state-to-state cases, including the United Kingdom in the *Fisheries Jurisdiction Case* (*U.K. v. Ice.*), Memorial on the Merits of the Dispute Submitted by the Government of the United Kingdom, 1975 I.CJ. Pleadings 266, ¶¶ 153–54 (July 31, 1973); Liechtenstein in the *Nottebohm Case* (*Liech. v. Guat.*), Memorial Submitted by the Government of the Principality of Liechtenstein, 1955 I.CJ. Pleadings 21, ¶ 51 (Jan. 26, 1952); Norway in the *Certain Norwegian Loans Case (Fr. v. Nor.)*, 1957 I.C.J. 9, 73 (July 6, 1957) (dissenting opinion of Judge Basdevant); Liberia and Ethiopia in the *South West Africa Case (Eth. v. S. Afr.; Liber. v. S. Afr.)*, Second Phase, Judgment, 1966 I.C.J. 6, at 10 (July 18); Belgium in *Barcelona Traction, Light and Power Co., Ltd. (Belg. v. Spain)*, Second Phase, Judgment, 1970 I.CJ. 3, 17 (Feb. 5); and Australia in the *Nuclear Tests Case, see Nuclear Tests (Austl. v. Fr.)*, Judgment, 1974 I.C.J. 253, 362 (Dec. 20); and the Federal Republic of Yugoslavia in the *Genocide Case, see Application of the Convention on the Prevention and Punishment of the Crime of Genocide (Bosn. & Herz. v. Serb. & Montenegro)*, Provisional Measures, Order, 1993 I.C.J. 325, ¶ 19 (Sept. 13).

118 *See, e.g., Fisheries Case (U.K. v. Nor.)*, Judgment, 1951 I.CJ. 116, 141–42 (Dec. 18).

119 *See, e.g., Canada v. France*, 82 Int'l L. Rep. 590, ¶ 28 (1986).

120 *See, e.g., Saipem S.p.A. v. People's Republic of Bangladesh*, ICSID Case No. ARB/05/07, Award, ¶ 160 (June 30, 2009) (concluding that when a State exercises a right for a purpose that is different from that for which that right was created, this constitutes an abuse of rights).

121 *See, e.g., The Gibraltar Football Association (GFA)/Union des Associations Européennes de Football (UEFA)*, Arbitration CAS 2002/O/410.

Although a right can be used maliciously with the intent to cause injury, it is more often used as an artifice, with the "form of the law . . . being used to cover the commission of what in fact is an unlawful act."[122] For instance, although a State is permitted by international law to take private property for the public good under certain circumstances, it cannot pretextually invoke the public good to take property for private profit.[123] Inherent in the cabined right to expropriate is the bona fide pursuit of a legitimate sovereign interest; where that interest is absent, the State lacks the right to expropriate and its false invocation of the right is necessarily abusive.[124] Similarly, Article XX of the General Agreement on Tariffs and Trade (GATT) allows States to impose trade measures that would otherwise conflict with broader GATT provisions to the extent that they are necessary to protect human, animal, or plant life, or exhaustible natural resources. The chapeau to the Article states that the excepted measures are not to be applied in a manner that "would constitute . . . a disguised restriction on international trade." The WTO Appellate Body has interpreted this to be an "expression" of the "general principle of law" prohibiting the abusive exercise of rights: "To permit one member to abuse or misuse its right to invoke an exception would be effectively to allow that member to degrade its own treaty obligations as well as to devalue the treaty rights of other Members."[125] The general principle thus serves to provide "additional interpretative guidance" in determining the precise line between the rights and obligations of WTO members.[126]

Given their corrosive effect on the system of law in general, abuses of rights are roundly condemned. It has been recognized since Roman times *that acts taken under the pretense of law, but for an illicit purpose, are not to be countenanced*—malitis non est indulgendum and ex re sed non ex nomine.[127] Numerous countries from the civil law tradition have provisions

122 CHENG, *supra* note 2, at 122.

123 *Id.* at 123 (citing the *Walter F. Smith Case*, UNRIAA 913, 917–18 (1929)).

124 *Kelo v. City of New London*, 545 U.S. 469, 490 (2005) (Kennnedy, J., concurring) ("transfers intended to confer benefits on particular, favored private entities, and with only incidental or pretextual public benefits, are forbidden").

125 Appellate Body Report, *United States—Import Prohibition of Certain Shrimp and Shrimp Products*, ¶¶ 156–59, WT/DS58/AB/R (Oct. 12, 1998) (*adopted* Nov. 6, 1998).

126 *Id.* ¶¶ 156–59.

127 CHENG, *supra* note 2, at 122–23. *See also* Alexandre Kiss, *Abuse of Rights*, *in* 1 ENCYCLOPEDIA OF PUBLIC INTERNATIONAL LAW (R. Burnhardt ed., 1992).

expressly barring abuse of rights,[128] and the principle has attained a special status under European Union law.[129] Illustrative is Article 7 of the Spanish Civil Code:

> The law does not protect abuse of rights or the antisocial exercise of rights. Every act or omission that, by virtue of the intention of the actor, the object thereof, or the circumstances in which it is undertaken manifestly surpasses the normal limits of exercise of a right, causing damage to a third party, shall give rise to liability in damages and to the adoption of judicial or administrative measures that will prevent persistence in the abuse.

Although not as readily apparent in the common law, the principle operates there as well in the form of torts such as nuisance, duress, and abuse of process.[130] Sir Hersch Lauterpacht wrote that "[t]he law of torts . . . is to a large extent a list of wrongs arising out of what society considers to be an abuse of rights."[131] Almost universally, then, parties must not be allowed to abuse the legal process so as to harm or harass others—in other words, to invoke a "right, power, or competency

128 Bolivian Civil Code art. 107 (a party "is not allowed to exercise their right in a manner contrary to economic or social purpose in which view the right has been given"); German Civil Code art. 226 ("the exercise of a right cannot be allowed when it has the purpose of causing harm to another"); Greek Civil Code art. 281 ("It is prohibited to exercise a right if this exercise clearly exceeds the limits imposed by good faith, good morals or social and economic order of law."); Mexican Civil Code art. 840 ("It is not lawful to exercise property rights so that their application does not give any result other than to cause harm to a third party, without utility to the owner."); Civil Code of the Netherlands § 3.13.2 ("A right can be abused, among others, when it is exercised with no other purpose than to damage another person or with another purpose than for which it is granted."); Paraguayan Civil Code art. 372 ("[R]ights shall be exercised in good faith. Abusive exercise of rights is not protected under the law and involves liability of the person exercising it for the resulting damages, whether he exercises such right for the purpose of causing damages, even if without benefit for himself, or if his actions are contrary to the purposes for which the law recognized such rights."); Portuguese Civil Code art. 334 ("The exercise of a right is illegitimate when the holder clearly exceeds the limits imposed by good faith, good customs or the social or economic goal of that right."); Swiss Civil Code art. 2 of preliminary title ("Everyone must, in the exercise of his rights and in the performance of his duties, act with truth and faith. The open misuse of a right finds no protection in the law."). *See generally* Byers, *supra* note 116, at 395 (surveying a number of civil law jurisdictions, and observing that although the principle "means somewhat different things in different civil law systems, it remains an enduring element of the civil law"); *Emsland-Stärke GmbH v. Hauptzollanmt Hamburg-Jonas*, Case C-110/99, 2000 E.C.R. I-1595, I-1615 (European Court of Justice (ECJ) holding that a German company's transportation of materials into Switzerland to obtain an export refund only to immediately return the materials to Germany was abusive because it ran against the purpose of the export refund (objective element) and was done with the intent of taking unfair advantage of the benefit (subjective element)); *accord Halifax plc, Leeds Permanent Development Services Ltd., Country Wide Property Investments Ltd v. Commissioners of Customs & Excise*, Case C-255/02, 2006 E.C.R. I-1655.

129 *See, e.g., Kofoed Case*, 321/05, 2007 E.C.R. I-5795, ¶ 38 (July 5, 2007).

130 *See* Byers, *supra* note 116, at 394–97 (citing Australian, U.S., and English authorities, and observing that "regardless of the label used, it appears that the same general principle is at work").

131 Hersch Lauterpacht, The Function of Law in the International Community 297 (1933).

whose form or purpose is not consistent with the purposes of the right, power, or competency concerned, for instance, if it is exercised for the purpose of evading an . . . obligation or obtaining an undue advantage."[132]

Although private parties can be (and often are) accused of abusing their rights,[133] in the modern regime of investment arbitration, States are also frequently accused of the same in the exercise of official legislative or administrative powers.[134] In either case, analysis of the accusation focuses on two salient questions.

First, does the invocation of the right conform to the scope and purpose of the right? This element was discussed in *PSEG v. Turkey*, where the tribunal found that the Turkish Ministry of Energy and Natural Resources had engaged in an "abuse of authority" by making demands for renegotiation of the claimant's contract—as it was permitted to do—that "went far beyond the purpose of the Law and attempted to reopen aspects of the Contract that were not at issue in this context or even within [its] authority."[135] Similarly, in *Metalclad v. Mexico*, the tribunal concluded that a Mexican municipal government violated the minimum standard of treatment when it denied the claimant's application for a construction permit on the basis of alleged "environmental impact considerations."[136] According to the *Metalclad* tribunal, the right to deny permits had been granted to the municipal government only for purposes of addressing "appropriate construction considerations," and its reliance on environmental considerations was therefore "improper."[137]

Second, even if the exercise of a right conforms to its scope and purpose, is the stated reason for the invocation of the right truthful? An exercise of authority

132 JEAN SALMON, DICTIONNAIRE DE DROIT INTERNATIONAL PUBLIC 3–4 (2001).

133 In the investment-treaty context, for instance, investors are often accused of abusing the rights of procedure to access international arbitration proceedings. *See, e.g., Phoenix Action, Ltd. v. Czech Republic*, ICSID Case No. ARB/06/5, Award, ¶ 143 (Apr. 15, 2009) (concluding that Claimant incurred in an abuse of rights (détournement de procédure) by creating a "legal fiction in order to gain access to an international arbitration procedure to which it was not entitled"); *Cementownia "Nowa Huta" S.A. v. Republic of Turkey*, ICSID Case No. ARB (AF)/06/2, Award, ¶ 159 (Sept. 17, 2009) ("[T]he Claimant has intentionally and in bad faith abused the arbitration; it purported to be an investor when it knew that this was not the case. This constitutes indeed an abuse of process.").

134 Michael Akehurst, *Jurisdiction in International Law*, 46 BRIT. Y.B. INT'L L. 145, 189 n.3 (1972–1973) ("legislative jurisdiction . . . can give rise to genuine examples of abuse of rights").

135 *PSEG Global Inc. et al. v. Republic of Turkey*, ICSID Case No. ARB/02/5, Award, ¶ 247 (Jan. 19, 2007).

136 *Metalclad Corp. v. United Mexican States*, ICSID Case No. ARB(AF)/97/1, Award, ¶ 86 (Aug. 30, 2000).

137 *Id. See also Phoenix Action, Ltd. v. Czech Republic*, ICSID Case No. ARB/06/5, Award, ¶ 144 (Apr. 15, 2009) (concluding that the claimant's restructuring after the dispute arose but before the initiation of arbitration "was an abuse of the system of international ICSID investment arbitration"); *Mobil Corp., Venezuela Holdings B.V. et al. v. Bolivarian Republic of Venezuela*, ICSID Case No. ARB/07/27, Decision on Jurisdiction, ¶¶ 169–85 (June 10, 2010).

that could ostensibly be aimed at achieving a legitimate purpose may nevertheless be abusive if the State is unable to demonstrate that this was the actual purpose.[138] This issue arose in the *ADC v. Hungary* case. There, the respondent State defended that the regulatory measures at issue were in "the strategic interests of the State,"[139] undertaken pursuant to its right to "regulate its own economy, to enact and modify laws, [and] to secure the proper application of law."[140] Nevertheless, the tribunal held that Hungary had unlawfully expropriated the claimant's investment in violation of the standard of fair and equitable treatment:

> Although the Respondent repeatedly attempted to persuade the Tribunal that the Amending Act, the Decree and the actions taken in reliance thereon were necessary and important for the harmonization of the Hungarian Government's transport strategy, laws and regulations with the EU law, it failed to substantiate such a claim with convincing facts or legal reasoning.... If mere reference to "public interest" can magically put such interest into existence and therefore satisfy this requirement, then this requirement would be rendered meaningless since the Tribunal can imagine no situation in which this requirement would not have been met.[141]

In *S.D. Myers v. Canada*, the respondent State similarly argued that its import ban "was made because Canada believed PCBs are a significant danger to health and the environment when exported without appropriate assurances of safe transportation and destruction,"[142] and that it was "necessary to protect human, animal or plant life or health or was necessary for the conservation of living or non-living exhaustible natural resource."[143] In evaluating this line of argument, the tribunal first noted that "[t]he intent of government is a complex and multifaceted matter," and that it could "only characterize Canada's motivation or intent fairly by examining the record of the evidence as a whole."[144] After carrying out that (comprehensive) examination,[145] the tribunal determined:

> Insofar as intent is concerned, the documentary record as a whole clearly indicates that the Interim Order and the Final Order were intended primarily to protect the Canadian PCB disposal industry from U.S. competition.

138 *See EDF (Servs.) Ltd. v. Romania*, ICSID Case No. ARB/05/13, Award, ¶ 303 (Oct. 8, 2009).

139 *ADC Affiliate Ltd. v. Republic of Hungary*, ICSID Case No. ARB/03/16, Award, ¶ 392 (Oct. 2, 2006).

140 *Id.* ¶ 384.

141 *Id.* ¶ 430.

142 *S.D. Myers Inc. v. Gov't of Canada*, UNCITRAL, Partial Award, ¶¶ 152, 155 (Nov. 13, 2000).

143 *Id.* ¶ 155.

144 *Id.* ¶ 161.

145 *Id.* ¶¶ 162–92.

> Canada produced no convincing witness testimony to rebut the thrust of the documentary evidence. The Tribunal finds that there was no legitimate environmental reason for introducing the ban. Insofar as there was an indirect environmental objective . . . it could have been achieved by other measures.[146]

Relying on this finding, the *S.D. Myers* tribunal concluded that Canada had violated both the national treatment standard and the minimum standard of treatment of aliens.[147]

Despite its widespread recognition, the notion of an *abuse* of rights may be a misnomer because what is in fact at issue is the *absence* of the right asserted. The principle thus has its detractors. Some consider it an oxymoron or "*logomachies*."[148] "A speaker who uses 'abuse of rights' to refer to conduct that is outside the scope of the right is simply talking nonsense."[149] It is true that, in most cases, an abuse of rights could be recast in terms of the party acting without any right at all. For example, under international law, a State has no power to expropriate except where necessary and in the public interest; nor can a State, consistent with the national treatment standard, exercise its regulatory powers so as to protect domestic producers from foreign competition. But this reconception of the issue does not alter the unlawfulness of the conduct, and the doctrine of abuse of rights continues to persist as a general principle notwithstanding the theoretical issues surrounding it. This is a reflection of the reality that rights today are rarely absolute. In most circumstances, a party's rights in one area are limited by its obligations in another, including respect for the potentially conflicting rights of others.[150] The specific exercise of a legal entitlement must therefore be measured on its own terms and relative to other pertinent legal interests, which is exactly what the abuse of rights doctrine does. The phrase "abuse of rights," moreover, goes some way in capturing the perniciousness of the wrong. The doctrine focuses upon the conduct and intent of the actor, who is attempting to commit an unlawful act—with impunity—through the pretense of exercising a legal right. It is precisely the beguiling invocation of a legal entitlement that makes the conduct so abusive and corrosive.[151]

---

146 *Id.* ¶¶ 194–95.

147 *Id.* ¶¶ 256, 268.

148 MARCEL PLANIOL ET AL., TRAITÉ PRATIQUE DE DROIT CIVIL FRANÇAIS, vol. II, No. 871 (1952).

149 Frederick Schauer, *Can Rights Be Abused?*, 31 PHIL. Q. 225, 227 (1981).

150 *See* CHENG, *supra* note 2, at 131.

151 Some jurists have considered the passage of time and presentation of stale claims to be an abuse of right. *See, e.g.*, George P. Fletcher, *The Right and the Reasonable*, 98 HARV. L. REV. 949, 980 (1985).

2. The Principle of Proportionality

The process of identifying the abusive exercise of legal rights is one of discernment, and it has given rise to its own (related) general principle of law. "In simplest terms, *the proportionality principle requires some articulable relationship between means and ends, specifically that the means chosen by an administration be suitable or appropriate, and no more restrictive than necessary to achieve a lawful end.*"[152] Applying this principle typically involves an inquiry into whether there is a rational and appropriate relationship between the means chosen and the ends being pursued (suitability); a test of the means chosen to determine if it curtails the right at stake more than necessary (least restrictive means); and a final weighing of all circumstances (balancing stricto sensu).[153] This standard of proportionality—insofar as it gauges the proper exercise of a legal right—can be viewed as a subset of abuse of rights.

The notion of proportionality traces back to Aristotle[154] and Cicero,[155] and has emerged in modern times as a general principle of law.[156] It is found in

---

Indeed, Cheng included the principle of extinctive prescription as a fundamental tenet of judicial process in his 1953 work. Cheng, *supra* note 2, at 373. It is open to question whether this is a fundamental tenet of international due process. To be sure, it is "[a] universally recognised principle" that where a party fails to bring a timely claim and the delay places his adversary in a disadvantageous position, the claim may be forfeited. *Id.* But that principle does not rely on any feature of municipal law (such as statutes of limitations), nor does it place any outer limit on the length of delay that will bar a claim. Instead, it simply limits the exercise of a right when doing so would be abusive, and is therefore more properly seen as an extension of the principle of abuse of rights rather than a general principle of law unto itself.

152 Ralph G. Steinhardt, Book Review, *European Administrative Law*, 28 Geo. Wash. J. Int'l L. & Econ. 225, 231–32 (1994) (emphasis added).

153 Gebhard Bücheler, Proportionality in Investor-State Arbitration 1-2 (Oxford 2015) ("First, the relevant measure must be a *suitable* means to achieve a *legitimate* goal. Second, the chosen measure must be the *least restrictive* means to attain the relevant goal.... Third, the measure adopted must be proportionate in the narrow sense (*proportionality stricto sensu*), which involves a weighing and balancing of the different interests at stake."); Alec Stone Sweet & Giancinto della Cananea, *Proportionality, General Principles of Law, and Investor-State Arbitration: A Response to Jose Alvarez*, Yale Law School, Public Law Research Paper No. 507, May 9, 2014, at 5, *available at* http://papers.ssrn.com/sol3/papers.cfm?abstract_id=2435307.

154 *See* Aristotle, The Nicomachean Ethics: Book V ("We do not allow a man to rule, but rational principle, because a man behaves thus in his own interests and becomes a tyrant.").

155 *See* Cicero, De Republica (Commonwealth) (describing law as the *recta ratio naturae congruens*—meaning the right ratio, the proper proportion).

156 *See generally* Bücheler, *supra* note 153, at 28–62; Eric Engle, *The History of the General Principle of Proportionality: An Overview*, 10 Dartmouth L.J. 1 (2012). Proportionality has not been accepted as a freestanding doctrine in the U.S. Supreme Court given concerns over the scope of judicial power and the focus upon constitutional provisions. *See, e.g., District of Columbia v. Heller*, 554 U.S. 570,

both common[157] and civil law[158] systems, and has been applied by national courts[159] and international tribunals.[160] The international development of the principle has been largely organic. The European Court of Human Rights regularly evaluates whether state actions that interfere with human rights are "proportionate to the legitimate aim pursued."[161] These decisions are in turn regularly cited and relied upon by investment tribunals in applying the principle of proportionality to claims of expropriation.[162] The concept of proportionality, furthermore, is now frequently included in the text of modern international investment agreements.[163]

The principle of proportionality plays a role in assessing performance and breach in private contract claims. Although a party may be permitted to withhold contract

634 (2008) ("The very enumeration of the right takes out of the hands of government—even the Third Branch of Government—the power to decide on a case-by-case basis whether the right is *really worth* insisting upon."). Nonetheless, in various areas of law, including issues of free speech and equal protection, the Court applies a balancing test that is quite similar to the principle of proportionality. *See* BÜCHELER, *supra* note 153, at 50–58.

157 *See The Eighth Amendment, Proportionality, and the Changing Meaning of Punishments*, 122 HARV. L. REV. 960, 960 (2009) ("In . . . *Solem v. Helm*, Justice Powell traced the history of the Cruel and Unusual Punishments Clause back to the Magna Carta and the English Bill of Rights of 1689, which he found to have embodied a strong principle of proportional punishment."); *see also Harmelin v. Michigan*, 501 U.S. 957, 967 (1991) (citing the Magna Carta as an early source of its Eighth Amendment proportionality analysis).

158 *See* Susanne Baer, *Equality: The Jurisprudence of the German Constitutional Court*, 5 COLUM. J. EUR. L. 249, 261–64 (1999).

159 *See* Margherita Poto, *The Principle of Proportionality in Comparative Perspective*, 8 GERMAN L.J. 835 (2007).

160 *See* Mads Andenas & Stefan Zleptnig, *Proportionality: WTO Law: In Comparative Perspective*, 42 TEX. INT'L L.J. 371, 372 (2007); Alec Stone Sweet & Jud Mathews, *Proportionality Balancing and Global Constitutionalism*, 47 COLUM. J. TRANSNAT'L L. 72, 72 (2008) ("From German origins, proportionality analysis spread across Europe into Commonwealth systems (Canada, New Zealand, South Africa) and Israel; it has also migrated to treaty-based regimes, including the European Union, the European Convention on Human Rights, and the World Trade Organization.").

161 *See James and Others v. United Kingdom*, App. No. 8793/79, Eur. Ct. H.R., Judgment of the Grand Chamber, ¶¶ 50, 77 (Feb. 21, 1986) (holding that a legislative scheme that allowed leaseholders to acquire their properties from their landlords was not in breach of the Convention because there was a "reasonable relationship of proportionality between the means employed and aim sought to be realized"); *Lingens v. Austria*, App. No. 9815/82, ¶ 37 Eur. Ct. H.R., Judgment of the Grand Chamber (July 8, 1986) (holding that the German Chancellor's prosecution of the applicant was a disproportionate response to the applicant's publication of criticisms of the Chancellor based on undisputed facts and made in good faith).

162 *See, e.g., Técnicas Medioambientales Tecmed, S.A. v. United Mexican States*, ICSID Case No. ARB (AF)/00/2, Award, ¶ 122 (May 29, 2003) and *Azurix Corp. v. Argentine Republic*, ICSID Case No. ARB/01/12, Award, ¶ 311 (July 14, 2006).

163 Carmen Martinez Lopez & Lucy Martinez, *Proportionality in Investment Treaty Arbitration And Beyond: An "Irresistible Attraction"?*, 2 BCDR INT'L ARB. REV. No. 2, 261 (December 2015).

performance based upon the other party's breach, it would be contrary to good faith and the principle of proportionality "to rely on . . . the non-performance of a relatively minor obligation . . . in an attempt to avoid performance of an essential obligation of one's own."[164] The same applies to the exercise of sovereignty by States. An ICSID tribunal found the proportionality principle violated when Ecuador terminated an oil participation agreement in response to the claimants' failure to receive advance state approval for a farmout agreement—a breach from which Ecuador "did not suffer any quantifiable loss."[165] The *Occidental v. Ecuador* tribunal reasoned:

> It can be accepted that some punishment or other step may well have been justified, or at the very least defensible. . . . But the overriding principle of proportionality requires that any such administrative goal must be balanced against the Claimants' own interests and against the true nature and effect of the conduct being censured. The Tribunal finds that the price paid by the Claimants—total loss of an investment worth many hundreds of millions of dollars—was out of proportion to the wrongdoing alleged . . . , and similarly out of proportion to the importance and effectiveness of the "deterrence message" which the Respondent might have wished to send to the wider oil and gas community.[166]

Although a State may of course exercise its contractual, regulatory, and police powers, the reasonableness of that exercise will be measured against the specific circumstances facing it. As the *Occidental* tribunal explained, quoting Lord Steyn, "'[i]n law, context is everything.'"[167] Like the overarching principle of abuse of rights, the principle of proportionality is used to determine the proper relationship between the means and ends of state action with respect to private rights.

This principle was also explored in the *Tecmed v. Mexico* case. There, the Mexican National Ecology Institute (INE) issued a resolution in which it refused to renew the operating permit of the claimant's subsidiary, citing certain violations of the terms

164 Philippe Fouchard et al., Fouchard, Gaillard, Goldman on International Commercial Arbitration 829 (John Savage ed., 1999).

165 *Occidental Petroleum Corp. and Occidental Exploration & Prod. Co. v. Republic of Ecuador*, ICSID Case No. ARB/06/11, Award, ¶ 445 (Oct. 5, 2012).

166 *Id.* ¶ 450. Although there was a dissent on the quantification of damages, the tribunal was unanimous on the finding of disproportionality. *See id.* Dissenting Opinion of Brigitte Stern, ¶ 1 (Sept. 20, 2012).

167 *Id.* ¶ 451 (quoting *R. v. Secretary of State for the Home Department, ex parte Daly* [2001] 3 All ER 433, at 447).

of the permit. The claimant alleged that "the reasons invoked [in the resolution] are not proportional to the decision not to renew the Permit."[168] Mexico countered that other reasons to refuse the renewal existed, including "the protection of the environment and public health."[169] Ultimately, the tribunal concluded that the decision not to renew the permit was not primarily based upon the permit violations cited in the resolution, nor was it based upon any legitimate concerns about public health or environmental risks associated with the project. Instead, the tribunal concluded that the State's primary reason for denying the renewal was its concern "related to the social or political circumstances [associated with the claimant's project] and the pressure exerted on municipal and state authorities and even on INE itself created by such circumstances."[170] This conclusion undergirded the tribunal's ultimate holding on liability, which turned upon whether the non-renewal was a proportionate means of accomplishing the purpose of the measure. The pretextual justification for the action led in part to the finding of disproportionality.[171]

Issues of proportionality are ubiquitous in the trade context. GATT Article XX exempts certain government measures that are necessary to protect public morals or related to a legitimate aim. In reviewing claimed exceptions, the WTO Dispute Settlement Body and Appellate Body have applied a lenient proportionality test.[172] In one case, the WTO Panel found that restrictions imposed by Thailand on the importation of cigarettes were "necessary" so long as there were no other measures that Thailand could "reasonably be expected to employ to achieve its health policy objectives."[173] Whether other measures are reasonably available involves a weighing and balancing of factors including the effectiveness of the measure in achieving its purpose, the importance of the interests protected by the measure, and the impact of the measure on trade.[174]

---

168 *Técnicas Medioambientales Tecmed, S.A. v. United Mexican States*, ICSID Case No. ARB (AF)/00/2, Award, ¶ 98 (May 29, 2003).

169 *Id.* ¶ 125.

170 *Id.* ¶ 132.

171 *Id.* ¶ 133.

172 *See, e.g.*, Appellate Body Report, *Korea—Measures Affecting Imports of Fresh, Chilled and Frozen Beef*, WT/DS161/AB/R, WT/DS169/AB/R, DSR 2001: Section I, ¶ 5 (Dec. 11, 2000) (*adopted* Jan. 10, 2001); Appellate Body Report, *Brazil—Measures Affecting Imports of Retreaded Tyres*, ¶¶ 141–44, WT/DS332/AB/R (Dec. 3, 2007).

173 Report of the Panel, *Thailand—Restrictions on Importation of and Internal Taxes on Cigarettes*, ¶ 75, WTO Dispute Settlement Body Case No. DS10/R-37S/200 (Nov. 7, 1990).

174 Appellate Body Report, *Korea—Measures Affecting Imports of Fresh, Chilled and Frozen Beef*, ¶ 164, WT/DS161/AB/R, WT/DS169/AB/R, DSR 2001: I, 5 (Dec. 11, 2000) (*adopted* Jan. 10, 2001).

As these cases demonstrate, striking the appropriate balance between rights and competing obligations is often difficult.[175] Different rights carry different weight in different contexts, and unless a judge or arbitrator has some objective benchmarks against which to weigh the competing considerations, there is a risk that the exercise will become arbitrary and yield unpredictable results.[176] It has been argued that "the different steps of a proportionality analysis make the reasoning of tribunals more transparent and enhance the probability that all relevant factors will be taken into account."[177] In addition, as set forth in chapter 1.A, international jurists can glean insights from analogous constitutional and administrative law decisions in various domestic courts.[178]

The hardest cases arise when the sovereign power at issue allows for the exercise of discretion. But even in these cases, the discretion—like the right itself—must be exercised in good faith and "in conformity with the spirit of the law and with due regard for the interests of others."[179] When the invocation of discretion merely shrouds an unlawful design, there is an abuse prohibited by law.[180] It is a "long established principle" in nearly every legal system that "whenever ... discretionary principles ... [are] overstepped," "limitations ... founded on definite rules [will] ... reappear as the constant element of the construction."[181] The *Occidental* case, discussed above, illustrates the limitations placed on the exercise of discretion.

---

175 GEORG SCHWARZENBERGER & EDWARD D. BROWN, A MANUAL OF INTERNATIONAL LAW 84 (Professional Books 6th ed. 1976) ("it is difficult to establish what is supposed to amount to an abuse, as distinct from a harsh but justified use, of a right under international law").

176 *See generally* BÜCHELER, *supra* note 153, at 62–66.

177 *Id.* at 208.

178 *See generally* LAUTERPACHT, *supra* note 131; Wolfgang Friedmann, *The Uses of "General Principles" in the Development of International Law*, 57 AM. J. INT'L L. 279, 281, 284 (1963); BÜCHELER, *supra* note 153, at 33; Stephan W. Schill, *General Principles of Law and International Investment Law*, *in* INTERNATIONAL INVESTMENT LAW: THE SOURCES OF RIGHTS AND OBLIGATIONS 133, 134 (Tarcisio Gazzini & Eric De Brabandere eds., 2012).

179 CHENG, *supra* note 2, at 132–34. As noted, some scholars view such qualified rights to be incapable of abuse. In other words, if the right itself is stated in qualified terms (e.g., a state may take reasonable measures to expel aliens), an unreasonable action would not necessarily be an abuse of that right, but rather an act taken without any right whatsoever. Under this conception, the inclusion of the term "reasonable" serves the same purpose as the unstated principle of proportionality or abuse of rights. *See* OPPENHEIM'S INTERNATIONAL LAW 407 n.1 (Robert Jennings & Arthur Watts eds., Longman 9th ed. 1992).

180 CHENG, *supra* note 2, at 132–33.

181 *Conditions of Admission of a State to Membership in the United Nations (Charter, Art. 4)*, Advisory Opinion, 1948 I.C.J. 57, 80 (May 28) (individual opinion of Judge José Azevedo).

In any context, the principle of abuse of rights provides the threshold at which a lack of good faith gives rise to a violation of the international minimum standard of treatment, with all the attendant consequences.[182] The determination of when the exercise of a right becomes abusive will invariably turn upon the specific circumstances of each case,[183] and arbitrators and judges must act with a significant degree of "studied restraint."[184] But it is equally manifest that "[t]he power to apply some . . . principle as that embodied in the prohibition of abuse of rights must exist in the background in any system of administration of justice in which courts are not purely mechanical agencies."[185] Conduct that trades upon the appearance of law to undermine the rule of law is anathema, and the doctrine of abuse of rights appropriately guards against the fictitious or malicious invocation of legal rights.[186]

C. Estoppel

All were confus'd, and each disturb'd the rest.
For hot and cold were in one body fix'd;
And soft with hard, and light with heavy, mix'd.

—Ovid[187]

There is broad consensus that, as a "general principle," "no party may rely upon its own inconsistency to the detriment of another."[188] This principle has been traced back through 12 centuries of Islamic jurisprudence and has deep roots in Roman law, common law, and modern civil law.[189] Its "mandatory implication" occurs where a party "tries to undo what he previously undertook"; in that situation, the general principle of estoppel demands that the party's previous

182 Byers, *supra* note 116, at 411.

183 Friedmann, *supra* note 178, at 289–90.

184 LAUTERPACHT, *supra* note 112; *see also* Hersch Lauterpacht, *Droit de la paix*, 62 REC. DES COURS 95, 342 (Oxford 1937).

185 LAUTERPACHT, *supra* note 112, at 165.

186 *See generally* Fletcher, *supra* note 151.

187 METAMORPHOSES, Book I, ll. 22–24.

188 CRAIG, ET AL., *supra* note 22, § 35.02(xvii) (citing Emmanuel Gaillard, 1985 REV. ARB. 241, 248; Paul Bowden, *L'interdiction de se contredire au detriment d'autrui (estoppel) as a Substantive Transnational Rule in International Commercial Arbitration*, *in* TRANSNATIONAL RULES IN INTERNATIONAL COMMERCIAL ARBITRATION 125 (Emmanuel Gaillard ed., 1991)).

189 *See Desert Line Projects LLC v. Republic of Yemen*, ICSID Case No. ARB/05/17, Award, ¶ 207 (Feb. 6, 2008); *Case concerning the Temple of Preah Vihear (Cambodia v. Thai.)*, Merits, Judgment, 1962 I.C.J. 6,

act "shall be turned against him."[190] The principle "is yet another instance of the protection which law accords to the faith and confidence that a party may reasonably place in another, which ... constitutes one of the most important aspects of the principle of good faith."[191] At its essence, estoppel precludes a party from averring a particular state of things to another having previously, by words or conduct, represented a different state of things, thereby causing some form of prejudice.[192]

As with many general principles, the articulation and nuances of estoppel vary across different domestic systems. Anglo-Saxon jurisprudence characterizes this principle as equitable estoppel or estoppel in pais (estoppel by out-of-court conduct). In both circumstances, the common law typically requires actual reliance on the initial act or representation by the other party, although intent to deceive or defraud is unnecessary.[193] This is different under the civil law. The principle there, known as *actos propios*, bars a party from asserting a claim or defense

at 39, 43 (June 15) (separate opinion of Vice-President Ricardo Alfaro) ("I have no hesitation in asserting that this principle, known to the world since the days of the Romans, is one of the 'general principles of law recognized by civilized nations.'"); *North Sea Continental Shelf Cases (Ger./Den. and Ger./Neth.)*, Judgment, 1969 I.C.J. 3, 100, 120–21 (Feb. 20) (separate opinion of Judge Fouad Ammoun) ("Acquiescence flowing from a unilateral legal act, or inferred from the conduct or attitude of the person to whom it is to be opposed—either by application of the concept of *estoppel by conduct* of Anglo-American equity, or by virtue of the principle of western law that *allegans contraria non est audiendus*, which has its parallel in Muslim law—is numbered among the general principles of law accepted by international law as forming part of the law of nations, and obeying the rules of interpretation, relating thereto.") (emphasis in original).

190 *Desert Line Projects LLC v. Republic of Yemen*, ICSID Case No. ARB/05/17, Award, ¶ 207 (Feb. 6, 2008).

191 Cheng, *supra* note 2, at 144; *see also* D.W. Bowett, *Estoppel before International Tribunals and Its Relation to Acquiescence*, 33 Brit. Y.B. Int'l L. 176, 179 (1957) ("The basis of the rule is the general principle of good faith. . . ."); *Amco Asia Corp. et al. v. Republic of Indonesia*, ICSID Case No. ARB/81/1, Decision on Jurisdiction, ¶ 47 (Sept. 25, 1983), 1 ICSID Rep. 389 (1993) ("the concept [of estoppel], [while] derived from the Common Law, ... is based on the fundamental requirement of good faith, which is found in all systems of law, national as well as international").

192 Cheng, *supra* note 2, at 141–49.

193 *See, e.g.*, *Serbian Loans Case*, Judgment, 1929 P.C.I.J. (Ser. A) Nos. 20/21, 39 (July 12) (where there has been "no change in position on the part of the debtor State," then there is "no sufficient basis" to apply the principle of estoppel); *Tinoco Arbitration (Gr. Brit. v. Costa Rica)*, Award (Oct. 18, 1923), 1 R.I.A.A. 369, 383–84 (Taft, C.J.) ("An equitable estoppel ... must rest on previous conduct of the person to be estopped, which has led the person claiming the estoppel into a position in which the truth will injure him."); *Case concerning the Temple of Preah Vihear (Cambodia v. Thai.)*, Merits, Judgment, 1962 I.C.J. 6, 30 (June 15) (refusing to allow Thailand to take a certain position when it had "enjoyed ... benefits" for 50 years from its presumed acceptance and Cambodia had "relied on Thailand's acceptance"); *see also* *Pope & Talbot Inc. v. Gov't of Canada*, UNCITRAL, Interim Award, ¶ 111 (June 26, 2000) (citing Ian Brownlie, Principles of Public International Law 646 (5th ed.), and noting that "the essence of estoppel [under international law] is the element of conduct which causes the other party in reliance on such conduct detrimentally to change its position or to suffer some prejudice").

that contradicts its own prior conduct,[194] but, unlike common law estoppel, *actos propios* applies so long as the conduct is capable of creating an objective expectation in third parties—actual detrimental reliance by the other party based on its subjective expectations is not typically required.[195] A middle ground appears in German law, where the principle has "two constituents: some assertion of rights by one party inconsistent with his previous conduct and a balancing between the conflicting interests of both parties to determine which of the two deserves protection."[196] Under this balancing test, reliance that may have been placed by one party on the other's conduct is often taken into account.[197]

Despite these national variations, certain truths emerge: *venire contra factum proprium*, *nemo contra factum suum venire potest*, and *allegans contraria non est audiendus*. According to Judge Ricardo Alfaro of the ICJ, writing separately in the *Temple Preah Vihear* case, "[w]hatever term or terms be employed to designate this principle such as it has been applied in the international sphere, its substance is always the same."[198] The more demanding common law definition has tended to prevail on the international stage, such that *a party will be bound to its prior words or conduct if it has evinced (1) a clear and authorized statement, action, or omission with (2) reliance in good faith by another party (or court) on that statement, action, or inaction (3) to that party's detriment or to the advantage of the first party.*[199] A derivative of good

194 *See* HÉCTOR MAIRAL, THE DOCTRINE OF *ACTOS PROPIOS* AND THE ADMINISTRATION OF JUSTICE ¶¶ 2, 5 (1988) (analyzing the doctrine in Spain); MARCELO J. LÓPEZ MESA, THE DOCTRINE OF ACTOS PROPIOS IN JURISPRUDENCE 93–95 (1997) (analyzing the doctrine in Spain and Argentina); Rubén S. Stiglitz & Gabriel A. Stiglitz, *Actos Propios*, *in* CONTRACTS 491–512 (1994) (analyzing the doctrine in Spain and Argentina); MIGUEL PASQUAU LIAÑO, NULLITY AND VOIDABILITY OF CONTRACTS 246–51 (1997) (analyzing the doctrine in Spain and Germany). As the Ecuador Supreme Court has recognized, the principle of *venire contra factum proprium* is a "principle of universal law, accepted by all legal systems." *Cobos Peña v. Asociación Mutualista de Ahorro y Crédito*, R.O. No. 363, Decision No. 195-2001 (July 6, 2001).

195 *See* MAIRAL, *supra* note 194.

196 Bowden, *supra* note 188, at 128.

197 *Id.*

198 *Case concerning the Temple of Preah Vihear (Cambodia v. Thai.)*, Merit, Judgment, 1962 I.C.J. 6, 40 (June 15) (separate opinion of Vice-President Ricardo Alfaro).

199 *See* Bowett, *supra* note 191, at 201–02. *See also Pope & Talbot Inc. v. Gov't of Canada*, UNCITRAL, Interim Award, ¶ 111 (June 26, 2000); *Canfor Corp. v. United States of America, Tembec Inc. et al. v. United States of America* and *Terminal Forest Prods. Ltd. v. United States of America*, UNCITRAL, Order of the Consolidation Tribunal, ¶ 168 (Sept. 7, 2005); *Amco Asia Corp. et al. v. Republic of Indonesia*, ICSID Case No. ARB/81/1, Resubmitted Case, Award, ¶¶ 144–45 (June 5, 1990); *Ceskoslovenska Obchodni Banka, A.S. v. Slovak Republic*, ICSID Case No. ARB/97/4, Decision on Jurisdiction, ¶ 47 (May 24, 1999); *Philippe Gruslin v. Malaysia*, ICSID Case No. ARB/99/3, Award, ¶¶ 20.1–20.5 (Nov. 27, 2000); *SGS Société Générale de Surveillance S.A. v. Islamic Republic of Pakistan*, ICSID No. ARB/01/13, Decision

faith,[200] this is "a recognised general principle of law that has been applied by many international tribunals."[201]

This principle governs a host of juridical relationships between both private and sovereign entities. In the context of an adjudicatory proceeding, it means that "where a party assumes a certain position in a legal proceeding, and succeeds in maintaining that position, he may not thereafter, simply because his interests have changed, assume a contrary position, especially if it be to the prejudice of the party who has acquiesced in the position formerly taken by him."[202] Where, for instance, the claimant's original contention before the British prize court was not to challenge the seizure of a vessel, which it admitted was lawful, the same claimant could not, in a subsequent arbitration, challenge the lawfulness of the seizure.[203] Litigants cannot, consistent with good faith, "recover[] upon [a] claim" that they previously denied.[204] Nor can a person who has voluntarily assented to a contract and openly reaffirmed its validity thereafter oppose its performance or its ultimate juridical effect. For instance, in the *Shufeldt* case, the United States contended that Guatemala was precluded from denying the validity of a contract that Guatemala, inter alia, had benefited from and had recognized for six years—despite the fact that the contract had not been approved by the

---

on Jurisdiction, ¶¶ 122, 175–77 (Aug. 6, 2003); *SGS Société Générale de Surveillance S.A. v. Republic of the Philippines*, ICSID Case No. ARB/02/6, Decision on Jurisdiction, ¶ 109 (Jan. 29, 2004); *ADC Affiliate Ltd. and ADC & ADMC Mgmt. Ltd. v. Republic of Hungary*, ICSID Case No. ARB/03/16, Award, ¶¶ 474–75 (Oct. 2, 2006); *Duke Energy Int'l Inv. No. 1, Ltd. v. Republic of Peru*, ICSID Case No. ARB/03/28, Award, ¶¶ 231, 241–49 (Aug. 18, 2008); *Rachel S. Grynberg, Stephen M. Grynberg, Miriam Z. Grynberg and RSM Prod. Corp. v. Grenada*, ICSID Case No. ARB/10/6, Award, ¶ 7.1.2 (Dec. 10, 2010).

200 *Delimitation of the Maritime Boundary in the Gulf of Maine Area (Can./U.S.)*, Judgment, 1984 I.C.J. 246, ¶ 130 (Oct. 12) (explaining that "acquiescence is equivalent to tacit recognition manifested by unilateral conduct which the other party may interpret as consent, while estoppel is linked to the idea of preclusion").

201 *Pan American Energy LLC and BP Argentina Exploration Co. v. Argentine Republic*, ICSID Case No. ARB/03/13, Decision on Preliminary Objections, ¶ 159 (July 27, 2006).

202 *Davis v. Wakelee*, 156 U.S. 680, 689 (1895). *Compare* ICC Case No. 1512, Second Preliminary Award, 5 Y.B. Comm. Arb. 170, 174 (1980) (also published in: ASA Bull. 1992, at 505) (estopping litigant from positions taken in previous proceedings), *with Abrahim Rahman Golshani v. Gov't of the Islamic Republic of Iran*, Award, Iran-U.S. Cl. Trib. Case No. 812 (546-812-3) (Mar. 2, 1993), 19 Y.B. Comm. Arb. 421 (1994) (refusing to estop party).

203 *S.S. "Lisman," Disposal of Pecuniary Claims Arising Out of the Recent War (1914–1918) (U.S. v. Gr. Brit.)*, (Oct. 5, 1937), 3 R.I.A.A. 1767, 1790; *see also* Cheng, *supra* note 2, at 142 (discussing that case, and observing that where a claimant has previously "affirmed what he now denies," he thereby prevents himself from recovering "there or here upon the claim he now stands on"); *cf. Desert Line Projects LLC v. Republic of Yemen*, ICSID Case No. ARB/05/17, Award, ¶¶ 207–08 (Feb. 6, 2008).

204 *S. S. "Lisman," Disposal of Pecuniary Claims Arising Out of the Recent War (1914–1918) (U.S. v. Gr. Brit.)*, 3 R.I.A.A. 1767, 1790 (Oct. 5, 1937).

Guatemalan legislature. The arbitrator held the contention to be "sound and in keeping with the principles of international law."[205]

States today are also frequently estopped by their acts, words, and omissions with respect to customary international law,[206] territorial claims,[207] or the existence of bilateral treaties.[208] States may be estopped vis-à-vis private parties, too. Cheng concluded that "if a State, having been fully informed of the circumstances, has accepted a person's claim to the ownership of certain property and entered into negotiation with him for its purchase, it becomes very difficult, if not impossible for that State subsequently to allege that he had no title at the time."[209] The same rationale foreclosed Nicaragua's objections to an arbitral award six years after its issuance where its Government had previously expressed its gratitude to the King of Spain for having settled the dispute: "Nicaragua, by express declaration and

---

205 Cheng, *supra* note 2, at 143 (discussing *Shufeldt claim* (*Guat. v. U.S.*), Award (July 24, 1930), 2 R.I.A.A. 1079, 1094); *see also* Ad Hoc *Arbitration*, Award (Mar. 4, 2004), *reprinted in* The UNIDROIT Principles in Practice 1077, 1081 (Michael Joachim Bonnell ed., 2d ed. 2006) (applying UNIDROIT Article 1.8 to hold that where a party fails to enforce a contract clause throughout a four-year commercial relationship, it cannot later insist upon strict enforcement of that clause when an unrelated dispute under the contract arises). This principle has since found its way into various soft-law codifications. *See* U.N. Convention on Contracts for the International Sale of Goods art. 29(2) ("A contract in writing which contains a provision requiring any modification or termination by agreement to be in writing may not be otherwise modified or terminated by agreement. However, a party may be precluded by his conduct from asserting such a provision to the extent that the other party has relied on that conduct."); UNIDROIT Principles of International Commercial Contracts art. 1.8 (2010) (stating that "a party cannot act inconsistently with an understanding it has caused the other party to have and upon which that other party reasonably has acted in reliance to its detriment"). In this context, however, it must be noted that declarations, admissions, or proposals made in the course of negotiations that have not led to a written agreement (and cannot form an oral agreement) do not constitute admissions that could eventually prejudice the rights of the party making them. *See* Cheng, *supra* note 2, at 149.

206 *See, e.g.*, *Case of the Atlantic and Hope Insurance Companies v. Ecuador (case of the schooner Mechanic)*, Opinion of the Commissioner, Mr. Hassaurek (Jan. 25, 1862), 29 R.I.A.A. 108-14 ("Ecuador . . . having fully recognized and claimed the principle on which the case now before us turns, whenever from such a recognition rights or advantages were to be derived, could not in honor and good faith deny the principle when it imposed an obligation."); *see also* Cheng, *supra* note 2, at 142.

207 *See Fisheries Case* (*U.K. v. Nor.*), Judgment, 1951 I.C.J. 116, 139 (Dec. 18) (the "prolonged abstention" of the United Kingdom from protesting against the Norwegian system of straight base lines in delimiting territorial waters was one of the factors that "warrant Norway's enforcement of her system against the United Kingdom"); *Legal Status of Eastern Greenland* (*Den. v. Nor.*), Judgment, 1933 P.C.I.J. (Ser. A/B) No. 53, at 69 (Apr. 5) (when "Norway reaffirmed that she recognized the whole of Greenland as Danish, . . . she has [thus] debarred herself from contesting Danish sovereignty over the whole of Greenland").

208 Kenneth James Keith, *Succession to Bilateral Treaties by Seceding States*, 61 Am J. Int'l L. 521, 544 (1967) ("There is little doubt that . . . new states [may be] estopped by their actions . . . from denying the continued validity of [preexisting bilateral] treaties.").

209 Cheng, *supra* note 2, at 144 (quotation omitted). In support, Cheng cited an international tribunal that refused to hear a State's averment that a company did not comply with the terms of a concession, explaining that the State "should be estopped from going behind th[e] reports of its own officers

by conduct, recognized the Award as valid and it is no longer open to Nicaragua to go back upon that recognition and to challenge the validity of the Award."[210]

With the advent of investor-state treaties, application of the principle has flourished. For example, in *Southern Pacific Properties v. Egypt*,[211] the respondent argued that a private contract was a nullity because "certain acts of Egyptian officials upon which [petitioners relied were], under Egyptian law, legally nonexistent or absolutely null and void ... because they were not taken pursuant to the procedures prescribed by Egyptian law."[212] But the State's earlier acts indicated that it was committing to an agreement, and thus "created expectations protected by established principles of international law."[213] "[A]cts [that] ... create[] expectations [are] protected by established principles of international law.... If the municipal law does not provide a remedy [for such acts], the denial of any remedy whatsoever cannot be the final answer."[214] Accordingly, Egypt was barred from denying its obligations under the contract. The doctrine of acquiescence was invoked against Hungary in similar circumstances. Noting that "[a]lmost all systems of law prevent parties from blowing hot and cold," the tribunal in *ADC v. Hungary* stated that "[when] ... Hungary enters into and performs these agreements for years and takes the full benefit of them, it lies ill in

---

[acknowledging compliance] and from attacking their correctness without supplementary evidence tending to show that such reports were induced by mistake or were procured by fraud or undue influence." CHENG, *supra* note 2, at 147 (quoting *Salvador Commercial Co. Case* (1902)). This proposition holds where a State remains silent in the face of a state of affairs that it knew to be creating expectations in the other side. *See Case concerning the Temple of Preah Vihear (Cambodia v. Thai.)*, Merits, Judgment, 1962 I.C.J. 6, 30 (June 15).

210 *Case concerning the Arbitral Award Made by the King of Spain on 23 December 1906 (Hond. v. Nicar.)*, Judgment, 1960 I.C.J. 192, 213 (Nov. 18).

211 *S. Pacific Props. (Middle East) Ltd. v. Arab Republic of Egypt*, ICSID Case No. ARB/84/3, Award (May 20, 1992), 8 ICSID REV. 328, 351–52 (1993).

212 *Id.* at 351–52.

213 *Id.* at 352.

214 *S. Pacific Props. (Middle East) Ltd. v. Arab Republic of Egypt*, ICSID Case No. ARB/84/3, Award (May 20, 1992), 8 ICSID REV. 328, 352 (1993). *See also Fraport AG Frankfurt Airport Servs. Worldwide v. Republic of the Philippines*, ICSID Case No. ARB/03/25, Award, ¶ 346 (Aug. 16, 2007) ("There is, however, the question of estoppel. Principles of fairness should require a tribunal to hold a government estopped from raising violations of its own law as a jurisdictional defense when it knowingly overlooked them and endorsed an investment, which was not in compliance with its law."); *Inmaris Perestroika Sailing Maritime Servs. GmbH and others v. Ukraine*, ICSID Case No. ARB/08/8, Decision on Jurisdiction, ¶ 140 (Mar. 8, 2010); *Desert Line Projects LLC v. Republic of Yemen*, ICSID Case No. ARB/05/17, Award, ¶¶ 119–20 (Feb. 6, 2008); *Railroad Dev. Corp. v. Republic of Guatemala*, ICSID Case No. ARB/07/23, Second Decision on Objections to Jurisdiction, ¶¶ 146–47 (May 18, 2010); *The Gibraltar Football Association (GFA)/Union des Associations Européennes de Football (UEFA)*, Arbitration CAS 2002/O/410, Award (Oct. 7, 2003).

the mouth of Hungary now to challenge the legality and/or enforceability from these Agreements."[215]

Estoppel applies with particular force when the contract in dispute is one to arbitrate. The "international *ordre public* . . . vigorously reject[s] the proposition that a State organ, dealing with foreigners, having openly, with knowledge and intent, concluded an arbitration clause that inspires the co-contractant's confidence, could thereafter . . . invoke the nullity of its own promise."[216] Where, for instance, a State assents to arbitration by virtue of an official directive, and later seeks to undo the resulting award for want of capacity under its domestic law to agree to arbitration, the later act will be disregarded as ultra vires because it conflicts with this "deeply rooted general principle of law."[217] Application of this aspect of estoppel has been widespread.[218]

Perhaps the most vibrant modern affirmation of the principle of estoppel lies in the protection of "legitimate expectations" through the fair and equitable treatment (FET) standard in modern investment law. The FET standard has been read to capture a broad spectrum of state conduct, and has served as the legal

215 *ADC Affiliate Ltd. v. Republic of Hungary*, ICSID Case No. ARB/03/16, Award, ¶ 475 (Oct. 2, 2006).

216 Yves Derains, *Le Statut des Usages du Commerce International Devant Les Jurisdictions Arbitrales*, 1973 REV. ARB. 145 (quoting ICC Case No. 1939/1971); *see also* Andreas Lowenfeld, *International Arbitration and International Law*, *in* LOWENFELD ON INTERNATIONAL ARBITRATION 226 (Juris 2005) ("a state party cannot by its unilateral act free itself from its obligations [to arbitrate]; even if the underlying act was justified—a conclusion [that the obligation is void] must come from the agreed arbitral forum, not from a party itself"); Mustill, *supra* note 6, at 112.

217 *Desert Line Projects LLC v. Republic of Yemen*, ICSID Case No. ARB/05/17, Award, ¶ 207 (Feb. 6, 2008).

218 *Benteler v. Belgian State*, Award (Nov. 18, 1983), 1 J. INT'L ARB. 184, 190 (1984); *see also Treatment of Polish Nationals and Other Persons of Polish Origin or Speech in the Danzig Territory*, Advisory Opinion, 1932 P.C.I.J. (Ser. A/B) No. 44, at 24–25 (Feb. 4) ("a State cannot adduce as against another State its own Constitution with a view to evading obligations incumbent upon it under international law or treaties in force"); ICC Case No. 7263 of 1994, Interim Award, 22 Y.B. COMM. ARB. 92, 98 (1997) ("In the field of international commercial arbitration, . . . states and public bodies as defendants . . . cannot avail themselves of the incapacity and lack of authorization [to contract] deriving from their national laws."); *Company Z and Others v. State Organization ABC*, Award (Apr. 1982), 8 Y.B. COMM. ARB. 94, 108–09 (1983) (applying local law to the dispute but recognizing the "general principle, universally recognized nowadays in both inter-State relations and international private relations . . . [that] would in any case prohibit the Utopian State [*sic*] . . . to repudiate the undertaking to arbitrate which it made itself"); *Khoms el Mergeb v. Societe Dalico*, 1994 REV. ARB. 116 (Cour de Cassation 1994) (the "existence and effectiveness" of an international arbitration clause with the State is to be addressed "according to the common intention of the parties, without need to refer to national law"); Court of Appeal, Stockholm (June 19, 1980), 20 I.L.M. 893 (1981); *see also* Swiss Private International Law Act art. 177(2) (1987); CRAIG ET AL., *supra* note 22, § 35.02(v).

basis for decisions in numerous cases, including *Southern Pacific Properties*[219] and *ADC*.[220] A quintessential example of general principles playing a definitional role, investor-state tribunals have interpreted FET to require "stability, predictability, and consistency of the legal framework"; "protection of legitimate expectations"; "due process, and the prohibition of denial of justice"; "transparency"; and "reasonableness and proportionality."[221] Consanguineous with estoppel, *the principle governing the protection of legitimate expectations applies "to a situation where a [State's] conduct creates reasonable and justifiable expectations on the part of the investor . . . to act in reliance on said conduct," and then the State fails to honor those expectations and thereby "cause[s] the investor . . . to suffer damages."*[222] Thomas Wälde, in his separate opinion in the *Thunderbird* case, likened the protection of "legitimate expectation" to common law estoppel, the Latin maxim "*venire contra factum proprium*," the civil law concept of *actos propios*, and the German phrase "*Vertrauensschutz*."[223] Other decisions, however, have deemed the protection of legitimate expectations to be a principle unto itself when a private party relies on the representations of a sovereign. Like estoppel, this principle is "based on converging considerations of good faith," and finds its roots in the legal traditions of many national jurisdictions, including German, French, English, and Venezuelan law;[224] Brazilian law;[225] Argentine law; and the law of the European Union.[226] Although the proper categorizations can be

---

219 *S. Pacific Props. (Middle East) Ltd. v. Arab Republic of Egypt*, ICSID Case No. ARB/84/3, Award (May 20, 1992), 8 ICSID Rev. 328 (1993).

220 *ADC Affiliate Ltd. v. Republic of Hungary*, ICSID Case No. ARB/03/16, Award (Oct. 2, 2006).

221 Schill, *supra* note 178, at 148, 165–80.

222 *Int'l Thunderbird Gaming Corp. v. United Mexican States*, UNCITRAL, Award, ¶ 147 (Jan. 26, 2006); *see also Total S.A. v. Argentine Republic*, ICSID Case No. ARB/04/01, Decision on Liability, ¶ 128 (Dec. 27, 2010); *Gold Reserve Inc. v. Bolivarian Republic of Venezuela*, ICSID Case No. ARB(AF)/09/1, Award, ¶ 576 (Sept. 22, 2014).

223 *Int'l Thunderbird Gaming Corp. v. United Mexican States*, UNCITRAL, Separate Opinion of Thomas Wälde, ¶¶ 25–30 & nn.19, 30, 32 (Dec. 1, 2005). Wälde also anchored the principle of "legitimate expectations" in the principles of good faith and estoppel through a review of comparative contract law, administrative law, and ECJ case law.

224 *See Gold Reserve Inc. v. Bolivarian Republic of Venezuela*, ICSID Case No. ARB(AF)/09/1, Award, ¶ 576 (Sept. 22, 2014).

225 *Recurso em Mandado de Segurança*, nº 6183-MG—4ª Turma Cível—Judge Ruy Rosado de Aguiar Júnior (Nov. 14, 1995).

226 *Total S.A. v. Argentine Republic*, ICSID Case No. ARB/04/01, Decision on Liability, ¶¶ 128–30 (Dec. 27, 2010). Conversely, in some national courts, there exist higher thresholds to estop the government to perform governmental acts, but these rules are typically a function of internal political doctrines such as the separation of powers, see *Office of Pers. Mgmt. v. Richmond*, 496 U.S. 414, 423 (1990), and do not denigrate the general principle that the government can be estopped when it deals with private parties.

debated, the decisional law concerning legitimate expectations and the FET standard illuminates the general principle of estoppel.[227]

Of the three basic elements of estoppel described above, two have received considerable attention and explication in this context. *First*, the existence of a statement, position, or action that induces reliance has been broadly construed. In the FET context, those clear representations must of course come *from the government*, but they need not be formal affirmations such as the grant of a license or permit. All that is necessary is "[a] representation of fact [that is] unequivocal in the sense that it can reasonably support the meaning attributed to it by the party raising the plea of estoppel[,] and that party must satisfy the court that it understood the statement to have that meaning."[228] In some situations, the behavior of government officials over the course of a relationship, and even their lack of action in the face of an open and continuous situation, can suffice to induce reliance by a foreign investor (so long as the officials have apparent authority to bind the government).[229] It is possible to discern from the various decisions assessing whether particular sovereign conduct fairly gives rise to a violation of the FET standard that specific and official undertakings are more likely to generate legitimate expectations than general and informal ones,[230] and the fact that the

227 One tribunal seemed to categorize the protection of legitimate expectations as a separate principle, expressly noting that it was "akin to the principle of estoppel," and "may lead to the same result." *Total S.A. v. Argentine Republic*, ICSID Case No. ARB/04/01, Decision on Liability, ¶ 131 (Dec. 27, 2010). But some considerations may counsel that the principles of estoppel and legitimate expectations remain separate, but related, legal cognates. In the case of estoppel arising from a relationship between two private parties, because those parties occupy roughly equal positions, each of them can be expected, in turn, to employ an equal degree of due diligence to minimize the ambiguities in their respective undertakings and representations. Where, however, one party is a State and the other a foreign investor, the threshold for finding a legitimate expectation arising from an official representation may be lower because the former occupies a superior position of authority and cannot readily be approached for any clarification. *See Int'l Thunderbird Gaming Corp. v. United Mexican States*, UNCITRAL, Separate Opinion of Thomas Wälde, ¶ 33 (Dec. 1, 2005).

228 Bowett, *supra* note 191, at 184–85.

229 *Metalclad Corp. v. United Mexican States*, ICSID Case No. ARB(AF)/97/1, Award, ¶¶ 85–87, 101 (Aug. 30, 2000); *Gold Reserve Inc. v. Bolivarian Republic of Venezuela*, ICSID Case No. ARB(AF)/09/1, Award, ¶¶ 577–615 (Sept. 22, 2014).

230 *See Int'l Thunderbird Gaming Corp. v. United Mexican States*, UNCITRAL, Separate Opinion of Thomas Wälde, ¶¶ 31–32 (Dec. 1, 2005) ("The greater the formality of an assurance, the greater its ability to trigger a legitimate expectation. . . . The threshold for . . . informal and general representations is quite high."); *Gold Reserve Inc. v. Bolivarian Republic of Venezuela*, ICSID Case No. ARB(AF)/09/1, Award, ¶ 571 (Sept. 22, 2014) ("Undertakings and representations made explicitly or implicitly by the host State are the stronger basis for legitimate expectations."); *see also Nagel v. Czech Republic*, SCC Case No. 49/2002, Award, ¶¶ 293, 326 (Sept. 9, 2003) (informal representations from "influential personal friends and contacts within the [government]" may provide an "over-optimistic" view of an investment, but rarely lead to a "legitimate expectation").

offending conduct is related to the public interest and is nondiscriminatory militates against finding a violation.[231]

Second, and relatedly, international tribunals have repeatedly drawn a clear line between unjustified expectations (which neither receive protection under the FET standard nor support the invocation of the doctrine of estoppel) and legitimate expectations (which do both).[232] Every foreign investor at the time of contracting is, or is deemed to be, aware of the conditions of the host State—such as the political situation, the general business climate, and the overall legislative and administrative framework. These factors provide the lens through which the law views the investor's expectations for that investment.[233] Without a clear commitment, no investor can reasonably expect a State's regulatory regime to remain static over the course of a long-term investment—this is precisely why investors often seek fiscal stability.[234] Nor, within limits, can an investor in a developing State expect the same level of administrative stability and efficiency as found in a developed country.[235] But, at the same time, sovereigns cannot invoke an investor's ex ante knowledge of country conditions to excuse inconsistent behavior,[236] such as by changing a tariff regime when it previously told an investor that that regime would remain unchanged[237] or by arbitrarily revoking prior concessions,

231 *Continental Casualty Co. v. Argentine Republic*, ICSID Case No. ARB/03/9, Award, ¶¶ 260–66 (Sept. 5, 2008). *See also* Kenneth J. Vandevelde, *A Unified Theory of Fair and Equitable Treatment*, 43 INT'L L. & POL. 43, 79–80 (2010) ("Applying these factors, the [*Continental Casualty*] tribunal found that, for the most part, the claimant had no legitimate expectations that were frustrated by Argentina.").

232 Tribunals have interchangeably used the words "justified," "reasonable," "basic," and "fundamental" as expressions of the "legitimacy" of an expectation. *See* IOANA TUDOR, THE FAIR AND EQUITABLE TREATMENT STANDARD IN THE INTERNATIONAL LAW OF FOREIGN INVESTMENT (2008), at 165.

233 *See generally id.* at 164–65 (citing *Técnicas Medioambientales Tecmed, S.A. v. United Mexican States*, ICSID Case No. ARB (AF)/00/2, Award, ¶ 154 (May 29, 2003)); *see also Duke Energy Electroquil Partners and Electroquil S.A. v. Republic of Ecuador*, ICSID Case No. ARB/04/19, Award, ¶ 340 (Aug. 18, 2008) (stating that the legitimacy and reasonableness of an expectation must be judged against the "political, socioeconomic, cultural and historical conditions prevailing in the host State").

234 *See, e.g., Saluka Investments B.V. v. Czech Republic*, UNCITRAL, Partial Award, ¶ 305 (March 17, 2006); *Total S.A. v. Argentine Republic*, ICSID Case No. ARB/04/01, Decision on Liability, ¶¶ 135–58 (Dec. 27, 2010).

235 TUDOR, *supra* note 232, at 165; *see also Parkerings-Compagniet v. Lithuania*, ICSID Case No. ARB/05/8, Award, ¶¶ 333–37 (Sept. 11, 2007) (when investing in a country undergoing a change from a Soviet State to a market economy and EU member, legislative changes were likely, and the expectation of a static regulatory framework was unreasonable).

236 *EnCana Corp. v. Republic of Ecuador*, LCIA Case No. UN3481, UNCITRAL, Award, ¶ 158 (Feb. 3, 2006) ("One arm of the State cannot finally affirm what another arm denies to the detriment of a foreign investor.").

237 *See CMS Gas Transmission Co. v. Argentine Republic*, ICSID Case No. ARB/01/8, Award, ¶¶ 275–81 (May 12, 2005).

permits, licenses, and approvals upon which the investor detrimentally relied.[238] In between these poles lie the harder cases, which require "a weighing of the Claimant's legitimate and reasonable expectations on the one hand and the Respondent's legitimate regulatory interests on the other."[239]

The U.S. Supreme Court, for instance, held that the U.S. Government was responsible for breach-of-contract damages stemming from the enactment of legislation that revoked certain regulatory benefits that had been promised to thrift banks during the savings-and-loan crisis in the early 1980s.[240] The rationale for the result, however, did not attract a majority of the Supreme Court. Writing for a plurality of four justices, Justice David Souter stated that the banks were not arguing that Congress was prevented from enacting the legislation, but merely that the Government had an obligation to pay for the damages resulting from the legislative change: "The Government cannot make a binding contract that it will not exercise a sovereign power, but it can agree in a contract that if it does so, it will pay the other contracting party the amount by which its costs are increased by the Government's sovereign act."[241] This accords with the tendency in investment arbitration to award damages rather than specific performance, as noted in chapter 2.A. Three other justices concurred in the result because, per Justice Antonin Scalia, it was unmistakably clear that the Government "made promises to *regulate* in a certain fashion, into the future," such that "unless the Government is bound as to that regulation, an aspect of the transactions that reasonably must be viewed as a *sine qua non* of the [banks'] assent becomes illusory."[242] A similar result was reached by the Colombian Constitutional Court, which determined that stability contracts could not restrict the power of the Government to regulate,

238 *See, e.g., Waste Mgmt. Inc. v. United Mexican States* ("Number 2"), ICSID Case No. ARB(AF)/00/3, Award, ¶¶ 98–99 (Apr. 30, 2004); *CME Czech Republic B.V. v. Czech Republic*, UNCITRAL, Partial Award, ¶¶ 155–57, 170 (Sept. 13, 2001); *Metalclad Corp. v. United Mexican States*, ICSID Case No. ARB(AF)/97/1, Award, ¶¶ 89–90, 99–101 (Aug. 30, 2000).

239 *Saluka Investments B.V. v. Czech Republic*, UNCITRAL, Partial Award, ¶ 306 (Mar. 17, 2006); *see also Int'l Thunderbird Gaming Corp. v. United Mexican States*, UNCITRAL, Separate Opinion Thomas Wälde, ¶ 30 (Dec. 1, 2005). The difficulty in applying this balancing test is exemplified by the Czech Republic cases decided almost simultaneously in 2001. In one case, the tribunal held that regulatory changes surrounding the restructuring of a television station violated the investors' legitimate expectations and the host State's promise of fair and equitable treatment, *see CME Czech Republic B.V. v. Czech Republic*, UNCITRAL, Partial Award, ¶ 624 (Sept. 13, 2001), whereas the tribunal in the other case assessed the same legislative changes and found no basis for reasonable reliance by the investor, *see Ronald S. Lauder v. Czech Republic*, UNCITRAL, Award, ¶ 295 (Sept. 3, 2001).

240 *See United States v. Winstar Corp.*, 518 U.S. 839–41 (1996).

241 *Id.* at 881 (plurality op.), quoting *Amino Bros. Co. v. United States*, 372 F.2d 485, 491 (Ct. Cl. 1967).

242 *Id.* at 921–22 (Scalia, J., concurring in the result).

but that the investor could demand a proper compensation when a change of legislation affected the expected economic benefit from the investment.[243]

Even representations that fail to estop a party (because of, say, their relative ambiguity or their failure to induce detrimental reliance) may still constitute evidence of the fact represented.[244] Such evidentiary use is not conclusive and does not foreclose a party from arguing to the contrary. It rather is directed at a tribunal's sense of consistency, or what in logic is paradoxically called the "principle of contradiction."[245] Although more limited, such evidentiary use falls within the principle of *allegans contraria non est audiendus*. Some basic evidentiary principles concerning this concept are discussed in chapter 3.E.

D. The Prohibition on Advantageous Wrongs and Unjust Enrichment

> *[It is among] the most exceptionable of all principles, that he who does wrong shall be at liberty to plead his own illegal conduct on other occasions as a partial excuse.*
>
> —Commissioner William Pinkney[246]

Nemini dolos suus prodesse debet and *nemo auditur propriam turpitudinem allegans*: these central tenets mean, inter alia, that a party cannot build a case upon a fraud, cannot cause the nonperformance of a condition precedent to its own obligation, and cannot invoke its own malfeasance to diminish its liability. Although expressed in myriad ways, *it is basic that "[n]o one can be allowed to take advantage of his own wrong."*[247]

Cheng illustrated this principle by reference to the seminal *Chorzów Factory* case. In the wake of World War I, the Polish Government had expropriated the

243 *See* Eduardo Zuleta, *International Jurisprudence, Global Governance, and Global Administrative Law*, *in* 94 Practicing Virtue: Inside International Arbitration (David D. Caron et al. eds., 2015).

244 *See* Bowett, *supra* note 191, at 185–86, 188–90, 194–97 (citing and discussing cases).

245 Cheng, *supra* note 2, at 147.

246 *The Betsy Case* (1797).

247 Cheng, *supra* note 2, at 149 (quoting *The Montijo Case* (1875)); *see also* Edwin M. Borchard, The Diplomatic Protection of Citizens Abroad or the Law of International Claims 713 (Bankslaw 1915) ("It is an established maxim of all law, municipal and international, that no one can profit by his own wrong.").

Chorzów Factory without following the procedure laid down in the Geneva Convention of 1922, which required prior notice to the real or apparent owner so as to permit an appeal to the Germano-Polish Mixed Arbitral Tribunal.[248] By failing to provide such notice, Poland had illegally deprived the expropriated party of the opportunity to be heard.[249] Yet, when Germany espoused its citizen's claim before the Permanent Court of International Justice (PCIJ), Poland contested jurisdiction on the ground that the Mixed Tribunal was the competent forum to hear the claim.[250] The PCIJ dismissed the objection because

> [i]t is . . . a principle generally accepted in the jurisprudence of international arbitration, as well as by municipal courts, that one Party cannot avail himself of the fact that the other has not fulfilled some obligation or has not had recourse to some means of redress, if the former Party has, by some illegal act, prevented the latter from fulfilling the obligation in question, or from having recourse to the tribunal which would have been open, to him.[251]

As Cheng observed, this principle is a corollary to estoppel and an application of the principle "*nullus commodum capere potest de sua iniuria propria.*"[252] Also a facet of the overarching principle of abuse of rights, the prohibition against use of an illegal act was cited by the PCIJ on several occasions.[253]

Although capacious enough to capture the full gamut of inequitable conduct, the principle has been specifically applied to (1) deny a private action based upon a fraud or other unlawful conduct, (2) forbid a contracting party from blocking

---

248 *Factory at Chorzów (Fed. Rep. Ger. v. Pol.)*, Merits, Judgment, 1928 P.C.I.J. (Ser. A.) No. 17, at 13 (Sept. 13).

249 *Id.* at 31–32.

250 *Id.* at 30.

251 *Id.* at 31. Cheng cited two other illustrative examples. In the *Frances Irene Roberts Case*, the United States-Venezuelan Mixed Claims Commission (1903) rejected a plea of prescription in a case that, though diligently prosecuted by the claimants for over 30 years, had not yet been resolved: "The contention [made by Venezuela] that this claim is barred by the lapse of time would, if admitted, allow the Venezuelan Government to reap advantage from its own wrong in failing to make just reparation to [claimant] at the time the claim arose." The conduct in *The Tattler Case* (1920) was equally notorious: "It is difficult to admit that a foreign ship may be seized for not having a certain document when the document has been refused to it by the very authorities who required that it should be obtained." *See* Cheng, *supra* note 2, at 150.

252 Cheng, *supra* note 2, at 155.

253 *See Free Zones Case*, 1930 P.C.I.J. (Ser. A) No. 24, at 12 (Dec. 6, 1930); and 1932 P.C.I.J. (Ser. A/B) No. 46, at 167 (June 7, 1932).

a condition precedent to its own contract performance, and (3) prevent unjust enrichment. Each application of the principle will be discussed in turn.

First, no cause of action will succeed if the claim is founded upon an unlawful act. This legal principle was first articulated in Roman law and can also be traced to tenth century Chinese customary law.[254] It sounds in equity and can take many forms.[255] Thus, when a State asks a tribunal to prohibit allegedly breaching behavior by its treaty partner, its claim will be denied where it, too, is "engaged in taking precisely similar action, similar in fact and similar in law."[256] In the same way, an investor's claim against a State will not lie where that investment was procured by fraud.[257]

The application of the principle nonetheless calls for case-specific discretion, and there is no strict or uniform principle in national legal orders that prohibits judicial relief whenever a claimant has contravened the law or failed to fulfill its contractual obligations.[258] Anglo-Saxon jurisprudence, for instance, "closes the door of a court of equity to one tainted with inequitableness or bad faith relative to the matter in which he seeks relief, however improper may have been the behavior of the defendant."[259] As U.S. Supreme Court Justice Louis Brandeis explained, "[aid] is denied in order to maintain respect for law; in order to promote confidence in the administration of justice; in order to preserve the judicial process from contamination."[260] Sir Gerald Fitzmaurice likewise noted that "a [party] which is guilty of illegal conduct may be deprived of the necessary *locus standi*

254 Rahim Moloo, *A Comment on the Clean Hands Doctrine in International Law*, *in* 8 Transnational Dispute Management, Issue 1 (Feb. 2011); T. Leigh Anenson, *Treating Equity Like Law: A Post-merger Justification of Unclean Hands*, 45 Am. Bus. L.J. 455, 478 (2008); Ralph A. Newman, Equity and Law: A Comparative Study 250 n.19 (Oceana 1961).

255 Aloysius Llamzon, *The State of the "Unclean Hands" Doctrine in International Investment Law:* Yukos *as both Omega and Alpha*, 30 ICSID Rev. 315, 316–27 (2015).

256 *Diversion of Water from the Meuse (Neth. v. Belg.)*, Judgment, 1937 P.C.I.J. (Ser. A/B) No. 70, at 78, ¶ 325 (June 28) (individual opinion of Manley Hudson); *see also Military and Paramilitary Activities in and against Nicaragua (Nicar. v. U.S.)*, Merits, Judgment, 1986 I.C.J. 14, 268–72 (June 27) (dissenting opinion of Judge Schwebel) ("Nicaragua has not come to Court with clean hands" and its "claims against the United States should fail").

257 *See World Duty Free Co. Ltd. v. Republic of Kenya*, ICSID Case No. ARB/00/7, Award, ¶¶ 161, 181 (Oct. 4, 2006); *Inceysa Vallisoletana S.L. v. Republic of El Salvador*, ICSID Case No. ARB/03/26, Award, ¶ 240 (Aug. 2, 2006); *Metal-Tech Ltd. v. Republic of Uzbekistan*, ICSID Case No. ARB/10/3, Award, ¶ 373 (Oct. 4, 2014).

258 *See, e.g.*, Zachary Douglas, *The Plea of Illegality in Investment Treaty Arbitration*, 29 ICSID Rev. 155 (2014).

259 *Precision Instrument Mfg. Co. v. Auto. Maint. Mach. Co.*, 324 U.S. 806, 814 (1945).

260 *Olmstead v. United States*, 277 U.S. 438, 484 (1928) (Brandeis, J., dissenting).

in judicio for complaining of corresponding illegalities on the part of other [parties], especially if these were consequential on or were embarked upon in order to counter its own illegality—in short were provoked by it."[261]

But the concept of "unclean hands" has been circumscribed in the international setting. One tribunal held that the doctrine applies only where (1) the claimant is seeking specific performance against future conduct, as opposed to reparation for an alleged past injury; (2) the claimant's alleged malfeasance is ongoing; and (3) the claimant's conduct relates to the same reciprocal obligation on which it is bringing suit.[262] Elements such as these go to the broader question whether sustaining the claim will perpetuate or reward an unlawful act.[263] The requirement that there be a nexus between the malfeasance and the cause of action serves to limit the number of situations in which the doctrine might apply,[264] thereby lessening the tension with the "principle of international law that any breach leads to an obligation to make reparation."[265] For instance, a diplomatic protection action on behalf of an alien who is subjected to torture after being arrested on criminal charges would not be barred because, even ignoring the fiction that the claim belongs to the protecting State (such that the alien's conduct is legally irrelevant), the alien's alleged crime is not commensurately related to the State's alleged international delict.[266]

Even with these qualifications, the application of "unclean hands" has been rare, raising the question whether this specific manifestation of *ex dolo malo non oritur actio* qualifies as a general principle.[267] The answer may turn in part upon the *procedural use* of the claimant's alleged malfeasance, that is, whether it bars the admission of a claim altogether or whether it is to be considered as part of the merits. Although the doctrine is traditionally understood as one of admissibility,[268]

261 Sir Gerald Fitzmaurice, 92 Recueil des Cours 119 (1957-II) (citations omitted).

262 *Guyana v. Suriname*, PCA, Award, ¶¶ 420–21 (Sept. 17, 2007).

263 Cheng, *supra* note 2, at 157–58.

264 *Niko Resources (Bangladesh) Ltd. v. People's Republic of Bangladesh et al.*, ICSID Case Nos. ARB/10/11 and ARB/10/18, Decision on Jurisdiction, ¶ 483 (Aug. 19, 2013) (rejecting "unclean hands" defense because, inter alia, "there is no relation of reciprocity between the relief which the Claimant now seeks in this arbitration and the acts in the past which the Respondents characterise [*sic*] as involving unclean hands").

265 *Guyana v. Suriname*, PCA, Award, ¶ 420 (Sept. 17, 2007).

266 *See* International Law Commission, *Sixth Report on Diplomatic Protection by Mr. John Dugard, Special Rapporteur* ¶¶ 8–9 Doc. A/CN.4/546 (57th Sess., Aug. 11, 2004).

267 *Guyana v. Suriname*, PCA, Award, ¶ 418 (Sept. 17, 2007).

268 *See Report of the International Law Commission on the Work of Its 51st Session*, U.N. GAOR, 54th Sess., Supp. No. 10, ¶ 411, U.N. Doc. A/54/10 (May 3–July 23, 1999).

recent authorities have indicated that a claimant's allegedly unlawful acts bear upon the substance of its claim and the relief that it seeks. The ICJ, for instance, deferred consideration of a "clean hands" argument to the merits phase in the *Concerning Oil Platforms* case.[269] Similarly, the tribunal in *Hulley Enterprises v. Russia* declined to recognize as a general principle the doctrine of "unclean hands" as "a complete bar" to claimants' claims as a "preliminary objection"—"whether as a matter of jurisdiction, admissibility or otherwise"[270]—but it considered the claimant's alleged malfeasance as part of its "assessment of liability and damages."[271] And although the principle of "clean hands" was considered and rejected for inclusion in the International Law Commission Draft Articles on Diplomatic Protection, the Special Rapporteur acknowledged that "the doctrine would more appropriately be raised at the merits stage, as it relates to attenuation or exoneration of responsibility rather than to admissibility."[272] These authorities suggest a dichotomy under which a claimant's "unclean hands" may not necessarily act as a threshold bar to jurisdiction or admissibility, as is the orthodox approach, but can instead be taken into account in considering the availability, scope, and nature of the relief.[273] Consistent with the reality that a claimant's conduct with respect to a dispute invariably affects some aspect of its resolution, it may be said that "as a doctrine dealing with substantive law in international

269 *Case concerning Oil Platforms (Iran v. U.S.)*, Judgment, 2003 I.C.J. 161, 177–78 (Nov. 6) (deferring resolution of claim by the United States that Iran's conduct precludes it from obtaining relief because it entailed examination of the actions of both States).

270 *See Hulley Enters. Ltd. (Cyprus) v. Russian Federation*, UNCITRAL, PCA Case No. AA226, Final Award, ¶¶ 1311, 1357–63, 1373 (July 18, 2014). Correctly noting that "[g]eneral principles of law require a certain level of recognition and consensus," the *Hulley Enterprises* tribunal found that there still exists "a significant amount of controversy" as to whether the doctrine may "bar an investor from making a claim before an arbitral tribunal under an investment treaty because it has so-called 'unclean hands.'" *Id.* ¶¶ 1358–59; *see also* Douglas, *supra* note 258, at 166–67.

271 *Hulley Enters. Ltd. v. Russian Federation*, UNCITRAL, PCA Case No. AA226, Final Award, ¶¶ 1276, 1373–74 (July 18, 2014); Llamzon, *supra* note 255, at 324–25 (noting that "the [*Yukos*] Tribunal did not engage with this argument [claimants' argument that the "unclean hands" doctrine required the Tribunal to consider the investor's illegality vis-à-vis the host State's original breach] but may have effectively conducted such an analysis through its findings on contributory fault").

272 *See* International Law Commission, *Sixth Report on Diplomatic Protection by John Dugard, Special Rapporteur* ¶ 16 (Aug. 11, 2004); *see also* International Law Commission, *Draft Articles on Responsibility of States for Internationally Wrongful Acts, with Commentaries*, 2(5) Y.B. INT'L L. COMM. 72, ¶ 9 (2001) ("The so-called 'clean hands' doctrine has been invoked principally in the context of the admissibility of claims before international courts and tribunals, though rarely applied. It also does not need to be included here.").

273 *World Duty Free Co. Ltd. v. Republic of Kenya*, ICSID Case No. ARB/00/7, Award, ¶ 161 (Oct. 4, 2006) (discussing "principle of public policy that courts will not assist a plaintiff who has been guilty of illegal (or immoral) conduct of which the courts should take notice" as it would be "an affront to public conscience to grant the plaintiff the relief which he seeks because the court would thereby appear to assist or encourage the plaintiff in his illegal conduct").

adjudication, the clean hands doctrine is an established part of international law."[274]

A similar nuance also exists where a party seeks to invalidate an agreement to arbitrate based upon its adversary's unlawful acts. The application of this general principle operates against the backdrop of another: *"It is a generally recognized principle of the law of international arbitration that arbitration clauses continue to be operative, even though . . . the contract containing the arbitration clause is null and void."*[275] When the agreement to arbitrate is found in a commercial contract, an arbitration tribunal will typically have the competence to adjudge the plea of illegality under the doctrine of separability, unless that illegality somehow impugns the validity of the arbitration provision and, therefore, the tribunal's jurisdiction.[276] For instance, *World Duty Free v. Kenya* concerned a contract secured through the claimant's U.S. $2 million "donation" to Kenya's head of state.[277] Although the tribunal determined that it had jurisdiction because the contract's arbitration clause was not the specific product of graft, it held that the "[c]laimant is not legally entitled to maintain any of its pleaded claims in these proceedings on the ground of *ex turpi causa non oritur actio*."[278]

Similarly, when consent to arbitration is contained in a treaty that applies to all foreign investors, only illegality that taints the "making" of an investment, and not the "performance" of the investor while in country, will divest a tribunal of

---

274 *See* Aleksandr Shapovalov, *Should a Requirement of "Clean Hands" Be a Prerequisite to the Exercise of Diplomatic Protection? Human Rights Implications of the International Law Commission's Debate*, 20 AM. U. L. REV. 829, 864 (2005); *see also* Stephen M. Schwebel, *Clean Hands in the Court*, 31 STUD. TRANSNAT'L LEGAL POL'Y 74, 74–78 (1999) (discussing role of the "clean hands" doctrine in international law generally).

275 *Elf Aquitaine Iran (Fr.) v. Nat'l Iranian Oil Co.*, Prelim-Award (Jan. 14, 1982), 11 Y.B. COMM. ARB. 97, 102–05 (1986); *see also* ICC Award No. 5485, 14 Y.B. COMM. ARB. 156–73 (1989) ("the separability (autonomy) of the arbitration clause has long been recognized as a general principle of international commercial arbitration"); *Libyan American Oil Co. (LIAMCO) v. Gov't of the Libyan Arab Republic*, Award (Apr. 12, 1977), 6 Y.B. COMM. ARB. 89–118 (1981) ("It is widely accepted in international law and practice that an arbitration clause survives the unilateral termination by the State of the contract in which it is inserted and continues in force even after that termination."); *see also* UNCITRAL Arbitration Rules art. 21.2; UNCITRAL Model Law on Int'l Commercial Arb. (1985) (amended 2006) art. 16(1) (2013); LCIA Arbitration Rules art. 23.1 (2014); ICC Rules of Arbitration art. 6(4) (2012); REDFERN & HUNTER ON INTERNATIONAL ARBITRATION §§ 2.88–2.98 (5th ed. 2015) (and sources cited therein).

276 *See generally* Douglas, *supra* note 258, at 159–60.

277 *World Duty Free Co. Ltd. v. Republic of Kenya*, ICSID Case No. ARB/00/7, Award, ¶ 66 (Oct. 4, 2006).

278 *Id.* ¶¶ 179, 187.

jurisdiction or otherwise defeat an investment claim.[279] This can be seen in three ICSID awards.

In *Inceysa v. El Salvador*, the claimant invoked the Spain-El Salvador BIT to protect an investment procured through a fraudulent bidding process. The tribunal dismissed the claim for lack of jurisdiction because, inter alia, the claimants had procured the investment through fraud. The tribunal underscored that the maxim *nemo auditur propriam turpitudinem allegans* prohibits an investor from benefitting from "an investment effectuated by means of one or several illegal acts."[280] Similarly, in *Plama v. Bulgaria*, the tribunal concluded that "the investment was obtained by deceitful conduct" and was thus ineligible for the substantive protections of the Energy Charter Treaty.[281] As in *Inceysa*, the *Plama* tribunal barred investor reliance on the substantive protections of the underlying investment treaty where the investment was made unlawfully.[282] And in *Metal-Tech v. Uzbekistan*, an ICSID tribunal declined jurisdiction where the investment was procured by payment of approximately U.S. $4 million of unlawful "consulting" fees to intermediaries of Uzbekistan public officials.[283] The *Metal-Tech* tribunal explained that "[t]he idea . . . is not to punish one party at the cost of the other, but rather to ensure the promotion of the rule of law, which entails that a court or tribunal cannot grant assistance to a party that has engaged in a corrupt act."[284]

In each case, the alleged malfeasance went directly to the threshold question whether a lawful "investment" had been made. By contrast, an investment lawfully made does not fall outside the ambit of treaty protection just because the investor's operations thereafter were allegedly "unclean." In that situation, as held in *Hulley*

279 *See Hulley Enters. Ltd. v. Russian Federation*, UNCITRAL, PCA Case No. AA226, Final Award, ¶¶ 1351–54 (July 18, 2014).

280 *Inceysa Vallisoletana S.L. v. Republic of El Salvador*, ICSID Case No. ARB/03/26, Award, ¶¶ 240–42 (Aug. 2, 2006).

281 *Plama Consortium Ltd. v. Republic of Bulgaria*, ICSID Case No. ARB/03/24, Award, ¶ 143 (Aug. 27, 2008).

282 *Id.* There is an active debate as to whether such illegality in making an investment goes to the tribunal's jurisdiction or rather to the merits of the claim. *See* Zachary Douglas, *The Plea of Illegality in Investment Arbitration*, 29 ICSID Rev. 155, 161–63, 170–71 (2014). In either case, however, the same result would obtain.

283 *Metal-Tech Ltd. v. Republic of Uzbekistan*, ICSID Case No. ARB/10/3, Award, ¶¶ 240, 373 (Oct. 4, 2013) (dismissing BIT claim for lack of jurisdiction where investment was tainted by corruption).

284 *Metal-Tech Ltd. v. Republic of Uzbekistan*, ICSID Case No. ARB/10/3, Award, ¶ 389 (Oct. 4, 2014) (dismissing BIT claim for lack of jurisdiction where investment was tainted by corruption); *see also World Duty Free Co. Ltd. v. Republic of Kenya*, ICSID Case No. ARB/00/7, Award, ¶ 181 (Oct. 4, 2006) (acknowledging that "'the objection, that a contract is immoral or illegal as between plaintiff and defendant, sounds at all times very ill in the mouth of the defendant,'" but reiterating the importance of a court not lending its aid to "'an immoral or illegal act'") (quoting *Holman v. Johnson*, (1775) 1 Cowp. 341, 343).

Enterprises, "the host state can . . . impose upon [the investor] sanctions available under domestic law," but the protections of the investment treaty, including the ability to challenge those sanctions under international law, continue to abide.[285]

Other principles of positive law also derive from this aspect of good faith. It is universally accepted in municipal legal orders that *legal protection will not be afforded agreements that have an immoral purpose or are performed through unethical means*.[286] For example, no court will "recognise an agreement between the highwaymen to . . . split the proceeds" of their crimes.[287] A venerable example of this principle is found in the *Pelletier* case of 1885, in which the United States took the position that an arbitral award against Haiti for the seizure of the vessel of an American claimant should not be enforced because the vessel was engaged in slave trading. According to the U.S. Secretary of State, the principle of *ex turpi causa non oritur actio* had been applied in "innumerable rulings under Roman common law, as held by nations holding Latin traditions, and under the common law as held in England and the United States."[288]

Second, "[n]o party can be allowed by its own [abusive] act to bring about a non-performance of a condition precedent to its own obligation."[289] International arbitration tribunals have invoked this principle, which they link to the doctrines of *actos propios* and estoppel.[290] Where some form of government approval is a legal

285 *Hulley Enters. Ltd. v. Russian Federation*, UNCITRAL, PCA Case No. AA226, Final Award, ¶ 1355 (July 18, 2014). The tribunal elaborated that "it would undermine the purpose and object of [such treaties] to deny the investor the right to make its case before an arbitral tribunal based on the same alleged violations the existence of which the investor seeks to dispute on the merits." *Id.*

286 *See* ICC Award No. 4145 (Second Interim Award), 12 Y.B. Comm. Arb. 97, 102 (1987) (also published in J. Droit Int'l (Clunet) 985 (1985)); ICC Award No. 11307 of 2003, 33 Y.B. Comm. Arb. 24, 36 (2008) ("An example of an agreement being illegal because the making of it is prohibited, is the sale of merchandise prohibited by statute. An example of illegality when performance renders it so is an agreement to commit a crime. An example of both parties intending to further a purpose contrary to law is [where] . . . a person giv[es] a prosecutor an inducement not to prosecute for a crime. Such contracts are void because they are based on a *turpis causa*.").

287 *Soleimany v. Soleimany*, [1999] Q.B. 785, 797; *see also Beresford v. Royal Ins. Co. Ltd.*, [1938] A.C. 586, 599 ("Court will not recognize a benefit accruing to a criminal from his crime.").

288 *Pelletier Case*, at 606–07 (U.S.F.R. 1887); *see also Legal Status of Eastern Greenland (Den. v. Nor.)*, 1933 P.C.I.J. (Ser. A/B) No. 53, at 95 (Apr. 5) (dissenting opinion of Judge Anzilotti) ("[A]n unlawful act cannot serve as the basis of an action at law.").

289 Mustill, *supra* note 6, at 113 (citing Philippe Fouchard, L'Arbitrage commercial international (Paris 1965)); Hugh Thirlway, The Sources of International Law 101 (Oxford 2014) (arguing that Article 60 of the VCLT "preserves and enacts the essence of the principle . . . that you cannot have the benefit of a contract if you don't fulfil your side of the bargain").

290 *See, e.g.*, ICC Case No. 10346, Award (Dec. 2000), 12 ICC Bull. 106, 108–10; *Desert Line Projects LLC v. Republic of Yemen*, ICSID Case No. ARB/05/17, Award, ¶¶ 119–20 (Feb. 6, 2008); *Railroad Dev. Corp.*

prerequisite to a contract, for instance, both parties are expected to collaborate in good faith to procure that approval. In a case concerning the provision of electricity in Colombia, when the seller sued the buyer for a breach of contract, the buyer defended on the ground that the contract was null and void for lack of governmental registration. The tribunal found that the seller "did everything within its power" to register the contract, but that the buyer "took no effective steps" to assist but instead "simply opted to hide behind" the non-registration in order to "wash[] its hands" of the agreement. Noting that the principle of *ut res magis valeat quam pereat* imposed a duty on both parties to bring the contract into effect, the tribunal ultimately upheld the contract because the "[buyer] [cannot] rely [] on its own inconsistency to the detriment of the [seller]."[291] Similarly, in the investment context, a State cannot plead the defense of necessity to justify its legislative act "if it has contributed to the situation giving rise to a state of necessity."[292] This rule is related to the notion of impossibility and other excuse concepts, discussed in chapter 2.A, but it is independently "a general principle of law devised to prevent a party from taking legal advantage of its own fault."[293]

The *third*, and perhaps most common, situation for invoking the prohibition of advantageous wrongs is in claims for unjust enrichment. In general, the law does not countenance a party enriching itself to the detriment of another through its own wrongful acts or without lawful cause. Restitutionary theories such as *enrichissement sans cause*, originated in Roman law, are now found in the laws of many nations[294] and in international law.[295] Accordingly, *the prohibition on unjust enrichment "is widely accepted as having been assimilated into the catalogue*

---

v. Republic of Guatemala, ICSID Case No. ARB/07/23, Second Decision on Objections to Jurisdiction, ¶¶ 146–47 (May 18, 2010).

291 ICC Case No. 10346, Award (Dec. 2000), 12 ICC Bull. 106, 108–10.

292 *See, e.g., Sempra Energy Int'l v. Argentine Republic*, ICSID ARB/02/16, Award, ¶ 353 (Sept. 28, 2007); *see also Enron Corp. and Ponderosa Assets, L.P. v. Argentine Republic*, ICSID Case No. ARB/01/03, Award, ¶¶ 311–13 (May 22, 2007).

293 *Sempra Energy Int'l v. Argentine Republic*, ICSID ARB/02/16, Award, ¶ 353 (Sept. 28, 2007).

294 *See Isaiah v. Bank Mellat*, 2 Iran-U.S. Cl. Trib. Rep. 232, 236 (1983) (citing J. Dawson, Unjust Enrichment: A Comparative Analysis (1951)); *Amco Asia Corp. et al. v. Republic of Indonesia*, ICSID Case No. ARB/81/1, Resubmitted Case, Award, ¶¶ 154–56 (June 5, 1990); *Southern Pacific Properties Ltd. v. Arab Republic of Egypt*, ICSID Case No. ARB/84/3, Award, ¶¶ 245–49 (May 20, 1992); *Inceysa Vallisoletana S.L. v. Republic of El Salvador*, ICSID Case No. ARB/03/26, Award, ¶ 254 (Aug. 2, 2006) ("[t]he written legal systems of the nations governed by the Civil Law system" recognize the principle of unjust enrichment, which provides that "when the cause of the increase in the assets of a certain person is illegal, such enrichment must be sanctioned by preventing its consummation").

295 *Id.* (citing Marjorie M. Whiteman, 8 Digest of International Law 1035–36 (1967)).

of general principles of law."[296] The raison d'être of the principle is "to re-establish a balance between two individuals, one of whom has enriched himself, with no cause, at the other's expense."[297] So, where a bank holds a person's funds and refuses to honor a check drawn on those funds, the creditor can typically make a claim against the bank for unjust enrichment.[298]

When the enrichment stems from fraud or turpitude, application of the principle of unjust enrichment follows a fortiori in accordance with the aphorism *nemini dolos suus prodesse debet.*[299] But the principle of unjust enrichment is broader than that. The duty to compensate can arise even in the absence of fraud, and turpitude is not always a prerequisite. The mere "unjust" retention of a monetary benefit—viz., to which one is not legally entitled—is sufficient to implicate the principle and require compensation. The remedy has been found to obtain where there is (1) an enrichment of one party to the detriment of the other, with both arising as a consequence of the same act or event; (2) no legal justification for the enrichment; and (3) no contractual or other remedy for the enrichment available to the injured party.[300] The principle is often applied where a foreign investor is deprived of the benefit of certain tangible objects—such as a port facility—that the State takes for its own enjoyment and profit. The prohibition on unjust enrichment requires the State to pay restitution to the investor in the amount it was enriched.[301] The principle might also be applied in favor a State, when, for example, an investor obtains an award of damages for an expropriated business that was delinquent in its tax and social security obligations. In that situation, it would be unjust if those payments were not deducted from the value of the expropriated enterprise.[302]

---

296 *Sea-Land Servs., Inc. v. Islamic Republic of Iran*, 6 Iran-U.S. Cl. Trib. Rep. 149 (1984) (citing sources); *see Saluka Investments B.V. v. Czech Republic*, UNCITRAL, Partial Award, ¶ 449 (March 17, 2006) ("The concept of unjust enrichment is recognised as a general principle of international law. It gives one party a right of restitution of anything of value that has been taken or received by the other party without a legal justification."); *Schlegel Corp. v. Nat'l Iranian Copper Indus. Co.*, 14 Iran-U.S. Cl. Trib. Rep. 176 (1987); *Flexi-Van Leasing, Inc. v. Islamic Republic of Iran*, 12 Iran-U.S. Cl. Trib. Rep. 335 (1986); *Shannon & Wilson, Inc. v. Atomic Energy Org. of Iran*, 9 Iran-U.S. Cl. Trib. Rep. 397, 402 (1985).

297 *Sea-Land Servs., Inc. v. Islamic Republic of Iran*, 6 Iran-U.S. Cl. Trib. Rep. 149, 168 (1984) (quoting Francesco Francioni, *Compensation for Nationalisation of Foreign Property: The Borderland between Law and Equity*, 24 INT'L & COMP. L.Q. 259, 273 (1975)).

298 *Isaiah v. Bank Mellat*, 2 Iran-U.S. Cl. Trib. Rep. 232 (1983).

299 *See, e.g., Tippetts et al. v. TAMS-AFFA Consulting Engineers of Iran*, 6 Iran-U.S. Cl. Trib. Rep. 219, 228 (1984) ("It is a well recognized principle in many municipal systems and in international law that no one should be allowed to reap advantages from their own wrong, *Nullus Commodum Capere De Sua Injuria Propria.*").

300 *Id.*

301 *See, e.g., Sea-Land Servs., Inc. v. Islamic Republic of Iran*, 6 Iran-U.S. Cl. Trib. Rep. 149, 169–70 (1984).

302 *See Tippetts et al. v. TAMS-AFFA Consulting*, 6 Iran-U.S. Cl. Trib. Rep. 219, 226–28 (1984).

E. Corporate Separateness and Limited Liability

The whole problem of the relation between parent and subsidiary corporations is one that is still enveloped in the mists of metaphor. Metaphors in law are to be narrowly watched, for starting as devices to liberate thought, they end often by enslaving it.

—Justice (then Judge) Benjamin N. Cardozo[303]

Corporate personhood is recognized to allow asset partitioning among related entities.[304] In all legal systems, corporate entities have "rights and obligations peculiar to themselves," separate and apart from their constituent owners.[305] This concept of "limited liability" allows owners to separate corporate assets and liabilities from their own.[306] For both private and public corporations, "[l]imited liability is the rule, not the exception."[307] Given its widespread acceptance, *separation of legal identity between different companies, and between a company and its shareholders, is a general principle of law.*[308]

---

303 *Berkey v. Third Avenue R. Co.*, 244 N.Y. 84, 94 (N.Y. 1926).

304 *Barcelona Traction, Light & Power Co., Ltd. (Belg. v. Spain)*, Second Phase, Judgment, 1970 I.C.J. 3, ¶ 56 (Feb. 5) (finding a "wealth of practice already accumulated on the subject" of corporate personhood in municipal law); *see also* Clive M. Schmitthoff's Select Essays on International Trade Law 137 (BRILL 1988) (noting "the universal application of the juridical concept of corporateness ... [in] all national legal systems"); Henry Hansmann & Reinier Kraakman, *The Essential Role of Organizational Law*, 110 Yale L.J. 387, 426, 440 (2000).

305 *Barcelona Traction, Light & Power Co., Ltd. (Belg. v. Spain)*, Second Phase, Judgment, 1970 I.C.J. 3, ¶ 39 (Feb. 5).

306 *Id.* ¶¶ 40–41.

307 *First Nat'l City Bank (FNCB) v. Banco Para El Comercio Exterior de Cuba*, 462 U.S. 611, 626 (1983); *see also Salomon Salomon v. Salomon & Co.*, [1897] A.C. 22 (H.L.) 30-31 (Eng.); Canada Business Corporations Act, R.S.C. 1985, c. C-44, § 15(1) ("A corporation has the capacity and, subject to this Act, the rights, powers and privileges of a natural person."), § 45(1) ("[t]he shareholders of a corporation are not, as shareholders, liable for any liability, act or default of the corporation"); Germany, Aktiengesetz [AktG] § 1, ¶ 1; GmbH-Gesetz [GmbHG] § 13, ¶ 2; Estonian Commercial Code §§ 135(2), 221(2); Ecuador Civil Code art. 568 ("The property of a corporation is not owned, in whole or in part, by any of the individuals who make up the corporation. Reciprocally, no one has the right to sue any of the individuals who make up a corporation, in whole or in part, to recover a debt owed by the corporation, nor does the debt give rise to an action against their personal assets, but instead the corporation's assets. . . .").

308 *See Lemire v. Ukraine*, ICSID Case No. ARB/06/18, Dissenting Opinion of Arbitrator Dr. Jürgen Voss, ¶¶ 65–67 (Mar. 1, 2011) (noting that "[m]ost municipal legal systems recognize corporations as legal persons distinct from their shareholders," such that it "pervades" those systems of law, and is thus "in principle recognized by international law"); *Ahmadou Sadio Diallo (Guinea v. Dem. Rep. Congo)*, Preliminary Objections, Judgment, 2007 I.C.J. 582, ¶¶ 61–63, at 605 (May 24) (holding that, under international law, "[c]onferring independent corporate personality on a company implies granting it rights over its own property, rights which it alone is capable of protecting," and looking to Congolese law for

As his book primarily concerned state-to-state relations, Cheng did not address corporate separateness or limited liability. But at that time the importance of these complementary principles was emerging as a practical necessity. In 1964, the ICJ noted that "there are almost as many different kinds of corporate entities as there are different systems of municipal law under which they are constituted and since their activities have been growing in complexity as well as in kind, the problem of protecting their legitimate interests in international law has been assuming increasing importance as well as endless complexity."[309] Although many of these variations remain today, certain basic principles pertaining to the corporate form were and are evident.

In 1970, the ICJ for the first time recognized "the corporate entity as an institution created by states" and began to "refer to the relevant rules of municipal law" in determining the rights and duties of corporate entities and their shareholders.[310] Drawing from "rules generally accepted by municipal legal systems,"[311] it held that, under international law, there is a "firm distinction between the separate entity of the company and that of the shareholders," such that the shareholder is "separated from the company" and "cannot be identified with it."[312] As a result, the "company alone, through its directors or management acting in its name, can take action in respect of matters that are ... [in the corporation's] best interests."[313] These precepts result in primary liability for the corporation.[314] They correspondingly circumscribe both the rights of shareholders with respect to corporate governance and the liability of shareholders with respect to corporate debt. To deny these principles is to deny the existence of the corporate

its treatment of companies); *Rompetrol Grp. N.V. v. Romania*, ICSID Case No. ARB/06/3, Decision on Respondent's Preliminary Objections on Jurisdiction and Admissibility, ¶ 90 (Apr. 18, 2008) (citing *Barcelona Traction* for the proposition that "a corporate entity has a legal personality, and a set of rights and obligations, which are separate from those of its shareholders"); *HICEE B.V. v. Slovak Republic*, UNCITRAL, PCA Case No. 2009-11, Partial Award on Jurisdiction, ¶ 147 (May 23, 2011) (discussing "the default position in international law that the corporate form is ... legally distinct").

309 *Barcelona Traction, Light & Power Co., Ltd. (Belg. v. Spain)*, Preliminary Objections, Judgment, 1964 I.C.J. 6, ¶ 12 at 55 (separate opinion of Vice-President Wellington Koo) (July 24).

310 *Barcelona Traction, Light & Power Co., Ltd. (Belg. v. Spain)*, Second Phase, Judgment, 1970 I.C.J. 3, ¶¶ 38, 41, 47 (Feb. 5).

311 *Id.* ¶ 50.

312 *Id.* ¶ 41.

313 *Id.* ¶ 42.

314 *See, e.g., First Nat'l City Bank (FNCB) v. Banco Para El Comercio Exterior de Cuba*, 462 U.S. 611, 628–29 n.20 (1983); *see also Doe v. Exxon Mobil Corp.*, 654 F.3d 11, 53 (D.C. Cir. 2011) (observing that "[l]egal systems throughout the world recognize that corporate legal responsibility is part and parcel of the privilege of corporate personhood").

form.[315] Because it is a "fundamental rule" of international law that the assets of a corporation are distinct from its shareholders, the only question is whether, under the pertinent domestic law, "a company possesses independent and distinct legal personality."[316]

All of this being said, the separate status of an incorporated entity may be disregarded in certain exceptional circumstances. "[I]nevitably there have arisen dangers of abuse . . . [so] the law . . . has had to provide protective measures and remedies in the interests of those within the corporate entity as well as those outside who have dealings with it."[317] Thus, by necessity, "'lifting the corporate veil' or 'disregarding the legal entity' has been found justified and equitable in certain circumstances or for certain purposes."[318] Although the contours of these exceptions vary across countries, they draw upon the more general concept of abuse of rights and from "[t]he wealth of practice already accumulated on the subject in municipal law."[319] Almost universally, the veil can be lifted "to prevent misuse of the privileges of legal personality, as in certain cases of fraud or malfeasance, to protect third persons such as a creditor or purchaser, or to prevent the evasion of legal requirements or of obligations."[320] As one court noted, however, this "must be done very carefully" and only in "extreme circumstances"—"the corporate veil may not be pierced in any situation and for any purpose, because making it so extensive would dislocate the entire legal structure of the corporation or company; this would entail practically abolishing this legal figure."[321] In this way, the "exceptional" principle of piercing the corporate veil itself is a reaffirmance of the general principle of corporate separateness.[322]

---

315 *See Barcelona Traction, Light & Power Co., Ltd. (Belg. v. Spain)*, Second Phase, Judgment, 1970 I.C.J. 3, ¶ 45 (Feb. 5) ("[E]ven if a company is no more than a means for its shareholders to achieve their economic purpose, so long as it is *in esse* it enjoys an independent existence. Therefore the interests of the shareholders are both separable and indeed separated. . . .").

316 *Ahmadou Sadio Diallo (Guinea v. Dem. Rep. Congo)*, Preliminary Objections, Judgment, 2007 I.C.J. 582, ¶¶ 61, 63, at 605–06 (May 24).

317 *First Nat'l City Bank (FNCB) v. Banco Para El Comercio Exterior de Cuba*, 462 U.S. 611, 628 n.20 (1983) (quoting *Barcelona Traction, Light & Power Co., Ltd.* (*Belg. v. Spain*), Second Phase, Judgment, [1970] I.C.J. Rep. 3, ¶ 56, at 38–39).

318 *Id.*

319 *Id.*

320 *Id.* (citing, inter alia, E. J. Cohn & C. Simitis, *"Lifting the Veil" in Company Laws of the European Continent*, 12 Int'l & Comp. L.Q. 189 (1963)).

321 *Encalada v. Encalada et al.*, Ecuador Supreme Court, Resolution No. 172-2004, R.O. No. 553 (Mar. 29, 2005).

322 *First Nat'l City Bank (FNCB) v. Banco Para El Comercio Exterior de Cuba*, 462 U.S. 611, 628 n.20 (1983). For examples of lifting the corporate veil in other common law jurisdictions, *see, e.g., Prest v. Petrodel*

F. The Principles of Causation and Reparation

> Felix, qui potuit rerum congoscere causas *(fortunate is the one who is able to know the causes of things).*
>
> —Virgil[323]

It is impossible to speak of liability without causation. An elusive concept, causation nevertheless encompasses an inviolable requirement to hold a party liable: a connection between its alleged act and the damage claimed. As Cheng observed, "*[i]n jure causa proxima non remota inspicitur*"[324]—*the proximate, and not the remote, cause is to be considered, and only those losses so occasioned are to be compensated.* The requirement that persons are obliged to redress the damage they cause is a general principle of law recognized by all civilized nations.[325]

The precise test of causation, however, has confounded jurists for centuries. An Anglo-American commission writing in 1904 observed "a striking absence of international precedent or authority" on the question, but noted that "in the continual litigation in the courts of our respective countries rules have gradually been established as to the damages that can or cannot be recovered in cases of wrongdoing."[326] Synthesizing these and other authorities, Cheng identified "the use of two criteria to determine proximate causality, the one objective and the other subjective."[327]

Res. Ltd., [June 12, 2013] UKSC 34 (UK); *Kosmopoulos v. Constitution Insurance Co. of Canada*, [1987] 1 S.C.R. 2 (Can.). Examples from civil jurisdictions include Italian Civil Code art. 2332 (stating that a sole shareholder can be held liable for the obligations of an underfunded and insolvent corporation), and The Company Law of the People's Republic of China (promulgated by the Standing Comm. Nat'l People's Cong., Oct. 27, 2005, effective Jan. 1, 2006) art. 20 (stating shareholders who abuse the advantages of corporate form can be held liable for the company's debts); Israel Companies Law 5759 (1999) § 6(c) (stating a court can lift the corporate veil if the use of the corporate form is for fraud or the company management took an "unreasonable risk in respect of the company's ability to pay its debts"). According to one tribunal, these decisions and statutes "progressively create . . . law, which should be taken into account, because [this law] draws conclusions from economic reality and in conformity with the needs of international commerce, to which rules specific to international arbitration, successively elaborated should respond." CRCICA Award No. 120/1998 (June 23, 2000), *in* ARBITRAL AWARDS OF THE CAIRO REGIONAL CENTRE OF INTERNATIONAL COMMERCIAL ARBITRATION II, at 32 (Mohie Eldin I. Alam Eldin ed., 2003).

323 GEORGICS, Book II, v. 490.

324 CHENG, *supra* note 2, at 245.

325 *Id.* at 241–53.

326 *Id.* at 249 (quoting Joint Report No. II of Aug. 12, 1904, Samoan Claims Award (1902), U.S. Department of State, National Archives, 210 Despatches, Great Britain, Ambassador Choate to Secretary Hay, Aug. 18, 1904, No. 1429, enclosure).

327 *Id.* at 245.

The objective criterion is whether the loss is a "normal and natural consequence" of the act. In commercial cases, this may be informed by the "usages, customs and laws of civilised countries"; in tort cases, it may also be informed by scientific, medical, or other technical evidence.[328] In both scenarios, the query is whether the loss (be it a loss of profit or loss of limb) "resulted through a line of natural sequences" from the act.[329] The subjective criterion, in turn, depends on the foreseeability of the harm. Despite its appellation, the second criterion calls for an objective analysis. According to Cheng, "[t]he proximate consequences of an act are not necessarily those which its author actually foresaw, but ... those which the judges consider he could and should have foreseen. In practice, therefore, it is ... the standard of the reasonable man."[330] In most cases, the two inquiries are interrelated, such that a natural consequence of an act will be foreseeable, and vice versa. "By thus introducing what may be called a minimum standard of foreseeability, the two criteria, objective and subjective, are in practice merged."[331] The notable exception is cases of intended harm, where satisfaction of the subjective criterion alone may suffice to establish causation.[332] Where a State "deliberately caused the loss of [claimant]'s rights," for instance, "[t]here is no question of remoteness or foreseeability of damage."[333] Within this framework, reparation ordinarily lies for loss that (1) is the normal and reasonably foreseeable consequence of the act or (2) is intended.[334]

Although there has been variance in nomenclature and emphasis, Cheng's distillation of the essential requirements of causation has endured over the past half-century, such that *the standard of proximate causality—defined with reference to natural consequences and foreseeability—must obtain before liability can attach.* Whether in word or in deed, courts and tribunals the world over have

328 *Id.* at 246–47 (citation omitted).

329 *Heirs of Jean Maninat Case* (July 31, 1905), 10 R.I.A.A. 55, 81.

330 Cheng, *supra* note 2, at 250–51.

331 *Id.* at 251.

332 *Id.* Reparation must be made for any consequences intended by the actor, however exceptional or remote. Stated another way, "'[i]nternational as well as municipal law denies compensation for remote consequences, in the absence of evidence of deliberate intention to injure.'" *Id.* at 252 (quoting *Dix Case*, Opinion of Commission, 9 R.I.A.A. 117, 121 (1903)); *see also* Ioannis *Kardassopoulos v. Republic of Georgia*, ICSID Case Nos. ARB/05/18 & ARB/07/15, Award, ¶¶ 468–69 (Mar. 3, 2010) (quoting Draft Articles on Responsibility of States, *supra* note 89, commentary to art. 31, ¶ 10).

333 *Ioannis Kardassopoulos v. Republic of Georgia*, ICSID Case Nos. ARB/05/18 & ARB/07/15, Award, ¶¶ 468–69 (Mar. 3, 2010).

334 Sergei Ripinsky & Kevin Williams, Damages in International Investment Law 137 (2008).

applied this standard in innumerable different circumstances.[335] For instance, while commenting that "the varying terminologies" concerning causation "often provide limited assistance in assessing specific situations," the *Eritrea-Ethiopia* Claims Commission concluded that "the necessary connection is best characterized through the commonly used nomenclature of 'proximate cause.'"[336] The Commission elaborated that it would "give weight to whether particular damage reasonably should have been foreseeable to an actor committing the international delict in question" as this element "provides some discipline and predictability in assessing proximity."[337]

Because the specific determination of causation and reparation calls for judgment and discernment, the principle of proximate cause necessarily operates at a high level of generality. With respect to "natural consequences," for instance, there is a robust debate on whether the action must be necessary in the sense of being a "but-for" condition of the outcome; whether it is sufficient for the action to be a necessary part of a complex set of conditions sufficient for the outcome; or whether it suffices for the action to be a "substantial factor in" or "contribute to" the outcome.[338] But however the factual link between action and outcome is measured, as a general principle of law it must exist. The same is true for imposing reasonable limits on the scope of liability by assessing the foreseeability of the harm. There had been a move away from the distinction between "direct" and "indirect" damages given its "ambiguity" and "scant utility,"[339] but in the International Law

335 *See Amco Asia Corp. et al. v. Republic of Indonesia*, ICSID Case No. ARB/81/1, Award on the Merits, 268 (Nov. 21, 1984), *reprinted in* 24 I.L.M. 1022, 1037 (1985) ("according to principles and rules common to the main national legal systems and to international law, the damages to be awarded must cover only the direct and foreseeable prejudice"); *BG Grp. Plc. v. Republic of Argentina*, UNCITRAL, Final Award, ¶ 428 (Dec. 24, 2007); *Lemire v. Ukraine*, ICSID Case No. ARB/06/18, Award, ¶¶ 155–72 (Mar. 1, 2011); *S.D. Myers Inc. v. Gov't of Canada*, UNICTRAL, Second Partial Award, ¶¶ 140–60 (Oct. 21, 2002); *LG&E Energy Corp. v. Argentine Republic*, ICSID Case No. ARB/02/01, Award, ¶ 50 (July 25, 2007) (applying proximate cause test); *CME Czech Republic B.V. v. Czech Republic*, UNCITRAL, Partial Award, ¶¶ 527, 584–85 (Sept. 13, 2001) ("Causation arises if the damage or disadvantage . . . is foreseeable and occurs in a normal sequence of events."); *Hoffland Honey Co. v. Nat'l Iranian Oil Co.*, 2 Iran-U.S. Cl. Trib. Rep. 41 (1983) (applying proximate cause test).

336 *Guidance regarding* Jus ad Bellum *Liability*, Eritrea-Ethiopia Claims Commission, Decision No. 7, ¶ 13 (July 27, 2007). Although the Commission stated that this "formulation" is not a general principle of law (¶ 9), it affirmed that "compensation can only be awarded in respect of damages having a sufficient causal connection with conduct violating international law" (¶ 7).

337 *Id.* ¶ 13.

338 *See generally* Antony Honoré, *Causation in the Law*, The Stanford Encyclopedia of Philosophy (Edward N. Zalta ed., Winter 2010 ed.).

339 Special Rapporteur, *Second Report on State Responsibility*, 2 Y.B. Int'l Law Comm'n 68–69 (1993) (by G. Arangio-Ruiz); *see also S.D. Myers Inc. v. Gov't of Canada*, UNICTRAL, Second Partial Award,

Commission's Second Report on State Responsibility, Special Rapporteur Gaetano Arangio-Ruiz reiterated that "an injury is . . . linked to an unlawful act whenever the normal and natural course of events would indicate that the injury is a logical consequence of the act or whenever the author of the unlawful act could have foreseen the damage his act would cause."[340] Although the limitations and imprecisions of language are especially conspicuous in this area, this does not detract from the essential requirement of proximate causation as a predicate to imposing liability.[341]

In some cases, determining causation is relatively straightforward. Where, for instance, the passage of a government decree expressly cancels existing contractual rights, "[t]here is no question of remoteness or foreseeability of damage," and a claimant's losses are the "direct and foreseeable consequence of the [law-making] process."[342] But with causal links rarely being so linear, the question frequently arises whether liability can attach in the face of complex chains of interrelated events. Take, for example, *Lemire v. Ukraine*, where the claimant was denied the ability to participate in Ukrainian radio frequency tenders. In determining whether compensation was due for the loss of the claimant's business enterprise, the majority of the arbitrators required that "two links in the causal chain be analyzed and proven": (1) if the tenders had been decided fairly, the claimant would have won them, and (2) with these frequencies, the claimant would have grown its business into the broadcasting company it had planned.[343] The majority sustained the claim, finding that the claimant had proven that "the initial cause (Ukraine's wrongful acts) and the final effect (the claimant's frustration to operate a nationwide FM channel . . .) [we]re linked through a chain of causation," with no "[intervening] causes other than [the respondent's] unlawful behavior."[344] *Lemire* thus affirms that the causal link between the wrongful act

¶ 160 (Oct. 21, 2002) ("a debate as to whether damages are direct or indirect is not appropriate"); *Guidance regarding* Jus ad Bellum *Liability*, Eritrea-Ethiopia Claims Commission, Decision No. 7, ¶ 10 (July 27, 2007) (observing that "many tribunals and commentators have criticized" the distinction between "direct" and "indirect" harm because "it lacks analytic power").

340 Special Rapporteur, *supra* note 339, at 69.

341 León Castellanos-Jankiewicz, *Causation and International State Responsibility*, ACIL Research Paper No. 2012-05 (SHARES Series) (Jan. 24, 2012) at 48 ("In the vastness of the causal universe, tribunals have rallied around and developed the notion of proximate causation. . . .").

342 *Ioannis Kardassopoulos v. Georgia*, ICSID Case Nos. ARB/05/18 & ARB/07/15, Award, ¶¶ 465–70 (Mar. 3, 2010).

343 *Lemire v. Ukraine*, ICSID Case No. ARB/06/18, Award, ¶ 171 (Mar. 28, 2011). It also remains a "general principle of . . . law" that the claimant bears the burden of demonstrating that "the causal relationship is sufficiently close (i.e. not 'too remote')" and that the claimed quantum of compensation flows from the defendants' conduct. *Id.* ¶ 155. Burdens of proof will be discussed in more detail in chapter 3.E.

344 *Id.* ¶ 208.

and ultimate loss may be transitive as long as there is no intervening cause to sever the chain.[345] "[I]t matters not how many links there may be in the chain of causation"—what matters is that there is "no breach in the chain and the loss can be clearly, unmistakably, and definitely traced" to the precipitating act.[346]

On the other end of the spectrum are cases such as *Biwater v. Tanzania*, where the claimant's investment encountered financial problems *before* the respondent State's wrongful act, so the proximate cause of the losses could not be traced through a natural sequence of events to the governmental act.[347] And the Iran-U.S. Claims Tribunal easily dispatched the claim of a Wisconsin farmer who complained that his bee colony had been harmed by agricultural chemicals derived from Iranian oil; quoting New York justice William Andrews's dissent in *Palsgraf v. Long Island Railroad*, it held that " 'because of convenience, of public policy, of a rough sense of justice, the law arbitrarily declines to trace a series of events beyond a certain point.' "[348]

Although causation is always an element of any claim, presumptions may be employed so long as they have a reasonable basis in fact.[349] In the absence of other possible causal agents, courts and tribunals today will "safely assume[] that a (rebuttable) presumption of causality between [two] events exists, and that the first is the proximate cause of the other," when "it can be proven that in the normal cause of events a certain cause will produce a certain effect."[350] In such

345 *See id.* ¶¶ 165–67.

346 *Id.* ¶ 166 (quoting Admin. Decision No. 2 of Nov. 1, 1923, U.S.-German Mixed Claims Comm'n, Doc. RLA 38, at 29).

347 *Biwater Gauff Ltd. v. United Republic of Tanzania*, ICSID Case No. ARB/05/22, Award (July 24, 2008); *see also Elettronica Sicula S.p.A. (ELSI) (U.S. v. It.)*, Judgment, 1989 I.C.J. 15, ¶¶ 100–01 (July 20) (a claimant's "headlong course toward insolvency; which state of affairs it seems to have attained even prior to the requisition" by the State, defeated any claim under the Treaty). At least one member of the tribunal in *Biwater*, though, deemed this question to be one of quantum of damages and not causation. *See Biwater Gauff Ltd. v. United Republic of Tanzania*, ICSID Case No. ARB/05/22, Concurring and Dissenting Opinion of Gary Born (July 18, 2008). In his view, an internationally wrongful act gives rise to an obligation to make reparation for any injury suffered, which may or not include a sum of money. That a proven injury does not include a quantifiable sum of monetary damages does not denigrate the occurrence of a wrongful act or its causal relationship to the actual injury suffered. Stated another way, "[t]he fact that [an] injury does not entail the monetary damage in no way implies that there was no injury." *Id.* ¶ 26.

348 *Hoffland Honey Co. v. Nat'l Iranian Oil Co.*, 2 Iran-U.S. Cl. Trib. Rep. 41, 42–43 (1983) (citation omitted).

349 The operation of presumptions is discussed in chapter 3.E.

350 *Lemire v. Ukraine*, ICSID Case No. ARB/06/18, Award, ¶ 169 (Mar. 1, 2011).

cases, "offenders must be deemed to have foreseen the natural consequences of their wrongful acts, and to stand responsible for the damage caused."[351] There are, however, limits. In *Osorio v. Dole Food*, for instance, a group of Nicaraguan citizens alleged that they worked on Dole banana plantations in Nicaragua between 1970 and 1982, where they were exposed to the chemical DBCP, which in 1977 was shown to cause sterility.[352] A Nicaraguan court awarded damages to compensate for infertility under the auspices of Special Law 364, which established an irrefutable presumption of causation if the plaintiff established that he was (1) exposed to DBCP and (2) sterile. This presumption was "scientifically and medically impossible" for the U.S. court to accept in an action for enforcement because DBCP is only one of many genetic and environmental causes of sterility.[353] The *Osorio* court accordingly refused to recognize the Nicaraguan judgment, holding that an award of liability "in the face of clear scientific proof of the absence of causation" is the "antithesis of basic fairness" and violates "international due process norms."[354]

When adequately proven, causation must ultimately lead to reparation. After the causal thread is drawn from the act to the loss, the wrongdoer has "the duty to make reparation . . . to those damages which are legally regarded as the consequences of an unlawful act."[355] This, Cheng established after surveying the municipal law of both common and civil law countries, derives from "*the fundamental principle that there exists a remedy for the direct invasion of every right*"—*ubi ius ibi remedium est.*[356] *That remedy, furthermore, "must, as far as possible, wipe out all the consequences of the illegal act and re-establish the situation which would, in all probability, have existed had that act not been committed."*[357] These precepts continue to hold sway. In commercial disputes, for instance, restitutio in integrum includes not just the loss actually suffered due to the wrongful act (*damnum emergens*), but also the loss of future profits (*lucrum cessans*)—so long as they are the contemplated fruit of the contract and not too speculative.[358] In

351 *Id.* ¶ 170.

352 *Osorio v. Dole Food*, 665 F. Supp. 2d 1307 (S.D. Fla. 2009), *aff'd sub nom. Osorio v. Dow Chem. Co.*, 635 F.3d 1277 (11th Cir. 2011).

353 *Id.* at 1333.

354 *Id.* at 1335.

355 Cheng, *supra* note 2, at 253.

356 *Id.* at 233–34 & n.1 (citation and quotation marks omitted).

357 *Id.* (citing *Factory at Chorzów (Fed. Rep. Ger. v. Pol.)*, Merits, Judgment, 1928 P.C.I.J. (Ser. A.) No. 17, at 47 (Sept. 13)); *see also Sapphire Int'l Petroleum v. Nat'l Iranian Oil Co.*, Award, 35 Int'l L. Rep. 136, 186 (1963); *INA Corp. v. Islamic Republic of Iran*, 8 Iran-U.S. Cl. Trib. Rep. 373, 395, 411 (1985).

358 *See Amco Asia Corp. et al. v. Republic of Indonesia*, ICSID Case No. ARB/81/1, Resubmitted Case, ¶¶ 178–87; *see also* ICC Case No. 1526, Award (1068), 101 J. Droit Int'l (Clunet) 915 (1974).

computing lost future profits arising from an expropriation, a tribunal is not limited to the existing valuation and foreseeable profits at the time of the taking, but may in certain circumstances also take into account subsequent events (whether foreseeable or not) that affect the value of the dispossessed property.[359] Another permutation of this general principle is that interest on a contract price forms part of compensatory relief when payment on that contract is breached or delayed.[360]

Mathematical certainty on the computation of damages is an elusive if not delusive goal—especially for future and hypothetical injuries. But, as with the determination of causation, the complexity does not absolve judges and arbitrators of their obligation to ascertain an appropriate level of compensation.[361] The test for quantification of damages, however, is less exacting than that for causation. As noted by the *Amco v. Indonesia* tribunal, although foreseeability is often the touchstone for determining causation, it is an "inappropriate test for damages that approximate to *restitutio in integrum*."[362] Instead, once causation has been established, a claimant need only provide a reasonable basis upon which the tribunal can, with some confidence, estimate the extent of the loss.[363] Although the principle of integral reparation does not permit an award for "speculative or uncertain damage[s],"[364] there inevitably remains "a certain

359 *Amco Asia Corp. et al. v. Republic of Indonesia*, ICSID Case No. ARB/81/1, Resubmitted Case, ¶¶ 184–86. Of course, as a function of the principle of *nemo auditur propriam turpitudinem allegans*, the effects of the taking itself cannot diminish the valuation of *restitutio in integrum* or future lost profits. *Id.* ¶ 187.

360 *See generally Russian Indemnity Case (Russ. v. Turk.)*, PCA, Award (Nov. 11, 1912); ICC Award No. 5835, 10(2) ICC BULL. 33, 34–39 (1999) ("This understanding of Kuwaiti law is in accordance with internationally accepted principles."); *Sylvania Tech. Sys. Inc. v. Gov't of the Islamic Republic of Iran*, 8 Iran-U.S. Cl. Trib. Rep. 298, 320 (1985) (invoking public international law to hold that, "[i]n the absence of a contractually stipulated rate of interest, the Tribunal will derive a rate of interest based approximately on the amount that the successful claimant would have been in a position to have earned if it had been paid in time and thus have the funds available to invest in a form of a commercial investment in common use in its own country").

361 CHENG, *supra* note 2, at 239; *see also Lemire v. Ukraine*, ICSID Case No. ARB/06/18, Award, ¶ 249 (Mar. 28, 2011) (the "difficulty in calculation cannot . . . deprive an investor, who has suffered injury, from his fundamental right to see his losses redressed").

362 *Amco Asia Corp. et al. v. Republic of Indonesia*, ICSID Case No. ARB/81/1, Resubmitted Case, Final Award and Decision on Supplemental Decision and Rectification, ¶ 96 (June 5 & Oct. 17, 1990), 17 Y.B. COMM. ARB. 73 (1992).

363 *Lemire v. Ukraine*, ICSID Case No. ARB/06/18, Award, ¶ 246 (Mar. 28, 2011).

364 *Id.* ¶ 245 (quoting *Amoco Int'l Finance Corp. v. Islamic Republic of Iran*, Iran-U.S. Cl. Trib. Case No. 56, Partial Award, ¶ 238 (July 14, 1987)); and JAMES CRAWFORD, THE INTERNATIONAL LAW COMMISSION'S ARTICLES ON STATE RESPONSIBILITY: INTRODUCTION, TEXT AND COMMENTARIES ¶ 27 (2002).

amount of conjecture as to how things would have evolved 'but for' the actual behaviour of the parties."[365]

Two permutations on the principle of causation act to limit the quantum of damages. *First, a party claiming a breach of contract is obliged to take such measures as are reasonable in the circumstances to mitigate its loss resulting from the breach.*[366] This generally accepted principle of mitigation allows (and in some cases requires) a non-breaching party to take acts not contemplated by the contract so as to lower the damages resulting from the other party's breach.[367] Where a buyer fails to pay the balance of the purchase price when due, a seller may refuse to ship the contract goods in an effort to mitigate the costs associated with the nonpayment.[368] Similarly, where a party's profits depend upon the supply of goods that never arrive, that party must nevertheless try to "avoid . . . financial loss . . . by making better use" of other available suppliers, lest its damages against the breaching supplier be reduced for its failure to mitigate.[369] Although an injured party is not required to perform a futile or impossible act,[370] if it fails to act reasonably in the circumstances, the party in breach may claim a reduction in the damages in the amount at which the loss should have been mitigated.

Second, there is a general principle *prohibiting the compensation of the same damages twice.*[371] This well-established principle applies, for instance, where a claimant brings parallel arbitrations under different instruments with respect to the same governmental measure. When the first award is paid by the respondent and the second

365 *Lemire v. Ukraine*, ICSID Case No. ARB/06/18, Award, ¶ 249 (Mar. 28, 2011).

366 *See generally* ICC Award No. 2478 in 1974, 3 Y.B. COMM. ARB. 222 (1978) (also published in: J. DROIT INT'L (CLUNET) 925 (1975)); ICC Award No. 8817, 10(2) ICC BULL. 75 (1999) (also published in: 25 Y.B. COMM. ARB. 355 (2000)); *see also* UNIDROIT Principles of Int'l Comm. Contracts (2010) art. 7.4.8.

367 *Middle East Cement Shipping & Handling Co. S.A. v. Arab Republic of Egypt*, ICSID Case No. ARB/99/6, Award, ¶ 167 (Apr. 12, 2002), 7 ICSID Rep. 173 (2005) ("The duty to mitigate damages . . . can be considered as part of the General Principles of Law.").

368 *See* ICC Partial Awards in Case No. 7110, 10(2) ICC BULL. 39 (1999).

369 See ICC Award No. 5885, 16 Y.B. COMM. ARB. 91 (1991).

370 *Amco Asia Corp. et al. v. Republic of Indonesia*, ICSID Case No. ARB/81/1, Resubmitted Case, Final Award and Decision on Supplemental Decision and Rectification, ¶ 79 (June 5 & Oct. 17, 1990), 17 Y.B. COMM. ARB. 73 (1992) (no duty to sell shares or interests in a contract where such transaction was subject to the approval of the breaching party, which "would have made it virtually impossible to find interested purchasers").

371 CHENG, *supra* note 2, at 236; *see also Pan Am. Energy LLC and BP Argentina Exploration Co. v. Argentine Republic*, Decision on Preliminary Objections, ICSID Case No. ARB/03/13, ¶ 219 (July 27, 2006); *Sempra Energy Int'l v. Argentine Republic*, ICSID Case No. ARB/02/16, Award, ¶ 395 (Sept. 28, 2007); *LG&E Energy Corp. v. Argentine Republic*, ICSID Case No. ARB/02/01, Award, ¶ 90 (July 25, 2007).

award is larger, the latter must be reduced by the amount of the former so "[d]ouble recovery [can] thus be avoided."[372] And when a party mitigates its damages by reselling goods once subject to a (breached) contract, any damages it receives must be discounted by the amount it profits from the resale.[373] Failing to account for the money made on resale would overcompensate the plaintiff, and hold the defendant liable for more than it is responsible. At least conceptually, both of these principles are ultimately a function of causation, because undeserved or two-fold compensation holds a defendant liable for more than the direct consequences of its unlawful act.

G. The Principles of Responsibility and Fault

> *A great nation is like a great man: When he makes a mistake, he realizes it. Having realized it, he admits it. Having admitted it, he corrects it. He considers those who point out his faults as his most benevolent teachers.*
>
> —Lao Tzu[374]

A party is only responsible for its own acts and those of its agents, and thus cannot be liable to restore that which was never in its power to restore, or to compensate an injury that it did not cause.[375] Thus, "[i]f the damage cannot be attributed to the defendant or to the persons or things for which he is liable, he must necessarily be acquitted. No one questions this."[376] "[R]esponsibility must be based on a fault imputable to the person charged"—that is, the individual's failure to observe a personal obligation.[377] This universal rule defines the "very nature of law" and is "one of the most important institutions in any legal order."[378]

This is a relatively simple concept as applied to natural persons. Although an individual might incur personal liability for her violations of a legal duty or for wrongful

---

372 *Mobil Corp., Venezuela Holdings B.V. et al. v. Bolivarian Republic of Venezuela*, ICSID Case No. ARB/07/27, Award, ¶ 378 (Oct. 9, 2014) ("The prohibition of double recovery for the same loss is a well-established principle, also referred to *as enrichessement sans cause*.").

373 *CMI Int'l, Inc. v. Ministry of Rds. and Transp. (MORT) and the Islamic Republic of Iran*, 4 Iran-U.S. Cl. Trib. Rep. 263 (1983).

374 LAO TZU, TAO TE CHING (Stephen Mitchell, trans., Harper Collins 2000).

375 CHENG, *supra* note 2, at 208, 213, 218.

376 HENRI MAZEAUD ET AL., 2 TRATADO TEÓRICO Y PRÁCTICO DE LA RESPONSABILIDAD CIVIL DELICTUAL Y CONTRACTUAL [THEORETICAL AND PRACTICAL TREATISE ON CIVIL, CRIMINAL, AND CONTRACTUAL LIABILITY] 5, Part Two (1963).

377 CHENG, *supra* note 2, at 219.

378 *Id.* at 231.

acts, there is no fault if the act was done by another individual (provided that the second individual is not the agent of the first) or if the harm results from a force majeure (provided that the *vis major* was not foreseeable or within the individual's control). In such cases, personal responsibility does not exist, for a party can only do that which is possible—*ad impossibilia nemo tenetur.*[379]

But the principles of responsibility and fault become hoary when applied to sovereigns or juridical entities, which can act only through a human conduit.[380] Many of the issues regarding state responsibility and inter-state relations that Cheng discussed are neither derived from nor dependent upon municipal law, and are not the focus of this book. Still, a brief discussion of the general principles of state responsibility is warranted as they often come to the fore in modern global disputes. The work of the International Law Commission, and in particular its Draft Articles on Responsibility of States for Internationally Wrongful Acts (the ILC Articles), provides indispensable guidance in this area.[381] Although the purpose of the ILC Articles was to ascertain state responsibility in relation to other sovereigns, its precepts of imputability are relevant in many settings.[382]

The question of state responsibility begins with attribution.[383] As Cheng noted, although "the acts of the agents of a State are . . . to be considered as the acts of the State itself," the "[a]cts of private individuals, however numerous, cannot . . . be imputed to the State, notwithstanding the link of membership . . . between the individual and the State."[384] Whether a government official is acting on behalf of the State largely turns upon the nature of the act in question, the function that the official is authorized to discharge, and the question whether those spheres overlap

379 *Id.* at 223, 227.

380 *Id.* at 183–84.

381 Articles on Responsibility of States for Internationally Wrongful Acts, *in* Rep. of the Int'l Law Comm'n on the Work of Its Fifty-Third Session, U.N. GAOR, 56th Sess., Supp. No. 10, at 43 (UN Doc. A/56/10 (2001)).

382 *See Jan de Nul N.V. & Dredging Int'l N.V. v. Arab Republic of Egypt*, ICSID No. ARB/04/13, Award, ¶ 156 (Nov. 6, 2008). *See also Sergei Paushok, CJSC Golden East Co. & CJSC Vostokneftegaz Co. v. Gov't of Mongolia*, UNCITRAL, Award on Jurisdiction and Liability, ¶ 576 (Apr. 28, 2011) (stating that the ILC Articles are "generally considered as representing current customary international law").

383 Cheng, *supra* note 2, at 180–81 ("Imputability in international law is the juridical attribution of a particular act by a physical person, or a group of physical persons, to a state, or other international person, whereby it is regarded as the latter's own act."); *see also United States Diplomatic and Consular Staff in Tehran (U.S. v. Iran)*, Judgment, 1980 I.C.J. 3, 29 ¶ 56, 58 (May 24); Articles on Responsibility of States for Internationally Wrongful Acts art. 2, *in* Rep. of the Int'l Law Comm'n on the Work of Its Fifty-Third Session, U.N. GAOR, 56th Sess., Supp. No. 10 (UN Doc. A/56/10 (2001)).

384 Cheng, *supra* note 2, at 184.

such that the act was done in a public capacity.[385] For instance, subsequent to Cheng's book, the ICJ found that the attack on the U.S. Embassy in Tehran could not be imputed to Iran because "[n]o suggestion ha[d] been made that the militants, when they executed their attack on the Embassy, had any form of official status as recognized 'agents' or organs of the Iranian State."[386] In order to hold the State responsible for the militants' conduct, the ICJ held, it would have to be established that "on the occasion in question the militants acted on behalf of the State, having been charged by some competent organ of the Iranian State to carry out a specific operation."[387] The ICJ similarly held in *Nicaragua v. United States* that the United States did not direct or control the contras such that they could be equated, "for legal purposes, with an organ of the United States Government, or as acting on behalf of that Government."[388] In contrast, in an ICSID arbitration against Mongolia, a central bank charged with the issuance of currency and administering the State's monetary policy was deemed to have "assume[d] part of the executive responsibility of the State," so its acts were attributed to the State.[389] Other recent cases have emphasized the link between the particular action and sovereign power, explaining that "[s]uch a link can result from the fact that the person performing the act is part of the State's organic structure . . . or exercises governmental powers specific to the State in relation with this act . . . or . . . acts under the direct control . . . of the State, even if being a private party."[390]

These are ultimately questions of international law. How the municipal law of the relevant State might answer these questions cannot be dispositive. Although local

---

385 *Id.* at 198–200.

386 *United States Diplomatic and Consular Staff in Tehran (U.S. v. Iran)*, Judgment, 1980 I.C.J. 3, 29 ¶ 58 (May 24).

387 *Id.* It should be noted that the ICJ held Iran responsible on the basis of its failure to attempt to stop the attack. This inaction by itself constituted a violation of Iran's obligations to the United States under the Vienna Convention on Diplomatic Relations and the Vienna Convention on Consular Relations. *Id.* ¶ 67. The ICJ also found that Iran's subsequent endorsement of the Embassy occupation and the detention of hostages transformed them into acts of the State. *Id.* ¶ 71.

388 *Case concerning Military and Paramilitary Activities in and against Nicaragua (Nicaragua v. U.S.)*, Judgment, 1986 I.C.J. 14, 62–64 ¶¶ 109–15 (June 27).

389 *Sergei Paushok, CJSC Golden East Co. & CJSC Vostokneftegaz Co. v. Gov't of Mongolia*, UNCITRAL, Award on Jurisdiction and Liability, ¶¶ 582–83 (Apr. 28, 2011).

390 *Jan de Nul N.V. & Dredging Int'l N.V. v. Arab Republic of Egypt*, ICSID No. ARB/04/13, Award, ¶ 157 (Nov. 6, 2008). As the modalities of sovereign involvement in the marketplace become more complex, identifying and distinguishing between these links for purposes of state attribution has been a frequent topic for arbitrators. *See, e.g., Bayindir Insaat Turizim Ticaret Ve Sanayi A.S. v. Islamic Republic of Pakistan*, ICSID Case No. ARB/03/29, Award, ¶ 119 (Aug. 27, 2009); *EDF (Servs.) Ltd. v. Romania*, ICSID Case No. ARB/05/13, Award, ¶¶ 190–209 (Oct. 8, 2009); *Compañía de Aguas del Aconquija, S.A. and Vivendi (formerly Compagnie Générale des Eaux) v. Argentine Republic*, ICSID Case No. ARB/

law may provide some framework for the assessment—for example, what the individual or entity in question is authorized to do—it does not provide the rule of decision for the attribution inquiry. Surveying various authorities, Cheng found it "plain" that "international law, in order to determine whether or not a person is acting as a state official, whose acts may be imputed to the State, decides autonomously according to the facts of the case and not according to the municipal status of the individual concerned."[391] A sovereign cannot, for instance, disown an official's wrongful act done in his official capacity because he might have disobeyed superior instructions or violated a local code of conduct.[392] As set forth by James Crawford in the Commentary to Article 7 of the ILC Articles, States are responsible when "officials acted in their capacity as such, albeit unlawfully or contrary to instruction."[393] The Inter-American Court on Human Rights has affirmed that "under international law a State is responsible for the acts of its agents undertaken in their official capacity and for their omissions even when those agents act outside the sphere of their authority or violate internal law."[394] Were it otherwise, "a situation [would be] created wherein '[t]he *State* can do no wrong,' and any liability of the State for such acts would be purely *ex gratia*."[395] Such a rule would not only be an affront to basic notions of justice, but it would run squarely against other principles of law, such as estoppel or *nemo iudex in causa sua*.[396]

These precepts have given rise to at least one general principle of international law that has taken root since Cheng's 1953 study: *a State cannot cite its own internal law to evade an international obligation.* The PCIJ held that it is a generally accepted principle that States cannot invoke their own constitutions[397] or municipal laws[398] to justify a breach of international obligations. Subsequently

---

97/3, Award, ¶ 49 (Nov. 21, 2000); *Metalclad Corp. v. United Mexican States*, ARB (AF)/97/1, Award, ¶ 73 (Aug. 30, 2000), 16 ICSID REV. 1, 22 (2001).

391 CHENG, *supra* note 2, at 196–97.

392 *Id.* at 202.

393 CRAWFORD, *supra* note 364, at 108.

394 *Case of Velásquez Rodríguez v. Honduras*, Merits, Judgment, Inter-Am. Ct. H.R. (Ser. C) No. 4, ¶ 170 (July 29, 1988), 95 INT'L L. REP. 232, 296.

395 CHENG, *supra* note 2, at 206–07 (emphasis in original).

396 It may well be that the claimant's own misconduct prevents it from raising a claim against the State, as was the case in *World Duty Free Co. Ltd. v. Republic of Kenya*, ICSID Case No. ARB/00/7, Award (Oct. 4, 2006).

397 *Treatment of Polish Nationals and Other Persons of Polish Origin or Speech in the Danzig Territory (Polish Nationals in Danzig)*, Advisory Opinion, 1932 P.C.I.J. (Ser. A/B) No. 44, at 24 (Feb. 4).

398 *Interpretation of the Convention between Greece and Bulgaria Respecting Reciprocal Emigration, Signed at Neully-Sur-Seine on 27 November 1919 (the Greco-Bulgarian Communities Case)*, 1930 P.C.I.J. (Ser. B) No. 17, at 32 (July 31).

codified in the Vienna Convention on the Law of Treaties,[399] this principle is often invoked to hold States to their contractual obligations. The "international *ordre public* ... vigorously reject[s] the proposition that a State organ, dealing with foreigners, having openly, with knowledge and intent, concluded [a contract] that inspires the co-contractant's confidence, could thereafter ... invoke the nullity of its own promise."[400] For example, "[a] State which has subscribed to an arbitration clause ... would act contrary to international public order in later invoking the incompatibility of such an obligation with its domestic legal order."[401] In this scenario, the principle represents a mixture of estoppel and state responsibility. It prevents a sovereign from retracting its promises and requires it to answer for the acts attributable to it.[402]

Most of this subchapter differs from the rest of this book. These principles of *state* responsibility are not derived from a consensus of national laws elevated to the international plane. They are instead principles of the international *ordre public*; principles that must and do obtain to make the system of transnational justice efficacious. As best can be stated, they are general principles of international law—no less obligatory upon States on the international plane, albeit not derived from laws *in foro domestico.*

---

399 Vienna Convention on the Law of Treaties art. 27, *opened for signature* May 23, 1969, 1155 U.N.T.S. 331 (entered into force Jan. 27, 1980).

400 ICC Case 1939/1971, *quoted in* Derains, *supra* note 216, at 122.

401 *See Benteler v. Belgian State*, Award (Nov. 18, 1983), 1 J. INT'L ARB. 184, 190 (1984); *see also* ICC Case No. 7263 of 1994, Interim Award, 22 Y.B. COMM. ARB. 92, 97–98 (1997) ("In the field of international commercial arbitration, ... states and public bodies as defendants ... cannot avail themselves of the incapacity and lack of authorization [to contract] deriving from their national laws."); *Co. Z and Others v. State Org. ABC*, Award (Apr. 1982), 8 Y.B. COMM. ARB. 94, 108–09 (1983) (applying local law to the dispute but recognizing the "general principle, universally recognized nowadays in both inter-State relations and international private relations [that] would in any case prohibit the Utopian State ... to repudiate the undertaking to arbitrate which it made itself"); *Khoms el Mergeb v. Societe Dalico*, 1994 REV. ARB. 116 (Cour de Cassation 1994) (the "existence and effectiveness" of an international arbitration clause with the State is to be addressed "according to the common intention of the parties, without need to refer to national law"); CRAIG ET AL., *supra* note 22, § 35.02(v).

402 This does not mean, however, that the harm caused will ultimately be compensated. Although a State may be held to answer for its conduct before an arbitral tribunal, and that tribunal may render an award against the State, it does not follow that the award will be automatically enforced against the sovereign in a particular forum. Sovereign immunity exists in most national legal regimes that would be responsible for the enforcement of an adverse monetary award against a State; its application depends substantially on the law and procedural rules of the municipal forum. *See* JAMES CRAWFORD, BROWNLIE'S PRINCIPLES OF PUBLIC INTERNATIONAL LAW 488 (8th ed. 2012). It is also possible that a State may breach international law without causing monetary harm.

CHAPTER 3

Modern Applications of the Principles of International Due Process

Whatever disagreement there may be as to the scope of the phrase "due process of law", there can be no doubt that it embraces the fundamental conception of a fair trial, with opportunity to be heard.

—Justice Oliver Wendell Holmes, Jr.[1]

This Chapter reviews the attributes of international due process deriving from the adjectival norms common to all systems of law. A party must have notice of a proceeding against it. The court deciding the case must have jurisdiction, treat the parties equally, and impartially apply the law to the facts. In the mechanical processing of a case, each party has the burden of proving its own proffered facts, and there exist a number of general principles that prescribe the weight given to such proof. Once the proceedings end, it is universal that the decision is final—meaning that the issues actually decided cannot be relitigated and the operative part of the judgment must be carried out by the parties. As noted by Cheng, these are "the essential rules which govern the activity of every tribunal as a Court of Justice. They ensure the fulfilment of the fundamental purpose of all judicial proceedings, the final settlement of a dispute by an impartial authority in a manner just and equitable to the parties on the basis of respect for law."[2]

1 *Frank v. Magnum*, 237 U.S. 309, 347 (1915) (Holmes, J., dissenting).

2 Bin Cheng, General Principles of Law as Applied by International Courts and Tribunals 389–90 (Cambridge Univ. Press 1953).

A. Notice and Jurisdiction

The Court exercises its jurisdiction for the enforcement of the truth . . . .

—Sir John Romilly[3]

It is axiomatic that "a court of justice is never justified in hearing and adjudging the merits of a cause of which it has no jurisdiction."[4] This, Cheng found, was "common to all systems of jurisprudence."[5]

Jurisdiction is an either-or proposition that must be satisfied. Two implications arise from a tribunal's erroneous determination on jurisdiction, whether it be affirmative or negative. The first is that *any decision made without jurisdiction is a nullity.*[6] For example, if a tribunal enters interim orders to maintain the status quo between the parties prior to definitively addressing its own jurisdiction, those orders would "automatically lose their effect" if the tribunal eventually concludes that it lacks jurisdiction.[7] Similarly, if an arbitration award is rendered on a matter "not falling within the terms of the submission to arbitration," the award is unenforceable.[8] The second implication is that *a court's failure to decide a case that falls within its jurisdiction is an international delict.*[9] As declared in 1797 by Christopher Gore, a commissioner on the Mixed Commission set up under Article VII of the Jay Treaty, "'[t]o refrain from acting, when our duty calls us to act, is as wrong as to act where we have no authority.'"[10] What more

3 *Laver v. Fielder*, [1862] 32 Beav. 13.

4 Cheng, *supra* note 2, at 259 (citing *Mavrommatis Palestine Concessions Case (Greece v. U.K.)*, Objection to the Jurisdiction of the Court, Judgment, 1924 P.C.I.J. (Ser. A) No. 2 (Aug. 30) (dissenting opinion of M. Moore)).

5 *Id.*

6 *Id.* at 261; *see also Pennoyer v. Neff*, 95 U.S. 714, 733–34 (1878).

7 Cheng, *supra* note 2, at 273–74.

8 Convention on the Recognition and Enforcement of Foreign Arbitral Awards (New York Convention) art. V(1)(c), June 10, 1958, 330 U.N.T.S. 3.

9 Cheng, *supra* note 2, at 261–62. A tribunal might also fail to address all issues presented to it, known as *infra petita*. *See* BLC and ors v. BLB and anor, [2014] SGCA 40, 91 (Singapore Appellate Court) (holding that the failure to address an argument could be grounds for annulment where it caused actual prejudice); Gary B. Born, International Commercial Arbitration 3293 (2d ed. 2014) ("an arbitral tribunal's failure to consider issues presented to it in fact amounts to an excess of authority, even if it appears only to be the reverse, because it effectively rewrites the tribunal's mandate, which is an act beyond the arbitrators' competence"). A party's claim of *infra petita* should be first raised with the tribunal itself absent compelling circumstances, with the usual remedy being completion of the award by the tribunal rather than annulment.

10 Cheng, *supra* note 2, at 261–62 (quoting *Jay Treaty (Art. VII) Arbitration* (1794), 4 Int. Adj., M.S. 179, 193).

commonly occurs is an unreasonable delay in issuing judgment, which has been likened to the refusal to judge.[11] Arising from the very nature of jurisdiction, both of these implications are considered to be general principles of law and fundamental components of international due process.[12]

Civil law attorneys might refer to this concept as *competency*, whereas common law attorneys would view it as *jurisdiction*. At base, it is the power of the court over the parties and issues before it. Whether a tribunal or court derives its authority from the parties' consent (as in a commercial arbitration), a treaty (as in an investment arbitration), or positive law (as in a municipal litigation) is largely beside the point. In every case, there exists an external limit on the scope of jurisdiction, so questions of competence over particular parties or issues can be raised either by motion or *propio motu*.[13] And when those questions are raised, the tribunal seised of the matter has the authority to answer them in the first instance.[14] The competence to decide one's own competence (known as the doctrine of *Kompetenz-Komptenz*) is inherent in the very nature of adjudicatory authority and universally expressed in the institutional rules governing international arbitration.[15]

Although jurisdiction may be an either-or proposition, neither conclusion is necessarily absolute in a given case. That jurisdictional power has been exceeded on one issue does not affect the validity of decisions on other issues for which there is competence, just as a finding of jurisdiction does not necessarily extend to all parties or issues concerned.[16] That said, once jurisdiction is properly obtained,

11 *Antoine Fabiani (No. 1) (Fr. v. Venez.)*, *in* J.B. MOORE, HISTORY AND DIGEST OF INTERNATIONAL ARBITRATIONS TO WHICH THE UNITED STATES HAS BEEN A PARTY 4895 (1898) ("Upon examining the general principles of international law with regard to denial of justice, that is to say, the rules common to most bodies of law or laid down by doctrine, one finds that denial of justice includes not only the refusal of a judicial authority to exercise his functions and, in particular, to give a decision on the request submitted to him, but also wrongful delays on his part in giving judgment."); *see also White Indus. Australia Ltd. v. Republic of India*, UNCITRAL, Award (Nov. 30, 2011); *Chevron Corp. & Texaco Petroleum Co. v. Republic of Ecuador*, UNCITRAL, PCA Case No. 34877, Partial Award on the Merits (Mar. 30, 2010).

12 CHENG, *supra* note 2, at 261–62.

13 *Id.* at 266.

14 *See* REDFERN & HUNTER ON INTERNATIONAL ARBITRATION ¶¶ 5.104–5.109 (6th ed. 2015); *see also* CHENG, *supra* note 2, at 275–78.

15 *See, e.g.*, UNCITRAL Rules art. 23; ICC Rules art. 6(4)–(5); LCIA Rules art. 23.1; ICSID Convention Rule 41; *see also* Statute of the International Court of Justice art. 36(6); *see also* UNCITRAL Model Law art. 16.

16 *See, e.g.*, *ConocoPhillips Petrozuata B.V. et al. v. Bolivarian Republic of Venezuela*, ICSID Case No. ARB/07/30, Decision on Jurisdiction and Merits, ¶¶ 315–17 (Sept. 3, 2013) (interpreting treaty to limit scope of tribunal's review of tax measures, but proceeding to sustain jurisdiction over other claims).

the tribunal's power typically extends to all relevant and auxiliary questions necessary to decide the primary dispute—even when those questions technically fall beyond the scope of the tribunal's authority.[17]

A cardinal antecedent to the exercise of jurisdiction is "due notice" of the proceeding. This principle stands anterior to the equally important principle of *audi alteram partem.* In 1878, the U.S. Supreme Court surveyed the practices of foreign jurisdictions and championed proper service as the means by which to fulfill this fundamental requirement:

> [I]nternational law . . . as it existed among the States in 1790, was that a judgment rendered in one State, assuming to bind the person of a citizen of another, was void within the foreign State, when the defendant *had not been served with process or voluntarily made defence*; because neither the legislative jurisdiction nor that of courts of justice had binding force.[18]

The Court found this fixture of international law to be part of U.S. law as well, holding it to be no less than a "principle of natural justice" to "require[s] a person to have notice of a suit before he can be conclusively bound by its result" in order to "protect persons and property within one State from the exercise of jurisdiction over them by another."[19] Adequate notice is thus a necessary predicate to recognition of a foreign judgment: "Every foreign judgment, of whatever nature, in order to be entitled to any effect, must have been rendered . . . upon regular proceedings and due notice."[20] Indeed the twin requirements of notice and jurisdiction are universal prerequisites to enforcement of a foreign judgment, as reflected in the Montevideo Convention,[21] the

---

17 *See, e.g., Land, Island and Maritime Frontier Dispute (El Sal./Hond.)*, Order on Application for Permission to Intervene, 1990 I.C.J. 3, 134 (Feb. 28); *World Duty Free Co. Ltd. v. Republic of Kenya*, ICSID Case No. ARB/00/7, Award, ¶ 3 (Oct. 4, 2006); *Legal Consequences for States of the Continued Presence of South Africa in Namibia (South-West Africa) notwithstanding Security Council Resolution 276 (1970)*, Advisory Opinion, 1971 I.C.J. 16, ¶ 89 (June 21); *CMS Gas Transmission Co. v. Republic of Argentina*, ICSID Case No. ARB/01/8, Decision on Objections to Jurisdiction, ¶¶ 116–20 (July 17, 2003); *see also* Cheng, *supra* note 2, at 266–67 (citing cases).

18 *Pennoyer v. Neff*, 95 U.S. 714, 730 (1878) (emphasis added; quoting *D'Arcy v. Ketchum*, 52 U.S. 165, 176 (1851)).

19 *Id.* (quoting *Lafayette Ins. Co. v. Fench*, 59 U.S. 404, 406 (1856)).

20 *Hilton v. Guyot*, 159 U.S. 113, 166–67 (1895) (emphasis added).

21 Organization of American States, Inter-American Convention on Extraterritorial Validity of Foreign Judgments and Arbitral Awards of 1979 art. 2(d), O.A.S.T.S. No. 51 (entered into force June 14, 1980) ("The judge or tribunal rendering the judgment is competent in the international sphere to try the matter."); art. 2(e) ("The plaintiff has been summoned or subpoenaed in due legal form substantially equivalent to that accepted by the law of the State where the judgment, award or decision is to take effect.").

Kiev Treaty,[22] the Foreign Judgments Act of 1991,[23] and Council Regulation (EU) No. 1215/2012.[24] National laws are in accord.[25]

By virtue of this broad acceptance, due notice has long been a general principle of law, and its contours have been clarified through numerous applications on the international plane. The International Institute for the Unification of Private Law (UNIDROIT) Principles of Transnational Civil Procedure state that adjudicatory proceedings can commence only after notice that is "reasonably likely to be effective."[26] Although different legal systems allow different mechanisms to transmit notice of adjudicatory proceedings, those mechanisms must, in the circumstances, adequately inform the interested parties of the "procedure for response and the possibility of default judgment for failure to make timely response."[27] For example, in

22 Treaty concerning the Modalities of the Settlement of Disputes Related to the Exercise of Commercial Activity art. 9(c) (entered into force Dec. 19, 1992) (denial of enforcement of commercial decision from jurisdiction in the Commonwealth of Independent States where court was "incompetent according to this Treaty"); art. 9(d) (requiring that the judgment debtor "be served with a summons").

23 Foreign Judgments Act 1991 arts. 7(2)(a)(iv) and 7(3)–(4), No. 112, 1991 as amended, *available at* https://www.comlaw.gov.au/Details/C2013C00640 (last visited Aug. 30, 2015) (denying recognition to foreign judgments where the "original court had no jurisdiction in the circumstances of the case" and providing that such jurisdiction exists if the judgment debtor, inter alia, brought a counterclaim in the suit or maintained a residence or principal place of business in the country); *id.* art. 7(2)(a)(v) (denying recognition where judgment debtor "did not . . . receive notice of those proceedings in sufficient time to enable the judgment debtor to defend the proceedings and did not appear," irrespective of "whether or not process had been duly served on the judgment debtor in accordance with the law of the country of the original court").

24 Regulation (EU) No. 1215/2012 of the European Parliament and of the Council of December 12, 2012 on jurisdiction and the recognition and enforcement of judgments in civil and commercial matters, art. 45.1(b), 2012 O.J. (L 351) 1 (Member State commercial judgment shall not be enforced "if the defendant was not served with the document which instituted the proceedings or with an equivalent document in sufficient time and in such a way as to enable him to arrange for his defence."). Although the Council Regulation does not permit an enforcing court to review the jurisdiction of the Member State that issued the judgment, *id.* art. 45.2, chapter 2 of the Council Regulation is dedicated to setting forth the standards for when a Member State may exercise jurisdiction, *id.* arts. 4–35.

25 *See, e.g.*, Korean Code of Civil Procedure art. 217 (jurisdiction of foreign court must satisfy the principle of international jurisdiction, and legitimate service of process must have been effected); German Civil Code [ZPO] § 328(1) (requiring that the foreign court had jurisdiction as measured against German law and that service allowed sufficient time to defend); *Club Resorts Ltd. v. Van Breda* (2012), 343 D.L.R. 4th 577 (Can. Sup. Ct.) (foreign judgment recognition dependent upon foreign court having a "real and substantial connection" to the parties or the facts in dispute, and identifying the following presumptive connecting factors: (1) defendant is domiciled or resident in the jurisdiction, (2) defendant carries on business in the jurisdiction, (3) tort was committed in the jurisdiction, and (4) contract was made in the jurisdiction); *Adams v. Cape Indus. plc*, [1990] ch. 433 (U.K. Court of Appeal) (requiring that foreign court have the competence to summon the defendant before it and to decide such matters as it has decided).

26 ALI/UNIDROIT Principles of Transnational Civil Procedure princ. 5.1, 2004-4 UNIF. L. REV. 758.

27 *Id.*

Middle East Cement v. Egypt, the host State seized and auctioned the claimant's vessel after publicizing the proceeding in a newspaper as opposed to providing the claimant with personal service. An International Centre for Settlement of Investment Disputes (ICSID) tribunal found that this notice, and thus the resulting taking of the claimant's property, was not in accordance with the international concept of due process of law—even though service by publication was authorized by Egyptian law.[28]

The requirement of due notice extends beyond formal judicial proceedings. Any state organ exercising adjudicatory powers is subject to similar, albeit more flexible, due-process standards. France's *Conseil d'Etat* declared in 1944 that administrative measures with a material effect could be implemented only after notice, so that affected parties could defend their interests.[29] Article 41.2(a) of the Charter of Fundamental Rights of the European Union, concerning administration, likewise records the "right of every person to be heard, before any individual measure which would affect him or her adversely is taken."[30] For its part, the Inter-American Court of Human Rights has stated that "both the jurisdictional organs and those of any other nature that exercise functions of a substantially jurisdictional nature have the obligation to adopt just decisions based on full respect for the guarantee of due process."[31] This obligation goes unmet by an administrative process in which the claimant is "prevented from intervening, fully informed, in all the

28 *Middle East Cement Shipping & Handling Co. S.A. v. Arab Republic of Egypt*, ICSID Case No. ARB/99/6, Award, ¶¶ 142–43 (Apr. 12, 2002), 7 ICSID Rep. 173 (2005); *see also Generica Ltd. v. Pharm. Basics, Inc.*, 125 F.3d 1123, 1129–30 (7th Cir. 1997) ("[A]n arbitrator must provide a fundamentally fair hearing," defined as "one that meets the minimal requirements of fairness—*adequate notice*, a hearing on the evidence, and an impartial decision by the arbitrator.") (quotation marks omitted; emphasis added); *Hilton v. Guyot*, 159 U.S. 113, 158 (1895) (requiring "a full and fair trial abroad before a court of competent jurisdiction, . . . *after due citation or voluntary appearance of the defendant*") (emphasis added); *Pennoyer v. Neff*, 95 U.S. 714, 735 (1878) ("It is not contrary to natural justice that a man who has agreed to receive a particular mode of notification of legal proceedings should be bound by a judgment in which that particular mode of notification has been followed, even though he may not have actual notice of them.").

29 *Dame Veuve Trompier-Gravier*, CE Sect. (May 5, 1944), Rec. Lebon 133. Adjectival requirements such as this stem, as another decision made clear, from the proposition that the executive branch is bound by "applicable general principles of law, even in the absence of a [legal] text." *Aramu*, CE Ass. (Oct. 26, 1945), Rec. Lebon 213. Indeed, "[t]he doctrinal foundations of French administrative law are almost entirely the product of an ongoing jurisprudence of general principles." Alec Stone Sweet & Giacinto della Cananea, *Proportionality, General Principles of Law, and Investor-State Arbitration: A Response to José Alvarez*, 46 N.Y.U. J. Int'l L. & Pol. 911, 945–46 (2013–2014).

30 Charter of Fundamental Rights of the European Union (2000/C 364/01) art. 41.2(a), *signed and proclaimed by* the Presidents of the European Parliament, the Council and the Commission at the European Council meeting, Nice (Dec. 7, 2000).

31 *Case of Ivcher-Bronstein v. Peru*, Merits, Reparations and Costs, Judgment, Inter-Am. Ct. H.R. (Ser. C) No. 74, ¶ 104 (Feb. 6, 2001).

stages," because, inter alia, "he was not told about the charges of which he was accused."[32] The World Trade Organization (WTO) Appellate Body has also held that a U.S. regulatory requirement imposed upon shrimp-harvesting nets to protect turtles violated the General Agreement on Tariffs and Trade (GATT) because the United States had not observed basic notice and comment requirements.[33] And the tribunal in *Metalclad v. United Mexican States* condemned "procedural and substantive deficiencies" arising from inadequate notice of an administrative proceeding, noting that the permit at issue there "was denied at a meeting of the Municipal Town Council of which Metalclad received no notice."[34]

This does not mean than all decisions taken prior to due notice and before jurisdictional certainty are void ab initio. As noted, national courts and international tribunals may issue interim and provisional measures on an ex parte basis and prior to resolving a challenge to their jurisdiction. It is "certain," as Cheng wrote, that "an international tribunal need not be convinced, nor reasonably certain, that it would have jurisdiction before it can indicate interim measures."[35] Given the complexities of international commerce, requests for precautionary measures are often urgent, and in certain cases they may be needed to maintain the status quo and protect the tribunal's ability to provide meaningful relief at the end of the adjudicatory process. Although the formulation of the requisite jurisdictional showing has differed across fora and time, it may be stated as a general proposition that—given the immediacy with which these requests must be decided, their importance to the viability of the arbitration, and the inherent difficulties in resolving issues of jurisdiction on the hoof—a prima facie or reasonable possibility of jurisdiction suffices to allow an award of interim protection.[36] Prior notice

---

32 *Id.* ¶¶ 106, 107.

33 Appellate Body Report, *United States—Import Prohibition of Certain Shrimp and Shrimp Products*, WT/DS58/AB/R (Oct. 12, 1998) (*adopted* Nov. 6, 1998).

34 *Metalclad Corp. v. United Mexican States*, ICSID Case No. ARB(AF)/97/1, Award, ¶¶ 91, 97 (Aug. 30, 2000).

35 CHENG, *supra* note 2, at 273.

36 *See LaGrand Case (Ger. v. U.S.)*, Request for the Indication of Provisional Measures, Order, 1999 I.C.J. 9, ¶ 13 (Mar. 3) ("*LaGrand* Provisional Measures Order") ("[O]n a request for the indication of provisional measures the Court need not, before deciding whether or not to indicate them, finally satisfy itself that it has jurisdiction on the merits of the case, but that it may not indicate them unless the provisions invoked by the Applicant appear, prima facie, to afford a basis on which the jurisdiction of the Court might be founded."); *Perenco Ecuador Ltd. v. Republic of Ecuador*, ICSID Case No. ARB/08/6, Decision on Provisional Measures, ¶ 39 (May 8, 2009) ("While the Tribunal need not satisfy itself that it has jurisdiction to determine the merits of this case for the purposes of ruling on the application for provisional measures, it will not order such measures unless there is at least a *prima facie* basis upon which such jurisdiction might be established.").

can even be dispensed with in exceptional circumstances, provided that the party affected is promptly given notice of, and a chance to oppose, the continuation of the order.[37] This is less an exception to the general principle of jurisdiction than an affirmation that the parties must always respect the tribunal's jurisdiction—a reflection of the "universally accepted" principle that "[p]arties to a case must abstain from any measure capable of exercising a prejudicial effect in regard to the execution of the decision to be taken and, in general, not allow any step of any kind to be taken which might aggravate or extend the dispute."[38]

Given that jurisdiction must obtain before an adjudication can occur, there have been various attempts to identify some baseline normative standard to assess that jurisdiction—viz., that a meaningful connection exists among the court, the parties, and the matters involved. The UNIDROIT Principles of Transnational Civil Procedure call for a "substantial connection between the forum state and the party or the transaction or occurrence in dispute."[39] Such a "substantial connection" might exist when (1) "a significant part of the transaction or occurrence occurred in the forum state," (2) "an individual defendant is a habitual resident of the forum state or a jural entity has received its charter of organization or has its principal place of business therein," or (3) "property to which the dispute relates is located in the forum state."[40] These fact-laden examples are subject to varying degrees of satisfaction—for instance, it is not self-evident when a residence becomes "habitual," or when a "meaningful" or "substantial" connection to the forum state has been formed. Such nuance is not captured with a general principle. And the existence of permissible jurisdictional bases that fall outside the definition of a "substantial connection," such as universal jurisdiction over crimes against humanity and transient (or tag) jurisdiction, make the existence of a general principle in this respect difficult to endorse. Perhaps the most that can be said is that the exercise

---

37 ALI/UNIDROIT Principles of Transnational Civil Procedure princ. 5.8, 8.2, 2004-4 Unif. L. Rev. 758.

38 Cheng, *supra* note 2, at 268 (quoting *Elec. Co. of Sofia and Bulgaria*, Interim Measures of Protection, Order, 1939 P.C.I.J. (Ser. A/B) No. 79, at 199 (Dec. 5)).

39 ALI/UNIDROIT Principles of Transnational Civil Procedure princ. 2.1.2 & cmt. P2-B, 2004-4 Unif. L. Rev. 758. Scholars have stated the "substantial connection" standard differently, for example by requiring a "clear connecting factor," or a factual "linking point" "between the legislating state and the conduct that it seeks to regulate [abroad]." Vaughan Lowe, *Jurisdiction*, *in* International Law 342 (Malcolm D. Evans ed., 2d ed. 2006); *see also* Ian Brownlie, Principles of Public International Law 309–10 (4th ed. 1990) (requiring a "substantial and bona fide connection between subject matter and the source of the jurisdiction"); Francesco Francioni, *Extraterritorial Application of Environmental Law*, *in* Extraterritorial Jurisdiction in Theory and Practice 125 (Karl M. Meessen ed., 1996) (an assertion of extraterritorial jurisdiction over subjects who have no significant relation to the forum, except transitory presence or an indirect effect, may well constitute a breach of an international due process standard).

40 ALI/UNIDROIT Principles of Transnational Civil Procedure princ. 2.1.2, 2004-4 Unif. L. Rev. 758.

of jurisdiction without any articulable or logical connection to the parties and the dispute is rare, difficult to justify, and unlikely to be recognized elsewhere.

B. Judicial Impartiality and Judicial Independence

> *The Best Judge . . . shall know nothing about the parties, everything about the case. He shall do everything for justice; nothing for himself; nothing for his friend; nothing for his patron; nothing for his sovereign. If on one side is the executive power and the legislature and the people—sources of his honors, the givers of his daily bread—and on the other side an individual nameless and odious, his eye is to see neither, great nor small; attending only to the trepidations of his balance . . .—or there is no judge.*
>
> —Rufus Choate[41]

As reflected in the figure of Lady Justice, who is typically represented blindfolded while holding out scales in one hand and grasping a sword in the other, an impartial and independent judge has long been a fundamental tenet of international due process. As Cheng wrote, "[a] judge must not only be impartial, but there must be no possibility of suspecting his impartiality."[42] This includes, as emphasized by Rufus Choate, judicial partiality toward the sovereign. Lord Chief Justices William Scroggs and George Jeffreys were Choate's "exemplifications" of "judicial subserviency" during "the worst years of the Stuart dynasty."[43] As he explained, when there is judicial capture by the political branches, the judge becomes "the tool of the hand that made him and unmade him," sitting on a bench "packed for the enforcement of some new or more flagrant royal usurpation."[44] But even with the advent of republican forms of government, the companion principles of impartiality and independence are far too often honored in the breach.

The travails of Jacob Idler offer a historical lens into the "vicissitudes of revolution" in nineteenth century Latin America.[45] Idler was an American businessman

---

41 Rufus Choate, Speech Delivered to the Massachusetts Constitutional Convention of 1853: The Judicial Tenure.

42 CHENG, *supra* note 2, at 289.

43 Choate, *supra* note 41, at 12.

44 *Id.* at 10–11.

45 *See Jacob Idler v. Venezuela*, United States and Venezuela Claims Commission, *in* J.B. MOORE, HISTORY AND DIGEST OF INTERNATIONAL ARBITRATIONS TO WHICH THE UNITED STATES HAS BEEN A PARTY 3491 (1898).

who sold arms and munitions to Venezuela during its wars of independence, yet nearly U.S. $250,000 in invoices remained unpaid. The Venezuela Secretary of the Treasury explicitly acknowledged the propriety of Idler's claim and the Venezuela Supreme Court affirmed a lower court decision that the Government should pay its debt. But the Executive Branch disregarded the order and, in an ex parte petition, requested that the Supreme Court annul its decision. Two of the four justices on that Court recused themselves and were replaced, by the vote of the two remaining justices, with members of the Caracas bar. The newly constituted Court reversed the order and extinguished the debt.

An arbitral tribunal, convened by treaty to resolve the dispute, "ha[d] no hesitation in saying that the effect of these judgments was a denial of justice."[46] The first thing that engaged the attention of the tribunal was the reorganization of the Supreme Court prior to the reversal. The tribunal acknowledged that "there is a facility of substitution as to judges" in civil law countries unknown in common law countries, but that "such change is believed to be always regulated by law."[47] Here, "[w]hy any change at all was necessary was not apparent," and, furthermore, such change was done contrary to the Constitution and governing law:

> The difficulty is not that the court at Caracas was filled by members from the bar for this case, or that two judges made the appointments. [The difficulty is that] this was done *without the authority of the law*. . . . Venezuela could, of course, constitute her courts as she desired, but having established them, it was Idler's right, if his affairs were drawn into litigation there, to have them adjudicated by the courts constituted under the forms of law.[48]

Given the illegality of the "reorganization of the court so as to change its *personnel* . . . for this one case," the tribunal could not "escape the conviction that it was the voice of Idler's opponents which found expression in the [resubmitted] judgments . . . and not that either of justice or of the supreme court of justice."[49] This has properly been deemed one of the most "remarkable instance[s] of governmental manipulation of the judicial branch."[50]

---

46 *Id.* at 3516–17.

47 *Id.* at 3506.

48 *Id.* at 3508.

49 *Id.* at 3517.

50 Jan Paulsson, Denial of Justice in International Law 162 (2005). *See also* Restatement (Third) Foreign Relations Law of the United States § 711, Reporter's note 2(A) (Am. Law Inst.

Robert Brown faced similar tribulations at the turn of the twentieth century in South Africa.[51] An American businessman, Brown had sought and obtained gold mining concessions from the South African Government in 1895.[52] When the president of South Africa unilaterally terminated the concession—which the legislature affirmed—Brown brought suit in the High Court of the South African Republic.[53] That Court declared the termination of the concession unconstitutional and invited Brown to pursue a claim for damages.[54] What ensued, according to the arbitral tribunal charged with reviewing the case, was "an amazing controversy between the Court and the Executive," leading to a "unique judicial crisis" and the "virtual subjection of the High Court to the executive power."[55]

In response to the High Court's decision, the Legislature passed a law forbidding judges from striking down legislative enactments and, despite "a vigorous but vain fight for the independence of the judiciary . . . by [members of] the bench, the bar, and the press," the Executive Branch dismissed the Chief Justice of the Court.[56] When Brown sued for damages, as he was invited to do, the new High Court abandoned its previous decision and dismissed his case.[57] Once the case was elevated beyond the national courts, an arbitral tribunal declared that "Brown had substantial rights" and that "he was deprived of these rights by the Government of the South African Republic in such manner and under such circumstances as to amount to a denial of justice within the settled principles of international law."[58] When a judiciary is "reduced to submission and brought into line with a determined policy of the Executive to reach the desired result regardless of Constitutional guarantees and inhibitions," the tribunal held, the "interest of elementary justice for all concerned . . . disappear[s]."[59]

1987) (noting that in *Idler*, the State was held internationally responsible where its judicial tribunal was "manipulated by the executive").

51 *See Robert E. Brown (United States v. Great Britain)*, Decision (Nov. 23, 1923), 6 R.I.A.A. 120.

52 *See id.* at 121–22.

53 *See id.* at 122.

54 *Id.* at 120.

55 *Id.* at 124–25.

56 *Id.* at 125–26.

57 *See id.* at 126.

58 *Id.* at 128.

59 *Id.* at 129. Though a denial of justice was found, Brown was eventually denied recovery because the arbitration was lodged against the United Kingdom, the successor to the South African Republic after the Boer War, and the tribunal decided that—in that specific circumstance—a successor sovereign did not assume the liabilities of its predecessor. *Id.* at 131 ("The relation of suzerain did not operate to render Great Britain liable for the acts complained of.").

Today nearly every nation provides in its written law for an independent judiciary.[60] That consensus has been mirrored on the international plane, too, as intergovernmental and nongovernmental organizations have expressly recognized judicial impartiality and independence as integral to the basic right of access to justice. This began soon after World War II, when the United Nations promulgated the Universal Declaration of Human Rights. According to Article 10 of that instrument, "[e]veryone is entitled in full equality to a fair and public hearing by an *independent* and *impartial* tribunal, in the determination of his rights and obligations and of any criminal charge against him."[61] The countries of the Organization of American States also recognize the right to an impartial and public hearing as a fundamental "right and duty of Man,"[62] whereas the European Convention for the Protection of Human Rights and Fundamental Freedoms requires that, in both civil and criminal cases, "everyone is entitled to a fair and public hearing within a reasonable time by an independent and impartial tribunal established by law."[63] The more recent Charter of Fundamental Rights of the European Union states in its section on "Justice" that "[e]veryone is entitled to a fair and public hearing within a reasonable time by an *independent and impartial*

60 *See, e.g.*, Germany Judiciary Act § 25 (1972) ("A judge shall be independent and subject only to the law."); Code of Conduct for United States Judges, Canon 1 ("An independent and honorable judiciary is indispensable to justice in our society.") and Canon 2 ("A judge should respect and comply with the law and should act at all times in a manner that promotes public confidence in the integrity and impartiality of the judiciary."); Kazakhstani Constitutional Law on the Judicial System and Status of Judges art. I(3) (2000, amended 2014) ("In the administration of justice, judges shall be independent and subordinate only to the Constitution and the law."); Constitution of the French Republic art. 64 (Oct. 4, 1958) ("The President of the Republic shall be the guarantor of the independence of the Judicial Authority."); Russian Federal Constitutional Law on the Judicial System art. 1 (1996, amended 2011) ("The judicial power shall be separate and shall act independently of the legislative and executive powers."); Iceland Act on the Judiciary art. 24 (1998, as amended 2011) ("Judges shall discharge their judicial functions independently and on their own responsibility. They shall, in resolving a case, proceed solely according to law, and shall never be subject to the authority of any other person.").

61 Universal Declaration of Human Rights, G.A. Res. 217 (III) A, U.N. Doc. A/RES/217(III), art. 10 (Dec. 10, 1948) (emphasis added).

62 American Declaration of the Rights and Duties of Man, O.A.S. Res. XXX, *adopted by* the Ninth International Conference of American States (1948), *reprinted in* Basic Documents Pertaining to Human Rights in the Inter-American System, OEA/Ser.L./V/II.82, Doc. 6 rev. 1, art. XXVI (1992) (establishing the right to an impartial and public hearing) ("Every person accused of an offense has the right to be given an impartial and public hearing, and to be tried by courts previously established in accordance with pre-existing laws, and not to receive cruel, infamous or unusual punishment.").

63 Convention for the Protection of Human Rights and Fundamental Freedoms art. 6, as amended by Protocols No. 11 and 14, Nov. 4, 1950, 213 U.N.T.S. 221 (entered into force Sept. 3, 1953) (providing for right to a fair trial).

tribunal previously established by law."[64] The same standards apply to arbitrators as well.[65]

Despite these florid de jure pronouncements, undue executive and legislative pressure continues to be a de facto scourge on the judicial function.[66] Russian courts, for instance, have been found to have "bent to the will of Russian executive authorities to bankrupt [a privately-owned company (Yukos)], assign its assets to a State-controlled company, and incarcerate [its executive] who gave signs of becoming a political competitor."[67] Similarly, the Inter-American Court for Human Rights (IACHR) held that the Peruvian courts in a particular case "did not satisfy the minimum requirements of independence and impartiality that Article 8(1) of the Convention establishes as essential elements of due legal process."[68] In the late 1990s, the Peruvian Immigration and Naturalization Service revoked the citizenship of Baruch Ivcher Bronstein, a former Israeli citizen, which had the effect of ending his service as a director of a Peruvian television company that had aired programs critical of the Government.[69] When a case was brought challenging this government action, the IACHR found the domestic

---

64 Charter of Fundamental Rights of the European Union art. 47(2) (2000/C 364/01), *signed and proclaimed by* the Presidents of the European Parliament, the Council and the Commission at the European Council meeting, Nice (Dec. 7, 2000) (emphasis added).

65 *See, e.g.*, IBA Guidelines on Conflicts of Interest in International Arbitration, General Standard 1 (2014) ("Every arbitrator shall be impartial and independent of the parties at the time of accepting an appointment to serve and shall remain so until the final award has been rendered or the proceedings have otherwise finally terminated.").

66 Chapter 3.D contains various surveys and statistics on the general functioning of court systems around the world.

67 *See Hulley Enters. Ltd. v. Russian Federation*, UNCITRAL, PCA Case No. AA226, Final Award, ¶ 1583 (July 18, 2014). In the proceedings that led to the criminal prosecutions of Yukos executives, the individual defendants received "harsh treatment," were "remotely jailed and caged in court," and their counsel were routinely "mistreat[ed]" and encountered obstacles in "reading the record and conferring with [their clients]." *Id.* When Russia tried to extradite other executives for prosecution,

> courts in the United Kingdom refused [those requests] on the basis that the prosecutions were "so politically motivated that there is a substantial risk that the Judges of the Moscow City court would succumb to political interference in a way which would call into question their independence." Courts in Lithuania, Cyprus and the Czech Republic also refused to extradite former Yukos managers or former Yukos service providers on the basis of the political dimensions of the underlying requests.

Id. ¶ 786.

68 *Case of Ivcher-Bronstein v. Peru*, Merits, Reparations and Costs, Judgment, Inter-Am. Ct. H.R. (Ser. C) No. 74, ¶ 139 (Feb. 6, 2001).

69 *Id.* ¶ 3.

mechanisms for judicial review of the administrative decision wanting as they did not provide for a regular and impartial court: "[B]y creating *temporary* public law chambers and courts and appointing judges to them at the time that the facts of the case *sub judice* occurred, the State did not guarantee to Mr. Ivcher Bronstein the right to be heard by judges or courts 'previously established by law,' as stipulated in Article 8(1) of the American Convention."[70] Whatever the issue sub judice and whoever the parties to the suit, judicial subservience to political expediency is anathema to law.[71]

Domestic courts typically will not give res judicata effect to a foreign decision,[72] enforce a foreign judgment,[73] or transfer a case to a foreign court[74] without first reviewing the independence and impartiality of the foreign judicial system. Applying a universal, rather than parochial, concept of due process,[75] courts and tribunals have denied recognition to foreign judgments where judges are "subject to continuing scrutiny and threat of sanction" by the political branches

70 *Id.* ¶ 114. Contemporaneous with the revocation of his citizenship, "the Judiciary's Executive Committee modified the composition of the Constitutional and Social Chamber of the Supreme Court of Justice" and "adopted a norm giving this Chamber the power to create, on a '[t]emporary basis' superior chambers and courts of public law, and also to 'appoint and/or ratify' their members, which effectively occurred two days later." *Id.* ¶ 113. It was one of these temporary public law courts that heard Mr. Ivcher Bronstein's appeals.

71 *Id.* ¶¶ 113–14.

72 *See Chevron Corp. v. Donziger*, 886 F. Supp. 2d 235, 240 (S.D.N.Y. 2012) (a foreign judgment "may not be afforded *res judicata* or collateral estoppel effect unless it is entitled to recognition and enforcement here").

73 *See, e.g.*, *Hilton v. Guyot*, 159 U.S. 113, 2029 (1895) (requiring "a system of . . . impartial administration of justice"); *Chevron Corp. v. Donziger*, 974 F. Supp. 2d 362, 608–09 (S.D.N.Y. 2014); Restatement (Third) Foreign Relations Law of the United States § 482 cmt. b (Am. Law Inst. 1987) ("the judiciary [must not be] dominated by the political branches of government or by an opposing litigant"). Most countries deny recognition of foreign judgments that are contrary to universal standards of due process or public policy, and decisions issued by foreign judges who lack independence and impartiality necessarily fall within this proscription. *See, e.g.*, Regulation (EU) No. 1215/2012 of the European Parliament and of the Council of Dec. 12, 2012 on jurisdiction and the recognition and enforcement of judgments in civil and commercial matters, art. 45.1(a), 2012 O.J. (L 351) 1 (denying recognition to Member State judgments that are "manifestly contrary to public policy (ordre public)"); *Ellefsen v. Ellefsen*, Civil Jurisdiction 1993, No. 202 (Oct. 22, 1993) (denial of recognition in Bermuda of foreign judgments that are contrary to public policy and natural justice); Foreign Judgments (Reciprocal Enforcement) Act, ch. F35, Laws of the Federation of Nigeria art. 6(1)(a)(v) (denying enforcement of a foreign judgment that is "contrary to public policy in Nigeria").

74 *See, e.g.*, *Vidovic v. Losinjka Plovidka Oour Broadarstvo*, 868 F. Supp. 695, 699–702 (E.D. Pa. 1994) (denying dismissal on the *forum non conveniens* grounds because "the courts of the Republic of Croatia may be biased in favor of the government," rendering them an inadequate forum in a suit by a non-Croatian citizen against an instrumentality of the government).

75 *Soc'y of Lloyd's v. Ashenden*, 233 F.3d 473, 476–77 (7th Cir. 2000).

of government;[76] where "judges serve[] at the will of the leaders of [political] factions";[77] and where there is a "close interwovenness" of the parties and the machinery of justice.[78]

A recent example comes from a Moroccan judgment arising out of the Talsint oil project, which held such promise that the King of Morocco personally announced during a nationally televised speech the discovery of "copious and high quality oil," causing the Moroccan stock market to jump five percent.[79] When the anticipated oil did not materialize, the project disintegrated and the King's credibility suffered.[80] Two of the project's investors brought suit in Morocco against a third investor, John Paul DeJoria, on the theory that DeJoria had engaged in fraud and mismanagement.[81] The King had made similar accusations against DeJoria such that, if the co-investors' suit against DeJoria failed, the King could "appear foolish if not downright dishonest for having promised so much oil during his now infamous speech."[82] A Moroccan court ultimately entered a judgment of U.S. $122.9 million against DeJoria.[83]

The U.S. district court, hearing a request to recognize and enforce that judgment, explained that "[w]here there is evidence that a country's judiciary is dominated by the political branches of government or by an opposing litigant, or where a party cannot obtain counsel, secure documents, or secure a fair appeal, recognition of a foreign judgment may not be appropriate."[84] Although noting that "serious strides" had been made in Morocco to establish "a societal framework founded upon the rule of law," the court cited a 66-page report by

---

76 *Bank Melli Iran v. Pahlavi*, 58 F.3d 1406, 1412–13 (9th Cir. 1995) (where judges "under the post-Shah regime . . . are subject to continuing scrutiny and threat of sanction," they "cannot be expected to be completely impartial," which means that Iran's judiciary lacked fundamental notions of "civilized jurisprudence") (quotation marks omitted).

77 *Bridgeway Corp. v. Citibank*, 45 F. Supp. 2d 276, 287 (S.D.N.Y. 1999), *aff'd*, 201 F.3d 134 (2d Cir. 2000) (where "regular procedures governing the selection of justices and judges had not been followed"; where "justices and judges served at the will of the leaders of the warring factions"; and where "judicial officers were subject to political and social influence," the Liberian judicial system during the period in question "simply did not provide for impartial tribunals").

78 *Yukos Capital S.A.R.L. v. OAO Rosneft*, Amsterdam Court of Appeal, Case No. 200.005.269/01, Decision, ¶¶ 3.9.1, 3.8.9 (Apr. 28, 2009) (where "[t]here is a close interwovenness of [the claimant] and the Russian state," the respondent could not have expected to receive the process that was due).

79 *DeJoria v. Maghreb Petro.* Exploration S.A., 38 F. Supp. 3d 805, 808–09 (W.D. Tex. 2014).

80 *Id.* at 809.

81 *Id.*

82 *Id.* at 816.

83 *Id.* at 810.

84 *Id.* at 812.

the U.S. Government on the rule of law in Morocco, which concluded, inter alia, that the judicial system is "permeable to political influence" because "the mechanisms through which judges are appointed, promoted, sanctioned, and dismissed leave them vulnerable to political retribution."[85] The court found it significant that the King of Morocco "presides over . . . the body that appoints, disciplines, and promotes judges" and that roughly 1,000 Moroccan judges, armed with a petition signed by about two-thirds of all judges, had held a sit-in protest demanding structural reforms to guarantee their independence from the King.[86] The court also recited the admission by Morocco's Foreign Minister that "phone call justice"—that is, a call from the Ministry of Justice to a judge on how to rule—means that judicial independence "is not the reality today."[87] All of this raised in the court's mind "serious questions about whether any party that finds itself involved in a legal dispute in which the royal family has an apparent interest—be it economic or political—in the outcome of the case could ever receive a fair trial."[88] In light of the King's reputational interest in having the lawsuit against DeJoria succeed, the court refused to recognize the judgment: "Whether or not the King . . . or some other official picked up the phone and ordered the judge to find against DeJoria is, in some sense, beside the point. . . . Judges are not stupid people oblivious to outside pressures. . . . Moroccan judges are keenly aware that their livelihoods (present and future) depend on remaining in the good graces of the King and the royal family."[89] Notwithstanding these finding, the district court's judgment denying enforcement was reversed on appeal—a testament to the deference afforded to foreign courts under the doctrine of comity.[90]

From these and other authorities, it is possible to ascertain certain constitutive elements of judicial independence. *No one can be judge in his own cause.*[91] This constitutes "the most elementary and essential guarantee of impartiality in the administration of justice" by disqualifying interested parties from adjudicating

85 *Id.* at 812–13 (citation and quotation marks omitted).

86 *Id.* at 814.

87 *Id.*

88 *Id.* at 812.

89 *Id.* at 816–17.

90 *DeJoria v. Maghreb Petro. Exploration*, S.A., 804 F.3d 373 (5th Cir. 2015). Notably, unlike the district court, the Court of Appeals gave no heed to the specific nature of the underlying case, explaining that under the Texas Recognition Act "the court's inquiry . . . focuses on the fairness of the foreign judicial system as a whole, and we do not parse the particular judgment challenged." *Id.* at 381. The flaws of this approach are discussed in chapter 1.B(3)(b).

91 *See* Cheng, *supra* note 2, at 279–80.

disputes.[92] Where, for instance, a contract delegates adjudicatory authority to an arbitral panel appointed solely by one of the parties, and including that party's legal counsel as one of the arbitrators, the arbitration clause will be deemed invalid as an expression of the maxim nobody should be a judge in his own cause, which is one of the core elements securing the right to a fair hearing.[93] This is an extreme example, but the principle has greater scope than a literal interpretation of the Latin expression might suggest: it applies in all cases where judges and arbitrators have sufficient personal or pecuniary interest in the outcome of the proceedings so as to raise objective doubts as their independence and impartiality.

Impartiality means that "judges must not allow their judgment to be influenced by personal bias or prejudice, nor harbour preconceptions about the particular case before them, nor act in ways that improperly promote the interests of one of the parties to the detriment of the other."[94] This principle implies an unfettered freedom on the part of the judge to decide the case as she sees fit—according to the facts and the law, and not according to her own interests or the interests of one of the parties.[95] It is a species of the requirement that justice must not only be done, but appear to be done.[96] Thus, where a judge decides a case while at the same time being the director of one of the interested (if not nominal) parties, his judgment must be set aside where it was not first disclosed.[97] Similarly, the refusal of an arbitral tribunal to take any steps to address an apparent conflict of interest arising from the concurrent representation by the respondent's counsel of related

---

92 *Id.* at 284. *See also In re Pinochet*, [1999] UKHL 52 (Jan. 15, 1999) (Lord Hope of Craighead: "One of the cornerstones of our legal system is the impartiality of the tribunals by which justice is administered," and the "guiding principle is that no one may be a judge in his own cause").

93 *LLC First Excavator Co. v. JSC Union of Indus.* RosProm, Case No. 1308/11 (Russ.); *see also Sramek v. Austria*, App. No. 8790/79, Eur. Ct. H.R., Judgment, ¶ 42 (Oct. 22, 1984) ("Where, as in the present case, a tribunal's members include a person who is in a subordinate position, in terms of his duties and the organisation of his service, vis-à-vis one of the parties, litigants may entertain a legitimate doubt about that person's independence. Such a situation seriously affects the confidence which the courts must inspire in a democratic society.").

94 U.N. Human Rights Committee, *General Comment No. 32*, U.N. Doc. CCPR/C/GC/32, ¶ 21 (Aug. 23, 2007); *see also Karttunen v. Finland*, Communication No. 387/1989, U.N. Doc. CCPR/C/46/D/387/1989, ¶ 7.2 (Nov. 5, 1992); Office of the High Commissioner for Human Rights, Basic Principles on the Independence of the Judiciary princ. 2.

95 *See* ALI/UNIDROIT Principles of Transnational Civil Procedure princ. 1.1 & 1.3, 2004-4 Unif. L. Rev. 758.

96 Cheng, *supra* note 2, at 286.

97 *In re Pinochet*, [1999] UKHL 52 (Jan. 15, 1999) (Lord Hope of Craighead); *see also Micallef v. Malta*, App. No. 17056/06, Eur. Ct. H.R., Judgment (Oct. 15, 2009) ("the close family ties between the opposing party's advocate and the judge sufficed to justify objectively . . . fears that the presiding judge lacked impartiality"); *New Regency Prods., Inc. v. Nippon Herald Films, Inc.*, 501 F.3d 111 (9th Cir. 2007) (conflict where the sole arbitrator was simultaneously sitting in judgment over the New Regency

entities—including those in which all three arbitrators had an interest—led a reviewing court to vacate the ensuing award on grounds of evident partiality.[98]

Neutrality is necessarily a casuistic inquiry governed by the applicable disqualification standard, which varies by country and arbitral fora.[99] Bias may be visible against a certain class of parties (e.g., foreigners) or in certain types of cases (e.g., suits against state-owned entities).[100] Although disqualification applications have become "increasingly irksome" with the "extended growth of personal property and the wide distribution of interests in vast commercial concerns," the general principle necessarily abides in light of the foundational importance of a fair hearing and public confidence in the administration of justice.[101] At the same time,

---

dispute and serving as chief administrative officer for a company negotiating a substantial contract with New Regency). Of course not all relationships require disqualification. For example, an arbitrator's appointment as a nonexecutive director of a bank that had business dealings with, or held stock in, the claimant companies were held not to warrant disqualification under the ICSID Rules. *See EDF Int'l S.A., SAUR Int'l S.A. and León Participaciones Argentinas S.A. v. Argentine Republic*, ICSID Case No. ARB/03/23, Challenge Decision Regarding Prof. Gabrielle Kaufmann-Kohler (June 25, 2008); *see Suez et al. v. Argentine Republic*, ICSID Case Nos. ARB/03/19 & ARB/03/17 (July 30, 2010), and *AGW Grp. Ltd. v. Argentine Republic*, UNCITRAL, Decision on a Second Proposal for the Disqualification of a Member of the Arbitral Tribunal (May 12, 2008).

98 *TCR Sports Broadcasting Holding, LLP v. WN Partner LLC*, 2015 WL 6746689 (N.Y. Sup. Ct. N.Y. Co. Nov. 4, 2015).

99 *See, e.g., Suez et al. v. Argentine Republic*, ICSID Case Nos. ARB/03/19 & ARB/03/17, Decision on the Proposal for the Disqualification of a Member of the Arbitral Tribunal (Oct. 22, 2007) and *AGW Grp. Ltd. v. Argentine Republic*, UNCITRAL, Decision on a Second Proposal for the Disqualification of a Member of the Arbitral Tribunal (May 12, 2008) (holding that "the alleged connection [between arbitrator and party] must be evaluated *qualitatively*," and evaluating the proximity, intensity, and materiality of—as well as the arbitrator's dependence on—the alleged connection); *Micallef v. Malta*, App. No. 17056/06, Eur. Ct. H.R., Judgment, ¶ 93 (Oct. 15, 2009) ("the existence of impartiality for the purposes of Article 6 § 1 must be determined according to a subjective test where regard must be had to the personal conviction and behaviour of a particular judge, that is, whether the judge held any personal prejudice or bias in a given case; and also according to an objective test, that is to say by ascertaining whether the tribunal itself and, among other aspects, its composition, offered sufficient guarantees to exclude any legitimate doubt in respect of its impartiality"); *see generally* Chiara Giorgetti, Challenges and Recusals of Judges and Arbitrators in International Courts and Tribunals (2015); 2014 IBA Guidelines on Conflicts of Interest in International Arbitration.

100 *See, e.g., Loewen Grp., Inc. & Raymond L. Loewen v. United States*, ICSID Case No. ARB(AF)/98/3, Award, ¶ 135 (June 26, 2003) ("a judgment is manifestly unjust . . . if it has been inspired by ill-will towards foreigners as such or as citizens of a particular states"); A.O. Adede, *A Fresh Look at the Meaning of the Doctrine of Denial of Justice under International Law*, 14 Can. Y.B. Int'l L. 73, 91 n.83 (1976) ("a . . . decision which is . . . discriminatory cannot be allowed to establish legal obligations for the alien litigant").

101 *In re Pinochet*, [1999] UKHL 52 (Jan. 15, 1999) (Lord Hope of Craighead) (citation and quotation marks omitted).

abusive, frivolous, or dilatory motions for disqualification must be summarily rejected and appropriately sanctioned.[102]

The provision of neutral decision-makers is one aspect of a broader obligation on a sovereign to "guarantee" the independence of the judiciary.[103] To meet this obligation, a few fundamental components must obtain: *(1) a judiciary must be free from improper external political influences and (2) its judges must enjoy regularity of appointment and dismissal.* The violation of the *first* part of this principle was found in *Idler, Brown, Hulley,* and *DeJoria.* There can be no confidence in the administration of justice where undue pressure, whether political or otherwise, is brought to bear on the court.[104] "Evidence that the judiciary was dominated by the political branches of the government . . . would support a conclusion that the legal system was one whose judgments are not entitled to recognition."[105] As stated by the Office of the United Nations High Commissioner for Human Rights in its *Basic Principles on the Independence of the Judiciary,* in order to decide "on the basis of facts and in accordance with the law," a court must act "without any restrictions, improper influences, inducements, pressures, threats or interferences, direct or indirect, from [other] quarter[s]."[106]

The *second* part of this principle can be seen as a specific manifestation of the first. "Security of tenure is basic to judicial independence. It is universally accepted that when judges can be easily or arbitrarily removed, they are much more vulnerable to internal or external pressures in their consideration of cases."[107] This application of the principle must be handled with care, however, for there is no

---

102 *See generally* GIORGETTI, *supra* note 99.

103 European Charter on the Statute for Judges art. 1, 2 (1997); *see also* Office of the High Commissioner for Human Rights, Basic Principles on the Independence of the Judiciary princ. 1; U.N. Human Rights Committee, *General Comment No.* 32, U.N. Doc. CCPR/C/GC/32, ¶ 19 (Aug. 23, 2007).

104 *See, e.g., Sovtransavto Holding v. Ukraine,* App. No. 48553/99, Eur. Ct. H.R., Judgment, ¶ 82 (July 25, 2002) ("Having regard to interventions of the executive branch of the State in the court proceedings . . . the Court finds that the applicant company's right to have a fair hearing in public by an independent and impartial tribunal . . ., construed in the light of the principles of the rule of law and legal certainty, was infringed.").

105 RESTATEMENT (THIRD) FOREIGN RELATIONS LAW OF THE UNITED STATES § 482 cmt. B (AM. LAW INST. 1987).

106 Office of the High Commissioner for Human Rights, Basic Principles on the Independence of the Judiciary princ. 2; *see also Petrobart Ltd. v. Kyrgyz Republic,* SCC Case No. 126/2003, Award, 18 (Mar. 29, 2005) (holding that "Government intervention in judicial proceedings is not in conformity with the rule of law in a democratic society").

107 United States Agency for International Development, *Guidance for Promoting Judicial Independence and Impartiality,* at 19 (Jan. 2002). *See also* ALI/UNIDROIT Principles of Transnational Civil Procedure princ. 1.2, 2004-4 UNIF. L. REV. 758.

international consensus on either the appointment or removal of judges, and a polity may generally structure and staff its courts as it sees fit. With respect to dismissal, for example, it cannot be gainsaid that judges may be removed from office for cause; but the bells of caution ring when appointments or removals appear to be irregular, evince political capture, or are targeted toward the resolution of a particular case. A touchstone of judicial independence is security of tenure, so that judges—irrespective of their method of appointment or the length of their term—enjoy the confidence to decide the cases before them without fear of arbitrary removal or other reprisal.[108] At a minimum, "[s]ecurity of tenure means that a judge cannot be removed from his or her position during a term of office, except for good cause (e.g., an ethical breach or unfitness) pursuant to formal proceedings with procedural protections."[109] In those judicial systems marked by frequent removals, political pressure, and general instability, judges may lack the confidence needed to rule in accordance with the dictates of law and fact, especially in cases of political or social interest.

C. Procedural Equality and the Right to Be Heard

> *When the court sits, which ought to be by sunrising, proclamation is made for the two parties and their champions, who are introduced by two knights, and are dressed in a coat of armour, with red sandals, barelegged from the knee downwards, bareheaded, and with bare arms to the elbows. The weapons allowed them are only batons, or staves of an ell long, and a fore-cornered leather target; so that death rarely ensued from this civil combat.*
>
> —Sir James Dyer[110]

A related concept to judicial impartiality is juridical equality between the parties in their capacity as litigants—*audiatur et altera pars*. These are, as Cheng said, the "two cardinal characteristics of a judicial process."[111] "At the heart of due process is the idea that adjudication cannot be considered legitimate if it does

108 U.N. Human Rights Committee, *General Comment No. 32*, U.N. Doc. CCPR/C/GC/32, ¶ 20 (Aug. 23, 2007) (citations omitted); *see also* United States Agency for International Development, *Guidance for Promoting Judicial Independence and Impartiality*, at 19 (Jan. 2002); Council of Europe Recommendation No. R (94) 12, princ. VI (2).

109 United States Agency for International Development, *Guidance for Promoting Judicial Independence and Impartiality*, at 19 (Jan. 2002).

110 Describing a "trial by battel" in 1571 at the Westminster court of common pleas, as quoted by Sir William Blackstone, The Student's Blackstone 572 (Robert Malcolm Kerr ed., 1865).

111 Cheng, *supra* note 2, at 290.

not prevent arbitrariness from the standpoint of the parties."[112] As Jan Paulsson has argued, "[i]f a judgment is *grossly* unjust, it is because the victim has not been afforded fair treatment."[113] Adjudicators must be vigilant to maintain equality between the litigants over the entire span of the adjudicatory process because it is a key component of a fair hearing,[114] so much so that it sits astride the requirement of impartiality in virtually all of the human rights instruments discussed in chapter 3.B.[115]

At its core, juridical equality means that each party has a "reasonable opportunity of presenting [its] case ... under conditions which do not place [it] at a substantial disadvantage vis-à-vis [its] opponent."[116] As described by U.S. courts, it is the ability of the parties to be heard "at a meaningful time and in a meaningful manner"[117] during a "full and fair trial."[118] At the international level, this principle means that a decision cannot be made under the rubric of due process without taking into account the arguments of each party.[119] Courts and tribunals must *"ensure equal treatment and reasonable opportunity for litigants to assert or defend their rights."*[120]

---

112 Sweet & della Cananea, *supra* note 29, at 943–44.

113 PAULSSON, *supra* note 50, at 82.

114 CHENG, *supra* note 2, at 290–91; *see also* UNCITRAL Model Law on Commercial Arbitration art. 18 ("The parties shall be treated with equality."); 4 WILLIAM BLACKSTONE, COMMENTARIES, ch. 20 (1765) (reiterating foundational importance of *audiatur et altera pars*).

115 *See, e.g.*, Universal Declaration of Human Rights, G.A. Res. 217 (III) A, U.N. Doc. A/RES/217(III) (Dec. 10, 1948).

116 *Kaufman v. Belgium*, App. No. 10938/84, 50 Eur. Comm'n H.R. Dec. & Rep. 98, 115 (1986). *See also Dombo Beheer B.V. v. Netherlands*, App. No. 14448/88, Eur. Ct. H.R., Judgment, ¶ 33 (Oct. 27, 1993); *Delcourt v. Belgium*, App. No. 2689/65, Eur. Ct. H.R., Judgment, ¶ 34 (Jan. 17, 1970).

117 *See, e.g., Mathews v. Eldridge*, 424 U.S. 319, 333 (1976) (a fundamental requirement of due process is the opportunity to be heard "at a meaningful time and in a meaningful manner" (citing *Armstrong v. Manzo*, 380 U.S. 545, 552 (1965) and *Grannis v. Ordean*, 234 U.S. 385, 394 (1914)); *Am. Surety Co. v. Baldwin*, 287 U.S. 156, 168 (1932) (all litigants must be afforded "an opportunity to present every available defense"); *Philip Morris U.S.A. v. Williams*, 549 U.S. 346, 353 (2007) (the due process clause prohibits a state from punishing an individual without first providing that individual with "an opportunity to present every available defense"); *Tennessee v. Lane*, 541 U.S. 509, 523 (2004) (the State must afford litigants a "meaningful opportunity to be heard by removing obstacles to their full participation in judicial proceedings") (quotation marks omitted).

118 *Hilton v. Guyot*, 159 U.S. 113, 117 (1895).

119 *Dombo Beheer BV v. Netherlands*, ECtHR, App. No. 1448/88, Merits and Just Satisfaction, ¶ 33 (Oct. 27, 1993).

120 ALI/UNIDROIT Principles of Transnational Civil Procedure princ. 3.1, 2004-4 UNIF. L. REV. 758 (emphasis added); *see also id.* at princ. 5.4 ("The parties have the right to submit relevant contentions of fact ... and to offer supporting evidence."). The principle of course concerns the *opportunity* to be heard; if a party refuses to appear before a competent tribunal after due notification, it cannot thereafter challenges the default judgment as a violation of procedural equality. *See* CHENG, *supra* note 2, at 296.

The right to juridical equality begins with the right of equal access to courts, which is an affirmative obligation of every sovereign. In the words of Lord Diplock, "[e]very civilised system of government requires that the state should make available to all its citizens a means for the just and peaceful settlement of disputes between them as to their respective legal rights."[121] In *Golder v. United Kingdom*, the European Court of Human Rights, after an extensive analysis of state practice, concluded that the principle of access to courts is grounded in the right to a fair hearing, which "secures to everyone the right to have any claim relating to his civil rights and obligations brought before a court or tribunal."[122] This facet of procedural equality has a substantive component in that it is not particularly meaningful to speak of a right that cannot be vindicated.[123]

Juridical equality, however, requires more than an unlocked courthouse door. "It is [also] fundamental, as a matter of procedure, that each party is given the right to . . . state its [case] and to produce all arguments and evidence in support of it . . . on an equal level."[124] Breach of the principle is clear where a party is precluded from presenting her case, addressing key arguments, or introducing certain evidence.[125] Where one party is able to make a written submission to a

121 *Bremer Vulkan v. South India Shipping Corp. Ltd.*, [1981] A.C. 909 (H.L.) 917.

122 *Golder v. United Kingdom*, App. No. 4451/70, Eur. Ct. H.R., Merits and Just Satisfaction, Judgment, ¶¶ 18, 35–36 (Feb. 21, 1975).

123 *See* Resolution of the Presidium of the Supreme Arbitrazh Court of the Russian Federation, No. 1831/12, at 5 (June 19, 2012) (unofficial translation), *available at* http://www.msamoylov.ru/?p=3888 (the "[p]rinciples of adversarial nature and equality of the parties imply that the parties participating in the court hearing will be granted equal procedural opportunities to defend their rights and lawful interests").

124 *Wena Hotels Ltd. v. Arab Republic of Egypt*, ICSID Case No. ARB/98/4, Decision on Annulment, ¶ 57 (Feb. 5, 2002); *Application for Review of Judgement No. 158 of the United Nations Administrative Tribunal*, Advisory Opinion, 1973 I.C.J. 166, ¶ 36 (July 12) (equality of arms/procedural equality).

125 *China Property Development (Holdings) LTD. v. Mandecly LTD.*, CACV 92 & 9312012 (Hong Kong Court of Appeal, May 24, 2016) (partially setting aside an award where the arbitral tribunal ascribed liability to one party based upon arguments directed solely against another party: it is impermissible for a tribunal to "carr[y] out its own investigation or inquiry on primary facts, or decide[] a case based on a wholly new point of law or fact without giving the parties a fair opportunity to consider and respond to such point"); *Generica Ltd. v. Pharm. Basics, Inc.*, 125 F.3d 1123, 1130 (7th Cir. 1997) ("When the exclusion of relevant evidence actually deprived a party of a fair hearing, therefore, it is appropriate to vacate an arbitral award."); *Btp Structural Pvt. Ltd. v. Bharat Petroleum Corp. Ltd.*, Arb. Petition No. 442 of 2010, High Court of Judicature, Bombay Ord. Civil Jur. (Apr. 27, 2012) ("unilaterally pass[ing] [an] award after taking written argument of Respondent" but with "no opportunity given to Petitioner to submit arguments" is a "clear breach of the principle of natural justice"); Restatement (Third) Foreign Relations Law of the United States § 482 cmt. b (Am. Law Inst. 1987) (a defendant must be able to "secure documents or attendance of witnesses" for due process to obtain and allow a foreign judgment to be enforced).

tribunal without its adversary's knowledge or reply, or where the judge or arbitrator admits to not receiving or reviewing the submissions of one of the parties and thereafter ignores pertinent arguments made in those submissions, the subsequent award will generally be unenforceable, as a violation of due process and fundamental fairness.[126] Orders that whipsaw the litigants also run afoul of this principle. Where, for example, an arbitrator initially tells a party that invoices may be submitted in summary form to prove its claims, only to switch course at the hearing on the merits and deny the claims for failure to submit the original invoices, that party may be "so mis[led]" as to deprive it of its right to present its claim "in a meaningful manner."[127]

Just as when a party is denied the opportunity to marshal the necessary elements of its own case, due process is denied when the decision is based upon evidence and argumentation that a party has been unable to address.[128] An ICSID award, for instance, was annulled where the tribunal had relied upon evidence submitted after conclusion of the formal proceedings.[129] "The fundamentals of a trial [a]re denied" when a decision is made "upon the strength of evidential facts not spread upon the record," and thus not made available for one of the parties to appreciate and address.[130] "This is not the fair hearing essential to due process. It is condemnation without trial."[131]

---

126 *See* Judgment of Jan. 31, 2012, 4A_360/2011 (Switzerland, First Civil Law Court). Numerous other cases are discussed in Dirk Otto & Omaia Elwan, *"Article V(2)," in* RECOGNITION AND ENFORCEMENT OF FOREIGN ARBITRAL AWARDS: A GLOBAL COMMENTARY ON THE NEW YORK CONVENTION 345–414 (Herbert Kronke et al. eds., 2010).

127 *Iran Aircraft Indus. v. Avco Corp.*, 980 F.2d 141, 146 (2d Cir. 1992) (refusing recognition of arbitral award under the due process defense of the New York Convention).

128 *See Goldberg v. Kelly*, 397 U.S. 254 (1970) (holding that an individual is entitled to an oral hearing before an impartial decision-maker, the right to confront and cross-examine witnesses, and the right to a written opinion setting out the evidence relied upon and the legal basis for the decision); *Greene v. McElroy*, 360 U.S. 474, 496 (1959) (holding that "where governmental action seriously injures an individual, and the reasonableness of the action depends on factfindings, the evidence used to prove the Government's case must be disclosed to the individual so that he has an opportunity to show that it is untrue").

129 *Fraport AG Frankfurt Airport Servs. Worldwide v. Republic of the Philippines*, ICSID Case No. ARB/03/25, Decision on the Application for Annulment, ¶¶ 197–247 (Dec. 23, 2010) (citing UNCITRAL Model Law in interpreting right to be heard).

130 *Ohio Bell Tel. Co. v. Pub. Utils. Comm'n*, 301 U.S. 292, 300 (1937).

131 *Id.* This notion also incorporates the basic requirements that, except in emergent circumstances, cases should not be decided ex parte. As recently held by the UK Supreme Court,

> [t]he idea of a court hearing evidence or argument in private is contrary to the principle of open justice, which is fundamental to the dispensation of justice in a modern, democratic society. However, it has long been accepted that, in rare cases, a court has inherent power to receive

The result is less clear when a party is merely surprised by a decision made *sua sponte* by the adjudicators, on a theory that it may not have anticipated.[132] The party in the latter scenario may technically have been deprived of its "opportunity to be heard" on the particular ratio decidendi adopted by the court or tribunal, but whether that rises to the level of violating a general principle of law is open to debate.[133] Consistent with the maxim *iura novit curia*, judges and arbitrators must be given wide berth to, inter alia, independently research the law bearing upon the parties' arguments and to rely upon those sources in making and supporting their decisions.[134] As the ICJ held in rejecting an objection to a legal point being raised for the first time during the oral proceedings, "the matter is purely one of law such as the Court could and should examine *ex officio*."[135]

The practical reality is that in most cases "the duty to secure equality of arms for a litigant rests primarily on his or her advocate."[136] A court or tribunal will intervene only exceptionally to correct a grave and manifest juridical inequality, lest its efforts to ensure parity lead to accusations of partiality.[137] Despite uncertainty over the existence of an affirmative obligation for sovereigns to ensure parity between parties appearing before state adjudicative organs, a few rules have emerged under this principle that impose a negative obligation on States to refrain from actions that might upset the equality of arms. For example,

---

> evidence and argument in a hearing from which the public and the press are excluded, and that it can even give a judgment which is only available to the parties.

Judgment in *Bank Mellat v. Her Majesty's Treasury*, [2013] UKSC.

132 *See Lemire v. Ukraine*, ICSID Case No. ARB/06/18, Dissenting Opinion of Arbitrator Dr. Jürgen Voss, ¶¶ 224–25, 336, 350 (Mar. 1, 2011).

133 *Id.*

134 CHENG, *supra* note 2, at 229–301.

135 *Territorial Jurisdiction of the International Commission of the River Oder (United Kingdom, Czechoslovakia, Denmark, France, Germany, Sweden/Poland)*, P.C.I.J., Series A, No. 23, at 18–19 (1929). There has also been some debate over whether a litigant is denied access to justice when he is subject to conflicting decisions within a municipal legal system, but is thereafter denied any appellate right to resolve that inconsistency. *See Philip Morris Brands Sàrl v. Oriental Republic of Uruguay*, ICSID Case No. ARB/10/7, Award (July 8, 2016). Although, on one hand, inconsistent decisions is a natural feature of federalized or hierarchical court systems, *see id.* ¶¶ 528–29, where different decisions are made against the same party and applying the same law, with no right of appeal, it may offend the "basic requirements of fairness and access to justice that international law demands." *Id.* Concurring and Dissenting Op. of Gary Born, ¶¶ 40–72.

136 *Richardson v. Lynda Rivers*, A1993/02 (Aug. 23, 2004).

137 *Id.*; *see also* Thomas W. Wälde, *"Equality of Arms" in Investment Arbitration: Procedural Challenges*, *in* ARBITRATION UNDER INTERNATIONAL INVESTMENT AGREEMENTS: A GUIDE TO THE KEY ISSUES 180 (Katia Yannaca-Small ed., 2010).

because the right to legal representation is a fundamental tenet of due process,[138] the equality of arms principle will be breached if a State substantially interferes with a party's counsel.[139] Even in international arbitration, outright intimidation of lawyers, or obstruction of access to them, violates the principle because such state action "strikes at principles which lie at the very heart of the ICSID [and other] arbitral processes," including procedural fairness and the integrity of the tribunal.[140] Interference may come in more insidious ways as well. For instance, a NAFTA tribunal observed that "it would be wrong for the [State] ex hypothesi to misuse its intelligence assets to spy on [the claimant] (and its witnesses) and to introduce into evidence the resulting materials."[141] Although a State may exercise its investigative powers, "[t]he coin has two sides," and those powers must be exercised with "regard to [the] other rights and duties" of parties to an active arbitration—including access to counsel and equality of arms.[142]

In another modern twist that arises primarily in the investment-arbitration context, a more pronounced role has been given to the non-discrimination aspect of juridical equality, especially when alienage is at issue.[143] The UNIDROIT principles state that "[t]he right to equal treatment includes avoidance of any kind of illegitimate discrimination, *particularly on the basis of nationality or residence*."[144] Domestic courts are thus called upon to take "into account difficulties

---

138 *See, e.g.*, Eur. Ct. H.R. art. 6(3)(b)–(c).

139 *See* Wälde, *supra* note 137, at 171–72.

140 *Libananco Holdings Co. Ltd. v. Republic of Turkey*, ICSID Case No. ARB/06/8, Decision on Preliminary Issues, ¶ 78 (June 23, 2008); *see also* The Basic Principles on the Role of Lawyers princ. 16, adopted by the Eighth United Nations Congress on the Prevention of Crime and the Treatment of Offenders, Havana, Cuba, Aug. 27–Sept. 7, 1990, U.N. Doc. A/CONF.144/28/Rev.1 at 118 (1990) ("Governments shall ensure that lawyers (a) are able to perform all of their professional functions without intimidation, hindrance, harassment or improper interference; (b) are able to travel and to consult with their clients freely both within their own country and abroad; and (c) shall not suffer, or be threatened with, prosecution or administrative, economic or other sanctions for any action taken in accordance with recognized professional duties, standards and ethics."); Abba Kolo, *Witness Intimidation, Tampering and Other Related Abuses of Process in Investment Arbitration: Possible Remedies Available to the Arbitral Tribunal*, 26 ARB. INT'L 43, 53 (2010) (stating that counsel and witness intimidation "should be viewed as a fundamental threat to rule of law and due process").

141 *Methanex Corp. v. United States of America*, NAFTA, Final Award, ¶ 54 (Aug. 3, 2005) (stating that "the Disputing Parties each owed in this arbitration a general legal duty to the other and to the Tribunal to conduct themselves in good faith during these arbitration proceedings and to respect the equality of arms between them"); *see also Libananco Holdings Co. Ltd. v. Republic of Turkey*, ICSID Case No. ARB/06/8, Decision on Preliminary Issues, ¶ 72 (June 23, 2008).

142 *Libananco Holdings Co. Ltd. v. Republic of Turkey*, ICSID Case No. ARB/06/8, Decision on Preliminary Issues, ¶ 79 (June 23, 2008).

143 ALI/UNIDROIT Principles of Transnational Civil Procedure cmt. P-3B, 2004-4 UNIF. L. REV. 758.

144 *Id.* princ. 3.2 (emphasis added).

that might be encountered by a foreign party in participating in litigation."[145] In *Loewen*, for instance, the tribunal observed that "the trial court permitted the jury to be influenced by persistent appeals to local favouritism as against a foreign litigant."[146] These and other factors made the trial, "[b]y any standard of measurement . . . a disgrace"—"the trial judge failed to afford Loewen the process that was due."[147] The tribunal reaffirmed the "responsibility of the courts of a State to ensure that litigation is free from discrimination against a foreign litigant and that the foreign litigant [does] not become the victim of sectional or local prejudice."[148] Concerns of discrimination are not limited to foreigners. Addressing the judiciary of post-revolution Iran, a U.S. district court found that the local courts routinely denied fair treatment to the members of the Shah's family and concluded that the Shah's sister "could not personally appear" before Iran's courts, "obtain proper legal representation," or "even obtain local witnesses on her behalf."[149] The resulting Iranian judgment against her was deemed unenforceable because such procedural guarantees "are not mere niceties," but rather the "ingredients of 'civilized jurisprudence'" and "basic due process."[150]

It would be pollutive of the adjudicative process, however, if the principle of equality of arms were understood to prevent arbitrators and judges from following procedures that facilitate the orderly resolution of the case. A court does not violate the principle by refusing to consider an argument first made in a reply brief where the applicable procedure requires both sides to present all legal arguments and available evidence in their opening submissions. Nor does *audiatur et altera pars* demand that irrelevant evidence be considered or that dilatory

---

145 *Id.*

146 *Loewen Grp., Inc. & Raymond L. Loewen v. United States*, ICSID Case No. ARB(AF)/98/3, NAFTA, Award, ¶ 136 (June 26, 2003).

147 *Id.* ¶ 119.

148 *Id.* ¶ 123. *See also Bird v. Glacier Elec. Coop. Inc.*, 255 F.3d, 1136, 1140, 1152 (9th Cir. 2001) (noting that "[t]he trial throughout had racial overtones that culminated a closing argument by Glacier Construction that repeatedly appealed to racial and ethnic prejudice" and concluding that "appeal to racial prejudice in closing argument in its civil case in tribal court offended fundamental fairness and violated due process").

149 *Bank Melli Iran v. Pahlavi*, 58 F.3d 1406, 1413 (9th Cir. 1995); *see also* Restatement (Third) Foreign Relations Law of the United States § 482 cmt. b (Am. Law Inst. 1987) (a defendant must be able to "secure documents or attendance of witnesses" for due process to obtain).

150 *Bank Melli Iran v. Pahlavi*, 58 F.3d 1406, 1413 (9th Cir. 1995) (citing *Hilton v. Guyot*, 159 U.S. 113, 205 (1895)). *See also Osorio v. Dole Food Co.*, 665 F. Supp. 2d 1307, 1336, 1341 (S.D. Fla. 2009) (where provisions of the Nicaraguan special law unfairly targeted "a narrowly defined group of foreign defendants and subject[ed] them to discriminatory provisions that d[id] not apply to domestic defendants," the law offended the general principle of equality before the law that is "basic to any definition of due process or fair play.").

requests go unsanctioned. Although the right to be heard is paramount, it is not implicated by reasonable orders that move the case forward and simplify the issues.[151]

Equality of arms often works in conjunction with other principles. It, along with the principle that no party may be judge in its own cause, can be seen in subparagraphs 2(e) and (f) of Article 9 of the IBA Rules on the Taking of Evidence in International Arbitration, which provide that claims of privilege relating to commercial or technical materials (often invoked by private parties) and to special governmental information (often invoked by sovereigns) will be recognized only if the tribunal itself finds the claims "compelling." By preventing parties from withholding relevant evidence without first justifying their assertions of privilege, the IBA Rules give effect to these twin aims.

D. Condemnation of Fraud and Corruption

Perplexed and troubled at his bad success
The Tempter stood, nor had what to reply,
Discovered in his fraud, thrown from his hope
—John Milton[152]

"The concept of fraud refers to situations in which a person attempts to gain rights granted by a rule of law on the basis of deception, malicious intent, or dishonesty."[153] Where a statement is solicited through fraudulent means, it may be inadmissible. Where a contract is induced by fraud or consummated to commit fraud, it is voidable. Where a judgment is procured by fraud, it can be nullified. *Fraus omnia corrumpit*—as Justice Samuel Miller wrote for the U.S. Supreme Court, "[t]here is no question of the general doctrine that fraud vitiates the most solemn contracts, documents, and even judgments."[154]

---

151 *See* Charles T. Kotuby Jr. & Luke A. Sobota, *Practical Suggestions to Promote the Legitimacy and Vitality of International Investment Arbitration*, 28 ICSID Rev. 454, 461 (2013).

152 John Milton, Paradise Regained, Book IV, ll at 1–3.

153 Annekatrien Lenaerts, *The Role of the Principle* Fraus Omnia Corrumpit *in the European Union: A Possible Evolution Towards a General Principle of Law?*, 32 Y.B. Eur. L. 460, 460 (2013).

154 *United States v. Throckmorton*, 98 U.S. 61, 64 (1878). *See also The Amistad*, 40 U.S. 518, 520 (1841) ("Fraud will vitiate any, even the most solemn transactions; and any asserted title founded upon it, is utterly void."); *The Amiable Isabella*, 19 U.S. 1, 27 (1821) ("Fraud will vitiate even a judgment, and the most solemn instruments and assurances. This is a principle of universal law. . . .").

As Cheng wrote, "[f]raud is the antithesis of good faith and indeed of law, and it would be self-contradictory to admit that the effects of fraud could be recognised by law."[155] Modern cases illuminate the types of fraud and corruption that "can have no countenance in any court . . . in any . . . civilised country."[156] In an ICC arbitration, for instance, the sole arbitrator found that a commission contract between an investor and a local agent was for the purpose of public bribery, and therefore dismissed the claim of the agent to collect under it.[157] "Parties who ally themselves in an enterprise of the present nature," the sole arbitrator wrote, "must realise that they have forfeited any right to ask for assistance of the machinery of justice (national courts or arbitral tribunals) in settling their disputes."[158]

As noted in the discussion of the prohibition on advantageous wrongs in chapter 2.D,[159] the tribunals in *World Duty Free v. Kenya, Inceysa v. El Salvador, Plama v. Bulgaria*, and *Metal-Tech v. Uzbekistan* arrived at similar conclusions,[160] affirming that fraud, bribery, and official corruption are contrary to "international *bones mores*"[161] and "the international public policy of most, if not all, States."[162] International law thus denies protection to an investment procured by bribery[163] or by the submission of doctored financial

155 Cheng, *supra* note 2, at 158.

156 ICC Case No. 1110, Award (1963), 10(3) Arb. Int'l 282, 294 (1994); *see also* ICC Case No. 6497 of 1994, Final Award, 24 Y.B. Comm. Arb. 71, 72 (1999) ("If the bribery nature of the agreements would be demonstrated, such agreements would be null and void in Swiss law. This is not because such bribe would be prohibited by the criminal law of the country in which bribes had been paid, but because the bribes in themselves cannot be, in Swiss law, the object of a valid contract. This is also admitted in most legal systems.") (citation omitted).

157 ICC Case No. 1110, Award (1963), 10(3) Arb. Int'l 282, 294 (1994).

158 *Id.* ¶ 23.

159 The overlap here with other general principles is evident. For instance, in some European countries, such as Belgium and France, the "principle *fraus omnia corrumpit* is perceived as a distinct corrective mechanism in relation to the general principle prohibiting the abuse of rights," whereas in others, such as Germany and the Netherlands, "the principle *fraus omnia corrumpit* is considered a specific application of the principle of good faith in its limitative function." Lenaerts, *supra* note 153, at 472, 473.

160 *Metal-Tech Ltd. v. Republic of Uzbekistan*, ICSID Case No. ARB/10/3, Award, ¶¶ 327, 373 (Oct. 4, 2014) (dismissing BIT claim for lack of jurisdiction where investment was tainted by corruption).

161 *Wena Hotels Ltd. v. Arab Republic of Egypt*, ICSID Case No. ARB/98/4, Award, ¶ 111 (Dec. 8, 2000).

162 *World Duty Free Co. Ltd. v. Republic of Kenya*, ICSID Case No. ARB/00/7, Award, ¶ 157 (Oct. 4, 2006) (where the tribunal dismissed an investor's claim after discovering that he had bribed the president of Kenya); *see also* Carolyn B. Lamm, Hansel T. Pham & Rahim Maloo, *Fraud and Corruption in International Arbitration*, TDM 3 (May 2013) ("The prohibition of bribery and corruption is widely recognized as a quintessential rule of transnational public policy. International consensus vehemently declares that bribery and corruption is morally and economically unacceptable [and] fundamentally wrong. [This view] is so universal that it has developed into a well-established example of a rule of transnational public policy.").

163 *World Duty Free Co. Ltd. v. Republic of Kenya*, ICSID Case No. ARB/00/7, Award (Oct. 4, 2006).

statements.[164] According to Emmanuel Gaillard, "[t]here is now little doubt that . . . a transnational rule has been established according to which an agreement reached by means of corruption of one of the signatories . . . is void."[165] The catholic condemnation of fraud can further be seen in the wave of increasingly stringent anti-bribery instruments on both the national and world stage.[166] As the *condemnation of bribery and corruption* emanates from a convergence in national laws, international conventions, arbitral case law, and scholarly opinion,[167] it must under any view be considered a general principle of law.

The remedy for fraud can take many forms, "vitiat[ing] judgments, contracts and all transactions whatsoever."[168] As noted, a contract aimed to further a corrupt scheme[169] or procured in the first instance by a corrupt scheme[170] can be denied effect as a general principle of law, irrespective of which municipal law governs the instrument. Judgments and arbitral awards are no different. "A judgment, which in principle calls for the greatest respect, will not be upheld if it is the result of fraud."[171] Where it is shown that a tribunal has been corrupted in its formation or operation, as occurred with respect to the United States-Venezuelan

---

164 *Inceysa Vallisoletana, S.L. v. Republic of El Salvador*, ICSID Case No. ARB/03/26, Award (Aug. 2, 2006).

165 Emmanuel Gaillard, *Thirty Years of Lex Mercatoria: Towards the Selective Application of Transnational Rules*, 10 ICSID Rev. 208, 214 (1995).

166 *See, e.g.*, Foreign Corrupt Practices Act (FCPA), Pub. L. 95-213, 91 Stat. 1494 (1977), as amended by Omnibus Trade and Competitiveness Act of 1988, Pub. L. 100-148, Title V, § 50003(c), 102 Stat. 11 07, 1419 (1988) (codified at 15 U.S.C. 78dd-1, 2), and further amended by The International Anti-Bribery and Fair Competition Act of 1998, § 2375; The Inter-American Convention against Corruption, done at Caracas on Mar. 29, 1996 (entered into force Mar. 6, 1997), 35 I.L.M. 724 (1996); OECD Convention on Combating Bribery of Foreign Public Officials in International Business Transactions, Dec. 17, 1997 (entered into force Feb. 15, 1999); Council of Europe Criminal Law Convention on Corruption, done at Strasbourg on Jan. 27, 1999 (entered into force Jan. 7, 2002), CETS No. 173, 38 I.L.M. 505 (1999); Council for Europe Civil Law Convention on Corruption, done at Strasbourg on Apr. 11, 1999 (entered into force Jan. 11, 2003), CETS No. 174; African Union Convention on Preventing and Combating Corruption, done at Maputo on July 11, 2003, 43 I.L.M. 5 (2004); United Nations Convention against Corruption, done at New York on Oct. 31, 2003 (entered into force Dec. 14, 2005), G.A. Res. 58/4, U.N. Doc. N58/422 (currently 140 Signatories, of which 137 have ratified).

167 Lamm et al., *supra* note 162, at 712.

168 *Lazarus Estates Ltd. v. Beasley*, [1956] 1 Q.B. 702, 712 per Denning L.J.

169 *E.g., id.; see also* ICC Case No. 1110, Award (1963), 10(3) Arb. Int'l 282, 294 (1994).

170 *See, e.g., Inceysa Vallisoletana S.L. v. Republic of El Salvador*, ICSID Case No. ARB/03/26, Award (Aug. 2, 2006); *World Duty Free Co. Ltd. v. Republic of Kenya*, ICSID Case No. ARB/00/7, Award (Oct. 4, 2006); *United States v. Mississippi Valley Generating Co.*, 364 U.S. 520 (1960) (deciding not to allow the enforcement of a government contract where, in the negotiations of the contract, the Government had been represented by a consultant to the Budget Bureau who was at the same time an officer in an investment bank that was expected to profit from the transaction by becoming a financial agent for the project).

171 Cheng, *supra* note 2, at 159.

Claims Commission of 1866,[172] "the entire proceedings will be regarded as null and void."[173] And where there is evidence of "fraud on the part of the parties and witnesses ... which ... has affected the decision,"[174] "no tribunal worthy of its name or of any respect may allow its decision to stand if such allegations are well-founded."[175]

The remedy of nullity befits the nature of the delict. Citing the "universally recognized need for correcting injustices," the U.S. Supreme Court in 1944 vacated a final judgment of patent infringement issued 12 years earlier based upon the subsequent revelation that an article trumpeting the patent's innovation and cited in the judgment had been secretly prepared by the patent holder's legal representatives.[176] Rejecting the views of the lower appellate court that the article was not "basic" to the challenged judgments, the U.S. Supreme Court wrote:

> Doubtless it is wholly impossible accurately to appraise the influence that the article exerted on the judges. But we do not think the circumstances call for such an attempted appraisal. [The patent holder]'s officials and lawyers thought the article material. They ... went to considerable trouble and expense to get it published.... They are in no position now to dispute its effectiveness. Neither should they now be permitted to escape the consequences of [the patent holder]'s deceptive attribution of authorship ... on the ground that what the article stated was true. Truth needs no disguise.[177]

The inverse of this final sentence is that fraud is borne of necessity: those with meritorious claims do not bear the costs and risks associated with manufacturing evidence or paying bribes. A party's resort to fraud thus gives rise to reasonable inferences about the strength of its case. And because fraud taints all that it touches, it is virtually impossible to expiate its effects ex post. "A malefactor, caught red-handed, cannot simply walk away from a case, pay a new docket fee, and begin afresh. History is not so glibly to be erased. Once a litigant chooses to practice fraud, that misconduct infects his cause of action, in whatever guises it

172 *Id.* at 358.

173 *Id* at 160.

174 *Id.* at 360.

175 *Id.* at 159. The ability to overturn an otherwise final judgment constitutes an exception to the competing principle of res judicata discussed in chapter 3.G. Although "error through fraud of the parties does not, strictly speaking, constitute a cause of nullity," it does, in this context, present "a cause of voidability." *Id.* at 360–61.

176 *Hazel-Atlas Glass Co. v. Hartford-Empire Co.*, 322 U.S. 238, 244 (1944).

177 *Id.* at 246–47.

may subsequently appear."[178] It follows that nearly every jurisdiction will refuse to enforce arbitral awards[179] or foreign judgments[180] that are tainted by fraud or the corruption of the rendering tribunal. Like contracts affected by graft, such judgments and awards are null and lose all value—even innocent third parties have no legitimate claim to benefit from a fraudulent decision.[181]

Permutations on *fraus omnia corrumpit* are intertwined with other general principles. For example, parties engaging in fraud may be denied the ability to invoke the benefit of otherwise applicable legal rules. The Belgian Court of Cassation held that where a seller overestimated the net value of a company through false statements, the buyer's gross negligence in failing to detect the fraud could not be invoked by the seller to prevent annulment of the contract—the seller's fraud deprived it of the ability to invoke the general rule that only parties committing

---

178 *Aoude v. Mobil Oil Corp.*, 892 F.2d 1115, 1121 (1st Cir. 1989).

179 *See, e.g.*, *European Gas Turbines v. Westman Int'l Ltd.*, ICC, REV. ARB. 359 (1994) (ICC award annulled by Paris Court of Appeal because Respondent had submitted fraudulent financial reports to the tribunal); Australian International Arbitration Act 1974 § 19 (stating that an award is in conflict with the public policy of Australia if it was "induced or affected by fraud"); Belgian Judicial Code art. 1717, § 3(b)(ii)–(iii) (stating that an arbitral award can be set aside if it was obtained by fraud or it is contrary to public policy); India Arbitration and Conciliation Act 1996 §§ 34(2)(b)(ii), 48(2)(b) ("for the avoidance of any doubt" "an award is in conflict with the public policy of India if the making of the award was induced or affected by fraud or corruption"); Netherlands Arbitration Act of 1986 art. 1068 (allowing for revocation of arbitral awards if fraud is discovered); New Zealand Arbitration Act of 1996 art. 36(3)(a) (stating that an award is in conflict with the public policy of New Zealand if it was "induced or affected by fraud"); United Kingdom Arbitration Act of 1996 § 68(2)(g) (providing the ability to challenge an award "obtained by fraud"); United States Federal Arbitration Act, 9 U.S.C. § 10(a)(1) (authorizing courts to set aside awards obtained by fraud); Zimbabwe Arbitration Act of 1996 arts. 34(5)(a), 36(3) (stating that if the making of the award was induced or effected by fraud or corruption, "the 'award is in conflict with the public policy of Zimbabwe'"); *see generally* Lamm et al., *supra* note 162, at 716–17.

180 *See, e.g.*, Uniform Foreign Money Judgments Recognition Act § 4(b)(2) (no recognition if "the judgment was obtained by fraud"); N.Y. CPLR § 5304(b)(3) (a foreign judgment need not be recognized or enforced if it was "obtained by fraud"); *Hilton v. Guyot*, 159 U.S. 113, 202–03 (1895) (stating that "fraud in procuring the judgment" will bar recognition); *de Manez Lopez v. Ford Motor Co.*, 470 F. Supp. 2d 917 (S.D. Ind. 2006); *Powell v. Cockburn* (1977) 2 S.C.R. 218 (Can.); *Abouloff v. Oppenheimer*, (1882) 10 Q.B.D. 295 (Eng.); *Price v. Dewhurst*, (1837) 8 Sim. 279 (Eng.); *Munzer Case*, Cour de Cassation (Fr.) (Jan. 7, 1964) (J. DROIT INT'L (CLUNET) 302 (1964)); Foreign Judgments Enforcement Act 5718-1958 § 6(1) (Israel); Italian Code of Civil Procedure arts. 798 & 395.

181 In light of the inherent wrongfulness of fraudulent conduct, the reasonable inferences that may be drawn from a party's decision to resort to fraud, and the need to deter future acts of fraud, the remedy for fraud is appropriately more exacting than that for abuse of rights. *See* Lenaerts, *supra* note 153, at 469, 493 ("[T]he principle of the prohibition of abuse of rights has a more limited corrective function than *fraus omnia corrumpit*: the judge may only limit the exercise of the subjective right to what would be reasonable and fair or refuse it to the extent that this is necessary to neutralize the improper conduct (reduction to zero). . . . On the contrary, the principle of *fraus omnia corrumpit* will totally exclude the application of a rule of law in the case of fraud.").

an excusable mistake may seek annulment of a contract.[182] In another case, a perpetrator who injured a bank through forged documents could not invoke the bank's own contributory negligence, which typically would have been available to limit tort liability.[183] These outcomes might be viewed as the procedural embodiment of *nullus commodum capere potest de sua iniuria propria*.[184] In all events, "a legal act which is fraudulently concluded, or a rule of law of which the application is obtained through fraudulent conduct, must be entirely deprived of legal effect in order to prevent the perpetrator from taking any profit from this legal act or rule."[185]

Garnering admissible proof of fraud, bribery, and corruption is exceedingly difficult. As Lord Coke noted, "secrecy is a mark of fraud."[186] Cognizant of their wrongdoing, perpetrators of fraud frequently go to great lengths to conceal their misconduct. Yet, presuming regularity,[187] many courts and tribunals have held that "the graver the charge, the more confidence there must be in the evidence relied on."[188] As a result, "[i]t is common in most legal systems for serious allegations such as fraud to be held to a high standard of proof,"[189] and some international tribunals have likewise required "more persuasive evidence" than that for other allegations.[190] The presumption seems to be more a creature of comity

182 Judgment of Sept. 23, 1977, Cour de Casssation (1978) Pasicrisie 100. Confirmed in Judgment of May 29, 1980, Cour de Cassation (1980) Pasicrisie 1190; Judgment of Mar. 18, 2010, Cour de Cassation (2010). Decisions from France are in accord. *See, e.g.*, Judgment of May 23, 1977, Cour de Cassation (Ch civ) (1977) Bulletin civil, I, 244. Confirmed in Judgment of Feb. 21, 2001, Cour de Cassation (Ch civ) (2001) Bulletin civil, IIII, 20.

183 Judgment of Nov. 6, 2002, Court de Cassation (2003) Journal des Tribunaux 310.

184 *See supra* chapter 2.D.

185 Lenaerts, *supra* note 153, at 466.

186 *Twyne's Case* (1601), 3 Co. 80, 81a.

187 *See* chapter 3.E.

188 *Case concerning Oil Platforms (Iran v. U.S.)*, 1996 I.C.J. 803, 856 (Dec. 12) (separate opinion of Judge Rosalyn Higgins); *see* Aloysius P. Llamzon, Corruption in International Investment Arbitration 233 (2014) ("When serious allegations of wrongdoing are involved in civil proceedings . . . both [national and international] systems generally demand a heightened standard of proof.").

189 *Waguih Elie George Siag and Clorinda Vecchi v. Arab Republic of Egypt*, ICSID Case No. ARB/05/15, Award, ¶ 326 (May 11, 2009) (applying a "clear and convincing" standard that was greater than "the balance of probabilities" but less than "beyond a reasonable doubt"); *see* Caroline E. Foster, *Burden of Poof in International Courts and Tribunals*, 29 Austl. Y.B. Int'l L. 27, 61 (2010) ("Where the charges leveled against a state are considered to be particularly serious there has been some inclination to maintain a higher standard of proof.").

190 *Libananco Holdings Co. Ltd. v. Republic of Turkey*, ICSID Case No. ARB/06/8, Award, ¶ 125 (Sept. 2, 2011); *see also Westinghouse and Burns & Roe (USA) v. Nat'l Power Co. and Republic of the Philippines*, ICC Case No. 640, Preliminary Award (Dec. 19, 1991); *Hilmarton Ltd. v. Omnium de Traitment et de Valorisation S.A.*, ICC Case No. 5622, ¶ 23 (1988); *EDF (Servs.) Ltd. v. Romania*, ICSID Case No.

than of experiential truth considering that, inter alia, 111 of 165 countries—over two-thirds of those surveyed—received scores below 50 on the 100-point scale of Transparency International's 2015 corruption perceptions index.[191] It is true that charges of fraud are serious, but it is also true that direct evidence of such malfeasance is rare. As the *Metal-Tech* tribunal observed, "corruption is by essence difficult to establish and [] it is thus generally admitted that it can be shown through circumstantial evidence."[192] An appropriate balance, it seems, would be to give the presumption no more than its due weight, that is, to presume normalcy only up and until there are evidentiary indications (direct or circumstantial) that something else is afoot. At that point the presumption drops away, and ordinary rules for weighing evidence should obtain.[193] A contrary approach would have the infelicitous effect of doubly immunizing malfeasants: *first*, by their own efforts at concealment and, *second*, by a heightened evidentiary standard that is made all the more difficult to satisfy in light of the first.[194] As in other areas, the

---

ARB/05/13, Award, ¶ 221 (Oct. 8, 2009); *Himpurna California Energy Ltd. v. Perusahaan Listruik Negara*, 25 Y.B. COMM. ARB. 11, 42 (2000).

191 Transparency International, Corruption Perceptions Index 2015: Results, *available at* https://www.transparency.org/cpi2015#results-table. The notorious presence of corruption in certain countries may be considered as circumstantial evidence of fraud in a particular case. *See, e.g., Rumeli Telekom A.S. and Telsim Mobil Telekomikasyon Hizmetleri A.S. v. Republic of Kazakhstan*, ICSID Case No. ARB/05/16, Award, ¶ 446 (July 29, 2008) (finding that international reports and articles indicated a general lack of impartiality in Kazakhstan's judiciary); *Yukos Capital S.a.r.l. v. OJSC Rosneft Oil Co.*, [2011] EWHC 1461, ¶ 36 (taking a country's reputation for corruption into account as circumstantial evidence because "partiality and dependency by their very nature take place behind the scenes"). A similar practice obtains in the United States, where generalized proof of systemic due process concerns can be sufficient to refuse recognition of a foreign judgment from that country. *See, e.g., Bank Melli Iran v. Pahlavi*, 58 F.3d 1406 (9th Cir. 1995).

192 *Metal-Tech Ltd. v. Republic of Uzbekistan*, ICSID Case No. ARB/10/3, Award, ¶ 243 (Oct. 4, 2014) (noting that, on the facts of that case, corruption had been established with "reasonable certainty").

193 *See* Constantine Partasides, *Proving Corruption in International Arbitration: A Balanced Standard for the Real World*, 25 ICSID REV. 47, 57 (2010) (noting that "those who presume that courts around the world unquestionably raise the standard of proof when dealing with serious allegations of fraud should tread with care") (citing *Sec. of State for the Home Dep't v. Rehman*, [2001] UKHL 47, [2002] 1 All ER 122, ¶ 55 (applying the "more probable than not" standard to allegations of fraud)); *Rompetrol Grp. N.V. v. Romania*, ICSID Case No. ARB/06/3, Award, ¶¶ 180–83 (May 6, 2013) (rejecting the argument that allegations of fraud and other serious wrongdoing, without more, require a heightened standard of proof and instead adopting a "more nuanced approach" to the balance-of-probabilities standard when deciding "whether an allegation of seriously wrongful conduct . . . has been proved on the basis of the entire body of direct and indirect evidence before it").

194 *See* LLAMZON, *supra* note 188, at 230, 237 ("The clandestine and highly complex nature of transnational corruption requires a candid admission that unless the evidentiary principles applied by the tribunal matches the ingenuity of those who are engaged in corruption, it will be difficult to find corruption in any arbitration. . . . [T]he degree of confidence a tribunal should have in the evidence of [] corruption must be high. However, this does not mean that the standard of proof should necessarily be higher, or that circumstantial evidence, inferences, or presumptions and indicators of possible corruption (such

truth-seeking function is best served by holistic consideration of all pertinent evidence.

E. Evidence and Burdens of Proof

Facts are stubborn things; and whatever may be our wishes, our inclinations, or the dictates of our passions, they cannot alter the state of facts and evidence.
—John Adams[195]

Evidentiary standards, burdens of proof, and myriad other procedural rules can be dispositive of the outcome of a case.[196] As Gustave Flaubert wrote, "[t]ruth lies as much in its shading as it does in vivid tones."[197] Uncovering this truth is the work of various adjectival rules. Both picayune and pivotal, procedural rules govern everything from a party's ability to obtain emails from its adversary to the presumptions that the fact-finder shall indulge in assessing the record evidence. These are the mechanics of the proceeding, and they can affect the due process rights of the participants, whether measured individually or systemically.[198] Certain of these rules, deriving from state practice *in foro domestic*, are properly deemed general principles of law and essential components of due process.[199]

The appropriate place to begin is with the lowest burden of proof: *courts and tribunals may take judicial notice of facts that are of common knowledge or public notoriety.*[200] Doing so does not offend due process and, conversely, a claim typically should not be dismissed based upon the claimant's inability to prove

as 'red flags') cannot come to the aid of the fact-finder. Tribunals are given the freedom and burden of choice, which they should not abdicate by rote reference to an abstract 'heightened' standard of proof.").

195 Argument in Defense of the British Soldiers in the Boston Massacre Trials (Dec. 4, 1770).

196 For the distinction between the *standard of proof* and the *burden of proof*, see *Rompetrol Grp. N.V. v. Romania*, ICSID Case No. ARB/06/3, Award (May 6, 2013) (establishing that the burden of proof defines which party has to prove what in order for its case to prevail, and the standard of proof defines how much evidence is needed to establish either an individual issue or the party's case as a whole).

197 Gustave Flaubert, Correspondence 1846, at 417 (1927).

198 *See, e.g., Caratube Int'l Oil Co. LLP v. Republic of Kazakhstan*, ICSID Case No. ARB/08/12, Decision on Annulment Application, ¶ 97 (Feb. 21, 2014) (noting that a reversal of the burden of proof could lead to a violation of fundamental rules of procedure).

199 *See* Cheng, *supra* note 2, at 302–03.

200 *Id.* at 303. With related transnational disputes often arising simultaneously in different fora, both international and municipal courts have shown a willingness to apply the holdings and accept evidence adduced at the parallel proceedings. *See, e.g., Mohle Case* (German-Venezuelan Commission), 10 Rec. des Sent's Arb. 113, 114 (1903); *Yukos Capital S.a.r.l. v. OJSC Rosneft Oil Co.*, [2011] EWHC

a self-evident and public fact.[201] Presumptions operate similarly but are more fraught. Whether forged in the crucible of experience or created for reasons of policy, presumptions that certain facts are true and that require the opposing party to rebut them are commonplace on the domestic and international plane. For example, it is trite to say that state actions enjoy a presumption of regularity and validity.[202] *Omnia praesumuntur rite esse acta* applies, for instance, "with respect to the validity of nationalisation and consular certificates as evidence of citizenship."[203] Similarly, deeds of ownership are entitled to a presumption of authenticity provided the party proffering it can offer some prima facie evidence to "inspir[e] a minimally sufficient degree of confidence" in the assertion.[204]

Allegations not admitted, noticed, or presumed must be proven. The traditional formulation of the principle governing the burden of persuasion is *actori incumbit onus probandi*.[205] This rule is universal save where, as noted, the burden

---

1461, ¶¶ 162, 173 ("I therefore accept Yukos Capital's submission that *Cherney* and like cases [that analyze 'whether substantial justice would or could be done in Russia'] provide powerful and principled general support for its case."); *Yukos Capital S.a.r.l. v. OAO Rosneft*, Amsterdam Court of Appeal, Case No. 200.005.269/01, Decision, ¶ 3.8.8 (Apr. 28, 2009); *Bank Melli Iran v. Pahlavi*, 58 F.3d 1406, 1410 n.3 (9th Cir. 1995) ("For purposes of this opinion, we will assume, without deciding, that the Banks are instrumentalities of Iran. Although they have not submitted evidence to that effect, other courts have said that they are.").

201 *See Application of the Convention on the Prevention and Punishment of the Crime of Genocide* (*Bosn. & Herz. v. Serb. & Montenegro)*, 2007 I.C.J. 43, ¶ 42 (Feb. 26) (separate order of Judge Lauterpacht) (advocating for the Court taking judicial notice of matters that are "public knowledge," provided that they are consistent with the main facts proven by evidence in the case); *Military and Paramilitary Activities in and Against Nicaragua* (*Nicar. v. U.S.*), Merits, Judgment, 1986 I.C.J. 14, ¶ 62, at 40 (June 27) (relying on press articles and extracts from books as corroborating material to evince the existence of a fact); *United States Diplomatic and Consular Staff in Tehran* (*U.S. v. Iran*), Judgment, 1980 I.C.J. 3, ¶¶ 12–13, at 9–10 (May 24) (same).

202 CHENG, *supra* note 2, at 305; Foster, *supra* note 189, at 36 ("The presumption of compliance is supported by the idea that what is normal is to be presumed and any other state of affairs is subject to proof."); DURWARD V. SANDIFER, EVIDENCE BEFORE INTERNATIONAL TRIBUNALS 144 (Univ. Press of Virginia rev. ed. 1975) ("Presumptions in favor of the validity of acts of various Government authorities are often invoked.").

203 *See* Foster, *supra* note 189, at 57.

204 *Abrahim Rahman Golshani v. Gov't of the Islamic Republic of Iran*, 29 Iran-U.S. Cl. Trib. Rep. 78 (1993).

205 CHENG, *supra* note 2, at 327 (citing 2 ARB. INT'L 706, 708 (Transl.)); *see also Tokios Tokelés v. Ukraine*, ICSID Case No. ARB/02/18, Award, ¶¶ 121, 124 (July 26, 2007); *Alpha Projektholding GmbH v. Ukraine*, ICSID Case No. ARB/07/16, Award, ¶¶ 236–37 (Nov. 8, 2010); *Tradex Hellas S.A. v. Republic of Albania*, ICSID Case No. ARB/94/2, Award, ¶ 74 (Apr. 29, 1999) (it "can be considered as a general principle of international procedure—and probably also of virtually all national civil procedural laws—[] that it is the claimant who has the burden of proof for the conditions required in the applicable substantive rules of law to establish the claim"); *Salini Costruttori S.p.A. and Italstrade S.p.A. v. Hashemite Kingdom of Jordan*, ICSID ARB/02/13, Award, ¶ 70 (Jan. 31, 2006) ("It is a well established principle of law that it is for a claimant to prove the facts on which it relies in support of his claim."); *Asian*

is removed by the provisions of a statute or other evidentiary presumption.[206] Although the U.S. legal system also places the burden of *production* on the plaintiff (or claimant), this is not generally supported in the continental system, nor is it supported as a general principle of law.[207] Rather, the burden of production of evidence typically falls on both parties, and, where necessary, international tribunals may require one or both parties to produce additional evidence or undertake appropriate inquiries or research *sua sponte*.[208] It nonetheless remains constant that, once the record has been assembled, the claimant must persuade the tribunal of the truth of its allegations.[209] A common standard of persuasion before international tribunals, at least in civil cases, is "reasonably convinced"—which is functionally the same as the "preponderance of the evidence" standard that

---

Agric. Prods. Ltd. v. Republic of Sri Lanka, ICSID Case No. ARB/87/3, Award, ¶ 56 (June 27, 1990), 6 ICSID Rev. 526 (1991); *Autopista Concesionada de Venezuela, C.A. v. Bolivarian Republic of Venezuela*, ICSID ARB/00/5, Award, ¶ 110 (Sept. 23, 2003); *Int'l Thunderbird Gaming Corp. v. United Mexican States*, UNCITRAL, Award, ¶ 95 (Jan. 26, 2006); ICC Award No. 1434, J. Droit Int'l (Clunet), at 978, 982 (1976); *Perenco Ecuador Ltd. v. Republic of Ecuador & Petroecuador*, ICSID Case No. ARB/08/6, Decision on Jurisdiction ¶ 98 (June 30, 2011) (stating that the burden to establish the facts supporting a claim lies with the claimant); *SGS Société Générale de Surveillance S.A. v. Republic of Paraguay*, ICSID Case No. ARB/07/29, Award, ¶ 79 (Feb. 10, 2012) (holding that the claimant bears the initial burden of proof in substantiating its claims); *Middle East Cement Shipping & Handling Co. S.A. v. Arab Republic of Egypt*, ICSID Case No. ARB/99/6, Award, ¶ 89 (Apr. 12, 2002); *Generation Ukraine, Inc. v. Ukraine*, ICSID Case No. ARB/00/9, Award, ¶¶ 19.1, 19.4 (Sept. 16, 2003); *Noble Ventures, Inc. v. Romania*, ICSID Case No. ARB/01/11, Award, ¶ 100 (Oct. 12, 2005); *Saipem S.p.A. v. People's Republic of Bangladesh*, ICSID Case No. ARB/05/7, Decision on Jurisdiction, ¶ 83 (Mar. 21, 2007).

206 Mojtaba Kazazi, Burden of Proof and Related Issues: A Study on Evidence before International Tribunals 72 (1996) (citing Jackson H. Ralston, The Law and Procedure of International Tribunals 220 (1973)); *see also id.* at 53–75 *et seq.*

207 *See* Juliane Kokott, The Burden of Proof in Comparative and International Human Rights Law: Civil and Common Law Approaches with Special Reference to the American and German Legal Systems 9 (1998); Foster, *supra* note 189, at 45. Cheng also distinguishes between the two, in particular, interpreting the meaning of the decision in the *Parker Case* where the Commission referred to the burden of production rather than persuasion. Consequently, he suggests that the universally accepted principle of *actori incumbit onus probandi* refers to the burden of persuasion. *See* Cheng, *supra* note 2, at 329 ("It means that a party having the burden of proof must not only bring evidence in support of his allegations, but must also convince the Tribunal of their truth, lest they be disregarded for want, or insufficiency, of proof."). *See also* K.P.E. Lasok, The European Court of Justice, Practice and Procedure 256 (2d ed. 1994).

208 Kokott, *supra* note 207, at 186 (referring to Durward V. Sandifer, Evidence Before International Tribunals 131 (1975) with references); *see also id.* at 154 (citing K.P.E. Lasok, The European Court of Justice Practice and Procedure 422 (2d ed. 1994) ("even in contentious proceedings, there is no allocation of the burden to produce evidence or sources of evidence as between the parties. Both lie under an equal duty to the court to produce evidence or sources of evidence relating to the issue of fact in the case")).

209 *Asian Agric. Prods. Ltd. v. Republic of Sri Lanka*, ICSID Case No. ARB/87/3, Award, ¶ 56 (June 27, 1990), 6 ICSID Rev. 526 (1991); *see also* ALI/UNIDROIT Principles of Transnational Civil Procedure princ. 21, 2004-4 Unif. L. Rev. 758.

obtains in most national legal systems.[210] The standard can, however, be altered depending upon the factual and procedural circumstances of the case; it is not considered a general principle of law.

It should be kept in mind that the nominal ordering of the parties in the case caption is irrelevant to the burden. It is not so much the "claimant" as it is the party who alleges a particular fact that must introduce sufficient evidence in support.[211] The requirement that a party establish the facts supporting its legal claims and defenses is found in, inter alia, the laws of France, Germany, Iran, Italy, and the Netherlands.[212] Article 1257 of the Iranian Civil Code provides that "[w]hosoever claims a right must prove it and if the defendant, in defence, claims a matter which requires proof it is incumbent upon him to prove the matter."[213] This could be the claimant trying to establish the tribunal's jurisdiction, but it could also be the respondent raising a counterclaim or an affirmative defense. In *Temple of Preah Vihear*, for example, the ICJ explained that "[t]he burden of proof in respect of [a particular matter] will of course lie on the [p]arty asserting or putting [the matter] forward," irrespective of whether that party is the claimant or the respondent.[214] And the *Tecmed v. United Mexican States* tribunal held

---

210 ALI/UNIDROIT Principles of Transnational Civil Procedure princ. 21 & cmt. P-21B, 2004-4 UNIF. L. REV. 758; *see also Inmaris Perestroika Sailing Maritime Servs. GmbH and Others v. Ukraine*, ICSID Case No. ARB/08/8, Award (Mar. 1, 2012).

211 *See, e.g.*, UNCITRAL Rules (1976) art. 27 (1) (holding that "[e]ach party shall have the burden of proving the facts relied on to support its claim or defence"); *Asian Agric. Prods. Ltd. v. Republic of Sri Lanka*, ICSID Case No. ARB/87/3, Award, ¶ 56 (June 27, 1990), 6 ICSID REV. 526 (1991); *William Nagel v. Czech Republic*, SCC Case No. 049/2002, Final Award, ¶ 177 (Sept. 9, 2003); *Saipem S.p.A. v. People's Republic of Bangladesh*, ICSID Case No. ARB/05/7, Award, ¶ 113 (June 30, 2009) (establishing that the burden of proof lies with the party alleging the fact, whether it is the claimant or the respondent); *Apotex Holdings Inc. and Apotex Inc. v. United States of America*, ICSID Case No. ARB(AF)/12/1, Award, ¶ 8.9 (Aug. 25, 2014) (This is "a generally accepted canon of evidence in civil law, common law and, in fact, most jurisdictions."); *Abrahim Rahman Golshani v. Gov't of the Islamic Republic of Iran*, 29 Iran-U.S. Cl. Trib. Rep. 78 (1993).

212 *See* Foster, *supra* note 189, at 42–44.

213 *Id.* at 44.

214 *Case concerning the Temple of Preah Vihear (Cambodia v. Thai.)*, Merits, Judgment, 1962 I.C.J. 6, at 16 (June 15); *Case concerning the GabčiKovo kovo-Nagymaros Project (Hung./Slovk.)*, Judgment, 1997 I.C.J. 7, at 42 (Sept. 25) (holding that Hungary bore the burden of proof regarding its defense of ecological necessity for breaching its obligations under a treaty); *Case concerning Pulp Mills on the River Uruguay (Arg. v. Uru.)*, Judgment, 2010 I.C.J. 14, ¶ 162 (Apr. 20) ("[I]t is the duty of the party which asserts certain facts to establish the existence of such facts."); Appellate Body Report, *United States—Measure Affecting Imports of Woven Wool Shirts and Blouses from India at pg. 14 (US-Wool Shirts)*, WT/DS33/AB/R (Apr. 25, 1997) ("[I]t is a generally-accepted canon of evidence in civil law, common law and, in fact, most jurisdictions, that the burden of proof rests upon the party, whether complaining or defending, who asserts the affirmative of a particular claim or defence."); *see also* Bin Cheng, *Burden of Proof before the I.C.J.*, 2 INT'L & COMP. L.Q. 595, 596 (1953); ICC Award No. 3344, J. DROIT INT'L

that the burden of proving an exception to the presumption of non-retroactivity "naturally lies with the party making the claim."[215] Consequently, the burden of proof may shift from one party to another in the course of a proceeding depending on which side asserts the fact or makes the request. At least a prima facie case is usually required on any matter before the burden shifts to the other party.[216]

International tribunals have leeway in assessing the weight of evidence they receive,[217] but when the question turns to whether the burden of proof is satisfied, the answer is again guided by a number of basic principles. For instance, an unsworn statement of fact from one of the parties is rarely regarded as conclusive proof without corroboration. Doing so, according to Cheng, would be a violation of the international minimum standard for the administration of justice.[218] Although more recent authority has undercut the extent of this concern,[219] tribunals continue to favor receipt of "contemporaneous evidence from persons with direct knowledge" of the facts being asserted, in a form capable of being tested for its veracity.[220] Evidence "obtained by examination of persons directly involved,

---

(Clunet) at 978, 983 (1982) (acknowledging the "rule of procedure, generally acknowledged in the various domestic legal systems, according to which every party must prove the facts which it alleges"); ICC Award No. 6653, J. Droit Int'l (Clunet) at 1040, 1044 (1993) (same).

215 *Técnicas Medioambientales Tecmed, S.A. v. United Mexican States*, ICSID Case No. ARB (AF)/00/2, Award, ¶ 63 (May 29, 2003).

216 *See, e.g., William A. Parker (U.S.A.) v. United Mexican States* (Mar. 31, 1926), 4 R.I.A.A. 35, 39 ("when the claimant has established a *prima facie* case and the respondent has offered no evidence in rebuttal the latter may not insist that the former pile up evidence to establish its allegations beyond a reasonable doubt without pointing out some reason for doubting"); *Tradex Hellas S.A. v. Republic of Albania*, ICSID Case No. ARB/94/2, Award, ¶ 84 (Apr. 29, 1999); *see also* Appellate Body Report, *United States—Measure Affecting Imports of Woven Wool Shirts and Blouses from India*, at 14, WT/DS33/AB/R (Apr. 25, 1997).

217 *See Tradex Hellas S.A. v. Republic of Albania*, ICSID Case No. ARB/94/2, Decision on Jurisdiction (Dec. 24, 1996) and Award (Apr. 29, 1999), 25 Y.B. Comm. Arb. 221, 240–41 (2000); *Case concerning Ahmadou Sadio Diallo (Rep. Guinea v. Dem. Rep. Congo)*, Merits, Judgment, 2010 I.C.J. 639, ¶ 54 (Nov. 30) ("The determination of the burden of proof is in reality dependent on the subject-matter and the nature of each dispute brought before the Court; it varies according to the type of facts which it is necessary to establish for the purposes of the decision of the case.").

218 Cheng, *supra* note 2, at 310.

219 *See Tradex Hellas S.A. v. Republic of Albania*, ICSID Case No. ARB/94/2, Decision on Jurisdiction (Dec. 24, 1996) and Award (Apr. 29, 1999), 25 Y.B. Comm. Arb. 221, 240 (2000); *Buckamier v. Islamic Republic of Iran et al.*, 28 Iran-U.S. Cl. Trib. Rep. 307 (1992); ALI/UNIDROIT Principles of Transnational Civil Procedure princ. 16 & cmt. 16-B, G, 2004-4 Unif. L. Rev. 758 (stating that, although it may be the rule in national systems, courts should not ascribe negative value to an interested party's testimony); *see also* Nathan D. O'Malley, Rules of Evidence in International Arbitration: An Annotated Guide 122 (2013) (noting the modern "departure from the view of early international tribunals," and citing Bin Cheng as ascribing to that earlier view).

220 *Case concerning Armed Activities on the Territory of the Congo (Dem. Rep. Congo v. Uganda)*, Judgment, 2005 I.C.J. 168, ¶ 61 (Dec. 19).

and who were subsequently cross-examined by [persons] skilled in examination . . ., merits special attention."[221] Also accorded great weight is contemporaneous documentary evidence, which is typically free from the "frailt[ies] of human contingencies" and "distrust."[222]

The ranking of preferred evidence is not a universal principle, but it is a reflection of one that is: *a litigant must produce the most trustworthy evidence to support its claim "tempered by considerations of possibility."*[223] The corollary to this principle is that a litigant who fails to produce the best evidence in its possession must "bear the consequences"[224] of that non-production—viz., an adverse inference "[w]hen it appears that a party has possession or control of relevant evidence that it declines without justification to produce."[225] As a result of a litigant's "duty to cooperate with international courts and tribunals in bringing forward evidence that will help them to decide the case," adverse inferences may even be drawn against the party that does *not* bear the burden of proof where it has better access to the pertinent evidence.[226] This is considered a general principle of law and due process "admitted in all systems of law."[227]

But sometimes the best evidence may not be all that good. Where direct evidence is unavailable, "*it is a general principle of law that proof may be administered by means of circumstantial evidence.*"[228] Appropriate inferences may be drawn from "a series of facts linked together and leading logically to a single conclusion."[229] For instance, evidence that there were sea mines in Albania's territorial waters

221 *Id.*

222 CHENG, *supra* note 2, at 318–19.

223 *Id.* at 322.

224 *EDF (Servs.) Ltd. v. Romania*, ICSID Case No. ARB/05/13, Procedural Order No. 3, ¶ 35 (Aug. 29, 2008).

225 ALI/UNIDROIT Principles of Transnational Civil Procedure princ. 21.3, 2004-4 UNIF. L. REV. 758; *see also* CHENG, *supra* note 2, at 325; CHRISTOPHER H. SCHREUER, THE ICSID CONVENTION: A COMMENTARY 656 (2001); *Europe Cement Inv. & Trade S.A. v. Republic of Turkey*, ICSID Case No. ARB(AF)/07/2, Award, ¶¶ 164–66 (Aug. 13, 2009); *Rompetrol Grp. N.V. v. Romania*, ICSID Case No. ARB/06/3, Award, ¶¶ 178–86 (May 6, 2013)); *Riahi v. Islamic Republic of Iran*, 37 Iran-U.S. Cl. Trib. Rep. 158, 176 (2003) (Brower, J., dissenting); *Marvin Feldman v. Mexico*, ICSID Case No. ARB(AF)/99/1, Award, ¶ 178 (Dec. 16, 2002).

226 *See* Foster, *supra* note 189, at 48.

227 *Corfu Channel Case (U.K. v. Alb.)*, Judgment, Merits, 1949 I.C.J. 4, 18 (Apr. 9); *see also* ALI/UNIDROIT Principles of Transnational Civil Procedure cmt. P.17B, 2004-4 UNIF. L. REV. 758.

228 CHENG, *supra* note 2, at 322; *see* ICC Award No. 4145 (Second Interim Award), 12 Y.B. COMM. ARB. 97 (1987) (also published in: J. DROIT INT'L (CLUNET), at 985 (1985)) (acknowledging the "general principle[] of interpretation [that] a fact can be considered as proven even by the way of circumstantial evidence").

229 *Corfu Channel Case (U.K. v. Alb.)*, Judgment, Merits, 1949 I.C.J. 4, 18 (Apr. 9). Although the ICJ in the *Corfu Channel* case included the caveat that such inference must leave "no room for reasonable doubt," that high threshold has disappeared in more recent cases; see also *Abrahim Rahman Golshani v. Gov't*

and that Albania carefully monitored those waters could support the (inferential) conclusion that Albania knew of the mines located in its waters.[230] The allowance of circumstantial evidence has a practical dimension in other contexts, too. Notorious corruption in a certain country can be considered as circumstantial evidence of corruption in a particular case arising from that country given that "partiality and dependence by their very nature take place behind the scenes."[231]

Where a party is "unable to furnish direct proof of facts giving rise to responsibility," it is typically "allowed a more liberal recourse to inferences of fact and circumstantial evidence."[232] This indirect evidence is "admitted in all systems of law, and its use is recognized by international decisions."[233] Although circumstantial evidence standing alone rarely carries the day, it may be sufficient where corroborative evidence lies solely within the hands of the party opposite but was not forthcoming, or where the circumstantial evidence is not contradicted by direct proof in the record.[234] The inferences to be drawn from circumstantial evidence will also vary in each case, depending on the other record evidence. The tribunal in *Oostergetel v. Slovak Republic*, for instance, found that although general reports of bribery of judges are relevant to a denial of justice claim, they cannot substitute for some direct evidence of a treaty breach in a specific instance, as mere insinuations cannot meet the burden of proof that rests with the claimant.[235]

One final note deserves mention. It should come as no surprise—based on previous discussions of good faith, procedural equality, and fraud—that *proof acquired by unlawful or otherwise improper means may be stricken out from the record or denied any weight.* Where, for example, a party acquires documentation "by successive and multiple acts of trespass, . . . it would be wrong to allow [that party] to introduce this documentation into the[] proceedings."[236] Any other conclusion would "offend[]

of the Islamic Republic of Iran, 29 Iran-U.S. Cl. Trib. Rep. 78 (1993); *Asian Agric. Prods. Ltd. v. Republic of Sri Lanka*, ICSID Case No. ARB/87/3, Award, ¶ 45 (June 27, 1990).

230 *Corfu Channel Case (U.K. v. Alb.)*, Judgment, Merits, 1949 I.C.J. 4, 18–20 (Apr. 9).

231 *Yukos Capital S.a.r.l. v. OJSC Rosneft Oil Co.*, [2011] EWHC 1461, ¶ 36.

232 *Corfu Channel Case (U.K. v. Alb.)*, Judgment, Merits, 1949 I.C.J. 4, 18 (Apr. 9).

233 *Id.*

234 *See* Michael P. Scharf & Margaux Day, *The International Court of Justice's Treatment of Circumstantial Evidence and Adverse Inferences*, 13 Chi. J. Int'l L. 123, 131 (2012).

235 *Jan Oostergetel and Theordora Laurentius v. Slovak Republic*, UNCITRAL, Award, ¶¶ 302–03 (Apr. 23, 2012).

236 *Methanex Corp. v. United States of America*, NAFTA, Final Award, ¶¶ 54–59 (Aug. 3, 2005). The Tribunal also noted, "*ex hypothesi*," that "[i]t would be wrong for the USA . . . to misuse its intelligence assets to spy on Methanex (and its witnesses) and to introduce into evidence the resulting materials."

basic principles of justice and fairness."[237] The same principle applies to evidence of questionable provenance. In *Libananco*, for example, the tribunal excluded from the record incomplete audio recordings whose authenticity was questioned in several expert reports.[238] This is not particularly controversional, and it might be argued that the principle is predicated less on evidentiary rules and more on the principles of "good faith," "equal treatment," and "procedural fairness."[239]

F. The Principle of Res Judicata

> *It appears to me that if there be a case in which it is legitimate to have recourse, in the absence of conventions and custom, to the "general principles of law recognized by civilized nations," [then it is with respect to] the binding effect of* res judicata.
>
> —Judge Dionisio Anzilotti[240]

The final principle is, according to Cheng and early twentieth century jurists, the least controversial: "There seems little, if indeed any question as to *res judicata* being a general principle of law."[241] It serves both a general and specific purpose. Generally, "the stability of legal relations requires that litigation come to an end"; specifically, "it is in the interest of [all] part[ies] that an issue which has already been adjudicated . . . be not argued again."[242] The rules defining this principle originate in Roman civil law, including several cases from the Digest of 541 A.D.[243] The principle has evolved little over the course of two millennia, leaving "no doubt that *res judicata* is a . . . general principle of law within the meaning of Article 38(1)(c) of the Statute of the International Court of Justice."[244]

Id. ¶ 54; *see also EDF (Servs.) Ltd. v. Romania*, ICSID Case No. ARB/05/13, Procedural Order No. 3, ¶ 38 (Aug. 29, 2008).

237 *Methanex Corp. v. United States of America*, NAFTA, Final Award, ¶ 59 (Aug. 3, 2005).

238 *See, e.g., Libananco Holdings Co. Ltd. v. Republic of Turkey*, ICSID Case No. ARB/06/8, Award, ¶¶ 383–84 (Sept. 2, 2011).

239 *Id.*; *see also EDF (Servs.) Ltd. v. Romania*, ICSID Case No. ARB/05/13, Procedural Order No. 3, ¶ 38 (Aug. 29, 2008).

240 Dissenting in *Factory at Chorzów (Fed. Rep. Ger. v. Pol.)*, Interpretation of Judgments Nos. 7 and 8, Judgment, 1927 P.C.I.J. (Ser. A) No. 13 (Dec. 16).

241 Cheng, *supra* note 2, at 336.

242 *Application of the Convention on the Prevention and Punishment of the Crime of Genocide (Bosn. & Herz. v. Serb. & Montenegro)*, Judgment, 2007 I.C.J. 43, 51 ¶ 116 (Feb. 26).

243 *See* 3 Digest of Justinian, Book 44, 2.6.

244 *See Waste Mgmt., Inc. v. United Mexican States* ("Number 2"), ICSID Case No. ARB(AF)/00/3, Decision on Mexico's Preliminary Objections concerning the Provisions Proceedings, ¶ 39 (June 26, 2002); *see*

Res judicata, has two consequences, both of which seek to avoid the repetition of what has already been raised and decided. *First*, as an affirmative matter, the terms of judgments and awards are binding and obligatory on the parties. By virtue of the general principle of res judicata, *parties to a final judgment or award are obligated to carry it out.*[245] This is not only a function of res judicata, but of other basic rules shared by all systems of law, including the principles of good faith and estoppel.[246]

Second, and as a negative corollary to the first, the same claims may not be tried again by another court or tribunal—*non bis in idem.*[247] In practice, *successive courts and tribunals are obligated to defer to the jurisdiction of the first if the same matter is submitted for adjudication a second time, and all of the rights, issues, and facts that were "distinctly put in issue and directly determined" by the first court or tribunal cannot be disputed again.*[248] To reopen the matter again undercuts the "seriousness and stability"[249] of adjudicated legal relationships—core notions of international due process.[250]

---

also Industria Nadonal de Alimentos, S.A. and Indalsa Peru, SA. v. Peru, ICSID ARB/03/4, Decision on Annulment, ¶ 86 (Sept. 5, 2007); *Apotex Holdings Inc. and Apotex Inc. v. United States of America*, ICSID Case No. ARB(AF)/12/1, Award, ¶ 7.11 (Aug. 25, 2014); *Amco Asia Corp. et al. v. Republic of Indonesia*, ICSID Case No. ARB/81/1, Resubmitted Case, Decision on Jurisdiction (May 10, 1988), 89 Int'l L. Rep. 552, 560; *Effect of Awards of Compensation Made by the U.N. Administrative Tribunal*, Advisory Opinion, 1954 I.C.J. 47, at 53 (July 13); *Case concerning the Arbitral Award Made by the King of Spain on 23 December 1906 (Hond. v. Nicar.)*, Judgment, 1960 I.C.J. 192 (Nov. 18); *Boundary Dispute between Argentina and Chile concerning the Frontier Line between Boundary Post 62 and Mount Fitzroy*, Award (Oct. 21, 1994), 22 R.I.A.A., ¶ 68. Buttressing this conclusion, the principle of res judicata is well established in the common law jurisdictions of England, Ireland, Canada, India, Australia, New Zealand, and the United States; the continental civil law systems of France, Belgium, the Netherlands, Germany, Italy, and Belgium; and the Latin American civil law systems of Mexico and Argentina, just to name a few. *See generally* ILA Berlin Conference, Interim Report on Res Judicata and Arbitration (2004).

245 *Effect of Awards of Compensation Made by the U.N. Administrative Tribunal*, Advisory Opinion, 1954 I.C.J. 47, 53 (July 13) (it is a "well-established and generally recognized principle of law [that] a judgment rendered by a judicial body is *res judicata* and has binding force between the parties to the dispute.").

246 *See Desert Line Projects LLC v. Republic of Yemen*, ICSID Case No. ARB/05/17, Award, ¶¶ 205-07 (Feb. 6, 2008). *See also* D.W. Bowett, *Estoppel before International Tribunals and Its Relation to Acquiescence*, 33 Brit. Y.B. Int'l L. 176, 177 (1957).

247 Cheng, *supra* note 2, at 337–38.

248 *Company General of the Orinoco Case*, 10 RIAA 184, 276 (July 31, 1905). Of course, where different legal systems are involved, the prior decision must be recognized before it will be given res judicata effect. *Chevron Corp. v. Donziger*, 886 F. Supp. 2d 235, 240 (S.D.N.Y. 2012).

249 Decision of Nov. 30, 1995, RDJ t. XCII sec. 1, at 116 (Chilean Supreme Court).

250 Like many general principles, this rule is not absolute, but those exceptions do not denigrate the principle of res judicata. Where, for instance, new facts have "come to light subsequent to [its] decision" that cast doubt as to the correctness of the decision, a case may be reopened and reconsidered. *Application of the Convention on the Prevention and Punishment of the Crime of Genocide*, Judgment, 2007 I.C.J. 43, 53 ¶ 120 (Feb. 26).

Though the principle itself is a general one, the precise elements for its application differ across jurisdictions.[251] Some basic precepts are nonetheless discernible. As to the threshold elements, only decisions on the merits, decided after full and fair adjudication, are entitled to res judicata effect. A dismissal by a court or tribunal for lack of jurisdiction, for example, is not a decision on the merits and does not preclude a subsequent airing of the issues before a tribunal that has jurisdiction.[252] Thus, if a claimant complains of a denial of justice before exhausting local remedies, and the claim is denied on that ground, the claimant may reinstate its claims after local claims have run their course.[253] The same is true of decisions regarding issues of admissibility,[254] such as instances where the claim advanced is "time-barred" under national law, but the same dispute may be brought before a tribunal under international law.[255] "The point is simply that a decision which does not deal with the merits of the claim, even if it deals with issues of substance, does not constitute *res judicata* as to those merits."[256] In *Bosh v. Ukraine*, the tribunal found that a Ukrainian court had not violated the principle of res judicata when it heard a case that had been previously dismissed by a prior Ukrainian judge. On reviewing Ukrainian civil procedure law, the tribunal found that res judicata does not attach to a case where the first judge declined to formally open proceedings, as was the case there.[257]

The requirement of a full and fair adjudication usually leaves default judgments outside the scope of the general principle. Though default judgments have the full effect of res judicata in some legal systems,[258] the existence of contrary

---

251 *See, e.g.*, Stavros Brekoulakis, *The Effect of an Arbitral Award and Third Parties in International Arbitration*, 16 AM. REV. INT'L ARB. 177, 182 (2005) (detailing the "great divergence among national legal regimes with regard to *res judicata*," with the "differences[] particularly marked between common and civil law jurisdictions").

252 *See, e.g., Trail Smelter Arbitration*, 3 RIAA 1905 (1953) (Mar. 11, 1941).

253 *Waste Mgmt., Inc. v. United Mexican States* ("Number 2"), ICSID Case No. ARB(AF)/00/3, Decision on Mexico's Preliminary Objections concerning the Previous Proceedings, ¶ 43 (June 26, 2002).

254 *Id.*

255 *Waste Mgmt., Inc. v. United Mexican States*, ICSID Case No. ARB(AF)/98/2, Dissenting Opinion of Keith Highet, ¶ 58 n.45 (May 8, 2000).

256 *Waste Mgmt., Inc. v. United Mexican States* ("Number 2"), ICSID Case No. ARB(AF)/00/3, Decision on Mexico's Preliminary Objections concerning the Previous Proceedings, ¶ 43 (June 26, 2002).

257 *Bosh Int'l, Inc and B&P Ltd Foreign Invs. Enter. v. Ukraine*, ICSID Case No. ARB/08/11, Award, ¶¶ 260–86 (Oct. 25, 2012).

258 *See, e.g.*, Code of Civil Procedure of Argentina art. 67; *Horton v. Horton*, 18 Cal. 2d 579, 585 (1941) (stating that "[i]t is immaterial that the judgment which is assailed was procured by default. The defendants in that action had an opportunity to appear and protect their interest. They deliberately waived the right to their day in court by failing to appear and answer the complaint. A default judgment is an estoppel as to all issues necessarily litigated therein and determined thereby exactly like any other judgment provided

authority[259] denies it the status of a general principle. Also, as Cheng noted, "not everything contained in [a] decision acquires the force of *res judicata*."[260] The claims and defenses decided by the court are res judicata.[261] Obiter dicta, however, do not have the effect of res judicata; views which are not relevant to the actual decision have no binding force. Preclusive effect typically attaches only to the operative portions of the judgment (*dispositif*) directed to matters fairly put before the court, and not to matters incidental and unnecessary to the ultimate decision.[262]

Almost all judicial systems require an identity of the parties (in the legal, not physical, sense), object (*petitum*), and grounds (*causa petendi*) between the first and the second suit before res judicata will apply. This is known as the "triple identity" standard, which was formulated by the Roman jurist Paolo,[263] redefined by the French jurist Pothier,[264] and applied by tribunals today.[265]

---

the court acquired jurisdiction of the parties and subject matter involved in the suit."); *Maddux v. County Bank*, 129 Cal. 665, 667 (1900) (finding that "[a] judgment by default stands on the same footing as a judgment after answer and trial with respect to issues tendered by the plaintiff's complaint"); *Kahn v. Kahn*, 68 Cal. App. 3d 373, Court of Appeals of California, First Appellate District, Division One (Mar. 24, 1977).

259 *See, e.g.*, Civil Procedure Rules 1998 of England art. 13.2.

260 Cheng, *supra* note 2, at 348.

261 ALI/UNIDROIT Principles of Transnational Civil Procedure princ. 28.2, 2004-4 Unif. L. Rev. 758, 804.

262 Cheng, *supra* note 2, at 349–50. Generally speaking, if the issue falls within the court's competence (i.e., it relates to the rights between the parties before the court and is not subject to the exclusive jurisdiction of another court), and is a necessary and essential condition to the determination of the principal question, then the decision on that issue is res judicata. Thus, if a tribunal holds that a claimant was denied justice, the essential holding that the claimant has exhausted his local remedies is likewise res judicata. *Id.* at 355. This is not collateral estoppel or issue preclusion—which generally obtains only in common law systems and is thus not a general principle of law; *see, e.g.*, ALI/UNIDROIT Principles of Transnational Civil Procedure princ. 28.3, 2004-4 Unif. L. Rev. 758, 806—but rather a holistic interpretation of the judgment and all things necessary to it. *See Delimitation of the Continental Shelf (U.K. v. Fr.)*, Decision (Mar. 14, 1978), 18 R.I.A.A. 271, 295 (although res judicata "attaches in principle only to the provisions of [the decision's] *dispositif* and not to its reasoning," it is equally clear that "having regard to the close links that exist between the reasoning of a decision and the provisions of its *dispositif*, recourse may in principle be had to the reasoning in order to elucidate the meaning and scope of the *dispositif*").

263 Eugene Petit, Tratado Elemental de Derecho Romano 630–31 (1994).

264 Robert Pothier, Tratado de las Obligaciones (1761).

265 *See Apotex Holdings Inc. and Apotex Inc. v. United States of America*, ICSID Case No. ARB (AF/12/1), Award, ¶¶ 7.10–7.32 (Aug. 25 2014); *Waste Mgmt., Inc. v. United Mexican States* ("Number 2"), ICSID Case No. ARB(AF)/00/3, Decision of the Tribunal on Mexico's Preliminary Objection concerning the Previous Proceedings, ¶¶ 40–41 (June 26, 2002); *Factory at Chorzów (Fed. Rep. Ger. v. Pol.)*, Interpretation of Judgments Nos. 7 and 8, Judgment, 1927 P.C.I.J. (Ser. A) No. 13 (Dec. 16) (dissenting opinion by Judge Dionisio Anzilotti); *Trail Smelter Case (U.S. v. Canada)*, Award (Mar. 11, 1941), 3 R.I.A.A. 1905, 1952–53; *see also* Cheng, *supra* note 2, at 339–40.

The first of the "triple identities" is usually the easiest: the requirement that the parties be the same between the first and second case means that the first judgment binds only the parties and their privies. This is not a nominal test, but a legal one—the first judgment covers not only the persons who actually appeared in the litigation, but those who were represented by, or in privity with, the litigating parties. It follows that a minor who is unsuccessfully represented in a personal-injury case by her father cannot later file the same claim when she comes of age, because she was the real party in interest in the first suit, even if she did not formally appear. An UNCITRAL tribunal applied the same principle to a government's settlement of a claim of diffuse environmental rights against an oil operator, holding that res judicata may extend to non-signatories seeking to raise the same diffuse rights against the same company.[266]

Moving to the second and third identities, the *causa petendi* is the reason or motive for requesting something in a complaint: in other words, the material facts in dispute between the parties that give rise to the legal claim. The legal rights implicated by a contract, a damaged plot of land, or a personal injury might all constitute the *causa petendi* of a complaint. The object, or *petitum*, is the legal benefit that the suit seeks to obtain. This requirement cannot be evaded through artful pleading. A claimant cannot seek money damages for environmental damage to real property in one suit, and then sue for remediation in another. Although the remedies sought may be different, the nature of the legal recourse is not, and the first suit (litigated to conclusion between the same parties) will typically bar the second. In some cases, the latter two elements of res judicata will collapse into a single inquiry regarding the general similarities between the substance of the two suits.[267] These elements dovetail with considerations of practicality and efficiency, as legal systems function more effectively if related claims are pursued together rather than piecemeal.

Despite its broad acceptance as a fundamental principle, res judicata does not prohibit a party from advancing in different legal systems a legally distinct cause of action arising from the same set of facts. "The doctrine applies only where a point

266 *See Chevron Corp. et al. v. Republic of Ecuador*, PCA Case No. 2009-23, First Partial Award on Track I, ¶¶ 94–108 (Sept. 17, 2013).

267 *See, e.g., Apotex Holdings Inc. and Apotex Inc. v. United States of America*, ICSID Case No. ARB (AF) 12/1, Award, ¶¶ 7.41–7.62 (Aug. 25, 2014) (finding that the triple identity standard provides a stringent test, and applying a simpler twofold test that only requires there to be an identity of the parties and an identity of the matter of the dispute); CHENG, *supra* note 2, at 339–40. Regardless of the articulation, the legal standard in those systems are functionally the same. Where the object and *causa petendi* are subsumed in a single question whether the "matter in dispute" is the same, the "matter" is interpreted to encompass the requests for a legal benefit arising out of a certain set of facts, so the difference in nomenclature does not denigrate the general principle or its application.

falls for decision twice within *one and the same legal context*, . . . [and] does not preclude the [re-]hearing of a claim on a *separate legal basis*."[268] It has thus been held that one tribunal hearing a dispute under an investment treaty cannot bind a second tribunal hearing the "same" dispute under a different treaty.[269] Or where a claimant initiates arbitration against a host State pursuant to a private contract or a domestic investment law, a decision from that tribunal will not bind a later tribunal convened under an investment treaty addressing different legal claims.[270]

One final point brings things full circle. Judgments from permanent courts are not the only form of formal dispute resolution. Settlement agreements may be more ubiquitous, and the policies behind res judicata (the advancement of stability and certainty in the legal process) are no less applicable when the parties settle their differences themselves. But although there is no consensus on whether such contracts are res judicata,[271] all agree that they are binding and enforceable, and therefore can act to bar subsequent litigation as a general principle of law. In this context, the finality and repose provided by res judicata are also provided through other general principles, such as estoppel and pacta sunt servanda.[272]

---

268 Vaughn Lowe, *Res Judicata and the Rule of Law in International Arbitration*, 8 Afr. J. Int'l & Comp. L. 38, 40–41 (1996). To avoid piecemeal litigation, in certain circumstances the alternative legal theory may be waived or barred if it could have been, but was not, brought at the same time.

269 *CME Czech Republic B.V. v. Czech Republic*, UNCITRAL, Final Award on Damages, ¶ 435 (Mar. 14, 2003).

270 *See Petrobart Ltd. v. Kyrgyz Republic*, SCC Arbitration No. 126/2003, Award, 65–68 (Mar. 29, 2005) (when a claimant initiates "two separate UNCITRAL proceedings, based on different arbitration clauses, one in the Foreign Investment Law and the other in the Treaty, the first one dealing with the question of investments under Kyrgyz law and the other one with compliance or not with the Treaty," a decision by one tribunal will not operate as res judicata over the other).

271 *Compare Carver v. Nall*, 172 F.3d 513, 515 (7th Cir. 1999) ("[T]he fundamental point remains that *res judicata* cannot operate in the absence of a judgment," and a "settlement agreement that has not been integrated into a consent decree is not a judgment and cannot trigger *res judicata*."); *Meyer v. Rigdon*, 36 F.3d 1375, 1379 (7th Cir. 1994) ("[S]ettlement agreements not approved by a court are not given preclusive effect."); *Frank v. United Airlines, Inc.*, 216 F.3d 845, 852 (9th Cir. 2000) ("[A] settlement [that] is not incorporated into a judgment . . . cannot have preclusive effect."); *with Chevron Corp. et al. v. Republic of Ecuador*, PCA Case No. 2009-23, First Partial Award on Track I, ¶¶ 107–08 (Sept. 17, 2013) (holding that, under Ecuadorian law, diffuse environmental claims had been extinguished by a settlement agreement); French Civil Code art. 2052 ("Transactions [a contract by which the parties put an end to an existing controversy, or prevent a future contestation] have, between the parties, the authority of res judicata of a final judgment."); Chilean Civil Code art. 2460 ("The transaction [a contract by which the parties extra-judicially put an end to an existing controversy, or prevent eventual litigation] has the effect of Res Judicata in last resort . . . ."); Ecuadorian Civil Code art. 2362 ("The transaction has the effect of Res Judicata in last resort . . . ."); Colombian Civil Code art. 2483 ("The transaction has the effect of Res Judicata in last resort . . . .").

272 *Desert Line Projects LLC v. Republic of Yemen*, ICSID Case No. ARB/05/17, Award, ¶¶ 205–07 (Feb. 6, 2008).

Epilogue

General Principles of Law and International Due Process as a Function of Private International Law

> *Private law, being in general more developed than international law, has always constituted a sort of reserve store of principles upon which the latter has been in the habit of drawing [because] a principle which is found to be generally accepted by civilized legal systems may fairly be assumed to be so reasonable as to be necessary to the maintenance of justice under any system.*
>
> —Judge Brett Kavanaugh[1]

Private international law usually does its part to resolve transnational disputes by pointing parties to the proper forum and the proper law. Its rules are adjectival and rarely provide the ultimate solution to a dispute. It has been said that this discipline of law "resembles the inquiry office at a railway station where a passenger may learn the platform at which his train starts"—it directs parties to the right court and the right law, "[b]ut it says no more."[2] Despite its limited functions, private international law does not always lead to clean and predictable results. "With regrettable frequency, traditional choice of law rules produce unsatisfactory decisions because mechanical precepts w[ith] hard and fast connecting factors indiscriminately invoke foreign law[s] . . . that may offend the foreign judiciary's sense of justice."[3]

1 *Doe VIII v. Exxon Mobil Corp.*, 654 F.3d 11, 54 (D.C. Cir. 2011) (Kavanaugh, J., dissenting).

2 James Fawcett et al., Cheshire, North & Fawcett: Private International Law 8-9 (14th ed., 2008).

3 Friedrich Juenger, *The Problem with Private International Law*, *in* Private Law in the International Arena—Liber Amicorum Kurt Siehr 296–97 (Jurgen Basedow et al. eds., Springer 2000).

In order to play a more meaningful role in aiding the resolution of modern transnational disputes, the authorities that encompass the rules of private international law might also play a role in determining the *substance* of those municipal laws applied. Like investment tribunals in the past two decades, municipal courts seised with transnational matters and asked to apply foreign law could develop interpretive, definitional, and corrective mechanisms grounded in positive law that ensure substantive justice from a universal perspective. Where the applicable law falls below accepted international norms, yielding to it can produce untoward results. If courts continue to hew to a mechanical application of the chosen municipal law, and excuse it with "meretricious concessions to cultural relativism," the law could find itself "complicit with dictators, fanatics and thugs" who have perpetrated the "fraudulent consensus on the rule of law" worldwide.[4] By the same token, if courts continue to rely on the "unruly horse" of local public policy,[5] or insist on parochial norms to stunt the movement of foreign judgments around the world, there is a threat to the very foundation of international law—that "systemic value of reciprocal tolerance and goodwill" that furthers the "mutual interests of all nations in a smoothly functioning international legal regime."[6]

To some extent, private international law organizations have already begun to play a more robust role in the substance of dispute resolution. The Hague Conference on Private International Law, for one, has recently acknowledged the "need, in practice, to facilitate access to foreign law" as an "essential component to . . . the rule of law and . . . the proper administration of justice."[7] Efforts such as this will make it easier for the national judge to apply the *whole law* to a particular case, including universal principles underlying it. Moving one step further, for almost a century the International Institute for the Unification of Private Law (UNIDROIT) has been modernizing, harmonizing, and coordinating the rules of private commercial law to formulate uniform law instruments, and numerous treaties have been concluded between States that effectively do the same.[8] And

4 Jan Paulsson, Speech at the Rule of Law Conference at the Univ. of Richmond: Enclaves of Justice 2 (Apr. 12, 2007), *available at* http://www.arbitration-icca.org/media/0/12254618965440/speech-richmond__enclaves_of_justice.pdf.

5 *Richardson v. Mellish* (1824), 2 Bing. 229, 252.

6 *Societe Nationale Industrielle Aerospatiale v. United States*, 482 U.S. 522, 555 (1987) (Blackmun, J., concurring in part and dissenting in part).

7 Hague Conference on Private International Law/European Commission, *Conclusions and Recommendations on Access to Foreign Law in Civil and Commercial Matters* (Feb. 15–17, 2012).

8 *See, e.g.*, Convention for the Unification of Certain Rules Relating to International Carriage by Air, signed at Warsaw on Oct. 12, 1929.

for centuries before that, *lex mercatoria* has provided rules of international trade that have long been used to "clarify, to fill gaps, and to reduce the impact of peculiarities of individual country's laws."[9]

But there is an inherent limitation to rules derived from scholarly consensus (in the case of uniform law instruments) and mercantile usage (in the case of *lex mercatoria*).[10] A municipal court may not recognize the choice of nonstate codifications to a particular dispute before it. In Europe, this comes from Article 1(1) of the Rome Convention, which stipulates that the Convention governs the "choice between the *laws* of different *countries*."[11] Other provisions, too, especially those dealing with contracts—such as Articles 3(3) and 7(1)—refer to the applicable law as "the law of a country." This is true in the United States as well. Section 187 of the *Second Restatement of Conflicts* and Sections 1-105 and 1-301 of the Uniform Commercial Code designate the law to which reference is made as the "law of a state." And because "state" is defined in that *Restatement* as a "territorial unit with a distinct body of law," this wording suggests that only the choice of applicable state law is contemplated.[12] There is a place, then, for an established source of domestic *positive* law to do what the *lex mercatoria* does.

This is precisely where the "general principles of law recognized by civilized nations" can fruitfully enter the field of private international law. These principles are, by definition, borne from *municipal* law—or, in the least, the distillation of

9 Andreas F. Lowenfeld, Lex Mercatoria: *An Arbitrator's View, in* 1990 ARB. INT'L 133, 149.

10 *See* Emmanuel Gaillard, *General Principles of Law in International Commercial Arbitration—Challenging the Myths*, 5 WORLD ARB. & MEDIATION REV. 161, 161–62 (2011) (noting that "it would be misleading . . . to equate general principles with *lex mercatoria*" because only the former is "rooted in national legal systems and identified through a comparative law analysis").

11 Convention 80/934/ECC on the law applicable to contractual obligations, opened for signature in Rome on June 19, 1980 (emphasis added). Some of these same national codes, however, do permit *arbitrators* to apply nonstate law in their decisions. *See, e.g.*, Austrian Code of Civil Procedure § 603(2); French Code of Civil Procedure art. 1496; Italian Code of Civil Procedure art. 822; Netherlands Code of Civil Procedure art. 1054(2); Swiss Fed. Code on Private International Law art. 187(2). A number of arbitration institutions have similar, liberal rules. *See, e.g.*, ICC Rules of Arbitration art. 21(1); LCIA Arbitration Rules art. 22.3; AAA/ICDR Procedures art. 28.1; HKIAC Arbitration Rules art. 31.1.

12 Case law is generally in accord. In *Trans Meridian Trading Inc. v. Empresa Nacional de Comercializacion de Insumos*, 829 F.2d 949, 953–54 (9th Cir. 1987), for example, the Court of Appeals for the Ninth Circuit refused to enjoin payment on an international letter of credit despite the fact that the contract had been expressly made subject to the "Uniform Customs and Practices for Documentary Credit (UCP)" published by the International Chamber of Commerce, which allowed issuance of an injunction under the given circumstances. The court held that the UCP was not the law "of a foreign jurisdiction, but rather . . . a compendium of commercial practices published by the International Chamber of Commerce." *Id.* Therefore, "a provision in a letter of credit that the UCP governs the transaction" did not "prevent application of California's Commercial Code." *Id.*

underlying legal principles that give shape to those positive laws. They stem from *international consensus*—before being characterized as general, the judge must deem them accepted by the vast majority of legal systems in the world. And they have been fashioned to function on the *international plane*. In a transnational case, involving litigants from differing legal traditions, a solution premised on international rather than municipal principles should be preferred given the competing interests of the two foreign parties to the dispute.[13] It could be argued that the category of international law set forth in Article 38(1)(c) of the International Court of Justice (ICJ) Statute is the best designed for private international law cases; it is, after all, the only source that derives from the world's many *municipal* codes, which in and of themselves are designed to apply to the conduct of *private relationships*.

The intent is not to formulate a new approach to the choice of law, even though on its face it may look like the "better law" approach championed by Robert Leflar a half-century ago[14] or the "principles of preference" introduced by David Cavers before that.[15] Both sought to announce criteria of rule-selection, a "choice between laws,"[16] a unified theory by which judges could choose the competing municipal law that would best effect "relevant multistate policies"[17] or some subjective notion of justice.[18] Instead what is suggested comes *after* the choice of law is made. At that point, the court ascertains—and, if necessary, adjusts—the content of the governing law by measuring it against "the general principles of

13 *See* Statute of the ICJ art. 38.

14 Robert Leflar, American Conflicts Law 258 (1968).

15 David Cavers, The Choice of Law Process 64 (1965).

16 Leflar, *supra* note 14.

17 Cavers, *supra* note 15.

18 There is no reason, however, that the general principles of law could not play an important role in the search for the appropriate choice of law. For example, in *Eli Lilly do Brasil, Ltda v. Fed. Express Co.*, 502 F.3d 78, 81–82 (2d Cir. 2007), Eli Lilly had contracted with FedEx to ship pharmaceuticals, which were stolen while being transported by truck in Brazil. Eli Lilly elected to sue in the Southern District of New York instead of Brazil, requiring the court to determine whether the federal common law or Brazilian law applied. In conducting its choice of law analysis, the court recognized that Brazil's interest under § 188 of the Restatement (Second) of Conflict of Laws was greater than that of the United States; however, the court noted that this was not the "end of [the] inquiry or determinative of its conclusion." *Id.* at 82. The court found that the expectation of enforceability of contracts should be afforded greater weight than Brazilian law. In reaching this conclusion, the court applied the following two general principles of law: (1) "the well-settled 'presumption in favor of applying that law tending toward the validation of the alleged contract,'" and (2) "the general rule of contract that 'presumes the legality and enforceability of contracts'"—pacta sunt servanda. *Id.*; *see also* Bin Cheng, General Principles of Law as Applied by International Courts and Tribunals 142 (1953). As these general principles favored enforcing the contract, they were weighed against Brazil's interest in having its own law applied. The principle of *locus regit actum* (the place governs the act) was thus displaced by

law recognized by civilized nations." The law is then applied in a manner that it is consonant with general principles, with the aim of achieving "justice, very simple, very fundamental, and of such general acceptance by all civilized countries as to form a part of the international law of the world."[19] At the very least, this methodology minimizes the risk of parochial outcomes in transnational disputes that have implications beyond one State's borders.

Nor is this an effort to craft a comparative code of conduct applicable to transnational relationships everywhere. The suggestion is more modest than that. *Principles* are distinguishable from *rules*. "A rule . . . is essentially practical and, moreover, binding."[20] Principles "express[] a general truth" and "serve[] as a theoretical basis" for binding rules.[21]

This is important, because when a municipal court is given the authority to apply a certain law to a transnational case—be it foreign or domestic—its authority is plenary, and it has the authority to *determine* the law before it applies it. This means that the *whole law*, including the foundational norms undergirding black-letter rules, may be applied.[22] A foreign law that purports to undo final decisions, for instance, may be rejected by the municipal court seised to apply it on the grounds that such a law violates the universal concept of res judicata. Thus whatever the fate of that (unprincipled) rule in the territory of the State that enacted it, it remains cabined there. The application of the general principles can thus keep *the law* in good health, even though imperfect laws may be passed from time to time.

General principles are most effective working *alongside* the positive rules of the governing law, guiding the application of municipal law rather than forming freestanding rules of decision themselves. In many contexts, only once challenges are raised to the legitimacy or propriety of municipal law is the "[a]ttention . . . immediately switched to international law, to see whether it may have a corrective effect, by operation of such things as international minimum

---

the general principle of law that the contract have effect rather than be nullified—*ut res magis valeat quam pereat*.

19 Elihu Root, *The Basis of Protection to Citizens Residing Abroad*, 4 PROC. AM. SOC. INT'L L. 16, 21 (1910).

20 CHENG, *supra* note 18, at 376.

21 *Id.*

22 *See generally* Jan Paulsson, *The Lalive Lecture, Geneva: Unlawful Laws and the Authority of International Tribunals (May 27, 2009)*, *in* 23(2) ICSID REV. 215 (2008).

standards or international public policy."[23] This is the norm in investment tribunals, where the general principles of law are often applied in an interpretive or corrective role. Indeed, general principles of law can correct a rule of law in an outcome-determinative way, even in municipal courts. When, for instance, an otherwise applicable foreign law would shield a state-owned corporation from liability, and allow it to benefit from its sovereign's international delicts, general principles step in to disregard the corporation's separate legal status.[24] "[L]imited liability is [still] the rule," but "controlling principles" imply an exception.[25] Similarly, when local notions of due process might render a foreign judgment unenforceable, a "less demanding standard" of "international due process"—derived from common principles and processes from around the globe—may be applied to recognize the judgment.[26] The acknowledgment and application of general principles derived from the positive laws of the forum and other legal traditions can be the difference between applying *a* rule of law, and applying *the* rule of law. Although the former can fall prey to political expediency (often to the detriment of the foreign litigant), the latter remains unyielding and constant.

The enterprise would benefit, though, from greater rigor. In the realm of public international law, where the general principles were originally meant to apply, their development has long been stunted by the truncated reasoning of international jurists. When international tribunals identify and apply a general principle of law, they typically do so without any express reference or label.[27] And rather than explain their comparative process in divining the principle, they typically assert, ipse dixit, that the principle is "admitted in all systems of law"[28] or that it is "widely accepted as having been assimilated into the catalogue of general principles of law."[29] To be sure, as Justice Ruth Bader Ginsburg noted in *Intel v. Advanced Micro Devices*, the "comparison of legal systems is slippery business."[30]

---

23 *Id.* at 215.

24 *See First Nat'l City Bank v. Banco Para el Comercio Exterior de Cuba (Bancec)*, 462 U.S. 611 (1983).

25 *Id.* at 626, 632.

26 *Soc'y of Lloyd's v. Ashenden*, 233 F.3d 473, 477 (7th Cir. 2000).

27 *See* Clarence Wilfred Jenks, The Prospects of International Adjudication 268–305 (Stevens & Sons Ltd. 1964); Hersch Lauterpacht, The Development of International Law by the International Court 158–72 (1958).

28 *Corfu Channel Case (U.K. v. Alb.)*, Judgment, Merits, 1949 I.C.J. 4, 18 (Apr. 9).

29 *Sea-Land Servs., Inc. v. Islamic Republic of Iran*, 6 Iran-U.S. Cl. Trib. Rep. 149, 168 (1984).

30 *Intel Corp. v. Advanced Micro Devices, Inc.*, 542 U.S. 241, 263 n.15 (2004).

But difficulty cannot be allowed to excuse the entire exercise.[31] Commentators have noted that "[i]t would be welcomed not only by the parties but also by the international legal world" if the reasoning of the ICJ's judgments were to explain *how* it had examined, by comparative methods, "the assertion that a general principle of law, having a specified meaning and significance, forms part of binding general international law."[32]

Perhaps more can be done with private international law. In helping to determine the substance of municipal laws applied in cross-border scenarios, private international law scholars, judges, and advocates might be better suited, and better situated, to explicate and elevate this source of law beyond its current state of arcane lore. They frequently scour transnational procedures and rules in the comparative search for commonality. Their reasoned work is another venerable source of international law—subsidiary, though complementary, to the general principles.[33]

Municipal courts are particularly well situated to find and apply general principles of law. International judicial bodies such as the ICJ depend upon the consent of States for their jurisdiction and their legitimacy. ICJ judges are understandably reluctant to find and expressly apply "new" substantive laws—especially those without a formal basis in state consent—lest they be accused of the unauthorized legislation of international law. For investment tribunals, too, which are subject to review and annulment, this is a real consideration. "The suspicion which states, especially those on the losing side, may entertain of indirect expansion of the scope of international law by a tribunal . . . no doubt largely accounts for the failure of the [international courts] . . . to make any significant use of this potentially very fertile source of development in international law."[34] Municipal

31 At least one arbitration case was annulled for that very reason, so the proper explication of the relevant principle as one that is indeed grounded in the positive law of all municipal systems is essential. *See Klöckner Industrie-Anlagen GmbH v. United Republic of Cameroon*, ICSID Case No. ARB/81/2, Award (Oct. 21, 1983), 2 ICSID Rep. 59-61; Decision on Annulment (May 3, 1985), 2 ICSID Rep. 95 (1994).

32 Hermann Mosler, *To What Extent Does the Variety of Legal Systems of the World Influence the Application of the General Principles of Law within the Meaning of Article 38(I)(c) of the Statute of the International Court of Justice?*, *in* INTERNATIONAL LAW AND THE GROTIAN HERITAGE 180 (T.M.C. Asser Instituut ed., 1985).

33 ICJ Statute art. 38(d).

34 Wolfgang Friedmann, *The Uses of "General Principles" in the Development of International Law*, 57 AM. J. INT'L L. 279, 280–81 (1963).

courts, however, are liberated of such concerns because their jurisdiction and authority is relatively stable. In the common law tradition, the discretion to resort to general principles to decide a transnational case is relatively unfettered. In the civil law tradition, that discretion is commonly enshrined in the applicable Civil Code. Because the rule of law is elusive in far too many jurisdictions, it would be a welcome development to see general principles progress and flourish on the domestic plane.

Annex of Cases

This Annex of Cases is intended to serve as a resource by summarizing illustrative decisions from courts and tribunals wherein general principles of law have been identified, explicated, or applied. Not all cases cited in the book appear in this Annex, and this is not a complete catalogue of all of the cases regarding these principles. The decisions highlighted in this Annex should nonetheless serve as a useful starting point for further understanding and study of the specific principles discussed in the book.

The General Principles of Good Faith and Responsibility

A. Good Faith in Contractual Relations

Pacta sunt servanda—agreements are to be observed

Arbitration Regarding the Iron Rhine Railway (Belg. v. Neth), P.C.A., Award, 14 (May 24, 2005) (observing that the principle of *pacta sunt servanda* would prohibit the Netherlands from building a tunnel on Dutch Iron Rhine territory to the extent that it interfered with a right of passage conferred to Belgium by treaty). **89n10, 92n27**

Dispute regarding Navigational and Related Rights (Costa Rica v. Nicar), Judgment, 2009 I.C.J. 213, ¶ 47 (July 13) (endorsing Articles 31 and 32 of the 1969 Vienna Convention on the Law of Treaties as reflecting the rules of customary international law and enforcing a treaty conferring on Costa Rica a right of passage over the San Juan River). **89n10**

Sovereignty over Pulau Ligitan and Pulau Sipadan (Indon. v. Malay), Judgment, 2002 I.C.J. 625, ¶¶ 37-38 (Dec. 17) (endorsing Articles 31 and 32 of the 1969 Vienna Convention on the Law of Treaties as reflecting rules of customary international law and enforcing a treaty containing territorial border delineation regarding Pulau Litigan and Pulau Sipadan). **89n10**

Kasikili/Sedudu Island (Bots. v. Namib), Judgment, 1999 I.C.J. 1045, ¶ 18 (Dec. 13) (II) (endorsing Article 31 of the 1969 Vienna Convention on the Law of Treaties as reflecting the rules of customary international law in order to determine the boundary between Namibia and Botswana as per the terms of a pre-Vienna Convention treaty). **89n10**

Territorial Dispute (Libyan Arab Jamahiriya/Chad), Judgment, 1994 I.C.J. 6, ¶ 41 (Feb. 3) (endorsing Article 31 of the 1969 Vienna Convention on the Law of Treaties as reflecting the rules of customary international law and enforcing a treaty delineating the boundary between Libya and Chad). **89n10, 97n56, 97nn61–62**

General Dynamics Corp. v. Islamic Republic of Iran, Award No. 123-283-3 (Apr. 13, 1984), 5 Iran-U.S. Cl. Trib. Rep. 386, 398 (observing that "general principles of law" obligated General Dynamics to perform its duties under a contract with the Iranian Navy satisfactorily and with due diligence, failing which a breach of contract and reduction in compensation might result). **46n240, 90n16**

Inceysa Vallisoletana, S.L. v. Republic of El Salvador, ICSID Case No. ARB/03/26, ¶¶ 49, IIC 134, 233 (2006) (affirming *pacta sunt servanda* as an internationally accepted principle, applicable to agreements to arbitrate contained within bilateral investment treaties). **2n2, 47–49, 47n245, 89n11, 94n38, 95n44, 96, 96n49, 101–102n83, 132n257, 136, 136n280, 138n294, 184, 185n164, 185n170**

Sapphire International Petroleums, Ltd. v. Nat'l Iranian Oil Co., 1963 Int'l L. Rep. 136, 186 (explaining that *pacta sunt servanda* required that Sapphire receive damages to compensate it for the consideration it would have received if NIOC had fully performed its contractual obligations). **33n177, 90nn16–17, 101n82, 148n357**

LIAMCO v. The Gov't of the Libyan Arab Republic, 1981 Y.B. COMM. ARB. 89, 101-03 (holding that *pacta sunt servanda* is a principle that applies to state-to-state agreements, as well as agreements between sovereign states and private parties). **29n159, 90n16, 90n18, 135n275**

Texaco Overseas Petroleum Co. (TOPCO) v. Gov't of the Libyan Arab Republic, 53 Int'l L. Rep. 420, 461-62 (1979) (holding that *pacta sunt servanda* operates as a "fundamental principle of international law" so as to require the Libyan government to honor its oil concessions with a private, foreign investor, and to preclude the use of sovereign expropriation power as a defense to non-performance of contractual obligations). **4n11, 17, 17n85, 21n112, 22, 22n116, 25n135, 28n152, 29n159, 45, 45n230, 89n11, 90n16, 106n107**.

Nuclear Tests (*New Zealand v. France*), Judgment, I.C.J. Reports 1974, 457, 472-73 (citing *pacta sunt servanda* to support the determination that France's public statements, made with the intent to be bound, obligated it to discontinue its South Pacific nuclear testing). **106n107**

Nuclear Tests (*Australia v. France*), Judgment, I.C.J. Reports 1974, 253, 268 (analogizing the good faith underpinnings of *pacta sunt servanda* to the "binding character of an international obligation assumed by unilateral obligation," so as to permit Australia to rely on statements made by France that it would cease its South Pacific nuclear tests). **90n16, 91n23, 108n117**

Zapata Hermanos Sucesores v. Hearthside Baking Co., 313 F.3d 385, 389 (7th Cir. 2002) (noting that *pacta sunt servanda* required one party to pay contractual debts incurred in its course of business with the other). **90n17, 106n105**

ICC Award No. 5485 (1987), *Bermudan Co. v. Spanish Co.*, XIV Y.B. Comm. Arb. 156, 168 (1989) (referring to *pacta sunt servanda* to support a finding that the Spanish Company must honor its agreement with the Bermudan Company to vote for the distribution of dividends in the joint venture between them). **90n17, 135n275**

ICC Award No. 3540 (1980), *French Contractor v. Yugoslav Contractor*, VII Y.B. Comm. Arb. 124, 128 (1982) (determining that the application of the *lex mercatoria*, as chosen by the arbitrators, was not inconsistent with the principle of *pacta sunt servanda* because the parties chose to defer to the choice of law of the arbitrators in their arbitration clause). **90n17, 101n82**

ICC Award No. 2321 (1974), *Two Companies v. A State Enterprise*, I Y.B. Comm. Arb. 133, 134 (1976) (expressing the view that the State Enterprise's sovereignty did not bar the enforcement of an arbitration agreement by private companies because the principle of *pacta sunt servanda* operated to make such agreements binding). **90n17**

Amco Asia Corp. v. Republic of Indonesia, ICSID Case No. ARB/81/1, Award (Nov. 20, 1984) (applying *pacta sunt servanda* as a long-settled principle of international law—noting its roots in civil, common, and Arabic law—so as to find the Republic of Indonesia liable for revoking Amco's investment authorization). **32n175, 40nn208–9, 41, 41–42n212, 41n210, 42n213, 44n228, 90nn17–18, 94n38, 100n79, 105n101, 120n191, 121n199, 138n294, 145n335, 148n358, 149n359, 149n362, 150n370, 197–98n244**

Desert Lines Projects, LLC v. Republic of Yemen, ICSID Case No. ARB/05/17, Award, ¶ 206 (2008) (citing *pacta sunt servanda* to enforce an agreement to arbitrate before a Yemeni tribunal, whose decision would be determinative as to Yemen's liability for non-payment for a road construction project). **90–91n19, 91n20, 119–20n189, 120n190, 122n203, 124n214, 125n217, 137n289, 198n246, 202n272**

Chilean-Peruvian Accounts Case (1875), *reprinted in* 2 J.B. Moore, History and Digest Of The Arbitrations To Which The U.S. Has Been a Party 2085, 2102 (recognizing, as a corollary principle of *pacta sunt servanda*, that commissioners appointed under a Peruvian-Chilean treaty possessed no authority that did not derive from the treaty itself; modifications of agreements, which change the enforceable obligations of the parties, cannot be made without the parties' consent, thus ensuring that only the original obligations are enforced). **98, 169**

The Oscar Chinn Case, 1934 P.C.I.J. (Ser. A/B, No. 63) 64, 87-88 (holding that Belgium was bound by the Convention of Saint-Germain and would be precluded from employing its sovereign authority as justification to modify or alter those obligations, or to disavow its obligation to respect vested rights, under the principle of *pacta sunt servanda*). **98**

Ambiente Ufficio S.P.A. et al. *v. The Argentine Republic*, ICSID Case No. ARB/08/9, Decision on Jurisdiction and Admissibility, ¶¶ 245-53, 362 (May 2, 2013) (dissenting Opinion of Santiago Torres Bernárdez) (arguing that the majority's finding of jurisdiction over Argentina threatens the very core of *pacta sunt servanda*, which supports the tribunal's jurisdiction only to the extent provided by the parties' consent, as evinced by the BIT). **91n22**

ICC Award No. 5953 (1989), *reprinted in* Sigvard Jarvin, Yves Derains, & Jean-Jeaques Arnaldez, Collection of ICC Arbitral Awards, 1986-1990, 441-42 (1997) (affirming that *pacta sunt servanda* governs the parties' dispute, not by virtue of its moral force alone, but because of its wide acceptance as a binding obligation). **91n23, 92n29**

Obligations should be carried out according to the good faith and mutual intention of the parties at the time the agreement was concluded

ICC Award No. 3131 (1979), IX Y.B. Comm. Arb. 109, 109-10 (1984) (applying the principle of good faith to determine that a French company failed to "maintain[] good commercial relations" with its Turkish business partner, and requiring the French company to pay damages for the latter's loss of business and reputation). **91n23**

Int'l Thunderbird Gaming Corp. v. Mexico, UNCITRAL, Award, ¶¶ 25-29, 31, 45, 46, 77, 123, 169 (Jan. 26, 2006) (separate opinion of Thomas Wälde) (elaborating upon the influence of principles of good faith to affirm that States must honor the legitimate expectations they create by their conduct toward investors, but agreeing that Mexico had not created any legitimate expectations in Thunderbird's gaming operation investments). **6n21, 76n431, 78n439, 78n441, 91n23, 99n70, 126, 126nn222–23, 127n227, 127n230, 129n239, 191–92n205**

Vivendi Universal S.A. v. Argentine Republic, Award, ICSID Case No. ARB/97/3, ¶¶ 7.4.3-4.3 (2007) (explaining that the fair and equitable treatment provision of the France-Argentine Republic BIT should be interpreted, not in isolation as a semantic exercise, but in good faith accordance with its "object and purpose," which was to "create favourable conditions for French investment in Argentina"). **95n43, 98n64, 153n390**

Methanex Corp. v. United States, Methanex Corporation v. United States, UNCITRAL, Final Award, ¶ 16 (Aug. 3, 2005), *reprinted at* 44 I.L.M. 1345 (affirming that treaty interpretation requires more than a semantic exercise but rather an examination of the terms in good faith and in light of the parties' object and purpose). **95n43, 98n64, 181n141, 196n236, 197n237**

Mendel Case, Germ-U.S. Cls. Comm. (1926) VII R.I.A.A. 1926, at 380, 384-87 (limiting the broad compensatory language provided for nations who suffered under "exceptional war measures" taken by Germany because one of the pervasive themes of the treaty, emanating from the language of the treaty as the touchstone of the parties' intent, was also to limit Germany's liability after World War II). **95n45**

Island of Timor (Portugal v. Netherlands) (1914), XI R.I.A.A. 1961, 481, at ¶¶ 20-24 (setting the boundaries of the Island of Timor in accordance with the intention of the Netherlands and Portugal, divined from a series of conventions between the two sovereigns, and going beyond the mere words of the agreements in order to promote good faith between the parties). **95n45**

Mavrommatis Palestine Concessions Case (1924), Collection of Judgments, I.C.J. (Ser. A) No. 2, 19 (deciding upon the more limited interpretation of treaty language because it "harmonized" both potential interpretations in a manner consistent with the intentions of the documents' drafters); Dissenting Opinion by Moore, at 62 (recognizing that a jurisdiction clause contingent upon the inability to reach a negotiated resolution could not, in a good faith understanding of the parties' intention and actions, be understood to allow the wrongdoer to "profess a willingness to negotiate" as a mere sham to purposefully delay the dispute's resolution). **38n199, 95n46, 158n4**

Asian Agricultural Prods. Ltd. v. Sri Lanka, ICSID Case No. ARB/87/3, Award, ¶ 40 (June 27, 1990) (noting that while the intention of the parties will be an essential part of interpreting the treaty, clear language should prevail despite any of the parties' stated intentions). **94n39, 97n57, 97n60, 191–92n205, 192n209, 193n211, 195–196n229**

Polish War Vessels in Danzig Case, PCIJ Adv. Op., A/B. 43, 144-45 (Dec. 11, 1931) (holding that the putative intent of the drafting parties regarding Poland's open access to the sea prior to entering into the Treaty of Versailles could not usurp the clear language of a treaty negotiated in good faith). **94n40**

Regina v. Immigration Officer at Prague Airport ex parte *European Roma Rights Centre*, UKHL 55, ¶ 19 (Dec. 9, 2004) (holding that a State's interpretation of its treaty, even if determined in good faith, still cannot create an obligation beyond that agreed to in the words and language used). **94n41**

Keith Cox v. Canada (Oct. 31, 1994), *reprinted in* Office of the United Nations High Commissioner for Human Rights, *International Covenant on Civil and Political Rights: Selected Decisions of the Human Rights Committee under the Option Protocol*, vol. 5, at 177-78 (2005) (concurring opinion of Messrs. Kurt Herndl and Waleed Sadi) (agreeing that Canada did not violate the Covenant when it extradited Cox, because the good faith interpretation of the words of the treaty provide the only obligations to which Canada is bound, and nothing outside the agreement may, in good faith, be imported into those obligations). **94n41**

Inceysa Vallisoletana S.L. v. Republic of El Salvador, ICSID Case No. ARB/03/26, Award, ¶¶ 177-83 (Aug. 2, 2006) (articulating that the principle of *pacta sunt servanda* and a good faith interpretation of a treaty must take into account consequences that the parties reasonably and legitimately contemplated when concluding it); *id.* ¶¶ 230-33 (noting that, implied in the general principle of *pacta sunt servanda* is the assumption by all contracting parties that contracts will be performed in good faith). **2n2, 47–48n245, 47–49, 89n11, 94n38, 95n44, 96, 96n49, 101n83, 132n157, 136, 136n280, 138n294, 184, 185n164, 185n170**

Amco Asia Corp. v. Republic of Indonesia, ICSID Case No. ARB/81/1, Decision on Jurisdiction, ¶ 14 (Sept. 25, 1983) (noting that, the principle of *pacta sunt servanda* requires treaties and arbitration agreements to be interpreted according to the expressed will of the parties, and the consequences of the commitments that they envisaged). **32n175, 40nn208–9, 41, 41–42n212, 41n210, 42n213, 44n228, 90nn17–18, 94n38, 100n79, 105n101, 120n191, 121n199, 138n294, 145n335, 148n358, 149n359, 149n362, 150n370, 197–98n244**

Territorial Dispute (Libyan Arab Jamahiriya/Chad), Judgment, 1994 I.C.J. Rep. 6, 21-23 (applying the general principle that treaties be interpreted in good faith according to their text and finding that the 1955 Libyan-Franco Treaty of Friendship and Good Neighbourliness provided evidence of the mutual intent between the parties regarding the Libya-Chad border). **89n10, 97n56, 97nn61–62**

Nuclear Tests (Austl. v. Fr), Judgment, 1974 I.C.J. 253, 268 (Dec. 20) (holding that France would be bound by its unilateral declaration that it would cease conduct of nuclear tests in the South Pacific on the basis of the principle of *pacta sunt servanda*). **90n16, 91n23, 108n117**

Fisheries Jurisdiction (Fed. Rep. Ger. v. Ice), Judgment, 1974 I.C.J. 175, ¶ 78 (July 25) (articulating that the principle of good faith governing the negotiation of a fair resolution to a maritime boundary dispute does not simply demand an equitable solution, but an "equitable solution derived from the applicable law"). **103n91**

Interpretation of the Agreement of March 25, 1951 between the WHO and Egypt, Advisory Opinion, 1980 I.C.J. 73, ¶ 43 (Dec. 20) (finding that the "very essence of the legal relationship between a host State and an international organization is a body of mutual obligations of cooperation and good faith," which specifically required Egypt and the WHO to consult and cooperate regarding the logistics of moving the WHO's Regional Office from Egypt, and included the obligation to give reasonable notice terminating that relationship). **89n10**

Legality of the Threat or Use of Nuclear Weapons, Advisory Opinion, 1996 I.C.J. 226, ¶ 99 (July 8) (holding that a treaty that requires "[e]ach of the Parties to . . . undertake[] to pursue negotiations in good faith on effective measures relating to . . . nuclear disarmament" imposes on them "an obligation to achieve a precise result—nuclear disarmament . . .—by adopting a particular course of conduct, namely, the pursuit of negotiations on the matter in good faith"). **89n10**

ICC Award No. 5953, 117 J. DROIT INT'L (CLUNET) 1056, 1060 (1990) (noting that while the principle of *pacta sunt servanda* requires parties to execute their contractual undertakings, it does not govern the modalities of this execution, which are informed by the principle of good faith). **91n23, 92n29**

Interpretation of Peace Treaties between Bulgaria, Hungary and Romania (Second Phase), Advisory Opinion, 1950 I.C.J. 221, 244 (July 18) (dissenting opinion of Judge Read) (disagreeing with the majority on the basis that the treaty was to be interpreted in good faith in order to give force to the dispute settlement mechanism that was the foundation thereof). **96n48**

Appellate Body Report, *Japan—Taxes on Alcoholic Beverages*, AB-1996-2, WT/DS8, 10 & at 9-11, 14-32 11/AB/R (1996) (applying the good faith principle of treaty interpretation to find that Japan's regulation of vodka was discriminatory under the GATT vis-a-vis its regulation of shochu). **97n56**

ICC Award No. 2291 (1975), 103 Clunet 989, 950, 951 (1976) (discussing the obligations of good faith as a general principle of contractual dealings, such that the parties cannot take action that would cause harm to the other person). **96n54**

ICC Award No. 9593 (1998), 10(2) ICC Bull. 107 (1999) (emphasizing that the general principle of good faith requires cooperation among the parties in achieving the "common goals contractually agreed upon"). **96n54**

ICC Award No. 4629 (1989), XVIII Y.B. Comm. Arb. 11, 18 (1993) (referencing the intentions of the parties, as evidenced by their conduct, to determine that the date of the contract was, in fact, earlier than the written "effective date" because of performance and other undertakings that took place prior to that date). **96n54**

Ut res magis valeat quam pereat—let the thing have effect rather than perish

Appellate Body Report, *Japan—Taxes on Alcoholic Beverages*, AB-1996-2, WT/DS8, 10 & 10, 16 11/AB/R (1996) (applying the principle of effectiveness to treaty interpretation of conflicting and ambiguous clauses and finding that Japan's regulation of vodka was discriminatory under the GATT vis-a-vis its regulation of shochu). **97n56**

Appellate Body Report, *Korea—Certain Dairy Products*, AB-1999-8, WT/DS98/AB/R, 24, ¶¶ 80-81 (1990) (applying the principle of effectiveness and reversing the panel's conclusion that rendered part of a treaty's language ineffective). **97n56**

Eli Lilly Do Brazil, Ltda v. Fed. Express Co., 502 F.2d 78, 81-82 (2d Cir. 2007) (emphasizing that the parties' contract should be interpreted to be effective; because US law would give full effect to the agreement, US law controls). **78n442, 147n347**

ICC Award No. 1434 (1975), Clunet 978 (1976) (referring to *ut res magis valeat quam pereat* as a general principle of law, useful for giving a meaningful interpretation to all aspects of the parties' agreement). **97nn58–59, 191–92n205**

ICC Award No. 3460 (1980), Clunet 939, 940 (1981) (giving effect to an ambiguous arbitration clause in order to fulfil the parties' intention to submit disputes to arbitration). **97n58, 98n68**

ICC Award No. 3380 (1980), 7 Y.B. Comm. Arb. 116, 118 (1982) (adopting the principle of effective interpretation to harmonize conflicting choice of law provisions and holding that the drafters of a works and supplies contract intended it to be governed by Syrian law, subject only to general principles of law and justice). **97n59**

ICC Award No. 8331 (1996), Clunet 1041 (1998) (explaining that where an MOU defines both specific terms of the parties' agreement and the parties' intention to enter into subsequent terms at a later stage, the principle of effectiveness means that the parties cannot be released from the latter obligation, but instead must use their best efforts to ensure that such intended terms become specific terms legally binding for each of them). **97n59**

Asian Agricultural Prods. Ltd. v. Sri Lanka, ICSID Case No. ARB/87/3, Award, ¶¶ 40, 52 (June 27, 1990) (referring to the principle of "effectiveness" to hold that the applicable treaty did not impose strict liability upon a host State for failure to provide "protection and security," as it would render meaningless the qualifications and exceptions located in other provisions of the BIT). **94n39, 97n57, 97n60, 191–92n205, 192n209, 193n211, 195–196n229**

Distributor v. Manufacturer, Partial Award, ICC Case No. 7920, XXIII Y.B. Comm. Arb. 80-85 (1993) (explaining that an application of Spanish law that would render the parties' ambiguous arbitration clause null violated the principle of *ut res magis valeat quam pereat*). **97n56**

Territorial Dispute (Libyan Arab Jamahiriya/Chad), Judgment, 1994 I.C.J. Rep., ¶ 51 (stating that when Parties to a treaty set defined borders by reference to other international instruments, rather than by reference to a map, the international principle of "effectiveness" requires giving meaning to those instruments listed by the Parties). **89n10, 97n56, 97nn61–62**

CBA Int'l Development Corp. v. Iran, Award No. 115-928-3 (Mar. 16, 1984), 5 Iran-U.S. Cl. Trib. Rep. 177, 180-81 (1984) (relying on the principle that the parties' intent should be respected by giving meaning to all words contained in their agreement in order to find that the parties had chosen to have their dispute heard by Iranian courts rather than the Iran-U.S. Claims Tribunal). **98n64**

Contra proferentem—the party who drafted an agreement cannot rely on its ambiguity, and any such ambiguity shall be interpreted against that party's interest

First Travel Corp. v. Islamic Repub. of Iran, Award, IUSCT Case No. 206-34-1 (Dec. 3, 1985), XII Y.B. Comm. Arb. 257, 258 (finding support in *contra proferentum* for the tribunal's decision that a contractual clause should be interpreted against the clause's drafter). **98n67**

ICC Award No. 7110 (1995), 10 ICC Bull. No. 2, 39, 44 (1999) (noting the applicability of the "widely accepted" principle of *contra proferentum* when deciding whether the parties' agreements support the tribunal's jurisdiction). **98n68, 150n368**

Cysteine Case, China CIETAC Arbitration Proceedings § 3(5) (Jan. 7, 2000) (finding that the seller's position as the drafter of a disputed provision meant that, because both parties' interpretations of the provision made sense, the clause should be construed against the seller in favor of the buyer). **98n68**

ICC Award No. 3460 (1980), Clunet 939 (1981) (finding that ambiguous provisions of a contract should be construed against the party who wrote them). **97n58, 98n68**

Int'l Thunderbird Gaming Corp. v. Mexico, UNCITRAL, Award, ¶¶ 50-51 (Jan. 26, 2006) (separate opinion of Thomas Wälde) (expressing the opinion that *contra proferentum* supports the conclusion that public authorities should bear the risk of ambiguities as the drafters of statutes and regulations, rather than those, such as private investors, who rely upon the provisions as drafted). **6n21, 76n431, 78n439, 78n441, 91n23, 99n70, 126, 126nn222–23, 127n227, 127n230, 129n239, 191–92n205**

Ceskoslovenska Obchodni Banka v. Slovak Republic, ICSID Case No. ARB/97/4, Decision of the Tribunal on Objections to Jurisdiction, ¶ 51 (May 24, 1999) (dismissing the respondent's argument that *contra proferentum* applies in its favor because the "Agreement was the subject of various drafts due to changes requested by Respondent"). **99n71, 121n199**

Parties can be held to contractual obligations when they conduct themselves as if a contract had entered into force

Futura Trading Inc. v. Nat'l Iranian Oil Co., Award No. 263-324-3 (Oct. 30, 1986), 13 Iran-U.S. Cl. Trib. Rep. 99, 112-13 (holding that the parties had conducted themselves in such a manner as to establish the existence of a contract for the purchase of electrical cables, despite the lack of a written agreement). **99nn73–74**

DIC of Delaware, Inc. v. Tehran Redevelopment Corp., Award No. 176-255-3 (Apr. 26, 1985), 8 Iran-U.S. Cl. Trib. Rep. 144, 161, 162 (noting that part performance of a contract can be evidence that the parties intended to make an agreement under international law, even if the applicable Iranian law prohibited oral contracts over a certain monetary threshold). **99n73, 100n75**

Framatome-Award, YCA 1983, at 94, 101 *et seq.* (finding that a party who acted as if a contract existed, including several months of performance of contractual duties, could not in good faith deny the existence of a contract). **99n74**

Kimberly-Clark Corp. v. Bank Markazi Iran, Award No. 46-57-2 (May 25, 1983), 2 Iran-U.S. Cl. Trib. Rep. 334, 338-39 (determining that Novzohour owed Kimberly-Clark royalties because the license agreement between the parties was a valid contract due, in part, to the fact that Novzohour's actions over the course of two years "constituted an unequivocal ratification of the agreement"). **99n73**

Iowa St. Univ. v. Ministry of Culture, Award No. 276-B72-2 (Dec. 16, 1986), 13 Iran-U.S. Cl. Trib. Rep. 271, 273-75 (explaining that the Embassy of Iran's conduct, in the form of a verbal offer to pay for the education of an Iranian student at the University of Iowa, was sufficient to establish a contract between the parties, and therefore the Ministry of Culture must pay its debt under that contract). **99n73**

Cal-Maine Foods, Inc. v. Iran, 6 Iran-U.S. Cl. Trib. Rep. 52, 61-62 (1984) (holding that Cal-Maine and an Iranian company had acted upon the provisions of a letter of intent, which included specific obligations, so as to demonstrate the creation of a contract). **99n73**

Chas. T. Main Int'l, Inc. v. Khuzestan Water & Power Auth., Award No. ITL 23-120-2 (July 27, 1983), 3 Iran-U.S.C.T.R. 156, 162 (holding that a contract existed based on the buyer's conduct and correspondence, which evinced its expectation that the seller would provide services in either Boston or Iran). **99n73**

R.N. Pomeroy v. Iran, Award No. 51-41-3 (June 8, 1983), 2 Iran-U.S. Cl. Trib. Rep. 372, 380 (recognizing as both a general principle of law and part of the Iranian code that the Iranian Navy could not deny the existence of a contract with R.N. Pomeroy when its actions were to the contrary, i.e., making payments and accepting R.N. Pomeroy's services). **99n73**

Pepsico, Inc. v. Iran, Award No. 260-18-1 (Oct. 13, 1986), 13 Iran-U.S. Cl. Trib. Rep. 3 (finding that Iranian companies owed Pepsico money under a loan because those companies received and enjoyed the loan proceeds). **46n240, 99n73**

Good faith implies a duty to maintain the status quo in juridical relations

Armed Activities on the Territory of the Republic of the Congo (Democratic Republic of the Congo v. Rwanda), Jurisdiction of the Court and Admissibility of the Application, Judgment, I.C.J. Rep. ¶ 8 (2006) (declaration of Judge Elaraby) (noting that States are required to settle their disputes "peacefully" and in accordance with international law, and through which the obligation to maintain the status quo is implied). **100n77, 194n220**

Electricity Co. of Sofia & Bulgaria (Belgium v. Bulgaria), Judgment, 1939, P.C.I.J. (Ser A/B) No. 79, 194, 199 (Dec. 5) (indicating that Bulgaria should respect the generally accepted principle that parties should not to permit any action that would prejudice the rights of other parties while suit is pending). **100n78, 164n38**

Holiday Inns S.A. and others v. Morocco, ICSID Case No. ARB/72/1, Decision on Provisional Measures (July 2, 1972) (confirming the jurisdiction of ICSID Tribunals to rule on requests for provisional measures pending jurisdictional objections). **100n79**

Amco Asia Corp. et al. *v. Republic of Indonesia*, ICSID Case No. ARB/81/1, Decision on Request for Provisional Measures, at 412 (Dec. 9, 1983), 1 ICSID Rep. 410 (1993) (holding that a press campaign by one of the parties does not necessarily affect the rights in dispute in the arbitration, notwithstanding the "good and fair practical rule" that parties to a legal dispute should refrain from aggravating or exacerbating the situation). **32n175, 40nn208–9, 41, 41–42n212, 41n210, 42n213, 44n228, 90nn17–18, 94n38, 100n79, 105n101, 120n191, 121n199, 138n294, 145n335, 148n358, 149n359, 149n362, 150n370, 197–98n244**

Plama Consortium Limited v. Republic of Bulgaria, ICSID Case No. ARB/03/24, Order, ¶¶ 38-40 (Sept. 6, 2005) (explaining that provisional measures are often necessary to preserve the status quo, but that such measures are limited to those rights in dispute—namely, damage claims under the Energy Charter Treaty—so ordering a stay of unrelated proceedings is unavailable). **49n256, 100–101n79, 136, 136n281, 184**

Occidental v. Ecuador, ICSID Case No. ARB/06/11, Decision on Provisional Measures, ¶¶ 60-61, 96 (Aug. 17, 2007) (denying Occidental's request for provisional measures because such measures are only available "to avoid aggravation of a dispute," not to mitigate damages). **100–101n79, 116, 116n165, 118**

City Oriente, Ltd. v. Ecuador, ICSID Case No. ARB/06/21, Decision on Provisional Measures, ¶ 55 (Nov. 19, 2009) (granting provisional measures to "prohibit[] any action that affects the disputed rights, aggravates the dispute, frustrates the effectiveness of the award or entails having either party take justice into their own hands"). **100–101n79**

Burlington Resources Inc. v. Republic of Ecuador, ICSID Case No. ARB/08/5, Proc. Order No. 1, ¶¶ 61-68 (June 29, 2009) (holding that Burlington was entitled to provisional measures to preserve the status quo, even if that means the tribunal interferes with Ecuador's ability to enforce its laws, under the theory that by ratifying the ICSID Convention Ecuador assented to certain intrusions by an ICSID tribunal). **100–101n80**

Quiborax S.A. v. Bolivia, ICSID Case No. ARB/06/2, Decision on Provisional Measures, ¶¶ 133-38 (Feb. 26, 2010) (ordering Bolivia to suspend domestic criminal proceedings that were pending related to the arbitration, in order to preserve the status quo and the procedural integrity of the ICSID proceedings). **100–101, 101n80**

Biwater Gauff v. Tanzania, ICSID Case No. ARB/05/22, Proc. Order No. 1, ¶¶ 84-88 (Mar. 31, 2006) (ordering that Tanzania take certain provisional measures in order to ensure that material evidence is preserved). **101n81, 147, 147n347**

AGIP S.p.A. v. People's Republic of the Congo, ICSID Case No. ARB/77/1, Decision, at 310 (Jan. 18, 1979) (ordering provisional measures to preserve access to and integrity of certain evidence). **101n81**

Clausula rebus sic stantibus—binding so long as circumstances remain the same

ICC Award No. 3540 (1980), VII Y.B. COMM. ARB. 124, 131-33 (1982) (affirming that *exceptio inadimplenti contractus*, that is, the right to withhold contractual performance in light of the counter-party's continuing breach, is a generally accepted principle of law, but one that is temporary and extinguishes once the counter-party has performed). **90n17, 101n82**

Sapphire Int'l Petrol., Ltd. v. Nat'l Iranian Oil Company, Ad Hoc Tribunal, 35 Int'l L. Rep. 136, 182-87 (1963) (finding that one party was justified in suspending its performance due to the uncertainty of its counter-party's performance, particularly in light of the risks undertaken by the first). **33n177, 90nn16–17, 101n82, 148n357**

Ministry of Def. and Support for Armed Forces of the Islamic Rep. of Iran v. Cubic Def. Sys., Inc., 65 F.3d 1091, 1101 (9th Cir. 2011) (acknowledging the general principle that performance may be excused when it becomes impracticable). **104n94**

Questech v. Ministry of Nat'l Def. of the Islamic Republic of Iran, Award No. 191-59-1 (Sept. 20, 1985), 9 Iran-U.S. Cl. Trib. Rep. 107 (applying the doctrine of *rebus sic stantibus* to limit Iran's damages owed to Questech to present harm and not future profits because Iran's need for highly sensitive intelligence software was drastically altered by the Iranian revolution—a changed circumstance Questech could have readily foreseen); *see also id.* at 286 (separate opinion of Howard M. Holtzmann) (criticizing the tribunal's application of *rebus sic stantibus* to a situation where the "changed circumstances" were within the control of the respondent). **46n240, 102n87**

Hungarian State Enter. v. Jugoslavenski Naftovod (Yugoslav Crude Oil Pipeline), Award, Ad Hoc Arbitration, IX Y.B. Comm. Arb. 69, 70 (1984) (determining that *rebus sic stantibus* did not excuse performance because the 1970s oil crisis, the alleged change in circumstance, was not a "social catastrophe," but a foreseeable market event). **102n87**

Scafom International BV v. Lorraine Tubes S.A.S., Belgium Court of Cassation [Supreme Court] (June 19, 2009) (finding that CISG Art. 79(1), which governed the contract for the sale of steel tubes, required buyer to renegotiate the price of steel in good faith with seller after the price of steel rose unexpectedly by 70%, causing severe hardship on the seller). **102n88**

ICC Award No. 1512, I Y.B. Comm. Arb., 128, 128-29 (1971) (explaining that while *rebus sic stantibus* is a generally accepted principle of law, it is an extreme derogation from the principle of sanctity of contract, and that a mere change in circumstance, rather than a change in the nature of the underlying obligation, was not enough to excuse an obligation). **102n86, 103n91, 122n202**

Fisheries Jurisdiction Case (United Kingdom v. Iceland), Jurisdiction of the Court, I.C.J. Reports 21, ¶¶ 35-40 (Feb. 2, 1973) (explaining that although Iceland's invocation of "changed circumstances," namely, increased exploitation of fishing waters and declining vital fishing stocks, could alter the terms of treaty obligations if the change was a fundamental one, such principle could not alter the jurisdiction of the Tribunal to adjudicate that obligation). **5, 5n17, 108n117**

Vine Wax Case, Bundesgerichtshof, Civil Panel VIII, CLOUT Case No. 271 (Germany, Mar. 24, 1999) (holding that the defect in the seller's vine wax was not an impediment beyond the seller's control, and could not therefore excuse its performance under CISG Art. 79(1)). **103n91**

Powder Milk Case, Bundesgerichtshof (Germany Jan. 9, 2002) (stating that the seller failed to carry its burden to demonstrate that the nonconformity of the powdered milk it sold was due to an impediment beyond its control, and that without such a showing, the court need not decide if CISG Art. 79(1) permits excuse regarding the nonconformity of goods delivered). **103n91**

Sempra Energy Int'l v. Argentine Republic, ICSID ARB/02/16, Award, ¶ 353 (Sept. 28, 2007) (explaining that, by preventing a State from invoking necessity as an excuse where it has contributed to the state of necessity, the tribunal merely gave expression to the general principle of law which prevents a party from taking legal advantage of its own fault). **102–3n89, 138nn292–93, 150n371**

The occurrence of unforeseen events that renders performance impossible constitutes force majeure, and is a valid excuse for the non-performance of a contract

Anaconda-Iran, Inc. v. Iran, Interlocutory Award No. ITL 65-167-3 (Dec. 10, 1986), 13 Iran-U.S. Cl. Trib. Rep. 199, 211 (explaining that force majeure was a general principle of law, not dependent upon consent of the parties or a contractual provision, but upon changed factual circumstances after the contract's entry into force; the claimant was thereby justified in suspending the performance of its services due to the developing situation in Iran in the 1970s). **103n92**

Sylvania Technical Sys., Inc. v. Iran, Award No. 180-64-1 (27 June 1985), 8 Iran-U.S. Cl. Trib. Rep. 298 (accepting Iran's claim of force majeure as to some events, but not others, because the circumstances outside of Iran's control causing both parties to suspend their performance, i.e., the Iranian Revolution, only existed for a certain period of time). **46n239, 103n92, 104n95, 149n360**

Queens Office Tower Ass'n (QUOTA) v. Iran Nat'l Airlines Corp., 2 Iran-U.S.C.T.R. 246, 254 (1983) (applying New York law to determine that Iran Air's lease of office space from QUOTA was frustrated by sovereign acts of the United States, which prevented Iran Air from paying rent; as a result, Iran was excused from its payment obligations). **46n239, 103n92**

Am. Bell Int'l, Inc. v. Islamic Republic of Iran, Award No. 37-172-1 (Apr. 15, 1983), 12 Iran-U.S. Cl. Trib. Rep. 170, 187, 193-96 (reducing the amount of damages Iran owed to AT&T for termination of a contract by the percentage of loss attributable to force majeure, where the contract contained a force majeure clause). **46n239, 103n92, 104n95**

ICC Award Nos. 3099 & 3100, VII Y.B. Comm. Arb. 87, 88-91 (1982) (holding that the defendants failed to demonstrate that they were excused from payment by virtue of force majeure because they should have been aware that the economic situation in Algeria was unstable and could prevent them from getting foreign currency to pay their obligations under the contract). **103n93**

ICC Award No. 4462, *Nat'l Oil Co. v. Libyan Sun Oil Co.*, Force majeure, XVI Y.B. Comm. Arb. 54 ¶ 26, 31, 48-50 (1985 & 1987) (determining that Sun Oil's assertion of force majeure failed because neither the Reagan administration's policies restricting U.S. passports to Libya nor the export-license regulations made it impossible for Sun Oil to continue working at the time when it stopped progress on the well project). **103n93**

Kel Kim Corp. v. Cent. Mkts., 70 N.Y.2d 900, 901-03 (1987) (holding that a commercial tenant could not assert impossibility to excuse its failure to secure an insurance policy within the terms of the lease because the "inability to procure and maintain requisite coverage could have been foreseen and guarded against when it specifically undertook that obligation in the lease, and therefore the obligation cannot be excused on this basis"). **103n93**

Gould Mktg. v. Ministry of Defense, Interlocutory Award No. ITL 24-49-2 (July 27, 1983), 3 Iran-U.S. Cl. Trib. Rep. 147, 153-54 (holding that the parties' contract was terminated by a force majeure—*viz.* the Islamic revolution—which prevented Gould from providing goods and services, and prevented Iran from making the contractual payments). **104n94**

Int'l Schs. Servs., Inc. v. Nat'l Iranian Copper Indus., Award No. 194-111-1 (Oct. 10, 1985), 9 Iran-U.S.C.T.R. 187 (explaining that force majeure consists of "social and economic forces beyond the power of the state to control through the exercise of due diligence," and excusing the obligation to operate schools because of "strikes, riots and other civil strife in the course of the Islamic Revolution"). **104n94**

Blount Bros. Corp. v. Iran, Award No. 215-52-1 (Mar. 6, 1986), 10 Iran-U.S. Cl. Trib. Rep. 56 (holding that a shortage of cement was a "classic" force majeure, and that the Iranian housing authority could not be held liable for the increased costs of cement, even though the government of Iran took over the cement industry). **104n94**

Exxon Research & Eng'g Co. v. Iran, Award No. 308-155-3 (June 9, 1987), 15 Iran-U.S. Cl. Trib. Rep. 3, ¶¶ 30-34 (holding that Exxon's agreement with Iran to provide professional research and program planning in the area of gasoline, asphalt, and related fields was suspended due to force majeure when Exxon personnel left Iran due to civil disturbances). **203n1**

Int'l Tech. Prod. Corp. v. Iran, Partial Award, Award No. 186-302-3, WL 324049 (1985) at 10-12 (finding that force majeure excused claimant from its performance under the contract because the events of the Islamic revolution expelled the company from Iran). **104n95**

Amoco Int'l Fin. Corp. v. Iran, Award No. 310-56-3 (14 July 1987), 15 Iran-U.S. Cl. Trib. Rep. 189 (holding that a joint venture agreement whereby claimant would provide various refined natural gas products was suspended by force majeure during the Islamic revolution, but that the agreement survived the later civil unrest conditions, rather than being entirely terminated by the force majeure's perpetuation). **104n95, 149n364**

Reparation is a necessary consequence of a party's failure to fulfill an agreement

Chorzow Factory (Germany v. Poland), Judgment No. 8, 1927 P.C.I.J. 5, 21 (June 1927) (holding that Article 23, paragraph 1, of the Geneva Convention gave the P.C.I.J. jurisdiction not only over disputes but also over the available remedies because it is "a principle of international law that the breach of an engagement involves an obligation to make reparation in an adequate form"). **8n38, 14, 14n70, 105n101, 106n106, 107n111, 130–31, 131n248, 148n357, 197n240, 200n265**

Amco Asia Corp. et al. *v. Republic of Indonesia*, ICSID Case No. ARB/81/1, Award, ¶¶ 265-68 (Nov. 20, 1984) (noting that "the principles governing damages for contractual liability hardly leave room for discussion," such that the breaching party is required to "compensate the whole prejudice," that is loss suffered and the expected profits not obtained). **32n175, 40nn208–9, 41, 41–42n212, 41n210, 42n213, 44n228, 90nn17–18, 94n38, 100n79, 105n101, 120n191, 121n199, 138n294, 145n335, 148n358, 149n359, 149n362, 150n370, 197–98n244**

Enron Corp. and Ponderosa Assets, L.P. v. Argentine Republic, ICSID Case No. ARB/01/03, Award, ¶ 360 (May 22, 2007) (being guided, in the absence of an agreed form of restitution for breach of the fair and equitable treatment standard, by the general principle of law that compensation should undo the material harm inflicted by a breach of an international obligation, and awarding the claimant for the difference in the fair market value of the investment as a result of the breach). **105n101, 106n107, 138n292**

Fedax N.V. v. Republic of Venezuela, ICSID Case No. ARB/96/3, Award, ¶ 30 (Mar. 9, 1998) (espousing general principles of law as part of a legal framework for determining the quantum of compensation owed for Venezuela's suspension of payments on promissory notes that it had issued). **105n100**

Zapata Hermanos Sucesores v. Hearthside Baking Co., 313 F.3d 385, 385-90 (7th Cir. 2002) (noting, as an ancillary principle to *pacta sunt servanda*, that the purpose of contracts is to create a system whereby damages caused by a breach of promise are to be repaid). **90n17, 106n105**

CRCICA Award No. 6/1985, in *Mohie Eldin I. Alam Eldin*, Arbitral Awards of the Cairo Reg'l Centre of Int'l Comm. Arb. 189, 190 (The Hague 2000) (noting that it is an "established principle of law" that the party in breach owes damages for the losses which were foreseeable, including loss profits, which in this case resulted from the respondent's breach of an agency agreement in favor of the claimant to provide building materials to an African State). **107n108**

Himpurna Cal. Energy, Ltd. v. Republic of Indonesia, Interim & Final Award, XXVII Y.B. Comm. Arb. 11, 205 (1999) (noting that damages are the remedy for breach of contract and that Indonesia had breached its contract with Himpurna when it failed to purchase energy as promised in an Energy Sales Contract). **188–89n190**

Rainbow Warrior Case (New Zealand v. France), Apr. 30, 1990 (United Nations) in XX Reports of International Arbitral Awards 215, 268-72 (2006) (determining that New Zealand's demand of specific performance of France's obligations to exile certain French agents for wrongful acts committed against New Zealand was within the tribunal's power, but nevertheless inappropriate in the circumstances). **106n107**

Ioan Micula v. Romania, ICSID Case No. ARB/05/20, Award, ¶ 1309 (Dec. 11, 2013) (explaining that the tribunal's "powers include all of those required to provide effective remedy in order to redress the injuries suffered," including non-pecuniary relief). **106n107**

Karaha Bodas Company L.L.C. v. Pertamina and PT. PLN (Persero), Int'l Arb. Rep., Mar. 2001, at C-2 ("[I]n case of breach of contract, the prejudiced party is entitled to damages. This [is a] general principle of law, which is part of Indonesian law. . . . Consequently, since the Respondents have been found in breach of their contractual obligations . . . they are liable for the damages resulting thereof"). **107n108**

B. Abuse of Rights and the Related Principle of Proportionality

Acts taken under the pretense of law, but for an illicit or dishonest purpose, constitute an abuse of rights

Anglo-Norwegian Fisheries Case (United Kingdom v. Norway), 1951 I.C.J. Rep. 116, 141-42 (holding generally that, when demarcating maritime boundaries, one must measure baselines according to the general direction of the coast, except in cases where such line-drawing is constitutes a "manifest abuse" of the right to do so). **5, 5n17, 103n91, 108nn117–18, 123n207**

La Bretagne Arbitration (Canada v. France), 82 Int'l L. Rep. 590, ¶ 28 (1986) (holding generally that treaty rights should not be exercised in an abusive manner but instead with "restraint and moderation . . . and in co-operating in the settlement of any disputes arising out of their exercise"). **108n119**

Waguih Elie George Siag & Clorinda Vecchi v. Arab Republic of Egypt, ICSID Case No. ARB/05/15, Decision on Jurisdiction, ¶¶ 119, 125, 213 (Apr. 11, 2007) (declining to assess the claimant's argument that Egypt's inconsistent application of its nationality law for the sole purpose of evading its international obligations constituted an abuse of rights under international law). **108n115, 188n189**

Saipem S.p.A. v. The People's Republic of Bangladesh, ICSID Case No. ARB/05/07, Award, ¶ 160 (June 30, 2009) (finding that even when a Bangladeshi court had discretionary and supervisory jurisdiction over the arbitration process, and could have legitimately revoked an arbitrator's authority in a case of misconduct, it constitutes an abuse of rights to use that jurisdiction to revoke arbitrators for reasons wholly unrelated with such misconduct). **108n115, 108n120, 191–92n205, 193n211**

Arbitration CAS 2002/O/410, *The Gibraltar Football Association (GFA)/Union des Associations Européennes de Football (UEFA)*, Award, 13 (Oct. 7, 2003) (holding that where a sports association has a duty to accept new members if they fulfill all statutory conditions to that effect, any exclusion that it is not grounded on objective and justified reasons is abusive and thus invalid). **108n121, 124n214**

United States—Import Prohibition of Certain Shrimp and Shrimp Products, WTO Case Nos. 58 (and 61), ¶¶ 156-59 (adopted Nov. 6, 1998) (where a treaty provision allows States to impose trade measures that would otherwise conflict with the broader aims of the treaty, that allowance must not be exercised in a manner which "would constitute . . . a disguised restriction" on those aims: "To permit one member to abuse or misuse its right to invoke an exception would be effectively to allow that member to degrade its own treaty obligations as well as to devalue the treaty rights of other members"). **92n27**

Case C-110/99 *Emsland-Stärke GmbH v. Hauptzollanmt Hamburg-Jonas* [2000] ECR I-1569 ¶¶ 43, 53, 59 (finding an intention on the part of an exporter to artificially create conditions to obtain a legal benefit, such as by selling a product into a non-member State and then re-importing the same to obtain export refunds, constitutes an abuse of rights). **110n128**

Case C-255/02 *Halifax plc, Leeds Permanent Development Services Ltd., Country Wide Property Investments Ltd v. Commissioners of Customs & Excise*, 2006 ECR I-1609 ¶¶ 69, 80, 85 (holding that transactions "essentially" conceived to recover input VAT under an EU Directive, with no independent business purpose and contrary to the purposes of the VAT Directive, constitutes an abuse of rights, thereby justifying the denial of the input VAT benefits). **110n128**

Case 321/05, *Kofoed* [2007] ECR I-5795, ¶ 38 (holding that while an exchange of shares is not normally taxed under a certain EU Directive, this advantage could be denied where the transactions were "carried out not in the context of normal commercial operations, but solely for the purpose of wrongfully obtaining advantages provided for by Community law"). **110n129**

Phoenix Action, Ltd. v. Czech Republic, ICSID Case No. ARB/06/6, Award, ¶ 143 (Apr. 15, 2009) (holding that where a claimant made an "investment . . . not for the purpose of engaging in economic activity, but for the sole purpose of bringing international litigation against the Czech Republic," and thereby transform a "pre-existing domestic dispute into an international dispute subject to ICSID arbitration," it has committed abuse of rights and its investment "cannot be a protected investment under the ICSID system"). **111n133, 111n137**

Cementownia "Nowa Huta" S.A. v. Republic of Turkey, ICSID Case No. ARB (AF)/06/2, Award, ¶ 159 (Sept. 17, 2009) (finding that a costs award was the appropriate sanction against a party that had committed an abuse of rights and abuse of process by claiming to be an investor, by fabricating a share purchase transaction in order to achieve investor status and take advantage of treaty protections). **111n133**

PSEG Global Inc. et al. *v. Republic of Turkey*, ICSID Case No. ARB/02/5, Decision on Jurisdiction, ¶ 247 (June 4, 2004) (finding that where the Turkish Ministry of Energy and Natural Resources made demands for renegotiation of the claimant's contract—as it was permitted to do by law—but where those demands went to aspects of the contract that were "far beyond . . . [its] authority," the Ministry has committed an abuse of rights). **111, 111n135**

Metalclad Corporation v. The United Mexican States, ICSID Case No. ARB(AF)/97/1, Award, ¶ 86 (Aug. 30, 2000) (holding that where a municipal government denied the claimant's application for a construction permit on the basis of alleged "environmental impact considerations" but its statutory authority only extended to "appropriate construction considerations," it has committed an abuse of right). **111, 111n136, 127n229, 128n238, 153–54n390, 163, 163n34**

ADC Affiliate Ltd. v. Republic of Hungary, ICSID Case No. ARB/03/16, Award, ¶ 384 (Oct. 2, 2006) (holding that even where a respondent State argues that its actions taken under the law were necessary to the government's transport strategy and harmonization with EU law, where it fails to substantiate such arguments with "convincing facts or legal reasoning," an abuse of rights may be found: a "mere reference to 'public interest' can[not] magically" justify the invocation of a right that is otherwise abusive). **112n139, 121–22n199, 125n215, 126n220**

S.D. Myers Inc. v. Gov't of Canada, UNCITRAL, Partial Award, ¶ 152 (Nov. 13, 2000) (finding that where the respondent State argues that its import ban was "necessary to protect human, animal or plant life," but the documentary record as a whole clearly indicates that the ban was intended primarily to protect the State's domestic industry from foreign competition, that State commits an abuse of rights). **77n438, 112–13, 112n42, 145–46n339, 145n335**

Técnicas Medioambientales Tecmed, S.A. v. The United Mexican States, ICSID Case No. ARB (AF)/00/2, Award, ¶ 98 (May 29, 2003) (determining that where a State refuses to renew a permit due to "the protection of the environment and public health," but the record evidence shows that the State's primary reason for denying the renewal was actually its concern for "social or political circumstances . . . and the pressure [being] exerted on municipal and state authorities," that State commits an abuse of rights). **115n162, 117n168, 128n233, 194n215**

Sovereign and private acts must be proportionate to the legitimate aim pursued

Técnicas Medioambientales Tecmed, S.A. v. The United Mexican States, ICSID Case No. ARB (AF)/00/2, Award, ¶ 149 (May 29, 2003) (finding that the denial of a license to operate a landfill was disproportionate to the reasons proffered by the State justifying its decision). **115n162, 117n168, 128n233, 194n215**

James and Others v. United Kingdom, ECHR Case No. 8793/79, Judgment of the Grand Chamber, ¶ 50 (1986) (holding that a mechanism which transfers property to a tenant with less than full compensation to the landowner is not necessarily a disproportionate legislative act when passed with the public interest and aims of economic reform in mind). **115n161**

Lingens v. Austria, ECHR Case No. 9815/82, Judgment of the Grand Chamber, ¶ 47 (1986) (holding that a conviction for publishing articles criticizing a political figure for defamation when the truth of the statements had been proven was not "necessary in a democratic society . . . for the protection of the reputation . . . of others" and was thereby "disproportionate to the legitimate aim pursued"). **115n161**

Azurix Corp. v. The Argentine Republic, ICSID Case No. ARB/01/12, Award, ¶¶ 311-30 (July 14, 2006) (observing that the standard for determining proportionality "provide[s] useful guidance for purposes of determining whether regulatory actions would be expropriatory and give rise to compensation"). **115n162**

Occidental Petroleum Corporation and Occidental Exploration and Production Company v. Republic of Ecuador, ICSID Case No ARB/06/11, Award, ¶ 445 (Oct. 5, 2012) (holding that when the respondent State terminated an entire oil participation agreement valued at many hundreds of millions of dollars in response to the claimants' failure to receive advance state approval for a farmout agreement—a breach from which the State "did not suffer any quantifiable loss"—the punishment is "out of proportion to the wrongdoing alleged"). **100–101n79, 116, 116n165, 118**

Thailand—Restrictions on Importation of and Internal Taxes on Cigarettes, WTO Dispute Settlement Body Case No. DS10/R–37S/200, Report of the Panel, ¶ 75 (Nov. 7, 1990) (finding that, in measuring the proportionality of a government measure, restrictions imposed on the importation of cigarettes may be deemed "necessary" so long as there were no other measures that the State could "reasonably be expected to employ to achieve its [stated] objectives"). **117, 117n173**

Korea—Measures Affecting Imports of Fresh, Chilled and Frozen Beef, WTO Case No. WT/DS161/AB/R, WT/DS169/AB/R), Appellate Body Report, ¶ 164 (Dec. 11, 2000) (noting that whether a trade restriction is a disproportionate measure to take against deceptive practices depends upon a weighing and balancing of factors including the effectiveness of the measure in achieving its purpose, the importance of the interests protected by the measure, and the impact of the measure on trade). **117nn172–73**

Appellate Body Report, Brazil—Measures Affecting Imports of Retreaded Tyres, ¶¶ 141-44, WT/DS332/AB/R (Dec. 3, 2007) (finding, after "weigh[ing] and balanc[ing]" the trade restrictiveness of an import ban on retreaded tyres against its stated objectives, and taking into account the importance of the underlying interests or values, that none of the less-restrictive alternatives were "reasonably available" and thus the measure was not disproportionate to its aim to protect human life or health). **117n172**

Admission of a State to the United Nations (Charter, Art. 4), Advisory Opinion, 1948 I.C.J. 57, 80 (May 28) (individual opinion of Judge Azevedo) (noting that every "legal system involves limitations and is founded on definite rules which are always ready to reappear as the constant element of the construction, whenever the field of action of discretionary principles, adopted in exceptional circumstances, is overstepped"). **118n181**

C. Estoppel: *Allegans Contraria Non Est Audiendus*

A person making contradictory statements is not to be heard

Desert Line Projects LLC v. Republic of Yemen, ICSID Case No. ARB/05/17, Award, ¶¶ 119-20, 207 (Feb. 6, 2008) (acknowledging that estoppel is a "deeply rooted general principle of law," and holding that a government should be estopped from raising violations of its own law as a jurisdictional defense when it knowingly overlooked them and endorsed an investment which was not in compliance with its law). **90–91n19, 91n20, 119–20n189, 120n190, 122n203, 124n214, 125n217, 137n289, 198n246, 202n272**

Temple of Preah Vihear (Cambodia v. Thailand), Judgment of June 15, 1962, 6, 30 & separate opinion of Vice-President Alfaro, 39, 43 (acknowledging that the principle of estoppel, "known to the world since the days of the Romans, is one of the 'general principles of law recognized by civilized nations,'" and will not allow a State to take a certain position when it had "enjoyed . . . benefits" from a contrary position, and another State had relied on that contrary position). **11n55, 106n107, 119n189, 120n193, 121, 121n198, 123–24n209, 124, 193, 193n214**

North Sea Continental Shelf Cases, 1969 I.C.J. Rep. 100, 120-21 (separate opinion of Judge Fouad Ammoun) (observing that estoppel "flowing from a unilateral legal act, or inferred from the conduct or attitude of the person to whom it is to be opposed . . . is numbered among the general principles of law accepted by international law as forming part of the law of nations"). **5, 5n16, 10n46, 10n49, 10n51, 119–20n189**

Davis v. Wakelee, 156 U.S. 680, 689 (1895) (holding that, "where a party assumes a certain position in a legal proceeding, and succeeds in maintaining that position, he may not thereafter, simply because his interests have changed, assume a contrary position, especially if it be to the prejudice of the party who has acquiesced in the position formerly taken by him"). **122n202**

S. S. "Lisman," Disposal of pecuniary claims arising out of the recent war (1914-1918) (*United States v. Great Britain*, Oct. 5, 1937), U.N. Reports of Int'l Arb. Awards, vol. III, 1767, 1790 (holding that the position deliberately taken by a party in an earlier proceeding—*viz.* that the seizure of the goods and the detention of the ship were lawful—thereby "prevented [it] from recovering there or here upon the claim he now stands on, that these acts were unlawful, and constitute the basis of his claim"). **122nn203–4**

Shufeldt claim (Guatemala v. USA, July 24, 1930), U.N. Reports of Int'l Arb. Awards, vol. III, 1079, 1094) (finding that Guatemala, which for six years recognized the validity of a contract and received benefits thereunder, as well as allowed the claimant to continue to spend money on its performance, was precluded from denying its validity, even despite the fact that the contract had not been officially approved by the Guatemalan legislature). **122, 123n205**

Case of the Atlantic and Hope Insurance Companies v. Ecuador (case of the schooner Mechanic) Commission established under the Convention concluded between the United States of America and Ecuador on January 25, 1862, U.N. Reports of Int'l Arb. Awards, vol. XXIX, 108-14 (opinion of Commissioner Hassaurek) (holding that, by openly acknowledging the continuing force of an older treaty, a State cannot later, "in honor and good faith," deny the existence of that treaty when it imposes an obligation). **123n206**

Anglo-Norwegian Fisheries Case (United Kingdom v. Norway), 1951 I.C.J. Rep. 116, 139 (holding that the "prolonged abstention" of the United Kingdom from protesting against the Norwegian system of straight base lines in delimiting territorial waters was one of the factors that "warrant Norway's enforcement of her system against the United Kingdom"). **5, 5n17, 103n91, 108nn117–18, 123n207**

Eastern Greenland Case (Denmark v. Norway), Judgement P.C.I.J. (Ser. A/B) No. 53, 50 (1933) (holding that when "Norway reaffirmed that she recognised the whole of

Greenland as Danish, . . . she has [thus] debarred herself from contesting Danish sovereignty over the whole of Greenland"). **123n207, 137n288**

Amco Asia Corp. v. Republic of Indonesia, ICSID Case No. ARB/81/1, Decision on Jurisdiction, ¶ 47 (Sept. 25, 1983) (explaining the contours and acceptance of the principle of estoppel as a general one, but holding that without a "benefit to the allegedly estopped party and/or prejudice to the other," there is no justification to apply it). **32n175, 40nn208–9, 41, 41–42n212, 41n210, 42n213, 44n228, 90nn17–18, 94n38, 100n79, 105n101, 120n191, 121n199, 138n294, 145n335, 148n358, 149n359, 149n362, 150n370, 197–98n244**

Serbian Loans Case (France v. Serb-Croat-Slovene State), 1929 P.C.I.J. (Ser. A) No. 20, ¶ 80 (holding that where there has been "no change in position on the part of the State [seeking to invoke the estoppel]," then there is "no sufficient basis" to apply the principle of estoppel in its favor). **120n193**

Tinoco Arbitration, 1 R.I.A.A. 375, 393-84 (1923) (Taft, C.J) (holding that "[a]n equitable estoppel . . . must rest on previous conduct of the person to be estopped . . . which has led the person claiming the estoppel into a position in which the truth will injure him"). **61n325, 120n193**

Pope & Talbot v. Canada, UNCITRAL, Interim Award, ¶ 111 (Mar. 5, 2002) (noting that "the essence of estoppel [under international law] is the element of conduct which causes the other party in reliance on such conduct detrimentally to change its position or to suffer some prejudice"). **120n193, 121n199**

Canfor Corporation v. United States of America, Tembec Inc. et al. *v. United States of America and Terminal Forest Products Ltd. v. United States of America*, UNCITRAL, Order of the Consolidation Tribunal, ¶ 168 (Sept. 7, 2005) (acknowledging that "estoppel is a recognized general principle of law that has been applied by many international tribunals," but holding that the United States is not estopped from seeking consolidation even though it may have previously indicated that it did not intend to do so). **121n199**

Ceskoslovenska Obchodni Banka, A.S. v. Slovak Republic, ICSID Case No. ARB/97/4, Decision on Jurisdiction, ¶ 47 (May 24, 1999) (acknowledging that "[a]n essential element of estoppel is that 'there must be reliance in good faith upon the statement either to the detriment of the party so relying on the statement or to the advantage of the party making the statement"). **99n71, 121n199**

Philippe Gruslin v. Malaysia, ICSID Case No. ARB/99/3, Award, ¶¶ 20.1-20.5 (Nov. 27, 2000) (noting that the requirements of an estoppel binding a State in international law are the same as with any estoppel but holding that the claimant had not established detriment in reliance upon any representation which might be constructed out of the Respondent's failure to plead an element of its defense at a particular time). **121–22n199, 137n289**

SGS Société Générale de Surveillance S.A. v. Islamic Republic of Pakistan, ICSID No. ARB/01/13, Decision on Jurisdiction, ¶¶ 122, 175-77 (Aug. 6, 2003) (holding that an estoppel would not be applied to a claim in the absence of specific treaty language or "fork in the road" provision, waiving an investor's right to initiate or continue an international arbitration claim once domestic court proceedings have been commenced). **39–40n206, 121–22n199**

SGS Société Générale de Surveillance S.A. v. Republic of the Philippines, ICSID Case No. ARB/02/6, Decision on Jurisdiction, ¶ 109 (Jan. 29, 2004) (finding that where an investor averred before local courts that it was not locally present for jurisdictional purposes, it was not estopped from asserting that an investment existed there for the purposes of the treaty because the State did not rely on those jurisdictional representations in order to exclude the possibility of an investment claim). **39–40n206, 121–22n199**

ADC Affiliate Ltd. and ADC & ADMC Mgmt. Ltd. v. Republic of Hungary, ICSID Case No. ARB/03/16, Award, ¶¶ 474-75 (Oct. 2, 2006) (noting that, having entered into an agreement and made certain representations and warranties, "[i]t would . . . be unconscionable to permit [Hungary] . . . to resile from these representations and warranties" on the basis that the investor should have been subject of a public procurement process). **112n139, 121–22n199, 125n215, 126n220**

Duke Energy Int'l Inv. No.1, Ltd. v. Republic of Peru, ICSID Case No. ARB/03/28, Award, ¶¶ 231, 241-49 (Aug. 18, 2008) (noting that the principle of *actos propios* "is implied [in] all contracts," and holding that unequivocal conduct by a state entity, acting within the sphere of its competence, that is perceived by reasonable third parties as an averment of the State's position, may preclude the State from contradicting that position in the future). **78n445, 128n233**

Rachel S. Grynberg, Stephen M. Grynberg, Miriam Z. Grynberg and RSM Prod. Corp. v. Grenada, ICSID Case No. ARB/10/6, Award, ¶ 7.1.2 (Dec. 10, 2010) (noting that "the doctrine of collateral estoppel is now well established as a general principle of law applicable in the international courts and tribunals," and finding that it operated as a species of *res judicata* against shareholder claims in relation to corporate assets). **121–22n199**

Delimitation of the Maritime Boundary in the Gulf of Maine Area (Can./U.S), Judgment, 1984 I.C.J. 246, ¶ 130 (Oct. 12) (acknowledging that, like the principle of acquiescence, estoppel flows from the fundamental principles of good faith and equity). **5n18, 122n200**

Case Concerning the Arbitral Award Made by the King of Spain on December 23, 1906 (Hond. v. Nicar), Judgment, 1960 I.C.J. 192, 210-13 (Nov. 18) (finding that Nicaragua, having recognized—by express declaration and by conduct—the validity of an arbitral award on the delimitation of its boundaries with Honduras, was precluded from challenging the validity of that award). **11n55, 124n210, 197–98n244**

Pan American Energy LLC and BP Argentina Exploration Company v. The Argentine Republic, ICSID Case No. ARB/03/13, ¶ 159 (July 27, 2006) (acknowledging that "[e]stoppel is a recognised general principle of law that has been applied by many international tribunals," but holding that none of the necessary elements of estoppel were proven in this case). **122n201**

Ad Hoc *Arbitration*, Award, Mar. 4, 2004, *reprinted in* The Unidroit Principles in Practice 1077, 1081 (Michael Joachim Bonnell ed., 2006) (applying UNIDROIT Article 1.8 to hold that where a party fails to enforce a contract clause throughout a four-year commercial relationship, it cannot later insist upon strict enforcement of that clause when an unrelated dispute under the contract arises). **102n87, 123n205**

ICC Second Preliminary Award in Case No. 1512, YCA 1980, 174, 175 (also published in: ASA Bull. 1992, at 505 *et seq)* (acknowledging estoppel as a general principle of law which may bind a litigant to positions taken earlier in the proceedings). **102n86, 103n91, 122n202**

Abrahim Rahman Golshani v. The Government of The Islamic Republic of Iran, Award No. 546-812-3 (Mar. 2, 1993), 29 Iran-U.S. Cl. Trib. 78, ¶¶ 42-45 (holding that, even though a related party may have acquiesced in the authenticity of a deed in a previous proceeding, the respondent State—who was not a party to those proceedings—is not later estopped from arguing that the same deed is a forgery). **122n202, 191n204, 193n211, 195n229**

Southern Pacific Properties Ltd. v. Arab Republic of Egypt, ICSID Case No. ARB/ 84/3, Award, ¶ 81 *et seq.* (May 20, 1992) (holding that, where a State argues that a private contract was a nullity because "certain acts of Egyptian officials . . . [were], under Egyptian law, legally non-existent or absolutely null and void . . . because they were not taken pursuant to the procedures prescribed by Egyptian law," but the State's earlier acts indicated that it was committing to an agreement, Egypt was barred from denying its obligations under the contract). **45n229, 124, 126, 138n294**

Fraport AG Frankfurt Airport Services Worldwide v. Republic of the Philippines, ICSID Case No. ARB/03/25, Award, ¶ 346 (Aug. 16, 2007) (holding that "principles of fairness should require a tribunal to hold a government estopped from raising violations of its own law as a jurisdictional defense when it knowingly overlooked them and endorsed an investment, which was not in compliance with its law"). **86, 86nn490–91, 124n214, 179n129**

Inmaris Perestroika Sailing Maritime Services GmbH and others v. Ukraine, ICSID Case No. ARB/08/8, Decision on Jurisdiction, ¶ 140 (Mar. 8, 2010) (determining that where a state institution enters a contract with the approval of other representatives of the State, and those representatives acknowledge the contract as valid, the respondent cannot later deem those contracts or the payment scheme contained in them to be illegal under its domestic law). **124n214, 193n210**

Railroad Development Corporation v. Republic of Guatemala, ICSID Case No. ARB/07/23, Second Decision on Objections to Jurisdiction, ¶¶ 146-47 (May 18, 2010) (holding that, even if claimant's actions with respect to its contract were in technical violation of domestic law, "principles of fairness should prevent the government from raising [those] violations of its own law as a jurisdictional defense when it knowingly overlooked them and effectively endorsed an investment which was not in compliance with its law"). **124n214, 137–38n290**

Arbitration CAS 2002/O/410, *The Gibraltar Football Association (GFA)/Union des Associations Européennes de Football (UEFA)*, Award, ¶ 11 (Oct. 7, 2003) (observing that the application of a retroactive procedural rule to deny a privilege to a petitioning party may "entail a violation of general principles of law which are widely recognized," in particular the "principle of *venire contra factum proprium*"). **108n121, 124n214**

Treatment of Polish Nationals and Other Persons of Polish Origin or Speech in the Danzig Territory, Advisory Opinion, 1932 P.C.I.J. (Ser. A/B) No. 44, 24-25 (holding that "a State cannot adduce as against another State its own Constitution with a view to evading obligations incumbent upon it under international law or treaties in force," which is why the question of the treatment of foreign nationals must be settled exclusively on the bases of the rules of international law and the treaty provisions in force between the two States). **94n40, 125n218, 154n397**

ICC Case No. 7263 (1994), Interim Award, 22 Y.B. Comm. Arb. 92, 98 (1997) (holding that, "[i]n the field of international commercial arbitration, . . . states and public bodies as defendants . . . cannot avail themselves of the incapacity and lack of authorization [to contract] deriving from their national laws"). **125n218, 155n401**

ADC Affiliate Ltd. v. Republic of Hungary, ICSID Case No. ARB/03/16, Award, ¶ 475 (Oct. 2, 2006) (observing that principles of good faith required that no person shall be entitled to refer to his own actionable conduct in order to obtain advantages, and finding that Hungary could not challenge the validity of agreements that it had observed, performed and benefitted from for years and, by its conduct, had led the investor to believe were effective). **112n139, 121–22n199, 125n215, 126n220**

Benteler v. Belgian State, Award, Nov. 18, 1983, 1 J. Int. Arb. 184, 190 (1984) (finding that where a state entity entered an international joint venture agreement with a private company, which included an agreement to arbitrate, that entity cannot thereafter assert that its own internal law "except[s] . . . public law entities" from any capacity to enter an arbitration agreement). **125n218, 155n401**

Company Z and Others v. State Organization ABC, Award, Apr. 1982 (1983) 8 Y.B. Comm. Arb. 94, at 108-09 (holding, within the framework of an agreement regarding the exploitation of natural resources between a private and state-owned entity, that a contract containing an arbitration clause cannot be contested on the basis that it had not been approved by a domestic legislature). **125n218, 155n401**

Where a State's conduct creates legitimate and justifiable expectations on the part of an investor, the State cannot later disavow that conduct to the investor's detriment

International Thunderbird Gaming Corporation v. The United Mexican States, UNCITRAL, Award, ¶ 147 (Jan. 26, 2006) (acknowledging that the frustration of legitimate expectations can give rise to a violation of fair and equitable treatment, but holding that where the government's prior statements were based on the claimant's misrepresentations, the claimant could not reasonably rely on the those statements). **6n21, 76n431, 78n439, 78n441, 91n23, 99n70, 126, 126nn222–23, 127n227, 127n230, 129n239, 191–92n205**

Total v. Argentina, ICSID Case No. ARB/04/01, Award, ¶¶ 113-34 (Dec. 27, 2010) (engaging "a comparative analysis of the protection of legitimate expectations in domestic jurisdictions," because "the concept . . . is based on the requirement of good faith, one of the general principles referred to in Article 38(1)(c) of the Statute of the International Court of Justice as a source of international law." The Tribunal acknowledged that a frustration of legitimate expectations can give rise to a violation of fair and equitable treatment, but held, *inter alia*, that claimant's expectations were "misplaced, especially in light of the growing difficulties experienced by Argentina's economy that were at the root of [its legislative changes]," and that Argentina's legal order could not serve as a basis for legitimate expectations absent more concrete assurances). **14n71, 126n222, 127n227, 128n234**

Gold Reserve Inc. v. Bolivarian Rep. of Venezuela, ICSID Case No. ARB(AF)/09/1, Award, ¶ 576 (Sept. 22, 2014) (acknowledging that the frustration of legitimate expectations can give rise to a violation of fair and equitable treatment, and holding that where a claimant has "good reasons to rely on the continuing validity of its mining titles . . . and an expectation that it would obtain the required authorization to start the exploitation of the concessions," the State cannot alter those expectations without giving rise to state responsibility). **126n222, 126n224, 127nn229–30**

Nagel v. Czech Republic, SCC Case No. 49/2002, Award, ¶¶ 293, 326 (Sept. 9, 2003) (holding that encouraging remarks on the part of government officials were not sufficient to constitute legitimate expectations that a crucial license would be granted by the government). **127n230, 193n211**

Metalclad Corporation v. The United Mexican States, ICSID Case No. ARB(AF)/97/1, Award, ¶ 85-87, 101 (Aug. 30, 2000) (finding that where the State denied a construction permit needed to operate a hazardous waste disposal site, but previously assured the investor that the site had been approved and no further permit would be required, the State violated the fair and equitable treatment standard). **111, 111n136, 127n229, 128n238, 153–54n390, 163, 163n34**

Continental Casualty Company v. The Argentine Republic, ICSID Case No. ARB/03/9, Award, ¶¶ 260-66 (Sept. 5, 2008) (acknowledging that a frustration of legitimate expectations can give rise to a violation of fair and equitable treatment, but holding that, *inter alia*, "political statements have the least legal value," so claimant "cannot invoke legitimate expectations as to [legislative] change[s]" based on previous "political declarations by various authorities"). **128n231**

Técnicas Medioambientales Tecmed, S.A. v. The United Mexican States, ICSID Case No. ARB (AF)/00/2, Award, ¶ 154 (May 29, 2003) (tying fair and equitable treatment to "the good faith principle established by international law" and concluding that fair and equitable treatment required "the Contracting Parties to provide to international investments treatment that does not affect the basic expectations that were taken into account by the foreign investor to make the investment"). **115n162, 117n168, 128n233, 194n215**

Duke Energy Electroquil Partners & Electroquil S.A. v. Republic of Ecuador, ICSID Case No. ARB/04/19, Award, ¶ 340 (Aug. 18, 2008) (acknowledging that the frustration of legitimate expectations can give rise to a violation of fair and equitable treatment, but those expectations must be gauged in light of the political and economic context at the time. Guarantees given by the State as a pre-condition to an investment may give rise to legitimate expectations). **78n445, 128n233**

Parkerings-Compagniet v. Lithuania, ICSID Case No. ARB/05/8, Award, ¶ 333-37 (Sept. 11, 2007) (observing that, while a State has the right to enact, modify, or repeal a law, it may not legislate in a manner that is inconsistent with a prior agreement, such as a stabilization clause, or in a manner that is unreasonable, unfair, or inequitable, or otherwise frustrates legitimate expectations that were reasonable in light of the circumstances. Where a Respondent State had given no assurances that the law would remain unchanged, and was in fact transitioning from a Soviet-style economy to an EU member State, legislative changes were likely, and any expectation that the laws would remain unchanged was illegitimate). **128n235**

Saluka Investments B.V. v. The Czech Republic, UNCITRAL, Partial Award, ¶ 305 (March 17, 2006) (acknowledging that a frustration of legitimate expectations can give rise to a violation of fair and equitable treatment, but holding that where the claimant knew that the minister of finance could not bind future governments, the claimant could not reasonably rely on his assurances). **128n234, 129n239, 139n296**

EnCana Corporation v. Republic of Ecuador, LCIA Case No. UN3481, UNCITRAL, Award, ¶ 158 (Feb. 3, 2006) (observing that, under the fair and equitable treatment standard, the State "must act with reasonable consistency and without arbitrariness in its treatment of investments," and "[o]ne arm of the State cannot finally affirm what another arm denies to the detriment of a foreign investor"). **128n236**

CMS Gas Transmission Company v. The Argentine Republic, ICSID Case No. ARB/01/8, Award, ¶¶ 275-81 (May 12, 2005) (holding that a change in a tariff regime contrary to commitments made by the State in an offer memo violated the fair and equitable treatment standard). **128n237, 160n17**

Waste Management, Inc. v. United Mexican States, ICSID Case No. ARB(AF)/00/3, Award, ¶¶ 98-99 (Apr. 30, 2004) (observing that, in applying this standard of fair and equitable treatment, "it is relevant that the treatment is in breach of representations made by the host State which were reasonably relied on by the claimant"). **77n438, 129n238, 197n244, 199n253, 199nn255–56, 200n265**

CME Czech Republic B.V. v. The Czech Republic, UNCITRAL, Partial Award, ¶¶ 155-57, 170 (Sept. 13, 2001) (determining that where a State initially approves a joint venture involving a foreign investor, but later asserts that the claimant was operating without a license and forces it out of the venture, the State "eviscerate[s] the arrangement upon which the claimant was induced to invest [and] violate[s] the fair and equitable treatment standard"). **40n208, 129nn238–39, 145n335, 202n269**

Ronald S. Lauder v. The Czech Republic, UNCITRAL, Award, ¶ 295 (Sept. 3, 2001) (finding no liability under the same facts as the CME Tribunal, because there were no specific undertaking by the State that it would not alter or enforce its regulations, and "[t]here cannot be any inconsistent conduct in a regulatory body taking the necessary actions to enforce the law, absent any specific undertaking that it will refrain from doing so"). **129n239**

D. The Prohibition on Advantageous Wrongs—*Nullus Commodum Capere Potest De Sua Iniuria Propria*—and Unjust Enrichment

Nullus commodum capere potest de sua iniuria propria—No advantage may be gained from one's own wrong

The Betsey Case (1797) (espousing the principle that a State may not invoke its own illegal act to diminish its liability because "[t]he most exceptionable of all principles [is] that he who does wrong shall not be at liberty to plead his own illegal conduct on other occasions as a partial excuse"). **130n246**

Chorzow Factory (Germany v. Poland), Judgment No. 8, 1927 P.C.I.J. 5, 21 (June 1927) (holding that where the Polish Government had expropriated a factory without following the procedure laid down in the Geneva Convention of 1922, which required prior notice to the real owner and thus affording it an opportunity of appealing to the German-Polish Mixed Arbitral Tribunal, the Government could not thereafter contest jurisdiction of the PCIJ on the ground that the Mixed Tribunal was the only competent forum to hear the claim). **8n38, 14, 14n70, 105n101, 106n106, 107n111, 130–31, 131n248, 148n357, 197n240, 200n265**

Free Zones Case, 1930 P.C.I.J. (Ser. A) No. 24, at 12; and 1932 P.C.I.J. (Ser. A/B) No. 46, at 167 (observing that, where a treaty allows tax but not customs duties in a free zone, neither State can be allowed to "evade the obligation to maintain the zones by erecting a customs barrier under the guise of a [fiscal tax]." This was not proven here, and "an abuse cannot be presumed by the Court"). **131n253**

Frances Irene Roberts Case IX R.I.A.A. 204, 207, United States-Venezuelan Mixed Claims Commission (1903) (rejecting a plea of prescription in a case which, though diligently prosecuted by the claimants for over 30 years, had not yet been resolved. If the plea were accepted, it would "allow the Venezuelan Government to reap advantage from its own wrong in failing to make just reparation to [claimant] at the time the claim arose"). **131n251**

The Tattler Case VI R.I.A.A. 48, 50 (1920) (holding that a foreign ship may not be seized for its failure to possess a certain document "when the document has been refused to it by the very authorities who required that it should be obtained"). **131n251**

Ex dolo malo non oritur actio—an action at law does not arise from grave deceit

ICC Award No. 4145 (Second Interim Award), YCA 1987, at 97 *et seq.* ¶¶ 24-26 (also published in: CLUNET 1985, at 985 *et seq)* (holding that where two parties agree to an immoral purpose to be achieved or an immoral means to be used in order to achieve a certain result, the legal process will not protect that agreement; the plea of illegality was nevertheless denied in this case, where defendant's accusation was not supported by direct evidence or even convincing circumstantial evidence). **136n286, 195n228**

ICC Award No. 11307 of 2003, YCA 2008, 24 *et seq.* ¶ 31 (holding that illegal contracts—*viz.* where performance requires the commission of a crime—are "void because they are based on a *turpis causa*"). **137n286**

Soleimany v. Soleimany, [1999] QB 785, 797 (reversing the High Court's decision to recognize an arbitral award which enforced a contract to illegally smuggle carpets out of Iran). **137n287**

Beresford v. Royal Ins. Co. Ltd., [1938] AC 586, 599 (holding that an insured may not recover under a policy of insurance in respect of loss intentionally caused by his own criminal or tortious act, however clearly the wording of the policy may suggest otherwise; in all cases "the absolute rule is that the courts will not recognise a benefit accruing to a criminal from his crime"). **137n287**

Pelletier Case (United States v. Haiti), 2 Moore, Int'l Arb. 1749, 1794-1800 (1898) (holding that an arbitral award against Haiti for the seizure of a vessel should not be enforced because the vessel was engaged in slave trading). **137, 137n288**

Diversion of Water from the Meuse (Neth. v. Belg), Judgment, June 28, 1937, P.C.I.J. (Ser. A/B) No. 70, at 77 (opinion of J. Hudson) (finding that when a State asks a tribunal to prohibit behavior by its treaty partner which contravenes the parties' agreement, its claim should be denied when it, too, is "engaged in taking precisely similar action, similar in fact and similar in law"). **101n82, 132n256**

Legal Status of Eastern Greenland (Den. v. Nor), 1933 P.C.I.J. (Ser. A/B) No. 53, at 95 (Sept. 5) (observing that because the Norwegian occupation of Greenland was effected "in violation of an undertaking validly assumed, it constitutes a violation of the existing legal situation, and it is therefore unlawful"; accordingly, such occupation cannot serve as a basis for a territorial claim, which should be rejected because "an unlawful act cannot serve as the basis of an action at law"). **123n207, 137n288**

Military and Paramilitary Activities in and against Nicaragua (Nicar. v. U.S), Merits, Judgment, 1986 I.C.J. 14, 268-72 (June 27) (dissenting opinion of Judge Schwebel) (disagreeing with the majority, and suggesting that Nicaragua's aid to rebels in El Salvador was an unlawful intervention that precluded judgment in its favor in relation to its claim of unlawful intervention against the United States). **132n256, 153n388, 191n201**

World Duty Free Co. Ltd. v. Republic of Kenya, ICSID Case No. ARB/00/7, Award, ¶¶ 161, 181 (Oct. 4, 2006) (espousing the public policy principle of *ex dolo malo non oritur actio*, that "[n]o court will lend its aid to a man who founds his cause of action upon an immoral or illegal act," and dismissing a claim based on the loss of an investment found to be procured by the payment of a bribe to the Kenyan President). **34n183, 42, 42n214, 43, 43–44n224, 101n83, 132n257, 134n273, 135, 135n277, 136n284, 154n396, 160n17, 184, 184nn162–63, 185n170**

Metal-Tech Ltd. v. Republic of Uzbekistan, ICSID Case No. ARB/10/3, Award, ¶¶ 327, 373 (Oct. 4, 2014) (finding that because the treaty defined investments to mean only those implemented in compliance with local law, this excluded an investment found to be procured by corruption from the tribunal's jurisdiction). **43n222, 132n257, 136, 136nn283–84, 184, 184n160, 189, 189n192**

Olmstead v. United States, 277 U.S. 438, 483 (1928) (Brandeis, J., dissenting) (suggesting in dissent that, where evidence used by a prosecutor in a criminal trial was illegally taken by federal agents, a judgment of conviction should be reversed under "the maxim of unclean hands, [which] comes from courts of equity [b]ut . . . prevails also in courts of law." While "[i]ts common application is in civil actions between private parties, [w]here the Government is the actor, the reasons for applying it are even more persuasive" because "[i]f the Government becomes a lawbreaker, it breeds contempt for law"). **132n260**

Guyana v. Suriname, PCA, Award, ¶¶ 420-21 (Sept. 17, 2007) (holding that "a violation must be ongoing for the clean hands doctrine to apply, . . . consistent with the doctrine's origins in the laws of equity and its limited application to situations where equitable remedies, such as specific performance, are sought"). **133n262, 133n265, 133n267**

Niko Resources (Bangladesh) Ltd. v. People's Republic of Bangladesh et al., ICSID Case Nos. ARB/10/11 and ARB/10/18, Decision on Jurisdiction, ¶ 483 (Aug. 19, 2013) (finding that the requirements for the application of the clean hands doctrine did not exist in this case, because the respondents were relying on a violation that occurred in the past, the remedy which the claimant was seeking did not concern this past violation, and there was no relation of reciprocity between the relief being sought by the claimant in the arbitration and the acts in the past which the respondents characterized as involving unclean hands). **133n264**

Oil Platforms (Iran v. U.S), Judgment, 2003 I.C.J. 161, 177-78 (Nov. 6) (observing that "in order to make [a] finding [of unclean hands]" a court needs to examine the parties' conduct during the relevant period. Accordingly, the "principle may have legal significance only at the merits stage, and only at the stage of quantification of damages, but does not deprive a [party] of locus standi in judicio"). **25n137, 134, 134n269, 188n188**

Hulley Enters. v. The Russian Federation, PCA Case No. AA 226, ¶¶ 1351-52 (2014) (holding that while an investor who has obtained an investment in the host State in violation of the local laws should not be allowed to benefit from an investment treaty, the violation of such law in the operation of the investment does not affect the jurisdiction of a tribunal). **134, 134nn270–71, 136, 137n285, 169n67, 175**

Inceysa Vallisoletana S.L. v. Republic of El Salvador, ICSID Case No. ARB/03/26, Award, ¶¶ 240-42 (Aug. 2, 2006) (dismissing a claim for lack of jurisdiction where a claimant invoked the mechanisms of the Spain-El Salvador BIT to protect an investment procured by a fraudulent bidding process, because, *inter alia*, the maxim *nemo auditur propriam turpitudinem allegans* (no one is to be heard relying on his own turpitude) prohibits an investor from benefitting from "an investment made by means of one or several illegal acts"). **2n2, 47–48n245, 47–49, 89n11, 94n38, 95n44, 96, 96n49, 101n83, 132n157, 136, 136n280, 138n294, 184, 185n164, 185n170**

Plama Consortium Limited v. Republic of Bulgaria, ICSID Case No. ARB/03/24, Award, ¶ 143 (Aug. 27, 2008) (holding that an investment obtained by "deceitful conduct" is ineligible for the substantive protections of the Energy Charter Treaty). **49n256, 100–101n79, 136, 136n281, 184**

No party can be allowed by its own abusive act to bring about a nonperformance of a condition precedent to its own obligation

ICC Award No. 10346 (Dec. 2000), 12 ICC Int'l Court of Arb. Bulletin 106, 108-10 (stating that where official registration of a private contract is a prerequisite for it to have any force and effect, and where both contracting parties undertake a "duty to collaborate" on that registration, a party that avoids taking any steps to collaborate on registration cannot thereafter "wash[] its hands" of the agreement. The Tribunal upheld the contract because the "Respondent cannot rely on its own inconsistency to the detriment of the Claimant"). **137–38n290, 138n291**

Desert Line Projects LLC v. Republic of Yemen, ICSID Case No. ARB/05/17, Award, ¶¶ 119-20 (Feb. 6, 2008) (holding that "[i]t would be extraordinary" to expect that a "project involving hundreds of millions of dollars . . . should be deprived of [BIT] protection due to the failure to have obtained some unspecified stamped or signed form from a governmental subdivision"). **90–91n19, 91n20, 119–20n189, 120n190, 122n203, 124n214, 125n217, 137n289, 198n246, 202n272**

Railroad Development Corporation v. Republic of Guatemala, ICSID Case No. ARB/07/23, Second Decision on Objections to Jurisdiction, ¶¶ 146-47 (May 18, 2010) (holding that, even if the claimant's actions with respect to its contract were in technical violation of domestic law, "principles of fairness should prevent the government from raising [those] violations of its own law as a jurisdictional defense when it knowingly overlooked them and effectively endorsed an investment which was not in compliance with its law"). **124n214, 137–38n290**

Sempra Energy International v. Argentina, ICSID ARB/02/16, Award, ¶ 353 (Sept. 28, 2007) (denying the defense of necessity because "the State cannot invoke [the defense] if it has contributed to the situation giving rise to [it]. This is of course the expression of a general principle of law devised to prevent a party from taking legal advantage of its own fault"). **102–3n89, 138nn292–93, 150n371**

Enron Corp. and Ponderosa Assets, L.P. v. Argentine Republic, ICSID Case No. ARB/01/03, Award, ¶¶ 311-13 (May 22, 2007) (holding that, as an expression of the general principle of law devised to prevent a party from taking legal advantage of its own fault, a State cannot invoke necessity if it has contributed to the situation of necessity. Where "the factors precipitating the crisis were [both] endogenous or exogenous," but there has been at least a "substantial contribution of the State to the situation of necessity," then the defense is unavailable to avoid liability). **105n101, 106n107, 138n292**

Where there is an unjustified and unjust enrichment of one party to the detriment of the other, and no contractual or other remedy available to the injured party, the law will demand reparation

Sea-Land Servs., Inc. v. Iran, Award No. 135-33-1, 6 Iran-U.S. Cl. Trib. Rep. 149, 168-69 (June 20, 1984) (acknowledging that the principle of unjust enrichment is "widely accepted as having been assimilated into the catalogue of general principles of law available to be applied by international tribunals," and applies where there is an unjustified enrichment of one party to the detriment of the other, with both arising as a consequence of the same act or event, and no contractual or other remedy at law available to compensate the loss). **139n301, 139nn296–97, 208n29**

Saluka Investments BV (The Netherlands) v. Czech Republic, UNCITRAL, Partial Award, ¶ 449 (Mar. 17, 2006) (acknowledging that "[t]he concept of unjust enrichment is recognised as a general principle of international law," but declining to find that such an enrichment occurred where a State transferred claimant's business to another private entity). **128n234, 129n239, 139n296**

Schlegel Corp. v. Nat'l Iranian Copper Indus. Co., Award No. 295-834-2 (Mar. 27, 1987), 14 Iran-U.S. Cl. Trib. Rep. 176, ¶ 16 (determining that a subcontractor who performed its obligation to a contractor could recover against respondent State on a theory of unjust enrichment because the link between the claimant's performance and the respondent's enrichment was "sufficiently direct" and unjust because the respondent had never paid either the contractor or the claimant for the work). **46n238, 139n296**

Flexi-Van Leasing, Inc. v. Islamic Republic of Iran, Award No. 259-36-1 (Oct. 13, 1986), 12 Iran-U.S. Cl. Trib. Rep. 335, 237-38 (acknowledging unjust enrichment as a general principle, and holding that, "[i]t is inherent in the principle . . . that there must have been an enrichment of one party to the detriment of the other"). **46n238, 139n296**

Shannon & Wilson, Inc. v. Atomic Energy Org. of Iran, Award No. 207-217-2 (Dec. 5, 1985), 9 Iran-U.S. Cl. Trib. Rep. 397, 402 (acknowledging the general principle of unjust enrichment, but rejecting a claim for lack of proof that the respondent had been unjustly enriched). **46n238, 139n296**

Isaiah v. Bank Mellat, Award No. 35-219-2 (30 March 1983), 2 Iran-U.S. Cl. Trib. Rep. 232 (finding that where a bank holds a person's funds and refuses to honor a check drawn on those funds, a claim can be made against the bank by the beneficial owner of those funds for an unjust enrichment). **138n294, 139n298**

Amco Asia Corp. v. Republic of Indonesia, ICSID Case No. ARB/81/1, Resubmitted Case, Award, ¶¶ 154-56 (June 5, 1990) (refusing to find an unjust enrichment in an investment arbitration regarding an expropriated hotel license because the subsequent hotel operator, and not the State itself, was the direct beneficiary of the allegedly wrongful act). **32n175, 40nn208–9, 41, 41–42n212, 41n210, 42n213, 44n228, 90nn17–18, 94n38, 100n79, 105n101, 120n191, 121n199, 138n294, 145n335, 148n358, 149n359, 149n362, 150n370, 197–98n244**

Southern Pacific Properties Ltd. v. Arab Republic of Egypt, ICSID Case No. ARB/84/3, Award, ¶¶ 245-49 (May 20, 1992) (holding that, although unjust enrichment has on infrequent occasion been used by international tribunals as a basis for awarding compensation, it is generally accepted that the measure of compensation should reflect the claimant's loss rather than the respondent's gain). **45n229, 124, 126, 138n294**

Inceysa Vallisoletana S.L. v. Republic of El Salvador, ICSID Case No. ARB/03/26, Award, ¶ 253 (Aug. 2, 2006) (holding that, where a claimant resorts to fraud to obtain a contract that it would not have otherwise obtained, providing BIT protection over that contract would provide that claimant with an unjust enrichment). **2n2, 47–48n245, 47–49, 89n11, 94n38, 95n44, 96, 96n49, 101n83, 132n157, 136, 136n280, 138n294, 184, 185n164, 185n170**

Tippetts et al. *v. TAMS-AFFA Consulting*, Award No. 141-7-2 (29 June 1984), 6 Iran-U.S. Cl. Trib. Rep. 219, 228 (holding that, where a claimant owes and has not paid tax and social security obligations owed to the State, it would be unjustly enriched and provide an advantage to an obvious wrong if, by virtue of the Tribunal's award, such amounts were not deducted from the final damage calculations). **139n299, 139n302**

Arbitration clauses continue to be operative, even though the contract containing the arbitration clause is null and void

Elf Aquitaine Iran (France) v. National Iranian Oil Company, Ad Hoc-Award of January 14, 1982, YCA 1986, at 97, ¶¶ 15-18 (holding that where an agreement is duly ratified by a national legislature, but later declared null and void *ab initio* as being at variance with other national law, the arbitration clause in that agreement still survives the termination; "[t]he jurisdiction of an arbitrator ... designated in accordance with [the] arbitration clause is unimpaired, even though the contract containing the arbitration clause is alleged to be null and void"). **135n275**

ICC Award No. 5485, YCA 1989, at 156, ¶¶ 9-12 (concluding that that separability of an arbitration clause from the main contract is recognized both in international commercial arbitration and under Spanish law). **90n17, 135n275**

LIAMCO v. The Government of the Libyan Arab Republic, YCA 1981, at 89, 96 (holding that an arbitration clause survives the unilateral termination by the State of the contract in which that clause is contained, and "continues in force after that termination"). **29n159, 90n16, 90n18, 135n275**

E. Corporate Separateness and Limited Liability

There exists a legal separation between a corporation and its shareholders

The Barcelona Traction, Light & Power Co. (Belg. v. Spain), 1970 I.C.J. 3, 38-39 (Feb. 5) (recognizing that legal separation of a corporation from its shareholders is accepted at international law and holding that only the State of incorporation, Canada, had standing to sue Spain for harm committed against the corporation; Belgium did not, despite being the State of citizenship for the majority of its shareholders). **5, 5n15, 17, 20n106, 27n150, 71n401, 108n117, 140nn304–5, 141nn309–10, 142n315, 142n317**

Lemire v. Ukraine, ICSID Case No. ARB/06/18, ¶¶ 65-67 (Mar. 1, 2011) (dissenting opinion of Dr. Jurgen Voss) (observing that "[m]ost municipal legal systems recognize corporations as legal persons distinct from their shareholders. . . . It pervades municipal legal systems in many areas and cannot be discarded as just a technicality"; thus, an individual "BIT protected investor may assert a violation of corporate rights under a BIT only in special qualifying circumstances"). **140n308, 145n335, 146–47, 146n343, 146n350, 149n361, 149n363, 150n365, 180n132**

Ahmadou Sadio Diallo (*Guinea v. Congo*), Decision on Preliminary Objections, I.C.J. Rep't 2007 (II), 502, 605, ¶¶ 61-63 (recognizing that Guinean shareholders of entities incorporated under Zaire law are separate legal entities from the corporation consistent with domestic law and international principles). **140n308, 142n316, 194n217**

Rompetrol v. Romania, ICSID Case No. ARB/06/3, Decision on Respondent's Preliminary Objections on Jurisdiction and Admissibility, ¶ 90 (Apr. 18, 2008) (finding that the separation of corporate and shareholder personalities allows contracting States to agree on allowing the place of incorporation as sufficient criterion of nationality in a treaty, notwithstanding the nationality of the controlling shareholders). **140–41n308, 189n193, 190n196, 195n225**

HICEE B.V. v. Slovak Republic, UNCITRAL, PCA Case No. 2009-11, Partial Award on Jurisdiction, ¶ 147 (May 23, 2011) (holding that the default position in international law is that a corporation is separate from its shareholders, and that a treaty will permit shareholders to sue for damages caused to the corporation only when the text of that treaty so provides). **140–41n308**

Salomon v. Salomon & Co., [1897] A.C. 22 at 30-31 (Eng. H.L) (holding that, once a corporation is established, it is a separate legal entity apart from the conduct or intent of the incorporators, and is not a mere alias of its shareholders). **140n307**

Doe v. Exxon Mobil Corp., 654 F.3d 11, 53 (D.C. Cir. 2011) (holding that corporate personhood, separate from stockholders, is a recognized principle of international law such that corporate liability in international law is possible under the Alien Tort Statute). **16n79, 51n268, 51n270, 141n314, 203n1**

CRCICA Award No. 120/1998, *Mohie Eldin I. Alam Eldin*, Arbitral Awards of the Cairo Regional Centre of International Commercial Arbitration II (1997-2000), The Hague 2003, 25 at 29-33 (finding that individual and corporate entities were so entwined that the corporations had become mere screens for the individual's doings, such that piercing the veil did not violate the international principle of separating corporations from their shareholders). **142–43n322**

First National City Bank (FNCB) v. Banco Para El Comercio Exterior de Cuba, 462 U.S. 611, 626 (1983) (holding that a Cuban state-owned bank, acting as a direct arm of a foreign sovereign, was subject to an exception to the general rule that corporations are separate entities from shareholders). **38n200, 53n277, 54n285, 140n307, 141n314, 142n317, 142n322, 208n24**

F. The Principles of Causation and Reparation

Jure causa proxima non remota inspicitur—the proximate cause rather than the remote one is to be looked to

Maninat Case (1905), R.I.A.A. 55, 81 (holding the Venezuelan Government liable for death of the claimant, who died of tetanus, because the tetanus flowed naturally from, and was thus proximately caused by, a machete wound he received while in the Government's care). **144n329**

Amco Asia Corp. et al. *v. Republic of Indonesia*, ICSID Case No. ARB/81/1, Award, ¶ 266 (Nov. 20, 1984) (observing the international principle that damages are limited to only that which was direct and foreseeable; in this case from a contract breach and license revocation by the Indonesian Government). **32n175, 40nn208–9, 41, 41–42n212, 41n210, 42n213, 44n228, 90nn17–18, 94n38, 100n79, 105n101, 120n191, 121n199, 138n294, 145n335, 148n358, 149n359, 149n362, 150n370, 197–98n244**

BG Group v. Rep. of Argentina, UNCITRAL, Final Award, ¶ 428 (Dec. 24, 2007) (noting that full reparation is limited to the harm that is proximately caused by the illicit act—in this case, a law passed to dismantle a regulatory scheme causing harm to a foreign corporation). **145n335**

Lemire v. Ukraine, ICSID Case No. ARB/06/18, Award, ¶¶ 155-72 (Mar. 28, 2011) (holding that, "[i]f it can be proven that in the normal cause of events a certain cause will produce a certain effect, it can be safely assumed that a (rebuttable) presumption of causality between both events exists, and that the first is the proximate cause of the other"). **140n308, 145n335, 146–47, 146n343, 146n350, 149n361, 149n363, 150n365, 180n132**

S.D. Myers Inc. v. Gov't of Canada, UNICTRAL, Partial Award, ¶¶ 140-59 (Oct. 21, 2002) (holding Canada liable for an investor's loss caused by the State's ban on exports of polychlorinated biphenyl, but only to the extent that the ban proximately caused that harm). **77n438, 112–13, 112n42, 145–46n339, 145n335**

LG&E Energy Corp. v. Argentine Republic, ICSID Case No. ARB/02/01, Award, ¶ 50 (July 25, 2007) (where a claimant suffers economic loss from the change in a tariff regime, but "it appears evident that the value of [those] assets . . . would have been negatively impacted by the economic situation [anyway]," the proper damages are determined by "the dividends they could have earned had the tariff regime not been abrogated"). **145n335, 150n371**

CME Czech Republic B.V. v. Czech Republic, UNCITRAL, Partial Award, ¶¶ 527, 584-85 (Sept. 13, 2001) (holding that "[c]ausation arises if the damage or disadvantage deriving from the deprivation of the legal safety of the investment is foreseeable and occurs in a normal sequence of events"; finding that the loss suffered by the investor was a foreseeable consequence of the acts of the State). **40n208, 129nn238–39, 145n335, 202n269**

Hoffland Honey Oil Co. v. Nat'l Iranian Oil Co., Award No. 22-495-2 (January 26, 1983), 2 Iran-U.S. Cl. Trib. Rep. 41 (holding that, in order to state a claim, a claimant must allege facts indicating that its property was lost through conduct attributable to the respondent that is wrongful as a matter of law; where the respondent merely sold oil to a third party, and those third parties used that oil to produce chemicals that damaged a claimant's business, the sales were not the proximate cause of the loss). **145n335, 147n348**

Guidance Regarding Jus ad Bellum Liability, Eritrea-Ethiopia Claims Commission, Decision No. 7, ¶¶ 7, 13 (July 27, 2007) (observing that "[c]ompensation can only be awarded in respect of damages having a sufficient causal connection with conduct violating international law" and finding that the necessary connection is best described as "proximate cause," which requires examination of whether the damage should have been reasonably foreseeable to the actor committing the delict in question). **145n336, 146n339**

Ioannis Kardassopoulos v. Georgia, ICSID Case Nos. ARB/05/18 & ARB/07/15, Award, ¶¶ 465-70 (Mar. 3, 2010) (finding that the value due to claimant was calculated in relation to the harm proximately caused by a decree that unfairly revoked oil export rights). **144nn332–33, 146n342**

Biwater v. Tanzania, ICSID Case No. ARB/05/22, Award, ¶ 778 (July 24, 2008) (holding that Tanzania was not liable for damages related to the failure of a water company where financial troubles began prior to the nation's wrongful acts such that resulting losses could not be fairly traced to Tanzania for purposes of proximate cause); *but see Biwater v. Tanzania*, ICSID Case No. ARB/05/22, ¶ 15-19 (July 18, 2008) (concurring and dissenting opinion of Gary Born) (asserting that the majority confused issues of causation with the calculation of damages). **101n81, 147, 147n347**

Elettronica Sicula S.p.A. (ELSI) (U.S. v. It), Judgment, 1989 I.C.J. 15, ¶¶ 100-01 (July 20) (finding that, because the claimant's own business decisions caused its insolvency, Italy could not be held liable for breaching a treaty, as the State's acts were not the proximate cause of the asserted loss). **78n442, 147n347**

Osorio v. Dole Food, 665 F. Supp. 2d 1307, 1333-35, 1345 (S.D. Fla. 2009), *aff'd sub nom. Osorio v. Dow Chem. Co.*, 635 F.3d 1277 (11th Cir. 2001) (refusing to recognize a foreign judgment given under a foreign law that established a presumption of causation between exposure to a chemical and sterility, because such a presumption was enacted against clear scientific proof to the contrary). **38n201, 83–84, 83n467, 148, 148n352, 182n150**

Wherever there is an invasion of a right, there is a remedy—*ubi ius ibi remedium est*—and that remedy must wipe out all the consequences of the illegal act and re-establish the situation which would have existed had that act not been committed

Chorzow Factory (Germany v. Poland), Judgment No. 8, 1927 P.C.I.J. 5, 21 (June 1927) (holding that Poland's seizure of a German company's factory in violation of a contract obligated reparations that negate the violation entirely, which includes interest). **8n38, 14, 14n70, 105n101, 106n106, 107n111, 130–31, 131n248, 148n357, 197n240, 200n265**

Sapphire Int'l Petroleum v. NIOC, 35 Int'l L. Rep. 136, 186-87 (1963) (holding that the claimant was due reparations for the full value of a breached contract as though it had been performed, but not for any damages that would put the claimant in a better position than if the contract had been performed). **33n177, 90nn16–17, 101n82, 148n357**

INA Corp. v. Islamic Republic of Iran, Award No. 184-161-1 (Aug. 13, 1985), 8 Iran-US Cl. Trib. Rep. 373, 395, 411 (holding that claimant was due reparations, including interest, for value lost when Iran nationalized a company it owned). **148n357**

Amco Asia Corp. v. Republic of Indonesia, ICSID Case No. ARB/81/1, Resubmitted Case, Award, ¶¶ 178-87 (June 5, 1990) (holding that Indonesia was required to pay all remedial costs, including lost profits, for its acts taken against a foreign investor). **32n175, 40nn208–9, 41, 41–42n212, 41n210, 42n213, 44n228, 90nn17–18, 94n38, 100n79, 105n101, 120n191, 121n199, 138n294, 145n335, 148n358, 149n359, 149n362, 150n370, 197–98n244**

ICC Award No. 1526 (1968), 101 Clunet 915, 918 (1974) (calculating damages for a breach of contract based on an evaluation of foreseeable events in the ordinary course of business). **148n358**

Russian Indemnity Case, Permanent Court of Arbitration, Award, 10-12 (Nov. 11, 1912) (holding that a respondent State was required to fulfill its obligations by compensating an investor for injuries sustained by during war, including interest). **8, 9n41, 149n360**

Sylvania Tech. Sys. Inc. v. Gov't of the Islamic Republic of Iran, Award No. 180-64-1, 8 Iran-U.S. Cl. Trib. Rep. 298, 320 (1985) (invoking international law to hold that, "[i]n the absence of a contractually stipulated rate of interest, the Tribunal will derive a rate of interest based approximately on the amount that the successful claimant would have been in a position to have earned if it had been paid in time and thus have the funds available to invest in a form of a commercial investment in common use in its own country"). **46n239, 103n92, 104n95, 149n360**

ICC Award No. 5835 (1999), 10 ICC Bull. No. 2, at 33, 39 (finding that Kuwaiti law compelling the payment of interest that accrued after the breach was in accordance with internationally accepted principles). **149n360**

Lemire v. Ukraine, ICSID Case No. ARB/06/18, Award, ¶ 249 (Mar. 28, 2011) (observing that the measure of compensation for breaches of the FET standard are complex, and typically require the Tribunal to accept certain reasonable assumptions and "conjecture as to how things would have evolved 'but for' the actual behaviour of the parties." However, "[t]his difficulty in calculation cannot . . . deprive an investor, who has suffered injury, from his fundamental right to see his losses redressed"). **140n308, 145n335, 146–47, 146n343, 146n350, 149n361, 149n363, 150n365, 180n132**

Amoco Int'l Fin. Corp. v. Iran, Award No. 310-56-3 (14 July 1987), 15 Iran-U.S. Cl. Trib. Rep. 189, ¶ 238 (holding, as a general principle of law, that reparations are not available for speculative or uncertain damages). **104n95, 149n364**

A party claiming a breach of contract is obliged to take such measures as are reasonable in the circumstances to mitigate its loss resulting from the breach

ICC Award No. 2478 (1974), YCA 1978, at 222, 223 (also published in: Clunet 1975, at 925 *et seq)* (holding that the duty to mitigate requires the injured party to take all necessary steps so as not to increase the injury). **150n366**

ICC Award No. 7110 (1999), 10 ICC Bull. No. 2, at 1029 *et seq.* (holding that the respondent's use of materials retained due to non-payment was consistent with duty to mitigate losses for a breach of contract). **98n68, 150n368**

ICC Award No. 8817 (1999), 10 ICC Bull. No. 2, at 75 *et seq.* (also published in: YCA 2000, at 355 *et seq.* ¶¶ 51-53) (holding that the claimant was not due compensation for loss that could have been reasonably avoided under the international duty to mitigate, despite a breach by respondent that interrupted claimant's business). **150n366**

Middle East Cement Shipping & Handling Co. S.A. v. Arab Republic of Egypt, ICSID Case No. ARB/99/6, Award, ¶ 167 (Apr. 12, 2002) (finding that although the duty to mitigate damages was not expressly mentioned in the treaty, "[t]his duty can be considered to be part of the General Principles of Law which, in turn, are part of the rules of international law which are applicable in [the] dispute according to Art. 42 of the ICSID Convention"). **32n174, 68n382, 78, 78n440, 150n367, 161–62, 162n28, 191–92n205**

ICC Award No. 5885, 16 Y.B. Comm. Arb. 91 (1991) (holding that although the claimant had rightfully terminated the contract due to lack of confirmed letters of credit, it had not met its burden of proving that it was unable to avoid the allegedly resulting loss of profit, because it could have capitalized on the rising market price of the commodity in question). **150n369**

AMCO Asia Corp. et al. *v. The Republic of Indonesia*, YCA 1992, at 73 (holding that the duty to mitigate was not violated when it would have been impossible to find purchasers that could have mitigated the loss, given the breach of contract). **32n175, 40nn208–9, 41, 41–42n212, 41n210, 42n213, 44n228, 90nn17–18, 94n38, 100n79, 105n101, 120n191, 121n199, 138n294, 145n335, 148n358, 149n359, 149n362, 150n370, 197–98n244**

The same damages may not be compensated twice

Mobil v. Venezuela, ICSID Case No. ARB/07/27, Decision on Jurisdiction, ¶ 378 (June 10, 2010) (holding that where one claimant had already been compensated for an injury, additional compensation threatened to award double recovery, which is prohibited under the well-established principle of *enrichessement sans cause*). **137n111, 151n372**

Pan American Energy LLC and BP Argentina Exploration Company v. Argentine Republic ICSID Case No. ARB/03/13, Decision on Preliminary Objections, ¶ 219 (July 27, 2006) (warning that a corporation's standing to make claims relating to acts prejudicial to both its shareholding and to the contractual rights of the subsidiary company of which it was a shareholder risks the possibility of an impermissible double or triple recovery by the claimants). **122n201**

Sempra Energy Int'l v. Argentine Republic, ICSID Case No. ARB/02/16, Award, ¶ 395 (Sept. 28, 2007) (noting that concerns about double recovery on account of renegotiated tariffs did not preclude an award, given the government's ability to negotiate such recovery in those external contexts). **102–3n89, 138nn292–93, 150n371**

LG&E Energy Corp. v. Argentine Republic, ICSID Case No. ARB/02/01, Award, ¶ 90 (July 25, 2007) (holding that the tribunal is not able to calculate compensation for the claimant's future, speculative losses, as doing so would create the potential for double recovery). **145n335, 150n371**

CMI Int'l, Inc. v. Ministry of Rds. and Transp. (MORT) and the Islamic Republic of Iran, Award No. 99-245-2 (Dec. 27, 1983), 4 Iran-U.S. Cl. Trib. Rep. 263, 270 (where a claimant successfully proved a breach of contract by virtue of non-payment, but had secured a "substantial[]" profit on the resale of the undelivered goods, "general principles of law . . . require[d] accounting for profits made on resale"). **47, 47n242, 151n373**

G. The Principles of Responsibility and Fault

A party is only responsible for its own acts and those of its agents, and thus cannot be liable to restore that which was never in its power to restore, or to compensate an injury which it did not cause

Jan de Nul NV and Dredging International NV v. Egypt, ICSID No. ARB/04/13, Award, ¶ 156 (Nov. 6, 2008) (finding that States are responsible for acts and omissions of organs and agents as determined by the State's organic structure, in their exercise of governmental powers). **77n438, 152n382, 153n390**

Sergei Paushok, CJSC Golden East Company, CJSC Vostokneftegaz Company v. Mongolia, UNCITRAL, Award on Jurisdiction and Liability, ¶ 576 (Apr. 28, 2011) (holding that Mongolia was liable for entities that could be deemed organs of the State, in this case a bank that was sufficiently connected to the State so as to establish state responsibility for its actions). **152n382, 153n389**

Case Concerning United States Diplomatic and Consular Staff in Tehran, Judgment, I.C.J. Rep., ¶ 56, 58 (1980) (holding that Iran cannot be held directly responsible for activities of individuals who overran American embassy because there was no indication those individuals were instructed to do so by a competent organ of the State). **152n383, 153nn386–87, 191n201**

Bayindir Insaat Turizim Ticaret Ve Sanayi A.S. v. Islamic Republic of Pakistan, ICSID Case No. ARB/03/29, Award, ¶ 119 (Aug. 27, 2009) (holding that a separate legal entity could not be considered an organ of the government of Pakistan, but that its actions were directly attributable to the government and therefore sufficient to sustain an action against Pakistan by those harmed by its acts). **153n390**

EDF (Services) Limited v. Romania, ICSID Case No. ARB/05/13, Award, ¶ 190 (Oct. 8, 2009) (holding that Romania could not be held liable for activities committed by an entity that was not an organ or instrumentality of the State, and whose acts could otherwise not be directly attributable to the State). **112n138, 153n390, 188–89n190, 195n224, 196–97n236, 197n239**

Compañía de Aguas del Aconquija, S.A. and Vivendi (formerly Compagnie Générale des Eaux) v. Argentine Republic, ICSID Case No. ARB/97/3, Award, ¶ 49 (Nov. 21, 2000) (holding that the Argentine federal government can be held liable for acts attributable to the Province of Tucumán and cannot use its internal constitutional structure to separate itself from liability for its political sub-divisions). **95n43, 98n64, 153n390**

Metalclad Corporation v. The United Mexican States, ICSID Case No. ARB(AF)/97/1 Award, ¶ 73 (Aug. 30, 2000) (holding that the Mexican federal government can be held liable for acts taken by a municipality even though municipalities are not explicitly named as organs of the State in the governing agreement). **111, 111n136, 127n229, 128n238, 153–54n390, 163, 163n34**

Case of Velásquez Rodríguez v. Honduras, Merits, Judgment, Inter-Am. Ct. H.R. (Ser. C) No. 4, ¶ 170 (July 29, 1988), 95 Int'l L. Rep. 232 (holding that "[u]nder international law a State is responsible for the acts of its agents undertaken in their official capacity and for their omissions, even when those agents act outside the sphere of their authority or violate internal law"). **154n394**

A State cannot cite its own internal law to evade an international obligation

Benteler v. Belgian State, Award, November 18, 1983, 1 J. Int. Arb. 184, 190 (1984) (finding that where a State entity entered an international joint venture agreement with a private company, which included an agreement to arbitrate, that entity cannot thereafter assert that its own internal law "except[s] . . . public law entities" from any capacity to enter an arbitration agreement). **125n218, 155n401**

Company Z and Others v. State Organization ABC, Award, April 1982, 8 Y.B. Comm. Arb. 94, 108-09 (1983) (finding that, within the framework of an agreement regarding the exploitation of natural resources between a private and state-owned entity, a contract containing an arbitration clause cannot be contested on the basis that it had not been approved by a domestic legislature; finding that it had jurisdiction over the dispute, because a state-entity cannot rely on its own errors, irregularities, acts or omissions to free itself of an arbitration clause on which the foreign co-contractor was entitled to rely in good faith, as an essential protection, without which there would be grounds for the presumption that the contract as a whole would never have been concluded). **125n218, 155n401**

Treatment of Polish Nationals and Other Persons of Polish Origin or Speech in the Danzig Territory, Advisory Opinion, P.C.I.J. (Ser. A/B) No. 44, 24-25 (1932) (holding that, because "a State cannot adduce as against another State its own Constitution with a view to evading obligations incumbent upon it under international law or treaties in force," the question of the treatment of foreign nationals must likewise be settled exclusively on the bases of the rules of international law and the treaty provisions in force between Poland and Danzig). **94n40, 125n218, 154n397**

Interpretation of the Convention between Greece and Bulgaria Respecting Reciprocal Emigration, Signed at Neully-Sur-Seine on November 27, 1919 (the Greco-Bulgarian Communities Case), 1930 P.C.I.J. (Ser. B) No. 17, 32 (July 31) (finding, in connection with its interpretation of the convention between Greece and Bulgaria respecting reciprocal emigration, that "[i]t is a generally accepted principle of international law that in the relations between Powers who are contracting Parties to a treaty, the provisions of municipal law cannot prevail over those of the treaty"). **154n398**

ICC Award No. 7263 (1994), Interim Award, 22 Y.B. Comm. Arb. 92, 98 (1997) (holding that, "[i]n the field of international commercial arbitration . . . states and public bodies as defendants . . . cannot avail themselves of the incapacity and lack of authorization [to contract] deriving from their national laws"). **125n218, 155n401**

The General Principles of Law in Judicial Proceedings and International Due Process

A. Notice and Jurisdiction

Any decision made without jurisdiction is a nullity

Mavrommatis Palestine Concession Case (Greece v. U.K), Judgment, 1924 P.C.I.J. (Ser. A) No. 2 (Aug. 30) (dissenting opinion of Judge Moore) (holding that no tribunal can hear or judge the merits of a case for which it has no jurisdiction, and that a tribunal has no jurisdiction to adjudicate a matter that arose before a treaty entered into force). **38n199, 95n46, 158n4**

Pennoyer v. Neff, 95 U.S. 714, 722, 733-34 (1878) (holding, as a "well established principle of public law," that a court must have jurisdiction prior to considering the merits of a particular cause and that any decision made without jurisdiction is a nullity: "[p]roceedings in a court of justice to determine the personal rights and obligations of parties over whom that court has no jurisdiction do not constitute due process of law"). **158n6, 160n18, 162n28**

A court or tribunal cannot refuse to decide a case that falls within its jurisdiction

White Industries Australia Limited v. The Republic of India, UNCITRAL, Award (Nov. 30, 2011) (holding that India violated its international law obligations when its judiciary delayed consideration of a case, over which it had jurisdiction, for nine years). **78n445, 159n11**

Chevron Corporation (USA) and Texaco Petroleum Company (USA) v. The Republic of Ecuador, UNCITRAL, PCA Case No. 34877, Partial Award (Mar. 30, 2010) (holding that the Ecuador violated its international law obligations when its judiciary delayed consideration of cases, over which it had jurisdiction, for nearly 15 years). **78n445, 159n11**

Antoine Fabiani (No. 1) (Fr. v. Venez), in Moore, Arbitrations 4895 (holding that "denial of justice includes not only the refusal of a judicial authority to exercise his functions and, in particular, to give a decision on the request submitted to him, but also wrongful delays on his part in giving judgment"). **159n11**

Due notice of the proceeding is a cardinal antecedent to a court or tribunal's competence

Pennoyer v. Neff, 95 U.S. 714, 730 (1878) (holding that a defendant cannot be bound by a court of law if the defendant had not been served with process: "[p]ersonal judgments rendered in another State against nonresidents, without service upon them . . . it has been held, without an exception, . . . that such judgments were without any binding force"). **158n6, 160n18, 162n28**

Hilton v. Guyot, 159 U.S. 113, 144 (1895) (holding that a foreign judgment cannot be recognized unless the foreign court fulfilled certain requirements of due process, including adequate prior notice of the judicial proceedings). **68n381, 69n390, 72n404, 79, 80n451, 81n458, 81n460, 160n20, 162n28, 170n73, 177n118, 182n150, 187n180**

Middle East Cement Shipping and Handling Co. S.A. v. Arab Republic of Egypt, ICSID Case No. ARB/99/6, Award, ¶¶ 143 *et seq.* (Apr. 12, 2002) (finding that Egypt's seizure of claimant's property and subsequent publication of the proceeding in a newspaper was not sufficient notice of the proceeding, under the international concept of due process of law). **32n174, 68n382, 78, 78n440, 150n367, 161–62, 162n28, 191–92n205**

Dame Veuve Trompier-Gravier, CE Sect. (May 5, 1944), Rec. Lebon 133 (finding that respect for the rights of defense requires that: the person must be informed early enough that a measure will be taken against him, and the facts against him, so as to be able to prepare his defense). **67, 162n29**

Generica Ltd. v. Pharm. Basics, Inc., 125 F.3d 1123, 1129-30 (7th Cir. 1997) (holding that arbitration requires fundamentally fair hearings including, at minimum, adequate notice prior to proceedings). **80n457, 85n484, 162n28, 178n125**

Ivcher-Bronstein Case, Judgment, Inter-Am. Ct. H.R. (Ser. C) No. 74, ¶ 104 (Feb. 6, 2001) (holding that due process was violated when, inter alia, the defendant in an administrative proceeding was not told in advance of the charges levied against him). **162n31, 169, 169n68, 170, 170n70**

Metalclad Corporation v. The United Mexican States, ICSID Case No. ARB(AF)/97/1, Award, ¶ 91 (Aug. 30, 2000) (holding that the denial of a construction permit "at a meeting of the Municipal Town Council of which [the applicant] received no notice, to which it received no invitation, and at which it was given no opportunity to appear, . . . demonstrates a lack of orderly process . . . in according with the NAFTA"). **111, 111n136, 127n229, 128n238, 153–54n390, 163, 163n34**

LaGrand Case (*Germany v. United States of America*), I.C.J., Request for the Indication of Provisional Measures, Order, Mar. 3, 1999, I.C.J. Reports 1999, 13, ¶ 13 (noting that the court need not make a final decision on jurisdiction before awarding provisional measures, but that it must only be satisfied of its *prima facie* jurisdiction). **163n36**

Perenco v. Ecuador, ICSID Case No. ARB/08/6, Decision on Provisional Measures, ¶ 39 (May 8, 2009) (noting that a court will not issue orders unless it has, at least, *prima facie* evidence of jurisdiction). **163n36, 191–92n205**

B. Judicial Impartiality and Judicial Independence

Nemo debet esse iudex in propria sua causa—No one should be the judge in his own case

In re Pinochet, [1999] UKHL 52 (Jan. 15, 1999) (holding that, because the judge had a stake in the outcome of litigation, he was sitting in violation of the principle that no one can be a judge in his own cause). **173n92, 173n97, 174n101**

New Regency Prods., Inc. v. Nippon Herald Films, Inc., 501 F. 3d 1101, 1109-111 (9th Cir. 2007) (holding that the arbitrator's failure to investigate and disclose to the parties to the arbitration any possible conflicts related to his recent employment with a company that was negotiating with one of the respondent's production executives to finance and co-produce a major motion picture, was sufficient to find evident partiality and invalidate the award). **173–74n97**

EDF Int'l S.A., SAUR Int'l S.A. and León Participaciones Argentinas S.A. v. Argentine Republic, ICSID Case No. ARB/03/23, Challenge Decision Regarding Prof. Gabrielle Kaufmann-Kohler (June 25, 2008) (finding that the economic or personal interest which an arbitrator had in one of the parties was insignificant and did not impugn her impartiality). **173–74n97**

TCR Sports Broadcasting Holding, LLP v. WN Partner LLC, No. 652044, 2015 WL 6746687, ¶¶ 70-74 (N.Y. Sup. Ct. N.Y. Co. Nov. 4, 2015 (observing that it is "[a]xiomatic that a neutral decision-maker may not decide disputes in which he or she has a personal stake"). **174n98**

Suez et al. *v. Argentine Republic*, ICSID Case Nos. ARB/03/19 & ARB/03/17, Decision on the Proposal for the Disqualification of a Member of the Arbitral Tribunal (Oct. 22, 2007) (holding that it was not sufficient to remove an arbitrator because of her award against the State in another arbitration). **173–74n97, 174n99**

AGW Grp. Ltd. v. Argentine Republic, UNCITRAL, Decision on a Second Proposal for the Disqualification of a Member of the Arbitral Tribunal ¶ 36 (May 12, 2008) (finding that a challenged arbitrator derived no economic benefit from her directorship and shareholding in a minority corporate shareholding in two of the claimants, and there was no justifiable doubt as to her independence and impartiality). **173–74n97, 174nn99**

LLC First Excavator Co. v. JSC Union of Industry RosProm, Case No. 1308/11 (Russia) (annulling an arbitration award where the appointed arbitrator was the chief executive of the respondent corporation; this close personal tie violated the principle that no one may be a judge in his own cause). **173n93**

Sramek v. Austria, ECHR Judgment on Application No. 8790/79, ¶ 42 (Oct. 22, 1984) (holding that where three of the judges were subordinate employees of one of the parties, the process violated the requirement that judges not have an interest in the outcome of a case). **173n93**

Micallef v. Malta, ECHR Judgment on Application No. 17056/06, ¶¶ 102-05 (Oct. 15, 2009) (finding that, although the judge did not display any personal bias, the "close family ties" of the judge to a party's advocate was sufficient to question the judge's impartiality and invalidate the judgment). **173n97, 174n99**

Karttunen v. Finland, Communication No. 387/1989, U.N. Doc. CCPR/C/46/D/387/1989 (1992), Report of the HRC, ¶ 7.2 (holding that a tribunal comprised of five judges, one of whom is an uncle of a party and a partner in a business also acting against the opposing party, "cannot normally be considered to be [a] fair or impartial" tribunal under international law). **173n94**

The Loewen Group, Inc. & Raymond L. Loewen v. United States, ICSID Case No. ARB(AF)/98/3, Award, ¶ 135 (June 23, 2003) (finding improper judicial bias shown where the trial court permitted consistent appeals to the jury based on local favoritism). **76, 76n430, 77, 77n433, 77n437, 82, 174n100, 182, 182n146**

A judiciary must be free from improper external political influences

Idler v. Venezuela, 4 MOORE'S INTERNATIONAL, ARBITRATIONS 3491, 3516-17 (1886) (finding that an unjustified change in the makeup of the court immediately prior to adjudicating a particular case constituted manipulation of the judicial branch by the Venezuelan government). **39, 39n202, 165–66, 165n45, 166–67n50, 175**

Robert E. Brown (U.S. v. Great Britain), VI R.I.A.A. 120 (1923), 129 (finding that executive and legislative manipulation of the South African courts in order to vacate a High Court opinion that would have subjected the executive to liability was in violation of international law obligations). **167, 167n51, 167n59, 175**

Ivcher Bronstein Case, Judgment of February 6, 2001, Inter-Am. Ct. H.R. (Ser. C) No. 74, at ¶ 3 (holding that, because a court was created specifically to review a decision to revoke citizenship, the result of the process was improperly manipulated by the government in violation of the requirement that tribunals be previously established by law). **162n31, 169, 169n68, 170, 170n70**

Hilton v. Guyot, 159 U.S. 113, 158-59 (1895) (holding that only foreign judgments rendered "by a court having jurisdiction of the cause, and upon regular proceedings," meaning those established by law, should be enforced in other States). **68n381, 69n390, 72n404, 79, 80n451, 81n458, 81n460, 160n20, 162n28, 170n73, 177n118, 182n150, 187n180**

Chevron Corp. v. Donziger, 974 F. Supp. 2d 362, at 557-66, 644 (S.D.N.Y. 2014) (holding that a judgment against petroleum company in Ecuador was procured by fraud and thus unenforceable due to the plaintiffs' interference with and influence over the judge). **170nn72–73, 198n248**

Hulley Enters. v. The Russian Republic, UNCITRAL, PCA Case No. AA226, ¶ 1583 (July 18, 2014) (holding that due process was lacking where local courts "bent to the will of the executive authorities" to bankrupt their political competitor). **134, 134nn270–71, 136, 137n285, 169n67, 175**

Vidovic v. Losinjka Plovidka Oour Broadarstvo, 868 F. Supp. 695, 699-702 (E.D. Pa. 1994) (holding that defendants' inability to demonstrate the impartiality of Croatian courts, in cases involving Croatian government and in face of evident bias, disqualified those courts from being an adequate forum to adjudicate a claim concerning government interests). **170n74**

Bank Melli Iran v. Pahlavi, 58 F.3d 1406, 1412-13 (9th Cir. 1995) (finding that questions as to the impartiality of Iranian judges where the bench was subject to scrutiny and threat of sanctions by the executive meant decisions made by those judges could not be recognized as a system that comports with due process). **72n403, 72n405, 81n460, 171n76, 182nn149–50, 189n191, 190–91n200**

Bridgeway Corp. v. Citibank, 45 F. Supp. 2d 276, 287 (S.D.N.Y. 1999) *aff'd*, 201 F.3d 134 (2d Cir. 2000) (finding inadequate due process in the Liberian judicial system because the judges and justices served at the will of competing parties and were subject to political and social influence; judgments from such a court could not be recognized as coming from a system that comports with due process). **39n202, 79n448, 171n77**

Yukos Capital S.A.R.L. v. Rosneft, Amsterdam Court of Appeal, Case No. 200.005.269/1, ¶¶ 3.9.1, 3.8.9 (Apr. 28, 2009) (finding inadequate due process when defendant was subject to a court that closely aligned with the Russian State and the interests of the state-owned entity, which was a party to the case). **69n387, 79n448, 132n255, 134n271, 169, 169n67, 171n78, 189n191, 190–91n200, 196n231**

Sovtransavto Holding v. Ukraine, ECHR Judgment on Application No. 48553/99 of July 25, 2002, ¶ 82 (holding that because Ukrainian officials intervened on a number of occasions with judicial proceedings, the parties were denied the right to an independent and impartial tribunal). **175n104**

Petrobart v. Kyrgyz Rep., SCC Arb. No. 126/2003, Award, 28, 75-76 (Mar. 29, 2005) (holding that the "direct and capricious intervention in its own court procedures by the Vice Prime Minister, . . . requesting [a] stay of execution of a valid judgment and the willingness of the . . . Court to readily accord the requested stay of execution, . . . cannot be regarded as anything other than . . . [a] perver[sion of the] administration of justice to which [that party] was entitled under any civilised system of law"). **78n444, 175n106, 202n270**

DeJoria v. Maghreb Petro. Exploration S.A., 38 F. Supp. 3d 805, 811-17 (W.D. Tex. 2014) (refusing to recognize a Moroccan judgment on the basis that it was not rendered under a system that provided impartial tribunals and procedures compatible with due process, because the judiciary was susceptible to the interference of the Moroccan king who had an apparent interest in the outcome of the case; the Moroccan constitution did not establish an autonomous judiciary; and the mechanisms for the appointment, promotion, sanction, and dismissal of judges left them vulnerable to political retribution if they ruled against the royal family), rev'd, 804 F. 3d 373 (5th Cir. 2015) (recognizing Moroccan judgment in part because under the Texas Recognition Act "the court's inquiry . . . focuses on the fairness of the foreign judicial system as a whole, and we do not parse the particular judgment challenged"). **171, 171n79, 172, 172n90, 175**

C. Procedural Equality and the Right to be Heard

Courts and tribunals must ensure equal treatment of litigants and a reasonable opportunity for them to assert and defend their rights

Kaufman v. Belgium, App. No. 10938/84, 50 Eur. Comm'n H.R. Dec. & Rep. 98, 115 (1986) (observing that "everyone who is a party to . . . proceedings shall have a reasonable opportunity of presenting his case to the Court under conditions which do not place him at substantial disadvantage vis-à-vis his opponent," but holding that the denial of an opportunity to submit a written memorial in reply to opponents' arguments did not necessarily violate this right). **177n116**

Dombo Beheer B.V. v. The Netherlands, ECHR, Judgment, ¶ 40 (Oct. 27, 1993) (holding that the refusal by the national courts to allow the applicant company's former managing director to give evidence, while the manager of the branch office of their opponent was so heard, was a failure to observe the principle of "equality of arms"). **177n116, 177n119**

Delcourt v. Belgium, App. No. 2689/65, Eur. Ct. H.R., Judgment, ¶ 34 (Jan. 17, 1970) (recognizing that "[a] trial would not be fair if it took place in such conditions as to put the accused unfairly at a disadvantage"). **177n116**

Amco Asia Corp. et al. *v. Republic of Indonesia*, ICSID Case No. ARB/81/1, Award, ¶¶ 196-98 (Nov. 20, 1984) (finding that where a sanction imposed by the State is "heavy" and "irremediable," an individual must have adequate warning of the contemplated action as an "element of due process"). **32n175, 40nn208–9, 41, 41–42n212, 41n210, 42n213, 44n228, 90nn17–18, 94n38, 100n79, 105n101, 120n191, 121n199, 138n294, 145n335, 148n358, 149n359, 149n362, 150n370, 197–98n244**

Mathews v. Eldridge, 424 U.S. 319, 324 (1976) (holding that an opportunity to be heard at a meaningful time in a meaningful manner is a requirement of justice that must occur before a person is finally deprived of a property interest). **65n357, 65n362, 115n160, 177n117**

Armstrong v. Manzo, 380 U.S. 545, 552 (1965) (holding that basic requirements of due process demand that all interested parties be provided an opportunity to be heard, so a party's complete inability to contradict a material claim made by his opponent was a denial of due process). **65n357, 177n117**

Philip Morris U.S.A. v. Williams, 549 U.S. 346, 353 (2007) (holding that due process requires the opportunity to put on all possible defenses, and does not allow for damages based on harm alleged on behalf of nonparties to the case). **65n358, 177n117**

Hilton v. Guyot, 159 U.S. 113, 202 (1895) (observing that for a judgment to be considered "civilized jurisprudence," it must be based on "due allegations and proofs and opportunity to defend against them"; where "the whole merits of the case [in the foreign court] were open . . . to the parties, however much they may have failed to take advantage of them," the judgment should be recognized and the matter not retried again in an enforcing court). **68n381, 69n390, 72n404, 79, 80n451, 81n458, 81n460, 160n20, 162n28, 170n73, 177n118, 182n150, 187n180**

Bremer v. South India Shipping Corp. Ltd., [1981] A.C. 909, 917 (H.L) (observing that "[e]very civilised system of government requires that the state should make available to all its citizens a means for the just and peaceful settlement of disputes between them as to their respective legal rights"). **178n121**

Golder v. The United Kingdom, ECHR, Judgment (Merits and Just Satisfaction), ¶¶ 18, 35-6 (Feb. 21, 1975) (holding that the right of access to a lawyer is a fundamental part of ensuring the right of access to the courts, and is thus a fundamental principle of due process). **178, 178n122**

Wena Hotels Ltd. v. Arab Republic of Egypt, ICSID Case No. ARB/98/4, Decision on Annulment, ¶¶ 56-57 (Feb. 5, 2002) (holding that it is a fundamental matter of due process that each party be given the equal right to state its case and produce arguments and evidence in support thereof, and that a decision can be annulled when a tribunal seriously departs from this principle). **40n208, 44–45n228, 178n124, 184n161**

Application for Review of Judgement No. 158 of the United Nations Administrative Tribunal, Advisory Opinion, 1973 I.C.J. 166, ¶ 36 (July 12) (finding that "[g]eneral principles of law and the judicial character of the Court do require that, even in advisory proceedings, the interested parties should each have an opportunity, and on a basis of equality, to submit all the elements relevant to the questions which have been referred to the review tribunal," but that this requirement was satisfied by the submission of written statements). **178n124**

Generica Ltd. v. Pharmaceutical Basics, 125 F.3d 1123, 1130 (7th Cir. 1997) (acknowledging that the exclusion of relevant evidence may deprive a party of a fair hearing, allowing the court to vacate an arbitral award, but that no such violation occurred in this case). **80n457, 85n484, 162n28, 178n125**

Btp Structural Pvt. Ltd. v. Bharat Petroleum Corp. Ltd., Arb. Petition No. 442 of 2010, §§ 18-21 (High Court of Judicature, Bombay Ord. Civil Jur., Apr. 27, 2012) (holding that where an arbitrator gave the petitioner no opportunity to submit arguments, but did allow respondent to do so, there was a clear breach of procedural equality). **178n125**

Lemire v. Ukraine, ICSID Case No. ARB/06/18, ¶¶ 224-25, 336, 350 (Mar. 1, 2011) (dissenting opinion of Dr. Jurgen Voss) (asserting that the respondent was misled in building its defense, and therefore deprived of its right to assert and defend its rights, when the tribunal asked for causation to be argued in the second phase of the proceedings but based its decision on facts and evidence presented only in the first phase of proceedings). **140n308, 145n335, 146–47, 146n343, 146n350, 149n361, 149n363, 150n365, 180n132**

Judgment of 31, 2012, 4A_360/2011 (Switzerland, First Civil Law Court) §§ 5.1, 6.2 (holding that where an arbitrator failed to take into account one party's post-hearing memorandum but considered the opposing party's, that arbitrator violated the fundamental right to procedural equality). **179n126**

Iran Aircraft Industries v. Avco Corporation, 980 F.2d 141, 146 (2d Cir. 1992) (refusing to recognize an arbitral decision where the arbitrator had misled one party as to what method of proof was sufficient by telling the party that actual physical evidence was not required but later requiring such evidence). **85n483, 179n127**

Ohio Bell Tel. Co. v. Public Utilities Comm'n, 301 U.S. 292, 303-04 (1937) (holding that fundamental trial rights were violated when a decision was made based on evidence not in the record). **179n130**

Goldberg v. Kelly, 397 U.S. 254, 267-71 (1970) (holding that an individual is entitled to an impartial decision-maker, the right to confront and cross-examine witnesses, and the right to a written opinion setting out the evidence relied upon and the legal basis for the decision as a matter of due process). **179n128**

Greene v. McElroy, 360 U.S. 474, 496-97 (1959) (holding that "where governmental action seriously injures an individual, and the reasonableness of the action depends on findings of fact, the evidence used to prove the Government's case must be disclosed to the individual so that he has an opportunity to show that it is untrue"). **65n359, 179n28**

Bank Mellat v. Her Majesty's Treasury [2015] UKSC 38, ¶ 2 (noting that, in the absence of rare and exigent circumstances, a court hearing evidence in private is contrary to the principles of fundamental justice). **138n294, 139n298**

Richardson v. Lynda Rivers, A1993/02, ¶ 21 (Aug. 23, 2004) (holding that the duty to secure equality of treatment is generally left to the advocates, and that it is not violated merely because one side's advocate was better than the other). **180n136**

Methanex Corp. v. United States, UNCITRAL, Final Award, ¶ 54 (Aug. 3, 2005) (noting that the United States government could not use its superior and governmental resources to intercept an adverse party's communications; doing so would be a violation of the principle that parties have equality of arms). **95n43, 98n64, 181n141, 196n236, 197n237**

Libananco Holdings Co. v. Turkey, ICSID Case No. ARB/06/8, Decision on Preliminary Issues, ¶ 72 *et seq.* (June 23, 2008) (observing that the Turkish government's interception of counsel's correspondence with a party to arbitration risked violating principles of fairness and equality among the parties). **181nn140–42, 188n190, 197, 197n238**

The Loewen Group, Inc. & Raymond L. Loewen v. United States, ICSID Case No. ARB(AF)/98/3, NAFTA, Award, ¶ 136 (June 23, 2003) (impugning the inequality of treatment suffered by foreigners in local courts, and holding that it is the "responsibility of the courts of a State . . . to ensure that litigation is free from discrimination against a foreign litigant and that the foreign litigant [does] not become the victim of sectional or local prejudice"). **76, 76n430, 77, 77n433, 77n437, 82, 174n100, 182, 182n146**

Bird v. Glacier Electric Cooperative Inc., 255 F.3d, 1136, 1140, 1152 (9th Cir. 2001) (impugning a judicial process that included "racial overtones [and] culminated in a closing argument . . . that repeatedly appealed to racial and ethnic prejudice," and concluding that such practice "offended fundamental fairness and violated due process"). **182n148**

Bank Melli Iran v. Pahlavi, 58 F.3d 1406, 1413 (9th Cir. 1995) (holding that Iranian courts did not comport with fundamental principles of fairness and due process where a party could not personally appear, obtain legal representation, or produce local witnesses on its behalf). **72n403, 72n405, 81n460, 171n76, 182nn149–50, 189n191, 190–91n200**

Osorio v. Dole Food, 665 F. Supp. 2d 1307, 1336, 1341-42 (S.D. Fla. 2009), *aff'd sub nom., Osorio v. Dow Chem. Co.*, 635 F.3d 1277 (11th Cir. 2001)(holding that where provisions of the Nicaraguan special law targeted "a narrowly defined group of foreign defendants and subject[ed] them to discriminatory provisions that d[id] not apply to [other] defendants," the law offended the general principle of equality before the law that is "basic to any definition of due process and fair play"). **38n201, 83–84, 83n467, 148, 148n352, 182n150**

D. The Prohibition of Corruption and the Nullifying Effect of Fraud: *Fraus Omnia Corrumpit*

ICC Award No. 1110 (1963), 10.3 Arb. Int'l 282, 294 (1994) (where an agent filed an arbitration claim seeking commissions with respect to public works contracts—commissions which were expressly intended to be used to bribe members of the local government—the contract calling for arbitration can be given no effect and an arbitral tribunal convened thereunder is without jurisdiction over the matter). **37n195, 184nn156–57, 185n169**

Wena Hotels Ltd. v. Arab Republic of Egypt, ICSID Case No. ARB/98/4, Award, ¶ 70 (Dec. 8, 2000) (holding that if an agreement for a consultant "to give advice and assistance to the [investor] as to opportunities available to the company for developing its hotel business in Egypt" constituted improper influence in the award of leases to the investor then this may be grounds for dismissing the investment claim, but finding that there was no evidence that the agreement was anything other than legitimate). **40n208, 44–45n228, 178n124, 184n161**

Metal-Tech Ltd. v. Republic of Uzbekistan, ICSID Case No. ARB/10/3, Award, ¶¶ 327, 373 (Oct. 4, 2014) (holding that payments to a public official designed to obtain his influence in support of obtaining claimant's investment violated local law and the legality requirement of the relevant Treaty). **43n222, 132n257, 136, 136nn283–84, 184, 184n160, 189, 189n192**

Plama Consortium Limited v. Republic of Bulgaria, ICSID Case No. ARB/03/24, Award, ¶ 143 (Aug. 27, 2008) (holding that an investment obtained by "deceitful conduct" is ineligible for the substantive protections of the Energy Charter Treaty). **49n256, 100–101n79, 136, 136n281, 184**

ICC Award No. 6497, 1999 YCA 71, 72 (observing that "[i]f the bribery nature of the agreements would be demonstrated, such agreements would be null and void in Swiss law. This is not because such bribe would be prohibited by the criminal law of the country in which bribes had been paid, but because the bribes in themselves cannot be, in Swiss law, the object of a valid contract. This is also admitted in most legal systems"). **184n156**

World Duty Free Company Limited v. The Republic of Kenya, ICSID Case No. ARB/00/7, Award ¶¶ 157, 188 (Oct. 4, 2006) (dismissing an investor's claim after discovering it had procured its investment by bribing the President of Kenya). **34n183, 42, 42n214, 43, 43–44n224, 101n83, 132n257, 134n273, 135, 135n277, 136n284, 154n396, 160n17, 184, 184nn162–63, 185n170**

Inceysa Vallisoletana S.L. v. Republic of El Salvador, ICSID Case No. ARB/03/26, Award, ¶ 239 (Aug. 2, 2006) (dismissing an investor's claim after discovering it had procured its investment by falsifying financial statements). **2n2, 47–48n245, 47–49, 89n11, 94n38, 95n44, 96, 96n49, 101n83, 132n157, 136, 136n280, 138n294, 184, 185n164, 185n170**

Lazarus Estates Ltd v. Beasley [1956] 1 QB 702, 712 (per Denning LJ) (holding that "[n]o Court in this land will allow a person to keep an advantage he has obtained by fraud. No judgment of a court, no order of a Minister, can be allowed to stand if it has been obtained by fraud. Fraud unravels everything. The court is careful not to find fraud unless it is distinctly pleaded and proved; but once it is proved it vitiates judgments, contracts and all transactions whatsoever). **185n168**

United States v. Mississippi Valley Generating Co., 364 U.S. 520, 562-66 (1960) (deciding not to allow the enforcement of a government contract where, in the negotiations of the contract, the government had been represented by a consultant to the Budget Bureau who was at same time an officer in an investment bank which was expected to profit from the transaction by becoming a financial agent for the project). **185n170**

Hazel-Atlas Glass Co. v. Hartford Empire Co., 322 U.S. 238, 244 (1944) (holding that equitable principles empower Courts to set aside judgments obtained by fraud, notwithstanding the general rule that judgments would not be altered or set aside after the expiration of the term at which the judgments were finally entered). **186n176**

Aoude v. Mobil Oil Corp., 892 F.2d 1115, 1121 (1st Cir. 1989) (finding that while, generally, "[i]t would be inappropriate and a deplorable kind of injustice mechanically to hold litigants bound by every lawyerly misdeed," the claimant—having masterminded a fraudulent evidential filing effected by his attorney—was jointly culpable in the fraud). **187n178**

European Gas Turbines, ICC, Rev. Arb. 359 (1994) (annulling an arbitration award because the respondent had submitted fraudulent financial reports to the tribunal). **187n179**

Hilton v. Guyot, 159 U.S. 113, 202-03 (1895) (observing that "fraud in procuring [a] judgment" will bar recognition of the same before a foreign court). **68n381, 69n390,**

72n404, 79, 80n451, 81n458, 81n460, 160n20, 162n28, 170n73, 177n118, 182n150, 187n180

Manez Lopez v. Ford Motor Co., 470 F. Supp. 2d 917, 929 (S.D. Ind. 2006) (refusing to recognize an order by a Mexican court when there was abundant circumstantial evidence that the judgment was obtained by fraud). **187n180**

Abouloff v. Oppenheimer, (1882) 10 Q.B.D. 295 (Eng) (holding that an English court would not recognize a judgment by a Russian court that was obtained by fraud). **187n180**

Price v. Dewhurst, (1837) 8 Sim. 279 (Eng), 309 (holding that a will executed in St. Croix and enforced through judicial proceedings there was fraudulent, suffered from self-dealing, and was therefore invalid in England). **187n180**

Judgment of September 23, 1977, Cour de Cassation (1978) Pasicrisie 100, 102-3 (holding that where a seller overvalued the net worth of a company through false statements, the buyer's gross negligence in failing to detect fraud could not be invoked by the seller to prevent annulment of the contract; the seller's fraud deprived it of the ability to invoke the general rule that only parties committing an excusable mistake may seek annulment of a contract). **188n182**

Judgment of May 29, 1980, Cour de Cassation (1980) Pasicrisie 1190 (finding that where a party has committed fraud it cannot invoke the negligence or carelessness of the adverse party to excuse the fraud). **188n182**

Judgment of March 18, 2010, Cour de Cassation (2010) (holding that a fraudulent actor is not permitted to reduce payments owed to defrauded plaintiffs due to plaintiffs own negligence). **188n182**

Judgment of May 23, 1977, Cour de Cassation (Ch civ) (1977) Bulletin civil, I, 244 (refusing to allow the negligence of the party purchasing shares to excuse the fraud of the party selling the shares). **188n182**

Judgment of February 21, 2001, Cour de Cassation (Ch civ) (2001) Bulletin civil, IIII, 20 (holding that fraudulent concealment by one party pardons the negligent error of an adverse party). **188n182**

Judgment of November 6, 2002, Cour de Cassation (2003) JOURNAL DES TRIBUNAUX 301, 310 (holding that a perpetrator who defrauded a bank through forged documents could not invoke the bank's own contributory negligence, which typically would have been available to limit tort liability). **134n269, 188n182**

Case Concerning Oil Platforms (Iran v. U.S), 2003 I.C.J. Rep. 225-34 (Nov. 6, 2003) (separate opinion of Judge Rosalyn Higgins) (observing that the "graver the charge, the more confidence there must be in the evidence relied on," and that the tribunal failed to properly inspect the evidence in this case so as to meet this burden). **25n137, 134, 134n269, 188n188**

Siag and Vecchi v. Egypt, ICSID Case No. ARB/05/15, Award, ¶¶ 325-26 (May 11, 2009) (holding that allegations that a Lebanese nationality application had been approved through fraud should be subject to a heightened standard of proof, and that Egypt failed to meet that standard with sufficient evidence). **108n115, 188n189**

Libananco v. Turkey, ICSID Case No. ARB/06/8, Award (Sept. 2, 2011) (requiring clear and convincing evidence to carry the burden of proving that a case had been fraudulently constructed). **181nn140–42, 188n190, 197, 197n238**

Westinghouse and Burns & Roe (USA) v. Nat'l Power Co. and the Rep. of the Philippines, ICC Case No. 6401, Preliminary Award (Dec. 19, 1991) (requiring that allegations of fraud be proven by clear and convincing evidence rather than a preponderance of the evidence). **188n190**

Hilmarton Ltd. v. Omnium de Traitment et de Valorisation S.A., ICC Case No. 5622, ¶ 23 (1988) (finding indirect evidence of fraud insufficient to prove that the Algerian government demanded bribes for public contracts). **188–89n190**

EDF (Services) Ltd. v. Romania, ICSID Case No. ARB/05/13, Award, ¶ 221 (Oct. 8, 2009) (noting that clear or convincing evidence of corruption is required to prove the allegation that a state official demanded a bribe). **112n138, 153n390, 188–89n190, 195n224, 196–97n236, 197n239**

Himpurnia California Energy Ltd. v. Perusahaan Listruik Negara, in Yb. Comm. Arb., vol. XXV, 11, 42 (Albert Jan van den Berg ed., The Hague: Kluwer 2000) (finding that, although several influential officials benefitted financially from commitments made to public-sector entities, there was no evidence of fraudulent behavior or bribery). **188–89n190**

E. Evidence and Burden of Proof

Actori incumbit onus probandi—the burden of proof belongs to the proponent

Rompetrol v. Romania, ICSID Case No. ARB/06/3, Award, ¶ 178 (May 6, 2013) 178 (explaining that, as a general principle, the burden of proof defines which party has to prove what in order for its case to prevail, and that the standard of proof defines how much evidence is needed to establish either an individual issue or the party's case as a whole). **140–41n308, 189n193, 190n196, 195n225**

Caratube v. Kazakhstan, ICSID Case No. ARB/08/12, Decision on Annulment Application, ¶ 97 (Feb. 21, 2014) (noting that a reversal of the burden of proof could lead to a violation of fundamental rules of procedure). **190n198**

Tokios Tokeles v. Ukraine, ICSID Case No. ARB/02/18, Award, ¶ 124 (July 26, 2007) (observing that "there can be no doubt that the [burden of proof] rests on the Claimant"). **191n205**

Alpha Projektholding GmbH v. Ukraine, ICSID Case No. ARB/07/16, Award, ¶¶ 236-37 (Nov. 8, 2010) (espousing the principle that the burden of proof rests upon the party alleging the particular fact, and also that "once a party adduces sufficient evidence in support of an assertion, the burden 'shifts' to the other party to bring forward evidence to rebut it"). **191n205**

Tradex Hellas S.A. v. Republic of Albania, ICSID Case No. ARB/94/2, Award, ¶ 74 (Dec. 24, 1996) (holding that "it can be considered as a general principle of international procedure—and probably also of virtually all national civil procedural laws—. . . that it is the claimant who has the burden of proof"). **194n219, 194nn216–17**

Salini Costruttori S.p.A. and Italstrade S.p.A. v. Hashemite Kingdom of Jordan, ICSID ARB/02/13, Award, ¶ 70 (Jan. 31 2006) (holding that "[i]t is a well-established principle of law that it is for a claimant to prove the facts on which it relies in support of his claim"). **191n205**

Asian Agricultural Products Limited v. Sri Lanka, ICSID ARB/87/3, Award, ¶ 56 (June 27, 1990) (explaining that while the burden of production may fall on both parties, it is always the claimant that is expected to persuade and convince the tribunal of the truth of its allegations, "lest [its claims] be disregarded for want, or insufficiency, of proof"). **94n39, 97n57, 97n60, 191–92n205, 192n209, 193n211, 195–196n229**

International Thunderbird Gaming Corp. v. Mexico, UNCITRAL, Award, ¶ 95 (Jan. 26, 2006) (applying the "well-established principle that the party alleging a violation of international law giving rise to international responsibility has the burden of proving its assertion" and that if the party "adduces evidence that prima facie supports its allegation, the burden of proof may be shifted to the other Party, if the circumstances so justify"). **6n21, 76n431, 78n439, 78n441, 91n23, 99n70, 126, 126nn222–23, 127n227, 127n230, 129n239, 191–92n205**

Autopista Concesionada de Venezuela, C.A. v. Venezuela, ICSID ARB/00/5, Award, ¶ 110 (Sept. 23, 2003) (observing that, "[a]s a matter of principle, each party has the burden of proving the facts upon which it relies"; it is up to the respondent which relies upon the force majeure excuse to prove that the conditions of force majeure are met). **191–92n205**

ICC Award No. 1434, Clunet 1976, at 978, 982 (acknowledging "the existence of a general principle according to which a claimant who claims damages for non-performance carries the burden of proving the existence and the contents of the obligation while it rests upon the defendant to claim and to prove the fact that he has performed this obligation"). **97nn58–59, 191–92n205**

Perenco v. Ecuador, ICSID Case No. ARB/08/6, Decision on Jurisdiction, ¶ 98 (June 30, 2011) (holding that "[t]he burden of proof to establish the facts supporting its claim to standing lies with the Claimant"). **163n36, 191–92n205**

SGS v. Paraguay, ICSID Case No. ARB/07/29, Award, ¶ 79 (Feb. 10 2012) (holding that the claimant bears the initial burden of proof in substantiating its claims). **191–92n205**

Generation Ukraine, Inc. v. Ukraine, ICSID Case No. ARB/00/9, Award, ¶¶ 19.1, 19.4 (Sept. 16, 2003) (holding that the claimant failed in discharging its burden of proving the nature and quantum of its investment in Ukraine by not furnishing corroborative evidence or actual documents). **191–92n205**

Noble Ventures, Inc. v. Romania, ICSID Case No. ARB/01/11, Award, ¶ 100 (Oct. 12, 2005) (holding that the claimant had "the burden of proof (i.e. the risk of non-persuasion of the tribunal)" in relation to its allegation that Romania was guilty of fraudulent misrepresentation). **40n207, 192n205**

Saipem S.p.A. v. People's Republic of Bangladesh, ICSID Case No. ARB/05/7, Decision on Jurisdiction, ¶ 83 (Mar. 21, 2007) (espousing as an "accepted international practice" the principle that "a party bears the burden of proving the facts it asserts" and finding that, at the jurisdiction stage, the claimant has to satisfy the burden of proof and make a *prima facie* showing of treaty violations). **108n115, 108n120, 191–92n205, 193n211**

Middle East Cement Shipping and Handling Co. S.A. v. Arab Republic of Egypt, ICSID Case No. ARB/99/6, Award, ¶¶ 89 *et seq.* (Apr. 12, 2002) (holding that, as "a general principle of international procedure—and probably also of virtually all national procedural laws—it is the claimant who has the burden of proof for the conditions required in the applicable substantive rules of law to establish the claim). **32n174, 68n382, 78, 78n440, 150n367, 161–62, 162n28, 191–92n205**

Inmaris Perestroika Sailing Maritime Services GmbH and others v. Ukraine, ICSID Case No. ARB/08/8, Decision on Jurisdiction, ¶ 69 (Mar. 8, 2010) (observing that "the burden of establishing that an express agreement of a commercial nature was not intended to create legal relations lies with the party that asserts that no legal effect was intended, and the burden is a heavy one"). **124n214, 193n210**

William Nagel v. Czech Republic, SCC Case No. 49/2002, Final Award, ¶ 177 (Sept. 9, 2003) (holding that, at the jurisdictional stage of an investment arbitration, the claimant "bears the burden of establishing that he made an investment in the Czech Republic, as that term is defined in the Investment Treaty, and if so, what his investment rights actually were"). **127n230, 193n211**

Saipem S.p.A. v. The People's Republic of Bangladesh, ICSID Case No. ARB/05/7, Award, ¶ 113 (June 30, 2009) (holding that the burden of proof lies with the party alleging the fact, whether it is the claimant or the respondent). **108n115, 108n120, 191–92n205, 193n211**

Apotex Holdings Inc. and Apotex Inc. v. United States of America, ICSID Case No. ARB(AF)/12/1, Award, ¶ 8.9 (Aug. 25, 2014) (holding that the fact that the party making the allegation bears the burden of proof is "a generally accepted canon of evidence in civil law, common law and, in fact, most jurisdictions"). **193n211, 197–98n245, 200n265, 201n267**

Abrahim Rahman Golshani v. The Government of The Islamic Republic of Iran, Award No. 546-812-3 (Mar. 2, 1993), 29 Iran-U.S. Cl. Trib. 78, (holding that"[t]he Claimant . . . has the initial burden of proving *prima facie* that [a document] is authentic. Once this is accomplished, . . . the burden of proving that [it] is a forgery shifts to the Respondent"). **122n202, 191n204, 193n211, 195n229**

Case Concerning the Temple of Preah Vihear (Cambodia v. Thailand), Judgment, Merits, 1962 I.C.J. 6 at 16 (June 15) (holding that "[t]he burden of proof in respect of [the particular matter] will of course lie on the [p]arty asserting or putting them forward"—irrespective of whether that party is the claimant or the respondent). **11n55, 106n107, 119n189, 120n193, 121, 121n198, 123–24n209, 124, 193, 193n214**

Pulp Mills on the River Uruguay (Arg. v. Uru), Judgment, 2010 I.C.J. 14, ¶ 162 (Apr. 20) (holding, "[i]n accordance with the well-established principle of *onus probandi incumbit actori*, [that] it is the duty of the party which asserts certain facts to establish the existence of such facts"). **12n64, 13n68, 193–94n214**

ICC Award No. 3344, Clunet 1982, at 978, 983 (acknowledging the "rule of procedure, generally acknowledged in the various domestic legal systems, according to which every party must prove the facts which it alleges"). **193–94n214**

ICC Award No. 6653, Clunet 1993, at 1040, 1044 (acknowledging, as a matter of French law and "a principle of international commerce," that it is upon the party that alleges the fact to furnish the relevant proof). **193–94n214**

Técnicas Medioambientales Tecmed, S.A. v. United Mexican States, ICSID Case No. ARB (AF)/00/2, Award, ¶ 63 (May 29, 2003) (finding that the burden of proving an exception to the general principle of non-retroactive application of treaties lies with the party claiming the exception). **115n162, 117n168, 128n233, 194n215**

Ahmadou Sadio Diallo (Guinea v. Dem. Rep. Congo), Merits, Judgment, 2010 I.C.J. 639, ¶ 54 (Nov. 30) (observing that the general rule that the party alleging a fact in support of his claim must prove the existence of that fact is not absolute, but varies depending on the subject matter and nature of the dispute, as well as the type of facts necessary to proven to resolve the case). **140n308, 142n316, 194n217**

Parker v. Mexico, 4 R. Int'l Arb. Awards 35, 39 (1926) (holding that, "[w]hen the claimant has established a prima facie case and the respondent has offered no evidence in rebuttal, the latter may not insist that the former pile up evidence to establish its allegations beyond a reasonable doubt without pointing out some reason for doubting"). **194n216**

United States—Measures Affecting Imports of Woven Wool Shirts and Blouses from India, WT/DS33/AB/R, 14 (May 23, 1997) (holding that "[i]f that party adduces evidence sufficient to raise a presumption that what is claimed is true, the burden then shifts to the other party, who will fail unless it adduces sufficient evidence to rebut the presumption"). **109n125, 163, 163n33**

Courts and tribunals may take notice of facts which are official or concern matters of common knowledge or public notoriety

Abrahim Rahman Golshani v. The Government of The Islamic Republic of Iran, Award No. 546-812-3 (Mar. 2, 1993), 29 Iran-U.S. Cl. Trib. 78 (observing that presumptive authenticity may attach to certain official documents, provided that they possess hallmarks of *prima facie* legitimacy). **122n202, 191n204, 193n211, 195n229**

Application of the Convention on the Prevention and Punishment of the Crime of Genocide (Bosn. & Herz. v. Serb. & Montenegro), 2007 I.C.J. 43, ¶ 42 (Feb. 26) (separate opinion of Judge Lauterpacht) (advocating that the Court take judicial notice of matters that are "public knowledge," provided that they are consistent with the main facts proven by evidence in the case). **108n117, 191n201, 197n242, 198n250**

Military and Paramilitary Activities in and Against Nicaragua (Nicar. v. U.S), Merits, Judgment, 1986 I.C.J. 14, ¶ 62, at 40 (June 27) (relying on press articles and extracts from books as corroborating material to evince the existence of a fact). **132n256, 153n388, 191n201**

United States Diplomatic and Consular Staff in Tehran (U.S. v. Iran), Judgment, 1980 I.C.J. 3, ¶¶ 12-13, at 9-10 (May 24) (finding that notwithstanding the United States' inability to present evidence of its diplomatic and consular staff being held hostage in Tehran due to its lack of access, the Court was entitled to and did take notice of the facts of the case as a matter of public knowledge, as demonstrated by the global press coverage of these events). **152n383, 153nn386–87, 191n201**

A litigant must produce the most trustworthy evidence in its possession to support its claim

Europe Cement Inv. & Trade S.A. v. Rep. of Turkey, ICSID Case No. ARB(AF)/07/2, Award, ¶¶ 164-66 (Aug. 13, 2009) (noting that by failing to produce the originals of share transfer agreements, a party gives rise to an "inference that the originals of the documents . . . either were never in the Claimant's possession or would not stand forensic analysis"). **195n225**

Rompetrol v. Romania, ICSID Case No. ARB/06/3, Award, ¶¶ 178-86 (May 6, 2013) (observing that "a given tribunal is specifically authorized to draw whatever inferences it deems appropriate from the failure of either party to produce evidence which that party might otherwise have been expected to produce"). **140–41n308, 189n193, 190n196, 195n225**

EDF (Servs) Ltd. v. Romania, ICSID Case No. ARB/05/13, Procedural Order No. 3, ¶ 35 (Aug. 29, 2008) (excluding, as unreliable and unauthenticated, an audiotape that had possibly been manipulated and from which a substantial part of the recorded conversation was missing). **112n138, 153n390, 188–89n190, 195n224, 196–97n236, 197n239**

Riahi v. Islamic Republic of Iran, Award No. 600-485-1 (Feb. 23, 2003), 37 Iran-U.S. Cl. Trib. Rep. 156, 176 (Brower, J., dissenting) (criticizing the majority for "rewarding" the respondent's "blatant stonewalling" of the Tribunal's production orders, and suggesting that adverse inferences should follow its refusal to produce "definitive records" necessary to the claimant's case and in the "actual possession" of the respondent). **195n225**

Marvin Feldman v. United Mexican States, ICSID Case No. ARB(AF)/99/1, Award, ¶¶ 662-63 (Dec. 16, 2002) (finding that negative inferences could be drawn from the State's failure to produce evidence that the investor was not being discriminated against on the basis of nationality). **195n225**

Corfu Channel Case (U.K. v. Alb), Merits, 1949 I.C.J. Rep. 4, 18 (Apr. 9) (in light of a State's exclusive territorial control within its frontiers, "[t]he other State, the victim of a breach of international law, is often unable to furnish direct proof of facts giving rise to responsibility. Such a State should be allowed a more liberal recourse to inferences of fact and circumstantial evidence" in order to prove its case). **11, 11n53, 14, 14n70, 49n258, 195n227, 195n229, 196n230, 196n232, 208n28**

Proof may be administered by means of circumstantial evidence

Corfu Channel (U.K. v. Alb), Merits, 1949 I.C.J. Rep. 4, 18 (April 9) (observing that, even without direct evidence, "[t]he proof may be drawn from inferences of fact, provided that they leave no room for reasonable doubt"). **11, 11n53, 14, 14n70, 49n258, 195n227, 195n229, 196n230, 196n232, 208n28**

Abrahim Rahman Golshani v. The Government of The Islamic Republic of Iran, Award No. 546-812-3 (Mar. 2, 1993), 29 Iran-U.S. Cl. Trib. 78 (inferring from the inconsistencies in corroborating evidence that an official document was not entitled to a presumption of authenticity). **122n202, 191n204, 193n211, 195n229**

Asian Agric. Prods. Ltd. v. Republic of Sri Lanka, ICSID Case No. ARB/87/3, Award, ¶ 45 (June 27, 1990) (adopting the "established international law rule[]" that "[i]n cases where proof of a fact presents extreme difficulty, a tribunal may thus be satisfied with less conclusive proof, i.e., prima facie evidence"). **94n39, 97n57, 97n60, 191–92n205, 192n209, 193n211, 195–196n229**

Yukos Capital S.A.R.L. v. Ojsc Rosneft Oil Company, [2011] EWHC 1461, ¶ 36 (rejecting the argument that direct evidence of partiality and dependence of the individual judges was required, because "partiality and dependency by their very nature take place behind the scenes"). **69n387, 79n448, 132n255, 134n271, 169, 169n67, 171n78, 189n191, 190–91n200, 196n231**

ICC Award No. 4145 (Second Interim Award), YCA 1987, at 97 ¶ 28 (acknowledging the "general principle[] of interpretation [that] a fact can be considered as proven even by the way of circumstantial evidence"). **136n286, 195n228**

Jan Oostergetel and Theordora Laurentius v. Slovak Republic, UNCITRAL, Award, ¶¶ 302-03 (Apr. 23, 2012) (espousing the view that corruption may be proved by circumstantial evidence but that such evidence was lacking in the case). **196, 196n235**

Proof acquired by unlawful or otherwise improper means should be stricken out from the record, as should evidence of questionable authenticity

Libananco v. Turkey, ICSID Case No. ARB/06/8, Award, ¶¶ 383-84 (Sept. 2, 2011) (excluding from the record incomplete audio recordings whose authenticity was questioned in several expert reports). **181nn140–42, 188n190, 197, 197n238**

Methanex Corp. v. United States, UNCITRAL, Award, ¶ 54 (Aug. 3, 2005) (holding that "[i]t would be wrong for the USA . . . to misuse its intelligence assets to spy on Methanex (and its witnesses) and to introduce into evidence the resulting materials"). **95n43, 98n64, 181n141, 196n236, 197n237**

EDF (Servs) Ltd. v. Romania, ICSID Case No. ARB/05/13, Procedural Order No. 3, ¶ 38 (Aug. 29, 2008) (excluding from the record an audiotape of a conversation allegedly containing evidence of a government official's demand for a bribe, on the basis that it was recorded without the official's consent and in breach of her right to privacy, and that its admission would be contrary to the principles of good faith and fair dealing required in international arbitration). **112n138, 153n390, 188–89n190, 195n224, 196–97n236, 197n239**

F. The Principle of *Res Judicata*

Chorzow Factory (Germany v. Poland), Judgment No. 8, 1927 P.C.I.J. 5, 21 (June) (observing that the principle of *res judicata* is a general principle of law). **8n38, 14, 14n70, 105n101, 106n106, 107n111, 130–31, 131n248, 148n357, 197n240, 200n265**

Waste Management, Inc. v. United Mexican States, ICSID Case No. ARB(AF)/00/3, Award, ¶ 39 (Apr. 30, 2004) (observing that the principle of *res judicata* is a general principle of law). **77n438, 129n238, 197n244, 199n253, 199nn255–56, 200n265**

Industria Nadonal de Alimentos, S.A. and Indalsa Peru, SA. v. Peru, ICSID ARB/03/4, Decision on Annulment, ¶ 86 (Sept. 5, 2007) (observing that the principle of *res judicata* is a general principle of law). **197–98n244**

Apotex v. United States of America, ICSID Case No. ARB (AF/12/1), Award, ¶ 7.11 (Aug. 25, 2014) (observing that the principle of *res judicata* is a general principle of law). **193n211, 197–98n245, 200n265, 201n267**

Amco Asia Corp. v. Republic of Indonesia, ICSID Case No. ARB/81/1, Resubmitted Case, Award (June 5, 1990) (observing that the principle of *res judicata* is a general principle of law). **32n175, 40nn208–9, 41, 41–42n212, 41n210, 42n213, 44n228, 90nn17–18, 94n38, 100n79, 105n101, 120n191, 121n199, 138n294, 145n335, 148n358, 149n359, 149n362, 150n370, 197–98n244**

Case Concerning the Arbitral Award Made by the King of Spain on December 23, 1906 (Honduras v. Nicaragua), 1960 I.C.J. Rep. 192, 21, 25-26 (applying the principle of res judicata). **11n55, 124n210, 197–98n244**

South West Africa Case (1966) I.C.J. Rep. 4, 240 (observing that the principle of *res judicata* is a general principle of law). **13n68, 22, 22n117, 108n117, 160n17**

Application of the Convention on the Prevention and Punishment of the Crime of Genocide (Bosn. & Herz. v. Serb. & Montenegro), Judgment, 2007 I.C.J. 43, ¶ 116 (Feb. 26) (observing that the principle of *res judicata* is a general principle of law). **108n117, 191n201, 197n242, 198n250**

Boundary Dispute between Argentina and Chile concerning the Frontier Line between Boundary Post 62 and Mount Fitzroy, Award, 22 R.I.A.A. ¶ 68 (Oct. 21, 1994) (observing that the principle of *res judicata* is a general principle of law). **197–98n244**

Parties to a final judgment or award are obligated to carry it out, and are prohibited from raising the same matter again

Effect of Awards of Compensation Made by the United Nations Administrative Tribunal, 1954 I.C.J. Rep. 47, 53 (holding that it is a "well-established and generally recognized principle of law [that] a judgment rendered by a judicial body is *res judicata* and has binding force between the parties to the dispute"; the obligation to carry out the award extends not only to the nominal parties to the dispute, but also those persons on whose behalf the parties act). **11, 11n54, 197–98n244, 198n245**

Desert Line Projects LLC v. Republic of Yemen, ICSID Case No. ARB/05/17, Award, ¶¶ 205-07 (Feb. 6, 2008) (the fact that an arbitral award "shall be implemented in its entirety, and be fully respected as definitively binding on both Parties," is not only a matter of *res judicata*, but ultimately derives from "the combined effect of two basic rules having paramount place within ... all ... systems of law as well as by international law"—*viz.* estoppel and *pacta sunt servanda*). **90–91n19, 91n20, 119–20n189, 120n190, 122n203, 124n214, 125n217, 137n289, 198n246, 202n272**

Successive courts and tribunals must defer to the jurisdiction of a prior court or tribunal if the same matter is submitted for adjudication a second time, and all of the rights, issues, and facts that were distinctly put in issue and distinctly determined in the prior case

Amco Asia Corp. v. Republic of Indonesia, ICSID Case No. ARB/81/1, Resubmitted Case, Award (June 5, 1990) (holding that *res judicata* is a general principle of law such that an unannulled award is binding between the parties and later tribunals, but that an annulled portion of an ICSID award has no *res judicata* effect and that there is no general principle giving such effect to a Tribunal's legal reasoning or preliminary or incidental determinations). **32n175, 40nn208–9, 41, 41–42n212, 41n210, 42n213, 44n228, 90nn17–18, 94n38, 100n79, 105n101, 120n191, 121n199, 138n294, 145n335, 148n358, 149n359, 149n362, 150n370, 197–98n244**

Case Concerning the Application of the Genocide Convention, Judgment, I.C.J., ¶ 120 (Feb. 26, 2007) (holding that, where new facts have "come to light subsequent to [the court's] decision" indicating that its "conclusions may have been based on incorrect or insufficient facts," the matter may be reopened and reconsidered notwithstanding the principle of *res judicata*, provided there are available procedures that allow for a judicial revision). **108, 117, 191n201, 197n242, 198n250**

Waste Management, Inc. v. United Mexican States, ICSID Case No. ARB(AF)/00/3, Decision on Mexico's Preliminary Objection concerning the Previous Proceedings (June 26, 2002) ¶ 43 (May 8, 2000) (holding that "there is no doubt that, in general, the dismissal of a claim by an international tribunal on grounds of lack of jurisdiction does not constitute a decision on the merits and does not preclude a later claim before a tribunal which has jurisdiction" and noting that the "same is true of decisions concerning inadmissibility"). **77n438, 129n238, 197n244, 199n253, 199nn255–56, 200n265**

Factory at Chorzów (Fed. Rep. Ger. v. Pol), Interpretation of Judgments Nos. 7 and 8, Judgment, 1927 P.C.I.J. (Ser. A) No. 13 (Dec. 16) (dissenting opinion by Judge Anzilotti) (finding that the Court's Judgment No. 7 establishing Oberschlesische's right of ownership to Chorzów factory was *res judicata*, and that Germany's request for interpretation of the Judgment called for the Court to consider this question afresh and should not have been entertained). **8n38, 14, 14n70, 105n101, 106n106, 107n111, 130–31, 131n248, 148n357, 197n240, 200n265**

Bosh International, Inc and B&P Ltd Foreign Investments Enterprise v. Ukraine, ICSID Case No. ARB/08/11, Award (Oct. 25, 2012) (holding that that a Ukrainian court had not violated the principle of *res judicata* when it heard a case which had been previously dismissed by a prior judge; *res judicata* does not attach to a case where a judge declined to formally open proceedings). **199, 199n257**

Delimitation of the Continental Shelf (UK v. France), 18 RIAA 271, 295 (1978) (holding that while *res judicata* attaches "only to the provisions of [the decision's] dispositif and not to its reasoning," it is equally clear that "having regard to the close links that exist between the reasoning of a decision and the provisions of its dispositif, recourse may in principle be had to the reasoning in order to elucidate the meaning and scope of the dispositif"). **200n262**

Apotex v. United States of America, ICSID Case No. ARB (AF/12/1), Award, ¶ 7.15 (Aug. 25, 2014) (holding that the triple identity standard provides a stringent test, and applying a simpler two-fold test that only required there to be an identity of the parties and an identity of the matter of the dispute before *res judicata* will attach). **193n211, 197–98n245, 200n265, 201n267**

Trail Smelter Case (U.S. v. Canada) 3 R.I.A.A. 1905, 1952 (dissenting opinion by Judge Anzilotti) (observing that a decision denying jurisdiction "can never constitute *res judicata*"; this principle is "undoubtedly correct"). **199n252, 200n265**

Chevron Corp. et al. *v. Republic of Ecuador*, PCA Case No. 2009-23, First Partial Award on Track I, ¶ 108 (Sept. 17, 2013) (holding that *res judicata* may extend to non-signatories of a settlement agreement that seek to raise the same diffuse rights against the same defendant). **201n266, 202n271**

CME Czech Republic B.V. v. Czech Republic, UNCITRAL, Final Award on Damages, ¶ 435 (Mar. 14, 2003) (holding that one tribunal hearing a dispute under an investment treaty cannot bind a second tribunal, hearing the "same" dispute, though under a different treaty). **40n208, 129nn238–39, 145n335, 202n269**

Petrobart Limited v. Kyrgyz Republic, SCC Arbitration No. 126/2003, Award, 65-68 (Mar. 29, 2005) (holding that, where a claimant initiates arbitration against a host State pursuant to a private contract or a domestic investment law, a decision from that tribunal will not bind a later tribunal convened under an investment treaty addressing different legal claims). **78n444, 175n106, 202n270**

SGS Société Générale de Surveillance S.A. v. the Islamic Republic of Pakistan, ICSID No. ARB/01/13, Award, ¶¶ 176-77 (Aug. 6, 2003) (holding that "the Claimant's conduct in previous Swiss legal proceedings and in a previous arbitration regarding contract and tort claims [cannot] preclude[] the Claimant from raising claims under the Bilateral Investment Treaty (BIT) between Switzerland and Pakistan"). **39–40n206, 121–22n199**

Name Index

General Principles of Law and International Due Process. Charles T. Kotuby Jr. and Luke A. Sobota. © Oxford University Press 2017. Published 2017 by Oxford University Press.

Subject Index

www.ingramcontent.com/pod-product-compliance
Ingram Content Group UK Ltd.
Pitfield, Milton Keynes, MK11 3LW, UK
UKHW051048150926
475595UK00005B/180